Do[illegible]rdan is a writer and filmmaker, most recently known fo[illegible] series of history books co-written with Michael Walsh. A[illegible]g them are *White Cargo*, acclaimed by Nobel laureate T[illegible] Morrison as 'an extraordinary book', *The King's Revenge* ar[illegible]*he King's Bed*.

Jo[illegible]'s work has won several awards, including two Blue R[illegible]ns at the New York Film and Television Festival. He is the c[illegible]ter and co-producer of the multi-award-winning feature fi[illegible]*ove is the Devil*, based on the life of the painter Francis Bac[illegible], starring Derek Jacobi and Daniel Craig.

[illegible]orn in Northern Ireland, Don has lived in England for more than thirty years, most of that time in London, and is married to Eithne, a hospital doctor.

Also by Don Jordan (with Michael Walsh)

Van Hoogstraten: Blood and Retribution

White Cargo: The Forgotten History of Britain's White Slaves in America

The King's Bed

The King's Revenge

THE KING'S CITY

London under Charles II

DON JORDAN

ABACUS

ABACUS

First published in Great Britain in 2017 by Little, Brown
This paperback edition published in 2018 by Abacus

1 3 5 7 9 10 8 6 4 2

A CIP catalogue record for this book
is available from the British Library.

ISBN 978-0-349-14137-4

Typeset in Electra by M Rules
Printed and bound in Great Britain by
Clays Ltd, Elcograf S.p.A.

Papers used by Abacus are from well-managed forests
and other responsible sources.

Abacus
An imprint of
Little, Brown Book Group
Carmelite House
50 Victoria Embankment
London EC4Y 0DZ

An Hachette UK Company
www.hachette.co.uk

www.littlebrown.co.uk

For Eithne

CONTENTS

PART 3 1667–1685: THE YEARS OF TURMOIL

PREFACE

On 29 May 1660, his thirtieth birthday, King Charles II of England, Scotland and Ireland rode across London Bridge, triumphantly entering a city he hardly knew and had not seen for almost twenty years. This book is about how the relationship between King and city subsequently developed, and about the remarkable people who helped London during his reign become the pre-eminent city in Europe.

Though it is difficult to say with certainty, London was possibly already the continent's largest city. It was not only the kingdom's capital, but its long-standing economic vibrancy had led it to become disproportionately large – perhaps nearly one-tenth of the entire English population lived in the city, making it 'a Head too big for the Body', according to one contemporary source. Owing to the scale of London, together with its satellite towns spread along the Thames Valley, in 1660 England was already beginning to look like a Monopoly board tipped up to let all the pieces fall to the bottom right-hand corner.* Of

---

* For this vivid image, I must thank that most distinguished British city planner and urban theorist, the late Professor Stuart Hall, who used it in a conversation with me.

all parts of the kingdom, London was therefore the one of key importance to the returning king.

London was one of a handful of 'world cities' scattered across the western hemisphere. Well-to-do Londoners drank tea from China and coffee from Arabia out of Chinese porcelain cups, enjoyed sack from Spain and the Canary Islands, put West Indian sugar in their drinks and syllabubs, smoked tobacco from Virginia, wore silks from Turkey and India, and flavoured their food with spices from Zanzibar and Indonesia. In the winter the wealthy kept their heads warm with hats made from beaver pelts from the far north of America. All this luxury was imported on English ships made watertight with tar and pitch from the Baltic, with sails hoisted aloft by ropes made with hemp from Russia to billow out from masts and spars made from Swedish pine. When Charles returned from exile, he was instantly involved in the commercial life of the city, particularly investing in and encouraging the slave trade, an issue examined here in some depth.

World cities – which at one time or another included, besides London, Venice, Lisbon, Antwerp and Amsterdam – owed their size and eminence to well-established long-range trading links across the world. With such trade came wealth, and with wealth came power. Such cities therefore tended to become the focus for all domestic policies, the hub for home markets in commodities and raw materials, and the centre of national political power. Some, like Venice, grew so powerful they could exist without a country or political hinterland attached; others drew power towards them over large geographic areas. In the case of London, by the time Charles II rode through its streets on that first occasion, the city had become the centre of England's economy, controlling markets in goods as far away as Cornwall and the Scottish borders, and even in Ireland. What made this possible, indeed inevitable, was the city's trade with Africa, America, Asia and the Far East.

As contemporary observers noticed, cities grew rich at a rate disproportionate to the growth of their populations. In other words, large cities created wealth more efficiently than less populated areas. London was like that: a magnet for wealth. Already, in the seventeenth century, England's economy depended upon its capital. In 1660, every thousand people living and working in London generated considerably more wealth than a similar number scattered through the villages and countryside.

Not unnaturally, London therefore had strong historic views about its own important place in the realm, its rights and its freedoms. It was Charles's misfortune to rule over a people he barely knew and who did not know him. It was the misfortune of Londoners to have a king who had grown to adulthood estranged from them.

While King Charles II was in exile in Europe, at home the genie had escaped from the bottle: large numbers of people, from politicians to the plainest folk, had started to believe that they could look after their affairs without a king, or at least without one who believed – as the Stuarts tended to do – in absolutist rule that saw little need for representation of at least some of the people through Parliament. After the execution of Charles's father, Charles I, following a protracted power struggle, England had been ruled without a monarch for eleven years, first as a republic and then as a form of military dictatorship. When this dictatorship collapsed in recriminations and further power struggles, the executed King's son was invited to return to put things right. From the royalist perspective, it looked as if the genie had been put back in the bottle. But it had not. In London's political and civic circles there were many who waited to see how an unpractised king would manage their needs and aspirations.

Charles was born in London on 29 May 1630, at St James's Palace, built by Henry VIII to the west of the City of London on the site of a leper hospital. As an infant, he was put into the care of the Countess of Dorset, wife to the 4th Earl of Dorset, Lord Chamberlain to Charles's mother, Queen Henrietta Maria. Charles was brought up at his own palace at Richmond, nine miles up the Thames from his parents' palace at Whitehall and a full ten miles from the Ludgate, the most westerly of the gates in the Roman walls containing the medieval heart of London.*

When the prince was aged about eleven, rumours spread through London that he had attended Catholic Mass in his mother's private chapel at Somerset House. Questions were asked in Parliament. The following year, civil war broke out, caused by a power struggle between Charles I and Parliament over the royal prerogative, the authority of Parliament and the right to levy taxes. The country split into forces loyal to the King and those loyal to Parliament. The King then went on a march through various counties to garner support. When his return to London was prevented by superior Parliamentarian forces at Turnham Green, Charles set up his headquarters at Oxford. This meant that from the age of about twelve, Prince Charles was brought up in a royal court at war with Parliament and about half the population, and unable to return to its main palace at the capital city. Within three years, with the war going badly for the Crown, the King dispatched his son to the West Country, as titular commander-in-chief. According to the courtier Edward

* Richmond Palace stood upstream of present-day Richmond Bridge, between the river and Richmond Green. It was demolished in the mid-seventeenth century.

Hyde, the Prince took little interest in discussions about the war, preferring to flirt with a former nurse.

By 1645 the situation had deteriorated so badly that the King ordered Prince Charles to leave for France. After much procrastination, the Prince sailed from England in March 1646 to live with his mother, now ensconced in a palace not far from Paris courtesy of her French royal relatives. Less than three years later, in January 1649, Charles I was tried and found guilty of treason against his people. He returned to the palace he had left seven years before to be executed. When the Prince heard the news, he was living in The Hague, thanks to the hospitality of his sister Mary, who was married to Prince William II of Orange. Two years later, Charles was crowned King of Scotland and led a Scottish Presbyterian army into England. Oliver Cromwell's superior forces crushed the invasion at Worcester. Charles had to escape like a criminal, hiding out until he sailed in disguise for France. He had been in England for just five weeks.

After the debacle of the failed invasion, Charles's return to the throne looked unlikely. Most European powers, including France, recognised the Commonwealth as the de facto ruling power in England. Charles, a king without a kingdom, became an isolated figure. With little future ahead of him, he took to a life of ease and debauchery. Then circumstances changed. Cromwell died in 1658 and his son Richard was appointed Lord Protector in his place. Richard lacked the drive and character to rule and was deposed by a group of army grandees. Many wondered where the country was heading next. An elite group of politicians, aristocrats and bishops, a sort of establishment clique, invited Charles to return for the good of the country. During this period, stability was ensured in London by an army under former Cromwellian general George Monck, who brought the city under martial law on behalf of the Crown.

Charles then returned and ruled for twenty-five exhilarating and tempestuous years, the period covered by this book.

The scene was set for London to develop into one of the greatest cities in the world – if not the greatest of them all. Though its fabric was medieval, in the minds of its people the modern world was taking shape. The great trading city, developed to a large extent by the materialist ideas of Puritanism, would now benefit from the power of royal authority to propel it into a new era.

Under the returned King, London looked forward to stability. The arts and sciences attracted some of the most brilliant minds in British history. Architecture flourished, with a cool, northern aesthetic drawn from hot, Mediterranean origins by men such as John Webb and most notably Christopher Wren, the father of English baroque and the designer of St Paul's Cathedral as it stands today. London's theatres, long closed, reopened to enchant with a saucy vigour and novelty of production thanks to impresarios such as Sir William Davenant, a man who claimed lineage from Shakespeare and happily rewrote his plays. Women played their part, within the constraints of seventeenth-century male society. Female playwrights including Aphra Behn appeared, together with that significant artistic innovation of the age – the female actor. Great artists of the stage rose up, including Elizabeth Barry, together with those who, like Nell Gwyn, became notorious for other reasons. Science blossomed, with the formation of the Royal Society; its members, including Robert Boyle and Robert Hooke, brought new insights into the workings of mankind and the universe. New music accompanied royal pageants and masques, and even the moribund world of English art began to revive. People poured in from all over the country and the city's ships and merchants expanded their international trade, growing fat on slavery, creating a new form of mercantile trade that would literally be the envy of the world. William Petty,

John Locke and others expounded new theories of commerce and wealth creation, leading towards modern economics and capitalism.

But it would not be all plain sailing. Under the rule of Charles II the city experienced some of the greatest cataclysms in its history. In 1660 London was still emerging from a depression that began in the early 1650s with the expansion of Dutch trade at the expense of its rivals, including England. In 1665–6 the city suffered an epidemic of bubonic plague, during which then-current medical remedies were tested and found wanting. Following the plague, the centre of the historic city burned down in one of the worst city fires in history. During these and other trials, Charles's character was tested to the full. He proved to be a paradox, being, for example, both selflessly brave and totally selfish.

London's wealth was based on international mercantile capitalism, 'the inhabitants of Europe being addicted to trade'. For this enterprise to work successfully, the state had to be intimately involved; in the case of London this meant Charles II.

The ruler's role was to regulate, to set taxes or enforce tariffs against foreign trade, and to help merchants increase their trade in the world by, if necessary, waging trade wars – and hence to increase London's profits. The person who sat at the apex of this great enterprise was therefore of supreme importance. In early 1660, that person was missing. It was as if Thomas Hobbes's Leviathan had no head on its shoulders to guide it.* It was therefore understandable that Londoners, the majority of whom had

---

* The frontispiece of the first edition of Thomas Hobbes's *Leviathan*, published in 1651, has a drawing of the state represented as a giant man whose body is made up of hundreds of little people gazing up reverently at the giant's face. The giant holds a sword representing armed strength and a bishop's crozier representing the Church, while its head wears a king's crown. Hobbes came up with the design himself. A more disquieting image of total power would be hard to conjure.

supported Parliament against the Crown in 1642, now wished for a king to give leadership again. In adopting this role, Charles was handed one of the most difficult tasks allotted to any monarch.

It is not possible to convey in one book all the many enterprises and innovations of an age, nor to include all the interesting or significant personalities – one can give only a snapshot. For example, Isaac Newton appears in these pages as a slightly peripheral figure. This is because his seminal work was done in Cambridge, not London, and to give full weight to the central place in modern physics he shares with Albert Einstein would require more than one book all to himself. Nor is it possible to delve into the twists and turns of political or ecclesiastical life to a great depth. What is attempted here is an impression of the vitality of early modern English life, and in particular in the place where everything was, or seemed to be, magnified – London. It is not fanciful to suggest that during Charles's reign much of what shapes modern Britain was first forged.

This book is the third and final part of a series about the reign of Charles II commissioned by Tim Whiting of Little, Brown. The first book in the series, *The King's Revenge,* told the neglected story of Charles's campaign for retribution upon the men who executed his father Charles I, while the second, *The King's Bed*, examined how Charles's notorious personal life influenced his reign. Both books were written in collaboration with Michael Walsh, who unfortunately has been unable to participate in this final part through illness. I say more about Michael and our long-standing collaboration on many projects in the Acknowledgements at the end of the book.

PART 1

1660–1663:
THE YEARS OF OPTIMISM

CHAPTER 1

A CITY OF EXPECTATION

In the spring of 1660 the city was enveloped in noxious fumes. Truth be told, the air was never good at any time, though the direction of the wind had a major influence upon its quality. When blowing from the west it carried acrid smoke across the city from limekilns sited in the grounds of Whitehall Palace, less than a mile from the city walls. When the wind veered to the south, it carried fumes from the leather tanneries, the kilns and factories in the industrial slums across the river.

When there was no wind at all, the furnaces of the trades inside the medieval city walls – the ironworkers, cutlery makers, leather workers, bakers, brewers, soap makers, glass blowers, silversmiths, goldsmiths, and anyone else who needed a flame – belched out a cloud of polluting chemicals that hung in the still air and sank into the streets and alleyways like a shroud. On Sundays the industrial smog died down, leaving the smoke from thousands of chimneys to puff sulphurous fumes from the sea-coal the inhabitants used to heat their homes and cook their dinner.

Beneath Londoners' feet the ground was as unwholesome as the air they breathed. Sanitation was rough and ready. Each house had a dry toilet at the back, in which human waste accumulated until collectors came round to shovel it up, load it onto carts and carry it out of the city. Collections could be irregular. In one repellent entry in his diary, Samuel Pepys described how his neighbour's heap of human waste broke through the adjoining cellar wall, causing an unholy mess in Pepys's cellar. Outside the city walls, at collection points too terrible to contemplate, human waste was mixed with horse manure to fertilise the fields in which the city's food was grown. In this way London helped to feed itself – and possibly to recycle its diseases. This was also the age of the plague, the dreadful disease that had swept Europe periodically since the Black Death in 1382 – there had been more than thirty outbreaks in England alone, several of them touching London, the most recent of which had taken place in 1637.

Londoners emptied their chamber pots into the open sewers that ran down the sides of the streets and sometimes through the middle. The contents routinely spilled out across the cobbles, covering them with a vile mixture of pig and horse manure mixed with rotting vegetables, animal entrails and human urine. Only rain could improve conditions, temporarily cleansing the air and washing away the hideous slush, sluicing it down to the choked rivers and culverts that ran under the streets into the Thames.

During the spring of 1660, nothing could wash away the persistent rumour that stuck to the city with an obstinacy that equalled of the tenacity of its smells: the King, it was said, was about to return from exile. Eleven years had passed since most of London had turned out to witness the old King, Charles I, beheaded on a scaffold outside his lavish Banqueting House, crowding Whitehall for a mile all the way from Charing Cross to the river. After that, London's population had been compelled to settle for a Puritan regime under which making money was good and frivolity was not. The great Maypole on the Strand had been pulled down, the theatres closed, and Christmas celebrations frowned upon.

It was not all bad; music was not only allowed, but encouraged. The people of London had need of a good tune to cheer their hearts. They had been through a great deal since the outbreak of civil war in 1642. The brilliant German artist and engraver Wenceslaus Hollar told a friend, biographer John Aubrey, that when he first came to England in 1636, it had been a time of peace and the people, rich and poor, looked cheerful. When he returned after the war he found 'the countenances of the people all changed, melancholy, spiteful, as if bewitched'.[1]

Bewitched or not, by early 1660, the Puritan experiment in governing without a king had spiralled into chaos. Following Oliver Cromwell's death in 1658 the army and Parliament began a protracted duel for supremacy, during which Cromwell's son Richard was appointed Protector, only to be roughly shooed away without a fight by a group of army heavyweights. The army then tightened its grip on London. Sir John Barkstead, a London-born goldsmith, who under Cromwell had become Lieutenant of the Tower, ran a cruel and corrupt administration. During the winter of 1659, Londoners got up petitions to complain about the army's repressive use of force. The army, in turn, fired on demonstrating crowds, causing several deaths. Feelings ran high. The need for change, for a new ruler to take hold of the deteriorating situation, was the talk of London.

It was far from certain that the young King, Charles II, would return from exile. He had been away from England since he was sixteen and had no experience of power. Some said Richard Cromwell should be given another chance. Others said that George Monck, the former Cromwellian general who now had an iron grip on London and whose troops were bivouacked throughout the capital, had designs on becoming another Cromwell. Though Monck publicly proclaimed his earnest allegiance to Parliament, his loyalty privately lay elsewhere. He ordered that the old city's defences be dismantled. Troops went to the city's eight gateways and lifted the great wooden gates, studded and reinforced with iron, off their hinges. With great difficulty, portcullises were removed from the gatehouses and broken up. London, the walled city that had closed its gates to a king during the civil wars, now lay defenceless, a fact not lost on the inhabitants of a city once described as 'England's Jerusalem'.[2]

There was no official census and hence no record of London's population. One of the inhabitants, a draper named John Graunt, wondered how many people lived in the city and decided to find out. Graunt ran a successful family haberdashery business in the heart of the old walled city. He had an inquiring mind and, though we have no record, seems to have been well educated. Apart from carrying out a full census, sending recorders door to door, there was no accurate means of estimating the population. So Graunt set out to invent a means of reaching such an estimate. He took as his starting point a trawl of the parish records of births and deaths. Then he estimated the average number of people living in each household. From this, Graunt was able to estimate the city's population at 384,000. The total population of England in the middle of seventeenth century was at most five million, and perhaps as low as four, meaning that between one in ten and one in thirteen of England's population lived in London.[3]

To gain a sense of London's great scale, we should remember that the next largest city in England was Norwich, with a population of 25,000.* Unlike London, with its many trades and industries, the economy of a city like Norwich tended to be based on one major industry. In the case of Norwich, this was the textile trade, mainly the weaving of worsted wool cloth. Norwich's population included a large number of foreign migrants, escaping religious persecution and attracted by the vibrant cloth industry.

In the north of England, among the largest towns was York. Though once a major ecclesiastical centre, York's significance had declined with the dissolution of the monasteries. Its seventeenth-century population of something over 10,000 was supported by an economy based on woollen manufacturing, leather tanning and general trade, both domestic and foreign; its significance as a trading centre was due to its location on the Great North Road and the River Ouse, which flowed eastwards into the Humber Estuary, enabling York to export cloth to the continent. In time even this trade would largely be taken over by Hull, owing to its situation on the coastal estuary. Perhaps greater in population than York was Newcastle, a major industrial hub and coal port.

Until the mid-1600s towns on the east coast tended to be of greater size and importance than those in the west, thanks to their proximity to continental Europe, with which England and Scotland had historically traded. By the middle of the century, Liverpool was a fishing town with a population of perhaps two

---

* Today, Greater London's population of 8.5 million is eight times that of the next largest city, Birmingham, which has a population of 1.1 million.

thousand. Growing trade with England's new colonies across the Atlantic meant that Liverpool's population would increase as it became a centre for refining sugar brought from the West Indies, the first so-called sugar houses appearing in the town in the 1670s. Sugar was later followed by the cotton imports that fed the industrial revolution in Lancashire. In a similar fashion, the seaport of Bristol became involved in the importation of sugar and tobacco. Like Liverpool, it would not grow significantly until the following century, when it became rich on slave trading on an industrial scale.

Larger than any town in England other than London was the Scottish capital of Edinburgh. In the mid-seventeenth century it was a walled city laid out on an east–west axis with its one grand street of handsome houses and public buildings rising up to the royal castle at its western end. Off this thoroughfare ran hundreds of narrow streets and alleyways like ribs from a spine. In all, the city housed somewhere from 30,000 to 40,000 inhabitants.

The city inhabited by John Graunt was clearly on a completely different scale from anywhere else in the kingdom. Even in Europe, only Naples and Paris competed for size. The population of the former was somewhere around 300,000, while that of the latter was variously estimated at between 180,000 in 1600 and 500,000 in 1700; the latter figure was probably wildly optimistic, because of the depredations of the civil war known as the Fronde.

There were other large cities in northern Europe. Amsterdam, the premier Dutch seaport, had a population of around 200,000. Leiden, the Dutch city where many Englishmen went to study medicine, had a population of more than 100,000. Because of their scale, these early megacities created environments unlike almost everywhere else. They offered totally different ways in which to live and to experience life. Not only that: long before the seventeenth century London had developed into the centre in which the entire country's political power resided and via which its economic life was channelled or controlled.

If it could be said that one city was obsessed with another, then the city with which London was obsessed was Amsterdam. By any measurement apart from size, Amsterdam was the most successful city in Europe. Trade, banking, culture, painting, crafts and medicine all flourished in what was to become known as the Dutch Golden Age. The Dutch had built on their commercially advantageous position next to Germany at the head of the Rhine and next door to the Baltic. They then branched outwards into the eastern spice trade, becoming wonderfully wealthy. Their society was far in advance of England's, their institutions in advance of London's. At any one time, among Amsterdam's population of 200,000 lived large numbers of English and other merchants from all across Europe. The English merchants in Amsterdam were able to examine Dutch society at first hand and admire its Calvinist orderliness and dedication to trade. They envied the Dutch for their commerce, their knowhow and their money. These preoccupations were to have significant ramifications for both countries during the ensuing years.

When not selling gentlemen's clothing, John Graunt continued to work on his mathematical obsessions. The intellectually curious Graunt seems to have hit upon the art of statistical analysis all by himself. His work – a form of proto-epidemiology – would later propel the shopkeeper into the circles of the scientific elite.

Graunt was an influential man in the meritocracy of city merchant life, a captain in the trained bands (London's part-time militia) and an alderman, one of the ruling elite, elected from among the city's common council members. London's establishment was based on the city's ancient social structure, centred on the Corporation. This was medieval in origin, hierarchical in form and fiercely independent. The Corporation was comprised of a pyramid of elected representatives, beginning with councilmen; one tier up were the aldermen, followed by two sheriffs and finally the Lord Mayor. Only those who were Freemen of the City of London could vote or stand for election. To become a Freeman was to enter a closed shop, based on the medieval system of guilds or livery companies, each representing a trade. The guilds were arranged in hierarchical order dependent upon social status, from humble wheelwrights and tin workers at the bottom to the grand mercers (international cloth merchants) and grocers (international spice merchants) at the top, wielding power and influence. To join a guild usually entailed having to serve a lengthy and often expensive apprenticeship. An apprenticeship with the grocers or mercers amounted to what would today be a university-level education in economics and commerce, together with the hands-on experience of a sandwich course. London was thus ruled by a self-perpetuating clique, which ran the city through the two powerful entities of the Corporation and the guilds. The system served London's interests well.*

Graunt had a friend with whom he could discuss his arithmetical problems. This was William Petty, a true renaissance man: colonial administrator, mathematician, surveyor, musician and leading exponent of the study of the finance of trade and the nation (what would in time become known as

* The Corporation of London continues to run the City of London, lobbying for its own privileges, overseeing its planning applications and finances. How well this sits in a modern democracy is open to debate.

economics). Petty had made his fortune in Ireland, surveying the island for Oliver Cromwell, in preparation for selling off the best arable land to English settlers. It was said, probably with good reason, that Petty had used his position deceitfully to enrich himself. His income from land rents was said to be £18,000 a year, putting him among the very top echelons of the contemporary rich list.

Petty's beginnings could not have been more different. His parents had, like Graunt's, been in the rag trade, and he had, like Graunt, largely educated himself in his early years. The difference was that Petty had started lower, as a cabin boy, and climbed higher; academically trained in Holland, he had become personal secretary to Thomas Hobbes, the mathematician and philosopher, before studying medicine at Oxford.

Petty, with his rigorous education, was better versed in mathematics than Graunt. Thanks to his status as an alderman, however, Graunt was able to help Petty – who was now, because of his wealth and education, his social superior – recommending him for the professorship in music at Gresham College, London's only institution of higher learning. The college had opened to promote the latest and most advanced learning at the beginning of the century, when the merchant philanthropist Sir Thomas Gresham bequeathed his mansion to the city. Gresham had made his money in several spheres of business, including the building of the Royal Exchange at the western end of Cornhill, where London's stock trading took place.

In the spring of 1660, Petty had a more mundane problem on his mind: he had been thrown out of his Gresham College rooms. Thanks to the military crackdown, the army had commandeered the college for barracks. The building was ideal for the purpose, being a large mansion with a courtyard, situated inside the city walls. Petty, along with his friend and fellow professor Christopher Wren, resigned from the college in protest at its requisitioning. His rooms having vanished, Petty's mind turned to staying with his friends, the Graunts.

The route of Petty's coach to the Graunt home in Birchin Lane would have taken him south along Bishopsgate and up the slight incline of Cornhill. Here Petty found himself atop the middle of the three hills on which medieval London was built. To his west was Ludgate Hill, crowned by St Paul's Cathedral, an ancient crumbling church of great significance to Londoners by virtue of its antiquity rather than its architecture; to his east, Tower Hill, named after the huge, grey Norman keep of the Tower that sat between it and the river.

At this point, Petty had to force his way across the constant stream of people, carriages and carts pouring into Leadenhall immediately to his left, one of the city's greatest streets, where once had stood the Roman forum. Now, together with Cheapside, Leadenhall was London's international shop window, selling the most exciting goods from around England and the world. Terraces of graceful, timber and plaster buildings rising six storeys high lined the road. Their pointed gable ends faced out onto the street, giving the roofline a vibrant rhythm. Foreign visitors marvelled at Leadenhall's luxury and vivacity.

Turning away from Leadenhall's delights, Petty would head west along Cornhill, one of the most congested parts of the city. A flood of humanity flowed past his carriage; shoppers, idlers, deliverymen with their barrows, draymen on their carts, pickpockets, the poor, the industrious and the rich. The streets, already narrow, were reduced to tracks by the hordes of street sellers, licensed and unlicensed, selling poultry, vegetables, butter, cheese, beer, cutlery and woollen cloth. Petty's coach turned south off Cornhill, leaving behind the merchants and millers haggling over seasonal prices, to descend into Birchin Lane, where he reached his destination, a substantial property on the west side of the street. This was Graunt's home and shop, just across the street from the house where he had been born.

Born on 24 April 1620, Graunt served in London's militia through the Civil War years and into the Commonwealth and Protectorate. He would therefore have been a Parliamentarian, like most of London's middle classes and proletariat. His friend Petty had worked directly for the Cromwellian regime in Ireland and so we can assume they shared political opinions. How strongly held these were we cannot say with certainty, but soon enough both men would be willing to accept privileges from the King.

London was a city of chiming clocks. Almost every parish church had a clock, which struck the hour and sometimes the half-hour and the quarter. They did not chime in unison, so Londoners took the time from each parish as they passed by the neighbourhood clock. London was a city in which timekeeping mattered.

While Petty fretted about his lodgings, Captain William Rider, seafarer and merchant, waited for the daily chime of the bell in the tower of the Royal Exchange, summoning all merchants to trade. The Exchange was the city's commercial heart, modelled on the great Burse at Antwerp, Europe's first stock exchange, which in its sixteenth-century heyday had attracted bankers from all over Europe.[4] London's Royal Exchange did not deal on such an international scale, but it was where London's business was done. It sat at the intersection of six streets, forming a natural focal point for the eastern portion of the walled city, just as St Paul's Cathedral did for the western end. Twice a day, at twelve noon and six in the evening, the bell in the Exchange's tower rang. In its Italianate piazza, stocks were traded, shares bought and sold, gossip exchanged.

Rider personified commercial London. For generations, the city's merchants had enjoyed elevated status, their prestige recorded in the city's ancient livery halls, grand homes of the city trade guilds. Stained glass windows, rich plateware in silver and gilt, ceremony and ritual marked their members out as nothing less than mercantile heroes.

We should define here what constituted a merchant in seventeenth-century London. A merchant was a wholesaler who almost certainly traded goods on the international market. Those who sold goods or services on the domestic market were never known as merchants; they were simply known after their trades, as haberdashers, shipwrights, vintners, tailors, and so on. A merchant had a status well above the average person in a trade. Some merchants, it was said, were as rich as princes.

Rider was not quite a merchant prince, but he was on the way up. With the knack of thriving in any weather, he had made his money under both monarchy and Commonwealth. During the reign of Charles I, Rider laid the foundations of his fortune as master of a ship trading in the Straights – the common name for the Mediterranean, so called after its narrow entrance from the Atlantic. The Mediterranean had been a mainstay of London's foreign trade for hundreds of years. Shakespeare nodded to this important link in several plays: *The Two Gentlemen of Verona*, *Romeo and Juliet* (set in Verona), *The Merchant of Venice* and *Othello* (whose full title was *Othello, the Moor of Venice*). Trade with Italy, Turkey and the Levant was well established from Tudor times, bringing spices, cloth and luxury goods for sale in the metropolis's upmarket shops, or to be sold on into other west European countries. Londoners were acquainted with the

Ottoman Empire both via the tales of those who went there – sailors, merchants and their factors – and by the goods that emanated from it. Queen Elizabeth had strengthened trade links between the vast empire and her small realm off the coast of Europe.

From his trading activities in the Mediterranean, Rider made sufficient money to become a major investor in the East India Company (EIC). This great speculative machine controlled the majority of London's eastern foreign trade, chiefly with the emperors, nabobs and sultans of countries such as China and India. Those who ran the EIC believed that no foreign ships should trade along routes or in foreign ports it considered as its own. Trading voyages might take two years or more, but the potential profits were great. So were the risks. The EIC allowed merchants like Rider to split the risk on voyages. Each year, the company would assemble a fleet bound for the east. The merchant princes and aristocrats who owned stock in the company shared in the profit – or loss – of all ventures. Later, the rules were altered to allow merchants to buy parcels of investment in each of the ships. Thus each merchant was not open to all the company's risk, but only to that in the voyages he helped finance.

With his fingers in many pies, Rider was far from unusual. Many wholesale merchants had multiple interests. In Rider's case, the business that had made him wealthy was the prosaic, everyday matter of supplying the navy. During the Commonwealth years, he imported timber, tar and pitch via the Baltic, chiefly from Sweden, making himself essential to government.

What men like Rider hoped was that any new government, especially a new monarchy, would continue to find them indispensable. In the meantime, impermanence in government was bad for business; orders were not made, bills not paid. For Rider, a political settlement of whatever nature was best arrived at soon. Merchants like him provided the economic powerhouse that made London what it was – a city grown fat on trade, where all social classes lived cheek by jowl in the maze of its medieval streets and the entrepreneur was never far from the next deal. For such men, a change of government was something to be weathered rather than feared.

The close proximity of London's social classes reflected the city's history. A wall around any city initially dictated the limits of building. The great and the wealthy lived cooped up with the low and the needy. When the threat of invasion receded and the city could expand outside the walls, the new suburbs tended to cater for a growing workforce rather than for the wealthy. Only with the western expansion of London towards Westminster in the early 1600s had an area grown up specifically for the aristocratic classes. The merchants, many of them spectacularly wealthy and members of merchant dynasties, tended to stay put in the original city, next to their businesses and close to their rivals. By and large, this meant they rubbed shoulders daily with the poor and the ordinary. All shared in the atmosphere of urban vibrancy on a level unknown anywhere else. The urgency, the fun, the immediacy, the opportunity and the unhealthy stench all made London what it was. There was simply nowhere else like it in England.

It was therefore no surprise that the retailer John Graunt and the plutocrat William Rider lived among the same crowded streets. In what had once been the heart of the Roman city, along Lombard Street and thereabouts, merchants built their houses of brick or dressed stone, marking them out among the medieval wood and plaster cityscape. These grand houses were generally set behind courtyards, distancing their inhabitants from the noise and bustle of the street.

For most who could afford it, that was not enough; taking a leaf from the aristocrats' book, a country house was required. Rider was one of those who could afford it. He could escape the old city's smells and filth by taking a coach through Bishopsgate and driving a mile north-east to his Elizabethan country house, Kirby Castle, in the pleasant agricultural hamlet of Bethnal Green.

A man like Rider spent most of the week at his city house, from where it would take minutes by carriage or sedan chair to the Royal Exchange or to a tavern where fellow merchants congregated to gossip and do deals, or else to the waterfront where the core of the city's business lay among the warehouses and shipping. From the Exchange, Rider's journey to his warehouses took him down Water Lane, where sat the headquarters of Trinity House.* This was the corporation that oversaw safety at sea, building lighthouses, marking channels and providing pilotage on the Thames. In the spring of 1660 Rider became a trustee of Trinity House, an honour that allowed him to take a small but important step into the establishment.

From Trinity House, Rider had only to turn the corner to enter Thames Street, fronting the river. If Leadenhall was the chief retail artery of the city, the Thames was its beating heart. So important was the Thames to London that the city's Lord Mayor was the 'conservator' of sixty miles of river from 'Gravesend in the East, to a place called Colme Ditch in Surrey' (possibly the point at which the River Colne joins the Thames at Staines).[5] Lining the old city's southern edge were the quays and docksides along the river. This was the Pool of London, the

* Trinity House came into being in 1514 by royal charter of Henry VIII.

deep anchorage stretching from London Bridge to the Tower. Standing on the quays, Rider could see before him a constantly changing scene of ships coming and going, barges putting in and out, wherries criss-crossing; the sky was filled with the persistent movement of masts, sails and spars.

On the landward side of Thames Street ran a continuous wall of solid buildings with small, barred windows. These were the warehouses. Ships and lighters tied up at the wharfs to unload pepper from Java, cinnamon from Istanbul or Malaya, sugar from Barbados and Jamaica, tobacco and indigo from Virginia, wool from Yorkshire, coal from Newcastle, tar and timber from Sweden, cotton, silk and saltpetre from the Bay of Bengal. Here could be found more of London's wealth than anywhere else in the city, except perhaps for the strongboxes of the goldsmiths in Cheapside, under the afternoon shadow of St Paul's Cathedral.

William Petty watched and wondered about the economic laws that underpinned the city's economic activity. Bringing his analytical mind to bear, he formulated theories about the nature of trade and the economic forces at work which would influence Adam Smith in the eighteenth century, Karl Marx in the nineteenth and John Maynard Keynes in the twentieth. In the 1660s the merchants of London worried about more immediate things: how the King would affect their business, what taxes might be imposed, and whether or not London could find a way to compete with its great rivals, the Dutch. Amsterdam's trade was greater than London's, its merchants wealthier, its global reach further and more secure, its shipping better developed and its navy stronger. As London waited to welcome its king, Amsterdam was the great cloud on the horizon.

*

For the warehouses to be filled, emptied and filled again required a huge army of workers, each one connected in some way to the next – chandlers, sailors, shipping agents, warehousemen, customs officials, carters, shipwrights, ropemakers, sailmakers, tavern owners, potboys, victuallers, cooks and more. Their living depended not only upon their own efforts, but on those of people from across the world whom they would never meet. London was the hub of a global economy, linking China, India, Java, Borneo, Zanzibar, West Africa, the Americas, the West Indies, Sweden, Turkey, the Levant and Russia. London was not simply a city, it was a great engine of trade.

There was one London trade in which the merchandise at its heart did not have to enter or leave the city to make money. This was the African slave trade. The business consisted of trading textiles from the East Indies and other goods for slaves in East Africa, who were then sold in the slave markets in the West Indies and America. The slaves were shipped across the Atlantic via what was known as the Middle Passage to English colonies. On the return voyage the ships were loaded with tobacco, sugar, indigo and other produce to be off-loaded in British ports, before completing the triangular journey back to Africa. The trade was slow and haphazard. For it to become an organised economic force a figurehead was required, someone who could give the trade new impetus and focus. In the spring of 1660 such a person was yet to appear.

As the spring days lengthened, there seemed no escape from the rumours and speculation. The gossip spread out beyond the city walls at Ludgate, across the Fleet River, and into the lawless alleys of the ragged urban slum known as Alsatia. Built across a former monastery garden, this was now home to some of the most villainous people in England. In a maze of streets sandwiched between the Tudor walls of the Bridewell prison on the east and the lawyers' leafy enclave of the Temple on the west, debtors, scroungers, murderers and thieves were left to manage their own affairs and think their own duplicitous thoughts. The area was so notorious that it would provide the material for a play, Thomas Shadwell's *The Squire of Alsatia*.

West again was the Strand, where speculation circulated among the wealthy aristocrats and gentry who inhabited fashionable modern mansions and older houses built in Tudor times. For aristocrats, the return of the King mattered a great deal, for without a king, the aristocracy had no meaning. The aristocratic system worked on patronage flowing downwards from the monarchy. If the King returned, patronage would flow once more; status and power would be restored to nobility who during the Cromwellian era had been seen as less valuable than, in Cromwell's famous dictum, 'the middle sort of men'.

North of the Strand lay the mildly disreputable area of Covent Garden. Only a few years before, it had been fashionable, after Francis Russell, 4th Earl of Russell, commissioned Inigo Jones to create a square with a church and a terrace of fine houses in the 1630s to replace a shanty town that had offended Charles I. The area had fallen down the social ladder once more when taverns and brothels opened up around the south end of Jones's innovative Italianate piazza, copied from that at Livorno. One of the inhabitants of the Piazza was the artist Peter Lely. If the King returned it could herald a great commercial opportunity for Lely, who had been making his living painting the portraits of wealthy merchants and Parliamentarian grandees. A reinstated royal court might be a major new source of commissions.

Lely was one of a large and varied population of foreigners living in the city. They included German merchants, Jewish traders, diplomats from many states, a handful of men of letters, and commercial agents and merchant seamen from many lands. A member of a small group of foreign, chiefly Dutch, artists who had come to earn their living in England, he was born in Germany to Dutch parents; his real family name was van der Faes. The name Lely derived from a lily carved over the door of the house where his father was born in The Hague.

Lely arrived in England in the early 1640s aged twenty-one, at what seemed an excellent time for an ambitious young artist. The arts were flourishing in England. Charles I was a great patron of painters, commissioning works from many of the finest European artists. England had few notable painters of its own: the break with Rome and the rise of Protestantism had seen to that. Only the great William Dobson rose out of a sea of home-grown mediocrity. With the death of Antony van Dyck in 1641, and Dobson five years after that, there was room for a new premier court painter.

Lely hoped his time had come, but within a year of his arrival civil war broke out. It had been a hardscrabble existence since then. He had been reduced to giving painting lessons, among his pupils being a keen boy of very limited financial means and a real aptitude for drawing: his name was Robert Hooke, the son of a curate and schoolteacher on the Isle of Wight. Perhaps with the return of the King, Lely could give up teaching and get back to producing the great landscapes he longed to paint.

Close to Lely's house in Covent Garden Piazza, in an alley off Drury Lane, Mrs Helena Gwyn struggled to bring up her two daughters Rose and Eleanor (the latter known either as Nell or Nellie). Mrs Gwyn had been born in the parish of St Martin in the Fields, and had lived in the parish almost all her life. Her husband, who was said to have been a Welsh army captain, had abandoned the family, leaving mother and daughters to fend for themselves. Mrs Gwyn took to the bottle and to keeping a brothel in Coal Yard Alley. It can't have been an easy business in a Puritan town. Her girls grew up knowing they had to make their own way in life without the expectation that anyone would help them. Families like the Gwyns had more to worry about than whether or not the King was likely to return.

Further west, in the drawing rooms along the well set-up streets around Whitehall Palace, political gossip competed with social chatter. Here were located the houses of the nobility most closely connected to the royal court. In 1660 the few former courtiers who remained in residence shared the comparatively clean streets and air of Westminster with the Parliamentarians, soldiers and political revolutionaries who had run the country under Oliver Cromwell. Included among them were those who had sat in judgement on the old King and sent his head rolling on a scaffold outside his own Banqueting House. Such men had especially good reason to ponder how the dead monarch's son might deal with them if and when he were restored to the throne.

The aristocrats, too, had reason to be wary; as the political wind backed and veered, it was not impossible that a more draconian regime might emerge that would not look kindly on the nobility. Many stayed out of town, glad to find an excuse to keep away.

Family matters called Katherine Jones, Viscountess Ranelagh, to Ireland and ensured she was well away from any unpleasant developments. She was one of the most important figures in Restoration London. The so-called 'invisible college' that preceded the Royal Society may have met at her house. London was her natural milieu; there she mixed in the circles of the most brilliant minds of the day. Her brother, Robert Boyle, who was yet to carry out the scientific work that would grant him lasting fame, was also in Ireland, finding life on the family estate increasingly unrewarding. A settlement that restored stability would attract those of wealth and status back to London.

Secrets, no matter how vital, were hard to keep. From drawing rooms, taverns and the teeming streets, talk of the King swirled down to the Thames, to be picked up in the hundreds of wherries that sculled across to the far bank of the river, taking the gossip to the industrial slums of Southwark, where the unskilled and the skilled worked and lived together. The rumours flowed down the river, to the shipyards where ships that sailed across the Atlantic or the Indian Ocean and beyond were built, maintained and lay at anchor between voyages. A procession of ship owners, captains, investors and merchants daily made its way up and downstream to see how their new ships were coming on, their rowers dodging between the hundreds of other wherries criss-crossing the river.

Downriver, beyond the Deptford shipyards, the land was low-lying and given to swampy pools; these harboured mosquitoes that caused malaria – swamp or campaign fever, as it was called. Yet the air here was cleaner than in the city. Here were several more of London's shipyards, some military, others commercial. Next to the shipyards of the East India Company, across two hundred acres of land, John Evelyn and his wife Mary had created their Garden of Eden, a unique collection of trees and shrubs, many of them rare species from overseas. Evelyn was a cultured man of inherited wealth. He and his wife had evaded the horrors of the Civil War and the subsequent problems associated with being Royalists by travelling in Europe. Evelyn was warm-hearted, a steadfast friend to those he considered worthy. He had a puritanical attitude to all forms of licentiousness, along with a well-developed sense of duty to the state – and on the debit side was as dreadful a snob as any man whose father made the family fortune from the manufacture of gunpowder.

When Evelyn was not thinking about horticulture and his beloved garden, he thought about London, its great capacity for wealth and its current parlous state. He compiled lists of the practical trades, the processes involved in manufacture, and the types of businesses undertaken. His hope was to produce encyclopaedic profiles of London's business and trades. The sheer diversity and complexity of the material defeated him, and he abandoned it. This allowed his inquisitive mind to be taken up with the unstable political situation. In the autumn of 1659 Evelyn had anonymously published a pamphlet entitled *An Apology for the Royal Party*, arguing that the interregnum had brought nothing but unfulfilled promises propped up by military might. Only the restoration of the monarchy could, he reasoned, bring the order and stability he saw all around him in his garden.

In his modest house in Holborn, John Milton had Evelyn's pamphlet read to him. The poet was now totally blind, but he could plainly see the way the political wind was blowing. He dictated a broadside in response to Evelyn, advocating a return to republican principles of equality.[6] But Milton was tarnished goods, having sold out in some eyes by becoming a minister in Cromwell's military Protectorate. There were few republicans – or Commonwealth men, as they were known – of any substance left to speak out. They were either dead, in retirement, or destroyed by events. The last of the breed, General John Lambert, had been ignominiously deserted the previous autumn by the army he hoped to lead against Monck and thrown in the Tower. There was some heroic spark left in the old soldier: on 3 March Lambert escaped and attempted to raise an army to overthrow Monck, only to surrender without a shot being fired.

Even though the republican cause was hopelessly compromised and fragmented, Milton felt he must reassert its values and warn against the re-establishment of monarchy, that 'unsound noxious humour of returning to old bondage, instill'd of late by some [cunning] deceivers'.[7] Others spoke out, but they were people without clout; men like Robert Locker, a labourer, who appeared before the Middlesex magistrates to answer the charge that he had spoken 'words against the King's Majesty'. Other men and women were heard saying uncomplimentary things and hauled before the magistrates. Only a month or two before, they would have been cheered for their egalitarian spirit. Those of more substance, and with more to lose, kept their heads down as events unfolded with astonishing rapidity.

Among them was John Thurloe, Cromwell's Secretary of State and spymaster. Throughout the growing turmoil, Thurloe had somehow managed to remain in government and, to everyone's surprise, in the spring of 1660 still occupied his post. Thurloe had information that might be worth a great deal to a returning monarch. But could it be parlayed into an agreement? And would Thurloe wish in any case to part with it? Even with his precious supply of intelligence, could Thurloe, the arch Commonwealth and Protectorate man, do anything to ensure his survival under a restored monarchy?

In London, royalist politicians secretly and tentatively felt their way towards an agreement with the exiled King, who resided in Holland. At the centre of these delicate negotiations, directing emissaries back and forth, was General Monck, a man proving himself to be more flexible than his physical bulk might indicate. At the start of the Civil Wars Monck had fought for the King, then for Parliament, becoming a bulwark of Cromwell's

Protectorate. What Monck seemed to hope for with the King's return was the introduction of a constitutional monarchy, encompassing a Parliament with ample powers, and a liberal atmosphere in which all political sides and creeds could get something of what they wanted, ensuring peace would reign. Like many old soldiers, Monck was more politically naïve than he liked to think.

Parliamentary elections were held. The country voted out numerous old Commonwealth men and Cromwellians and voted in many royalists and Presbyterians, men who favoured an agreement with the King. Among those elected was Thomas Bloodworth, an ambitious member of a very wealthy London merchant family whose fortune came from dealing in silk and lead, investment in property and membership of the East India Company. His father John had been master of the Vintners' Company, while his mother Anne was the daughter of the East India Company's bookkeeper, Andrew Ellam. The family were staunch royalists who supported the return of the King. Thomas, ambitious for influence as well as money, was one of five merchants who signed a credit note promising £25,000 for the King to assist his return. Within a few years Thomas Bloodworth would be Lord Mayor of London.

As spring wore on, despite the commercial activity in the streets, a stillness enveloped the city. It was a stillness of the mind, of expectation and suspense. The army was everywhere, its officer class noticeably culled of its Commonwealth men and replaced by royalists and trimmers. And, like the first sparrows of spring, a type of person long exiled from London began to appear on the streets. Threadbare figures who, despite their obvious dearth of funds, carried themselves with the assurance of those who had once been able to hold their own and were certain of their worth, some had the look – a sort of contained hauteur – of men who had once been able to persuade others to do their bidding, to turn the disposition of a crowd.

These were theatrical men, stalwarts of the playhouses that had existed before the wars. They had lost their livelihood when the Puritans closed the playhouses in 1642 to cut down on public licentiousness, 'Fasting and prayer having bin often tried to be very effectuall.'[8]

With rumours of the King's return, the theatricals emerged to sniff out the possibility of returning to their old profession. Among them was a tall, distinguished-looking figure, his dignified appearance let down by an oddly upturned nose. This was the theatrical producer and writer Sir William Davenant. At the age of fifty-four, Davenant was a link with the past, with the great period of Renaissance English theatre. William Shakespeare had been a friend of his parents. For a few years Davenant had been keeping the wolf from the door by staging semi-clandestine theatrical evenings in his home. In this way, he dodged precariously around the ban.

Sensing the royalist wind was picking up force, Davenant was keen to open a new public theatre. He knew that other former theatre owners were also anxious to resume business. Aware he had to beat the opposition, Davenant went to inspect a disused real tennis court at the end of Portugal Street to see if it could be turned into a theatre.*

Building a theatre inside such a tennis court was an idea copied from the French. Tennis courts proved ideal for the purpose, their long, high interiors lending themselves to the

---

* In Wenceslaus Hollar's perspective map of central western London of 1650, the tennis court can be seen on the western side of Lincoln's Inn Fields, protruding into the public spaces.

erection of a stage and a deep auditorium. Davenant signed a lease and began to look around for an architect and builder to turn the property into the theatre he had in mind.

Word spread that the wily impresario and poet was returning, planning to open a public theatre. The theatricals sensed their time was coming round again. And so, with Charles not yet back on the throne, theatrical life began to seep back into the city, coming up from below, without fanfare, whispering that fun was about to make a comeback.

Off the Kent coast meanwhile, at anchor in The Downs, the English navy awaited instructions.*

* The Downs was the sheltered stretch of water north of the English Channel, stretching between Dover and Deal. Here the fleet could maintain a state of readiness, while still taking on supplies.

CHAPTER 2

THE KING COMES IN

At his home in Axe Yard, not far from John Thurloe's official residence, a young man made preparations to accompany his employer on a voyage. This was 27-year-old Samuel Pepys, born in Salisbury Court off Fleet Street, the university-educated son of a tailor and a seamstress, now with several years' experience in government work as a teller in the Exchequer. Pepys arranged for his house to be shut up, while his nineteen-year-old French wife, Elizabeth de St Michel, was sent to stay with friends in the country. In his diary (which he had started to keep in January), he wrote on 6 March 1660 that he thought the King might return soon. It is safe to suppose that he based this speculation on information from his employer.

Edward Montagu was the son of an earl and held the rank of general-at-sea, recently bestowed upon him by the Council of State. Despite the great differences in their social status, Pepys and Montagu were related; Montagu's mother was Pepys's great-aunt. Pepys was Montagu's private secretary, and the two men shared an analytical and pragmatic turn of mind. Born in a house built by Oliver Cromwell's grandfather, Montagu had served as a general in the Parliamentary forces. In the heady and uncertain days of late 1659 and early 1660 he switched sides. Seeing the political chaos that had developed since Cromwell's death, Montagu was not alone in believing rule without a king had run its course.

Along with General Monck, a few among the nobility, and a few Anglican bishops, Montagu nursed a secret: he was in contact with the exiled King. Montagu was one of those planning, in the parlance of the time, 'the King's coming in'. At his desk at the Navy Office in Seething Lane, Montagu compiled lists of dyed-in-the-wool Cromwellian officers to be forcibly retired from the Navy. His view was that this was the time for flexible men like himself, men who knew how to bend with the wind, to take charge. On Montagu's hit list were those he could not trust to accept change, those firmly attached to the ideals of the Commonwealth or the rule of the Protectorate.

On 23 March, Montagu left his desk and took a boat down the Thames to join the fleet off Dover. Pepys accompanied him. Once on board his flagship, Montagu vigorously renewed his cull of officers with republican or suspect sympathies.

In the Dutch town of Breda, the exiled King was preparing his statement of intent, a letter setting out his objectives upon his return. Charles had lived in Breda for most of his exiled years, thanks to the support of his sister Mary, who had married William II, Prince of Orange and head of state of the Dutch United Provinces. Upon William's death, the country's republican leader and opponent of the House of Orange, Johan de Witt, extended his predecessor's courtesies towards the Stuarts. Owing to its historic connections to the House of Orange, Breda had once been an important city. Many noble families had resided there. Its glory days, though, were long over and the town in which Charles resided was a backwater, largely ruined by war, with only a few fine houses remaining.

Here, Charles drew up his calling card to his kingdom. His close advisors were his Civil War counsellor Edward Hyde, the Irish royalist James Butler, 1st Duke of Ormonde, who was a close friend of the King, and Sir Edward Nicholas, former Secretary of State to Charles I. The letter they produced promised freedom of religious expression for all who did not seek to overthrow the Crown, restoration of land and titles to dispossessed aristocracy, and a general amnesty for all who had fought on Parliament's side against Charles I. Those who had directly planned the execution of the King were to be exempted from the amnesty. An order to this effect was to be drawn up by Parliament, which would decide who was to receive exemption. Charles's document seemed to have something for everyone, including death for the regicides – except that the document was not quite what it seemed.

With hindsight, it would be realised that the document had one clear intention and one clouded exclusion. The clear intention was to ensure that soldiers like Monck, who had fought with Cromwell, would be immune from any future legal action for their part in the war against Charles II, and their subsequent part in the administration of the Commonwealth and Protectorate. The part that would later be seen to be important by omission was any guarantee for the actual role of Parliament in the future government of the country. The declaration mentioned a 'free parliament' by which Charles gave the word 'of a king' to be advised, but it did not spell out the actual relationship between Parliament and Crown concerning, for example, which took precedence over the other on important matters such as taxation or declaring war. In his clandestine negotiations, Monck had been too eager to safeguard his own position to think about that of the country as a whole. Charles and his advisors must have marvelled at an agreement so advantageous to the King and of such disadvantage to those old adversaries of the House of Stuart – the elected members of the House of Commons.

On 1 May the secret talks were made public. Rather than seeking to sharpen up a hazy document, the two Houses of Parliament, now replete with royalists, sought only to race one another for the honour of voting for the King's return. The House of Lords won by a whisker. Thirteen years had passed since the Cromwellian generals Henry Ireton and John Lambert had written a constitution that guaranteed rule by monarchy *and* Parliament. Charles I had turned it down and gone to his death. Now his son was to return on the basis of a document that did not spell out the constitutional arrangements for how the country would be governed. It was one of the greatest failures of oversight in the history of Parliament, and indeed of the country.[1]

On 9 May the Declaration of Breda was presented to Parliament in the form of a 'Bill of General Pardon, Indemnity and Oblivion'. Heated debates took place, with many showing their new zeal for the monarchy by calling for widespread retribution. Realising their days on earth were numbered, many of those who had signed Charles I's death warrant quietly began to leave the country, bound either for the Calvinist states of northern Europe or for Puritan New England. The round-up of those who stayed stretched from Yorkshire to Ireland. The changing of the political guard was taking place swiftly, although the King was still weeks away from landing on English soil.

A letter from the King was presented to London's Lord Mayor, the sheriffs, aldermen and common council men, promising to renew the city's charter and to allow the Corporation to retain its privileges. Commonwealth politicians of the upper social ranks kept their thoughts to themselves, but republicans from London's working classes made their views known in strong language. Many appeared in magistrates' courts, charged with treason. On 11 May, Edward Medburne, a glazier from Wapping, was arraigned in front of the Middlesex magistrates, accused of shooting his mouth off in the Gun Tavern in Wapping. According to witnesses, Medburne said he that if he met the King he would 'run his knife through him and kill him', and he did not mind if he was hanged himself. He also said that if the King and General Monck were hanged together he would 'spend that day five shillings for joy', a hefty sum for a working man.[2] Dorothy Phillips, the wife of a shoemaker, was brought in front of the magistrates for calling the King a bastard. It is not known what happened to Medburne and Phillips, but it was not a time for leniency.

Events were moving rapidly. On 12 May, Montagu's fleet set sail and two days later it arrived at the Dutch port of Scheveningen. A large retinue of members of the Houses of Lords and Commons and of assorted grandees from the merchant classes of London made their way to The Hague to greet the King, who had left Breda to base himself on the coast in preparation for returning to England. Businessmen always know on which side their bread is buttered. In their hearts, many – or even most – might have remained antagonistic to the House of Stuart and hostile to Episcopalian rule by the church of which the monarch was the figurehead, but in their heads they knew the direction in which power had shifted. Shrewd minds would have worked out that if London were to be able to go about its business unhindered by the change in government, it had better take the initiative. Thomas Bloodworth was among the eighteen 'commissioners' representing city merchants. If Charles was astonished to see them on Dutch soil, he let nothing show. He knighted all of them for their pains.

On 23 May, Charles, accompanied by his brother James, went on board Montagu's flagship. On the same day, in London, husband and wife Edward and Alice Jones appeared in court, charged with treason for saying that 'it was the King's time now to reign but it was upon sufferance for a little time.' Over the ensuing weeks, Londoners regularly appeared in court accused of similar crimes. Others rejoiced and paraded royalist banners in the streets.

As the royal entourage set sail from Holland, London's business elite busied itself getting rid of republican symbols. The arms of the Commonwealth were removed from the Guildhall and replaced with the yellow and blue Stuart royal standard. In New Palace Yard, in Cheapside and at the Old Exchange, the common hangman burned copies of the Parliamentarian Solemn League and Covenant. Not to be outdone, courtiers gathered in Whitehall Palace found a bust of Cromwell, strung it up by the neck and left it dangling from a window.

On 25 May the King landed at Dover. Monck was there to greet him. The King made Montagu and Monck Knights of the Garter. Montagu was created an earl and Monck, by dubious dint of descent from an illegitimate son of Edward IV, a royal duke. For his part in the voyage, Pepys received a sum of money, something always close to his heart.

Charles was astonished at the tumultuous welcome that greeted him. He had fled the country on 14 March 1646, pursued by Oliver Cromwell's Ironsides, with a £1000 price tag on his head. Now Cromwell's former flagship, the *Naseby*, renamed the *Royal Charles*, brought him back in triumph. He landed on the beach at Dover to the blare of trumpets and a salute of cannon. The huge throng of people gathered under the cliffs heaved with excitement as the King, whom most had never seen, sprang agilely ashore.

A press of courtiers and dignitaries jostled to kiss the hem of the King's slightly threadbare robes and deliver the humblest declarations of loyalty and love. Most were rewarded with a smile and a nod. The one exception was the King's friend from boyhood, George Villiers, 2nd Duke of Buckingham. Three years earlier Buckingham had made his peace with Oliver Cromwell and returned to England from exile. Charles found that hard to forgive. When Buckingham kneeled, Charles snubbed him.

There followed words of homage from the mayor of Dover and other dignitaries before a leisurely progress towards London, which Charles planned to reach on his thirtieth birthday, 29 May 1660. He made one lengthy stop en route. Six days earlier, at Charles's urging, his dead father had been canonised at Canterbury as a martyr of the Anglican Church. Charles's first task in England was to pay tribute to his father. During his three-night sojourn in the cathedral city, the King was presented by the mayor with 'a tankard of massy gold'. During the stopover, George Monck – along with three others, the Earl of Southampton, William Morrice and Sir Anthony Ashley Cooper – was made a privy councillor.

The Stuarts particularly valued the order, which bound its members, or knight companions, personally to the monarch. Charles I in particular had held great store by it, wearing the insignia to his death on the scaffold. On hearing of his father's death, nineteen-year-old Charles II had his portrait engraved by Wenceslaus Hollar. Charles I was depicted wrapped in a cloak on which was ostentatiously pinned the order's great star-like medallion, giving the little portrait an impressive symbolic meaning that indicated it was created to be distributed for propaganda.

Then it was on towards the capital. The King, now attired in a silver doublet and a gold-laced cloak, was accompanied by his two brothers, riding just behind and to either side; the humourless James, Prince of Wales, dressed all in white, and the boisterous Henry, Duke of Gloucester, in green silk, twenty years old and described by Edward Hyde as 'a prince of extraordinary hopes'.* Hyde later recalled: 'all the way from Dover thither being so full of people . . . it was as if the whole Kingdom was there.'[3] Samuel Pepys noted that, 'The shouting and joy expressed by all is beyond imagination.'[4]

Charles recorded his own reaction in a letter to his sixteen-year-old sister Henrietta Anne, written after his first day back in England: 'My head is so prodigious dazed by the acclamation and by the quantities of business that I know not whether I am writing sense or no.' He joked that it was clearly his own fault that he'd stayed away so long, since everyone he met in England had longed for his return.[5]

Meanwhile, from across the south and east, troops, militia and bands of rejoicing royalists were drawing towards Blackheath. This high expanse of heathland immediately to the south of London had been the scene of historic gatherings including the Peasants' Revolt in the fourteenth century and Jack Cade's Rebellion and the Cornish Rebellion in the fifteenth. Now it was the rendezvous for Charles to inspect an army that had been until days before, in name at least, that of a republic. It was to be the greatest demonstration of loyalty so far.

General Monck had spent five months purging the army of republican and other 'unhealthy' elements, cashiering hundreds of religious and political radicals and replacing them with

---

* Henry was to die three months later of smallpox.

royalists. At the same time, the delicate business had begun of disbanding all Cromwellian regiments, the continued existence of which was a permanent threat to the monarchy. Facing the King so soon after his arrival in the country with tens of thousands of battle-hardened Roundheads might prove a venture too far.

Charles's cavalcade lengthened as it reached the heath. But all was not unalloyed celebration. Macaulay's *History of England* gives us a typically vivid insight into the other side of the King's reception:

> Everywhere flags were flying, bells and music sounding, wine and ale flowing in rivers to the health of him whose return was the return of peace, of law, and of freedom. But in the midst of the general joy, one spot presented a dark and threatening aspect. On Blackheath the army was drawn up to welcome the sovereign. He smiled, bowed, and extended his hand graciously to the lips of the colonels and majors. But all his courtesy was vain. The countenances of the soldiers were sad and lowering; and, had they given way to their feelings, the festive pageant of which they reluctantly made a part would have had a mournful and bloody end.[6]

Macaulay's flowery description seems at first fanciful, but it was based to some extent on the eyewitness account of Edward Hyde, the King's loyal counsellor. Ever attentive to the political wind, Hyde detected hostility in the ranks. In more prosaic style than Macaulay, Hyde recorded that the expressions on soldiers' faces that day made plain that 'they were involved in a service they were not delighted in'.[7]

*

Charles reached London Bridge on his birthday, 29 May, riding a white stallion. Before him ran the River Thames, to which London owed its birth and on which it depended for its life. Beyond the river the city sloped upwards to the great cathedral, with the rooftops of the Guildhall and the other mansions of the guilds rising above close-packed streets, signifying wealth and commercial expertise reaching back hundreds of years. Above them jutted the spires of the parish churches; ninety-seven in all, with a few smaller ones besides. Outside the walls were thirty-three more, all testifying to the religious core of seventeenth-century society. Bells rang from scores of belfries. Banners fluttered everywhere.

At the south side of London Bridge, the Lord Mayor of London, Thomas Allen, offered the King his sword of office. In return the King knighted Allen and gave him back his sword. The mayor's act of greeting the King was no idle piece of theatre. It was based on the ancient ritual whereby in exchange for maintaining London's liberty as a self-governing city, the mayor once a year made the journey to Westminster to swear allegiance to the king. This annual journey soon became known as the Lord Mayor's Show, and is enacted to this day.

The Lord Mayor rode across the bridge in front of the King, to be greeted with jubilation. Among the crowds that lined the streets was John Evelyn. Always anxious to be at the heart of things, Evelyn had travelled up the river from his estate at Deptford to see the King's return. Wisely, he chose not to watch the King pass through the congested medieval city, instead picking the wide, modern road of the Strand, which followed the line of the river west to the King's destination at Whitehall. On the Strand, Evelyn found a celebratory mood prevailing among the rank and file stationed along the highway as Charles's cavalcade passed by:

> This day, his Majesty, Charles II came to London, after a sad and long exile and calamitous suffering both of the King and Church, being seventeen years. This was also his birthday, and with a triumph of above 20,000 horse and foot, brandishing their swords, and shouting with inexpressible joy; the ways strewn with flowers, the bells ringing, the streets hung with tapestry, fountains running with wine; the Mayor, Aldermen, and all the companies, in their liveries, chains of gold, and banners; Lords and Nobles, clad in cloth of silver, gold, and velvet; the windows and balconies, all set with ladies; trumpets, music, and myriads of people flocking, even so far as from Rochester, so as they were seven hours in passing the city, even from two in the afternoon till nine at night.
>
> I stood in the Strand and beheld it, and blessed God. And all this was done without one drop of blood shed, and by that very army which rebelled against him: but it was the Lord's doing, for such a restoration was never mentioned in any history, ancient or modern, since the return of the Jews from their Babylonish captivity; nor so joyful a day and so bright ever seen in this nation, this happening when to expect or effect it was past all human policy.[8]

Evelyn was correct – it was extraordinary and unexpected. The city that welcomed Charles II was wracked by divisions left intact by the war fought between Charles's father and major elements of Parliament. London, formerly the bedrock of Puritan opposition to monarchy, now rose in celebration of the return of the exiled King. Writing two decades after the event, Hyde recalled that from the time the Restoration looked certain, 'there was such an emulation in Lords, Commons and city and generally over the kingdom [on] who should make thee most lively expressions of their duty and of their joy.'[9] Writing from a royalist perspective, Hyde had inadvertently put his finger on an interesting phenomenon. As if overnight, the city outwardly changed from being pro-Parliament and republican to being for the King. Monck's purges of the upper echelons of the army had done their job, while London's Parliament-supporting trained bands were no match for Monck's military grip.

Lucy Hutchinson, a Latin scholar whose husband had been a Roundhead officer, wrote that Charles enquired, 'where were all his enemies?'. No wonder, she asked, 'for he saw nothing but prostraitive expressions of all the love that could make a prince happy'. 'Indeed,' she added, 'it was a wonder that day to see the mutability of some and the hypocrisy of others and the servile flattery of all.'[10]

Both the statesman and the army officer's wife alluded to the great divisions in the nation that had prevailed during the previous twenty years. The country had been split into opposing religious and political factions. In such conditions, where one came from and what one's parents' religion was were matters of great concern. Each person's upbringing defined how they lined up during the taking of sides that led to civil war in 1642, and where they stood afterwards. Now, with the return of the King, many found it in their interests either to change sides or to keep their mouths shut.

The key to why a city that had been staunchly nonconformist and Presbyterian during the Cromwellian years put on such a splendid show for a returning member of the hated House of Stuart lay in its ancient structures. The origins of London's self-governing charter were lost in time, but it may have first been granted by William the Conqueror. The city's rights were subsequently written into the Magna Carta in 1215. The livery companies, the ancient guilds regulating individual trades, also traced their power back to royal charters, the oldest of which was that granted to the mercers, or cloth merchants, by Richard II in 1394. Charles II and his advisors understood this and knew that support in London was vital to the success of his return. Therefore, the King had written a letter from Breda to the mayor, sheriffs and aldermen asserting the city's ancient rights to self-government by a corporation, and the renewal of its royal charter. The members of the livery companies saw royal acceptance as vital to their ability to protect their interests. Those at the forefront of corporate and commercial life in London were hardly supporters of the House of Stuart, but they knew they required validation from the King in order to perpetuate their ancient systems of independent governance and freedom to trade. A good show was one way of ensuring the returning King would look upon them kindly.

In this way, the city that greeted Charles was shaped by a dynamic past bound up with that of the monarchs of England. Its ancient origins lay in Roman settlement in AD 47, with its walls built in the time of the Emperor Claudius. Subsequently, it was sacked by Queen Boudicca, rebuilt and then abandoned by the Romans, before resettlement by Alfred the Great in the ninth century. All this explains why the city was a medieval jumble of streets inside Roman walls. By the seventeenth century its confined and twisted medieval heart was a far from ideal cradle for the creation of the modern world. But London was more than that; though the walled city was its core, its royal hub was to the west, with the 'West End' developed during the reign of Charles I. Thanks to the ribbon development that snaked along both the south bank of the Thames to the shipyards and the main roads out of the city, London was already in the process of turning itself into the multi-centred metropolis we see today.

The population was young; attracted by the chance of a job or a fortune, people flooded in from all over the country. Marriage took place comparatively late among the labouring classes (it was generally delayed until people were in their late twenties), so the greater part of the workforce was unattached and full of youthful vigour. This was a population ready to cast off Puritan shackles and have fun. Tavern keepers and street entertainers were ready to provide the sport they needed. At night there was no street lighting, so citizens had to beware of robbers. No gentleman of rank would venture out without a sword, and would preferably go in company.

Almost everything made in England was either sold or finished in London. The city's chief industry in the 1600s was cloth finishing – the messy and smelly business of cleaning, bleaching and dyeing woollen cloth into a finished product for domestic and foreign markets. Along with that went the trades making domestic items and luxury goods for home and abroad, and the shipbuilding trade along the Thames. This huge concentration of industry required large amounts of coal, brought by sea from Northumberland, and a banking system based around the goldsmith-bankers to finance it all.

The city that greeted the returning King was a mixture of the luxurious and the squalid. John Graunt thought it overcrowded. 'The old streets are unfit for the present frequency of coaches,' he wrote. Graunt considered overpopulation to be the cause of Londoners' ill-health. Tuberculosis was common, with an astounding 10,000 people per year dying from it. Plague returned with appalling regularity. Infections spread easily as the poor lived in houses of multiple occupancy, several families often inhabiting a space built for one. They shared latrines inadequate even for the original number for which they were intended. Basic hygiene was difficult for the poor, who could not afford piped water and had to depend upon public standpipes and pumps. In such households, coal to heat water for washing the body was a luxury.

On the late spring day of 29 May, however, London's usually filthy streets had been cleaned, flowers scattered along the royal route, flags and banners roped from house to house and rich tapestries hung from balconies. The King paused his horse continually; he kissed the beautiful wife and newborn baby of a tavern owner; he watched a spectacular pageant laid on by the Corporation in St George's Fields. Deep into the night giant bonfires burned, some two or three storeys high. Cavalier songs were sung and fountains reportedly flowed with wine. There was no let-up in the following weeks as nobles, courtiers and city grandees vied with one another to entertain the King and his brothers. To welcome the King, the city's livery companies put on grand banquets in their ancient guildhalls, each competing to be more lavish than the others. The poet John Dryden, who had walked in Cromwell's funeral cortège beside fellow poets Andrew Marvell and John Milton, now wrote a long panegyric to the King, entitled *Astraea Redux*:*

> Oh Happy Age! Oh times like those alone
> By Fate reserv'd for great Augustus throne!

Dryden celebrated what he perceived as the return of justice and order. Most of all, what the poet was looking for was political stability. He was not alone.

The return of monarchy after eleven years' absence caused those of a reflective turn of mind to wonder exactly what might

---

* Astraea was the Greek goddess of justice, hence 'Justice Returned'.

be in store. Charles II was something of an unknown quantity, a cipher onto whom great things were projected. But would an untested king have the personality and character to carry the people with him and heal the fractured kingdom? In the minds of the people of London, and in those of many who laid plans for his return, the unproven and largely unknown Charles was the perfect exemplar of a traditional king: a man who embodied God's rule on earth and was a regal symbol of that power. What most did not know – for how could they? – was that he was a playboy, carrying hardly a jot of statecraft within him.*

Though obsessed with carnal pleasure, this unlikely ruler was set to become a catalyst to whom London reacted favourably. The lives of a great many of its inhabitants would undergo radical changes – those of Montagu and his secretary, William Rider and other merchants, the experimenters in the new field of natural philosophy, at least one of the daughters of Mrs Gwyn the brothel-keeper, John Graunt, John Evelyn and many, many others. Under Charles II, London would enter an age of transformation.

---

* According to his boyhood friend, the 2nd Duke of Buckingham, Charles had no statecraft at all.

CHAPTER 3

THEATRUM REDUX!

The lavish arrival ceremony for the returning King signalled a return to London of crowd-pleasing spectacle. During the tight grip of Puritanism all grand public displays had been banned. With the return of the monarchy, public pageants and the playhouse were also set to make a comeback. Prominent among those anxious to bring the theatre back to London was the former theatrical impresario Sir William Davenant. Once a leading light in the world of the English stage, Davenant had been running a semi-clandestine theatre in the back salon of his rented home, Rutland House in Aldersgate, near Smithfield livestock market. Now that the Cromwellian ban had been lifted, he was keen to resume business.

With advanced ideas on staging, Davenant was to play a decisive role in the story of English theatre, changing the style of productions and the form of plays. Davenant's important role in the revival of the London theatre grew out of his colourful pre-Restoration career. Like many of those who were to make their mark in Restoration London (the polymath Christopher

Wren being a good example – his father having been Dean of Windsor, young Christopher spent some of his childhood living at Windsor Castle, where he would undoubtedly have met the King), Davenant was an important link between the Restoration and the pro-royalist antebellum.

Davenant was born in 1606, the year Ben Jonson's *Volpone* was first performed and William Shakespeare's *King Lear* was presented before James I. He was the son of a wine merchant who rose to be mayor of Oxford. Shakespeare was a family friend, often staying with the Davenants at the Crown Tavern.* The playwright reportedly took a shine to young William, who in later life liked to suggest that he might be the great man's son.[1] There is no proof of this, but the boy's life was to take on the semblance of a Shakespearian tragicomedy, with the protagonist suffering many misfortunes and misadventures before gaining his heart's desire. What Davenant desired was his own playhouse and company of players. By the age of seventeen or eighteen he was married, soon becoming a father. Ignoring his own father's wishes that he apprentice himself to a London merchant, he took service in aristocratic houses, learning the manners of the upper classes while pursuing literary ambitions. By the age of twenty-four he would be a published poet and dramatist.

On his way to achieving success young Davenant gained an enviable patron in Endymion Porter, the arch-courtier of the age, becoming a favourite of the Queen and part of her energetic social and cultural scene at court. Henrietta Maria loved to watch and take part in court masques. The chief designer and writer of these entertainments were respectively Inigo Jones and Ben Jonson. When Jonson tired of writing for the court,

---

* The building exists today at 3 Cornmarket, Oxford.

Davenant was ready to take his place, writing masques with parts written specifically for the Queen.

At the age of twenty-two, Davenant was appointed the Queen's vice-chamberlain. The King's Men performed his comedy *The Wits*, which was a success. All was going well with the young man's swift upward climb until he found himself in a horizontal position in Axe Yard, Westminster, with 'a black handsome wench' from whom he told John Aubrey he caught the pox.[2] Davenant was treated by the Queen's physician, Sir Thomas Cademan, undergoing expensive treatment with that 'devil mercury'.[3]

Though mercury possibly helped cure the initial onslaught of the disease, it may have contributed to the severe ill-health Davenant suffered for the next two years. He dropped out of his fashionable circle. Rumours circulated that he had died, and he had to write to his friends to assure them he had not.[4] When he returned to view, Davenant's physical appearance had changed dramatically. His nose was curiously flattened and upturned, giving him an unfortunately comical look. The syphilis bacteria had eaten away the cartilage supporting the bridge of his nose, causing it to collapse and create what is known as a saddle-nose deformity.

Davenant resumed work, and upon the death of Ben Jonson in 1638 became de facto poet laureate, writing masques performed at court, one of which included both the King and the Queen among its cast. The outbreak of civil war saw Davenant's fortunes decline disastrously. The King's Men joined the Royalist army *en masse*. Although some of the players saw action, the company became in essence an entertainment troop, giving performances at Oxford, where the King had his wartime headquarters.[5] Davenant fought on the Royalist side in the early stages of the war and went on to raise money for the purchase of guns; he was knighted for this service, but his personal money soon ran out.

The Puritans' closure of London's playhouses threw players, prompters, costume makers and the rest into a hand-to-mouth existence, 'Cause they can't work, but live by play.'[6] Despite the ban and the threat of public floggings, illicit performances were staged.[7] One way around the ban was to disguise plays as something else. As there was no prohibition on other forms of staged events, including music, actors rather cunningly put on what were known as 'drolls', a form of comic musical revue. Parliament passed ordinances against the players, branding them 'rogues'.

Davenant attempted to build a playhouse, but when the plan crashed and the investors lost their money, he decided he must hold theatrical events at his home. So he installed a temporary theatre in a long, narrow salon at the rear of the house. The small group of adventurous theatre fans who turned up on 23 May 1656 saw not a play in any conventional form but an assemblage of music, song and dramatic scenes, described by Davenant as 'opera' (but being more like a collection of set pieces resembling Davenant's court masques of old), at a stroke both referring to Italian musical theatre and distancing his work from the banned form of the play.[8] A government spy paid his five-shilling entrance fee and reported back to Cromwell's espionage chief, John Thurloe, that he had seen and heard nothing that smacked of the hated theatre.

Davenant had pulled it off. He had disguised theatre by calling it opera, and had incidentally begun the development of opera in England. There was another reason why Davenant was able to stage his theatrical events while others struggled to do so: he engineered them to ensure that they made some reference to Cromwellian government policies.

Davenant introduced the visual framework that would hold theatre in its grasp for the next three hundred years – the proscenium arch, or 'picture window' stage. With his new device, he put on one of the most important productions in the history of the English stage: *The Siege of Rhodes*, based loosely on events of 1522, when the Spanish blockaded the city. This entertainment in September 1656 not only referred disparagingly to England's arch-enemy Spain but marked the beginning of English opera, containing musical and recitative elements we would recognise today. A greater novelty was the appearance of the first Englishwoman on an English stage, a lady called Mrs Catherine Coleman.* John Webb, an architect who had learned his craft assisting Inigo Jones in the design of court masques that incorporated moveable scenery and other theatrical *tours de force*, designed the sets. Even the high-minded John Evelyn went to see *The Siege of Rhodes*, reporting that he had witnessed an opera 'after the Italian Way, in recitative music and scenes'.[9]

Davenant followed up this success by moving production out of his house and into one of the city's disused theatres for an opera about Sir Francis Drake. From there he planned the playhouse he was to build in Lisle's tennis court. It was to be a blend of the traditional and the innovative, designed to give London's public an entirely new theatrical experience. Davenant's wish was to take the English tradition of rhetorical theatre and build on top of it a new drama based on spectacle. This would require new forms of writing and acting. It would also require the shocking introduction of women players, in the European manner.

---

* French actresses had appeared on stage in London in the late 1620s.

Having once been unofficial poet laureate to Charles I, now, in the spring of 1660, Davenant felt sure Charles II would show him similar favour.

As he made his revolutionary plans, little did Davenant realise that a theatrical spectacular was being planned that would surpass any marvel he could produce. This was the trial and execution of the regicides, the men who had dared to execute the King's father, Charles I.

Immediately after Charles II's return, and in compliance with his wishes, a new Parliament set about compiling lists of the men who had allegedly played a part in his father's death. These were drawn up according to the clause in the King's declaration of general amnesty made at Breda, which stipulated that those involved in sentencing his father to death were exempt from pardon. One list was compiled in the House of Commons while another, longer one emerged from the House of Lords. Many of those who drew up the lists had fought on the Parliamentary side in the Civil War, or had taken part in the administration of the Commonwealth or Protectorate. Now they prepared to send their former friends and colleagues to the scaffold.

The combined Houses of Parliament identified fifty-six men they regarded as regicides. These were drawn largely from two groups: high-ranking officers in Cromwell's army and members of the House of Commons. A few unfortunates who were particularly hated by the new Parliament were included out of spite. The firebrand Roundhead preacher Hugh Peter was one of these, his name added to the list although he had not sat in judgement on the King. Some escaped the list by paying large bribes. Many evaded retribution by simply declaring it had all been a terrible mistake and they had now seen the error of their ways. In a particularly celebrated case, Richard Ingoldsby successfully claimed that Oliver Cromwell had held his hand and forced him to sign the King's death warrant. His signature on the document was notably florid.

Revenge was in the air. Many royalists looked forward to a bloodbath of Commonwealth men who had ruled after the execution of Charles's father. Wiser heads knew that political divisions had to be healed. Sheer numbers dictated that many of the most significant members of the previous administration would have to be pardoned, and perhaps – if the price were right – welcomed into the new administration. All sorts of former Commonwealth men were suddenly ardent royalists. With the change in government, men knew their fortunes could be made or ruined, dependent upon what they had done in the past – or more importantly how they were perceived now. Those who changed tack ranged from spies and diplomats like George Downing, or politicians and lawyers like Bulstrode Whitelock, to well-known poets like Andrew Marvell and John Dryden.

For a small but important group, the King's return signalled not an opportunity for a position at court, a monopoly of some sort, or a title, but a fight for life itself. Men who had run the country now had prices on their heads. Many fled to the continent, pursued by royalist spies, kidnap gangs and assassination squads. Their departure brought opportunities for others keen to pick over their abandoned estates and property.

When the regicide Sir James Harrington fled to the continent, his wife had no option but to sell their home to raise money. Swakeleys House was a red-brick mansion with Dutch gables built on an enormous scale at Twickenham, on the Thames to the west of London. It was bought by Robert

Viner, a talented and ambitious young London banker and goldsmith, whose family were already well established in both lines of business. Viner would later go on to become Lord Mayor of London and an important financial backer of the monarchy.

While Viner benefited from Harrington's escape, for the Puritan poet John Milton flight was not an option, as he was blind. Milton, who had served in Cromwell's government and had written extensively against tyranny and the rule of kings, knew he was unlikely to escape the hurtful attentions of the new regime. He went into hiding in a friend's house in West Smithfield. His friends claimed he was dead and staged a funeral to convince the authorities. After some weeks, Milton judged it safe to reappear. He had miscalculated and was promptly imprisoned in the Tower, where he was held under threat of execution for treason until the intervention of Viscountess Ranelagh, Andrew Marvell and others. Continuing anti-royalist sentiment among the lower classes was rewarded by prison, the stocks, flogging and, in some cases, death.

In October, those regicides who could be rounded up were subjected to a series of show trials at the Old Bailey. Twenty-eight had been selected for trial, chiefly because they had not run away and had been easily apprehended. On the evening of 9 October their guards gathered them together in the Tower of London and read them the indictment for high treason. It was the first time they had heard the charges against them. The trials began on the following morning at the Sessions House of the Old Bailey, giving the defendants no opportunity to hire lawyers or prepare a defence. Voices opposed to the Stuarts forecast that the proceedings would be rigged, and so it turned out. When they began, it became clear that every effort had been made to ensure guilty verdicts. The Solicitor-General, Sir Heneage Finch, and the Baron of the Exchequer, Sir Orlando Bridgeman, had secretly met with other senior lawyers to change the rules of evidence. They decided corroborating testimony was unnecessary, as was any legal defence for the accused.[10] Eleven judges sat on the bench, accompanied by thirty-four lay commissioners. A contemporary estimated that no fewer than fifteen of them had opposed Charles I, either fighting in the Parliamentary army, as members of Parliament or as judges who had sentenced him to death. Now they sat in judgement on their former friends and allies.

During the lead-up to the trials, Charles was surprisingly quiet on the subject. He had his partisan Houses of Parliament to do his work for him, with his brothers James and Henry as his go-betweens to ensure all went to plan. He also had personal matters on his mind. His chief distraction was his mistress, Barbara Palmer. The daughter of an ardent Royalist, she had returned from exile with him. According to one observer, the relationship 'did so disorder him that often he was not master of himself nor capable of minding business, which in so critical a time, required great application'.[11]

Charles had a yet more vexing matter to contend with. Anne, the daughter of his great advisor Edward Hyde, had become pregnant by James, Duke of York, who had secretly married her. For the House of Stuart, this was a serious matter, for it meant that James could not be married to some suitable foreign princess and so forge or strengthen an alliance. Courtiers suggested all sorts of stratagems to get James out of the marriage, but Charles declared that his brother had made his bed and must lie in it.

The trials were a sensation. Londoners flocked to the

courthouse to watch. The Sessions House was a peculiar building, with the courtroom open to the street, so the throng could press up against the perimeter railings and watch as those who had so recently run the country were tried for treason. Whenever the accused began to speak in their defence or to ask the court a question on a point of law they were quickly slapped down. The common hangman stood by the bar of the court, holding a noose, indicating to the accused what they could expect and to the jury what they should decide.[12]

The cases were quickly heard and death sentences were carried out in tandem with the hearings, designed to take place over ten days. On 13 October the executions began at Charing Cross, close to the spot where the King's father had been sent to his death in 1649. Londoners thronged to see the second great spectacle of the new King's reign. The first of the regicides to be executed was Thomas Harrison, a Cromwellian colonel and an ardent Puritan and anti-royalist. If the new government thought the imminent torture and slow death would show their old enemies to be men of straw they were mistaken. Harrison's brave demeanour and defiant speech were unexpected. 'God hath covered my head many times in the day of battle,' he declared. 'By God I have leaped over a wall, by God I have runned through a troop, and by my God I will go through this death.'[13] After being throttled on the end of a noose, Harrison was lain down on the scaffold, still conscious, to be disembowelled. As the executioner leant over him and with his knife began his task, with one last Herculean effort Harrison leapt up and hit him on the chin. This was not the sort of theatre Charles and the turncoat court had been hoping for.

Not all those condemned to death had signed Charles I's death warrant or taken part in his trial. Some were executed for other forms of involvement. John Cooke, the brilliant young lawyer who had written the case accusing the King of making war against his people, was among them. In his speech from the gallows he said he was the first man ever condemned to death for supporting justice. He admonished the former Commonwealth men who had sentenced him, saying, 'Brother hath betrayed brother to death'. Having learnt a lesson from Harrison's execution, the sheriff in charge interrupted Cooke several times before giving the order to have him hoisted by the neck and swung choking out over the crowd before being taken down and disembowelled.

Forced to watch Cooke's grisly death was Hugh Peters, whose crime was to have been Cromwell's favourite preacher. As Peters cried out, 'Oh, this is a good day. He is come that I have looked for and I shall be with Him in glory!' the crowd drowned him out with booing and jeering.

According to Evelyn, as the first of the men who had had the temerity to challenge the divine right of kings was tortured to death on the scaffold at Charing Cross, the King went to watch, hidden from the crowd behind a window. And so the executions took place 'in the presence of the king . . . whom they also sought to kill'.[14]

As the executioners went about their work, the smell became so bad that the site of the executions was removed from Charing Cross to Tyburn, the site of the ancient gallows to the west of the city on the road to Oxford. In all, ten regicides were hanged, drawn and quartered before the grisly exhibition was brought to a premature end, in fear that the London mob was turning against the display of violent revenge. According to a member of Charles's government, the King grew 'weary' of the killings.[15] Whatever the reason, Charles demonstrated what amounted to a degree of royal mercy, drawing back from revenge before the show trials moved towards their completion. Meanwhile, without fanfare or publicity, spies were dispatched to track down those regicides who had fled abroad. Plots were hatched to murder them or bring them home to face trial. Money was channelled to spies and kidnappers via Charles's sister Henrietta Anne, married to Louis XIV's brother Philippe. Charles may not have had the stomach for carnage upon a scaffold, but he had the heart for retribution.

CHAPTER 4

SOMETHING FOR EVERYONE?

When Charles returned, the question was, what would he do now? How would he reign? There is little evidence that he had given much thought to such matters. Fortunately, others had. Those with experience of government who were not on the run or in prison for their part in the trial and execution of Charles I had strong ideas about how the country should be ruled. The elected Cavalier Commons and the reinstated House of Lords knew exactly what to do, and a programme of reforming government structures and appointing new government officers was quickly under way.

Charles has often been portrayed as the Merry Monarch, the easy-going pleasure-seeker, but there was more to him. It is true he became the King of Fun, creating a court of carnal and sporting pleasure. But from the outset, he also became the King of Tolerance, allowing freedom of religious observance that helped heal the schisms of the past (though this tolerance would come under repeated pressure as his reign progressed). He became the King of War, prosecuting a series of conflicts with the Dutch in an attempt to win outright access to foreign trade and wealth. And he became the King of Commerce, presiding over state-sponsored mass slavery in order to provide a workforce for England's colonies, changing the social and political fabric of the nation for generations, and causing irreparable harm to West African societies, though few cared about or even recognised this at the time.

As soon as Charles was ensconced in Whitehall Palace, people who wanted something from him formed a metaphorical line at the palace door. But before he could dispense patronage, Charles had his own family to cater for. His brother, the Duke of York, was appointed Lord High Admiral, in charge of the navy, the single greatest organisational entity in the land. Then he turned to those who had stood by him in his exile, who had helped the royal cause on the battlefield or with money. These favourites were rewarded with titles, lands and jobs, as befitted their rank, role or abilities – and equally importantly, whether or not Charles liked them. The old guard was swept away and London saw a regiment of new faces take over the levers of power. Some, like the diplomat and spy George Downing, made the transition appear seamless, gliding from serving one administration to the next. Like many, Downing showed an aptitude for betraying his former friends that came as easily as changing his shirt. Thurloe, too tainted by Puritanism (and by his master Cromwell), was allowed to fade away, his intelligence-gathering ignored and his person shunned.

Some of the new faces were in fact quite old: Edward Hyde, now aged fifty-one, continued as Lord Chancellor, the office he had held in exile with the King (becoming the 1st Earl of Clarendon the following year), while 67-year-old Sir Edward Nicholas continued as Secretary of State, an office he now held jointly with 58-year-old Sir William Morrice, a relative of

Monck, who had helped arrange the King's return. These older men had great experience of office and were essential to Charles in arranging his new administration. He would soon tire of them, however, and replace them with younger men.

The arts, trades and sciences were all waiting for support from the King. Men of science and philosophy came calling, seeking a charter for a new society of learning and experimentation. Merchants and traders required the King's say-so – the granting of a warrant – to reopen businesses closed by the Puritans. Merchants trading with the East Indies and China wanted a new charter for their trading company, updating that granted by Elizabeth I. Those trading in Africa and the West Indies sought a charter for their new company. One group particularly close to the King's heart approached him for warrants to reopen the theatres.

Then there was Charles's own life to set in order. Ancient royal palaces needed reinstating as official residences. Charles's mistress, Barbara Palmer, needed to be set up in a grand house near Whitehall Palace. A suitable one was found in King Street, backing onto the palace gardens. Parliament had to agree an income for the King. It was set at a little over £1 million a year, a sum that seemed sufficient but was not – something which was to have profound repercussions for future relations between Crown and Parliament. Charles was not enamoured of Parliament. Like his father before him, he harboured ambitions of ruling as an absolute monarch. How, then, to find the money to rule? He had in his gift the incomes from various estates and from assorted taxes and duties. Would these be enough?

One man who thought he had an answer to making money for the royal coffers was Charles's irrepressible older cousin, Prince Rupert of the Rhine. Rupert was one of the most unfortunate of creatures, a prince without a principality, a warrior without a war. He was the third son of Frederick,

King of Bohemia and Elector Palatine, and Elizabeth, sister of Charles I.* Following battles in 1620 and 1622, Frederick had found himself deprived of both his titles and had to flee to The Hague, where Rupert was brought up. Rupert excelled at his lessons and grew to be a handsome man, exceptionally tall for the time (by the age of eighteen he was 6ft 4in in height). In later portraits we see a thin patrician face, with wide-set eyes above a long straight nose, a full wide mouth and a firm, cleft chin – a cavalier to the life.

Like many European nobles, Rupert was highly schooled in warfare. When the civil wars broke out in England, he volunteered his military prowess to his uncle Charles, acquitting himself ably, if erratically, on the field. Following the crushing defeat by Parliamentary forces at Marston Moor in 1644, he languished in Europe before returning to the British Royalist cause with the outbreak of the brief Second Civil War, taking command of a small fleet that harried Parliamentary shipping before turning to piracy. He then returned to Europe, latterly in service to the Holy Roman Empire in Vienna. With his cousin Charles seemingly miraculously recalled to power, Rupert left for England, where he was warmly welcomed and awarded an annual stipend of £4000. It was said he had turned up with some of his privateering money still intact, £2000 of which he used to bribe his way physically into apartments in the royal court. Comfortably bivouacked, and with a reasonable income, Prince Rupert found himself at the age of forty-one ensconced in the palace of his cousin the King, with an agile mind and little to occupy it.

To fill his days, Rupert took up alchemy, equipping a

---

* Rupert was therefore first cousin to King Charles II. His sister Sophia was mother to King George I of Great Britain.

laboratory in The King's Walk in the Temple, further developed his early method of printmaking by mezzotint, and endeavoured to keep himself busy. But he remembered his days in battle and those spent commanding his little Royalist fleet of privateers off West Africa. He had explored 150 miles of the Gambia River, caught malaria and heard stories of a mountain of gold somewhere in the interior. He added this legend to his cache of tales of heroic deeds.

There was gold indeed – although no mountain of it – in what are today Ghana, Togo and Benin. In the Precambrian era, enormous quantities of gold were deposited in quartz veins set in granite. By the seventeenth century, local people had begun hacking gold from surface veins, although most was laboriously sieved from deposits in the form of fine dust in sand and gravel. The Asante people, a sub-set of the Akan, made royal regalia out of gold so lavish they declared their land a Kingdom of Gold.*

Quite soon the stench of revenge faded away and the Palace of Whitehall became gripped by gold fever. The King's brother, James, Duke of York, found Rupert's stories particularly convincing. An expedition was planned to find the mountain of gold. Samuel Pepys noted, 'I heard the Duke speak of a great design that he and my Lord of Pembroke have, and a great many others, of sending a venture to some parts of Africa to dig for gold ore there. They intend to admit as many as will venture their (sic) per man.'[1]

The task of finding gold was entwined with a more general plan to establish trade links with various kingdoms in West

---

* In the nineteenth century a British envoy met an Akan chieftain whose gold bracelets were so heavy that he rested his arm on the head of a small boy. The British went on to fight several wars against the Asante's Kingdom of Gold, finally declaring it a Crown possession in 1901. Today, the Ashanti gold mine is one of the ten largest in the world.

Africa. This was not an easy matter. For many years, assorted Europeans, including the Dutch, the Swedes, the Danes, the Portuguese and the Spanish, had traded along the coast. In the late fifteenth century, the Dutch and Spanish sparred over trading rights for gold, slaves, ivory, pepper, mahogany and other commodities. In 1479 they fought the first European colonial war over access to the area's riches. The Dutch prevailed and in 1482 established a trading fort on the coast of present-day Ghana. Fort Elmina was the first European settlement in West Africa. The gold supply was controlled by, among others, the Asante nation, which coincidentally was one of the kingdoms in which slavery was traditionally practised.

Customarily, West African societies (but not all of them) acquired slaves in one of two ways, either by war between competing nations or via an hereditary system. In the seventeenth century, along the coast and in the immediate hinterland there were dozens of independent states, vying with one another for status and power. For example, the Fon dynasty of Dahomey only came into being at the beginning of the 1600s. The Fon, along with the neighbouring Asante, took slaves in battle. The first European nation to take advantage of African slavery for its colonies in the Americas was Spain, closely followed by Portugal, with the Dutch following suit much later, and only then the English.

Many ingenious justifications were to be made for colonising the Americas, exterminating the inhabitants and supplanting them with enslaved Africans. Aristotle was called upon for his authority: 'Those whose condition is such that their function is the use of their bodies and nothing better can be expected of them, those, I say, are slaves of nature. It is better for them to be ruled thus.'[2] This was taken as sanctioning the enslavement of all ordinary non-Christian foreign people. The fifteenth-century Spanish theologian Juan de Sepulveda built on those ideas, saying that the indigenous people of the Americas were 'natural slaves' as characterised by Aristotle: 'inferior to the Spanish ... as monkeys are to men'.[3]

Within a few decades of invading England, the Normans had sought justifications for conquering other nations. A twelfth-century Welsh monk named Gerald came up with excuses for sweeping the Irish off their lands and settling Anglo-Normans in their place. Here is one of the kinder things this factotum to Henry II had to say about the Irish: 'It should seem that by the just judgments of God, nature sometimes produces such objects, contrary to her own laws.'[4]

By Elizabeth I's reign, the English were not only spasmodically planting Ireland, but sporadically trading in West Africa, bringing slaves across the Atlantic to sell in the Spanish colonies in the West Indies or in England itself, though many more of these slaves were probably brought by Dutch traders. After a time, Elizabeth banned the use of slaves in England because their employment warped the home labour market, driving down the wages of labourers in East Anglia – an interesting early example of distortions arising from the internationalisation of commerce. From then on a desultory trade continued until the English civil wars reduced it to a trickle. Thanks to those domestic wars the English were unable to compete with other nations trading in West Africa, and so the Dutch became the dominant European trading nation in the region. This pre-eminence was what Charles, Prince Rupert and the Duke of York were keen to overthrow.

On 18 December 1660, Charles issued a charter setting up the Company of Royal Adventurers Trading to Africa. He bestowed on the company a monopoly on English trade running the length of West Africa from Cape Blanco (a peninsula north of the Gambia River), all the way south and east to Cape Castle (a trading fort built by the Swedes in Ghana in the 1650s). The monopoly, which was to last a notional thousand years, was to provide a platform from which to take on the Dutch East India Company, which was out-competing its rivals not only in Africa but in other territories.

The new company was very much a Stuart family initiative. The King promised to invest £800, the Duke of York, being the company's patron, £3600, Prince Rupert £800, and the Queen Mother, Henrietta Maria, £400. Characteristically, the King paid only £560 of the £800 he had pledged. Among the aristocratic investors attracted to the scheme were the Dukes of Albemarle and Buckingham and the Earls of Bath, Hawley, Ossory, Pembroke, St Albans and Sandwich. To these aristocratic investors (or adventurers, as they were called) were added a group of wealthy London merchants and senior members of guilds. They contributed not only their money but also their business acumen. Among them were the wealthy goldsmith and banker, Robert Viner, the Lord Mayor, Sir John Robinson, and Colonel Philip Frowde, the prominent East India Company investor. The company's books were to be kept by the able William Coventry, the Duke of York's secretary, who was no less ambitious than his father, the former Keeper of the Great Seal for Charles I. In all, the total amount in subscriptions promised by the primary investors was £17,400.

To confirm the royal family's commitment, James in his role as Lord High Admiral made it known he would lend the new company several Royal Navy ships to accompany its merchant vessels to Africa. The scene was set for the royal family's first commercial venture, albeit with the participation of experienced personnel from London's merchants, captains and seamen to carry out the task.

*

While the Stuarts put together the finances for their private money-making venture, there was one man long associated with the royal family who believed he richly deserved a job from the King. This was the architect John Webb. To begin with, it looked as if he was well on his way to royal preferment, for when it was known Charles was definitely on his way home, the government asked Webb to oversee the refurbishment of Whitehall Palace to make it once more fit for habitation by a king, to prepare 'ye Royall houses for yor Maties [Majesty's] reception'.[5] Whitehall Palace had been Oliver Cromwell's official residence as Lord Protector, but it had suffered neglect during the wars. After Cromwell's death in 1658 it had lain unoccupied. There followed a move to sell it off, which came to nothing. Now Webb oversaw an £8000 makeover. He claimed the work was done in the space of a fortnight, but quite how such a colossal sum of money could have been spent in so short a time is anybody's guess. At any rate, most of the money expended – including a sizeable sum out of Webb's own pocket – remained unpaid long after, setting a pattern to be repeated throughout the new King's reign.[6]

Webb was the most highly qualified architect of his generation. He was born in 1611 among the mansions and bookshops of a street called Little Britain, situated among the warren of narrow lanes to the north of St Paul's Cathedral. In terms of its inhabitants, Little Britain was a microcosm of the old city, where the wealthy and the not-so-well-off lived side by side. At the age of seventeen Webb went to live with his uncle, Inigo Jones, studying classical architecture under his tutelage. According to Webb, Charles I himself had demanded that he be 'brought up by his unckle

Mr Inigo Jones upon his late majestyes command in the study of architecture'.[7]

We only have Webb's word for this, but true or not, he was the first English architect to be trained by another in the classical architecture of Italy. Jones himself was the last of a breed: the master masons and carpenters who had built medieval Europe. These men, all learned in their trade, some of them geniuses, had remained mostly anonymous down the centuries. Jones's name, too, might not have come down to us had he not become a designer of court masques and gone on to become the protean force that brought a new style of architecture to England.

By dint of his studies with Jones, Webb could rightly be proclaimed as the first professionally trained architect in England. Like William Davenant, he was a link with the court of Charles I, and was perfectly equipped to introduce new forms of theatrical architecture. Webb was ambitious enough not to be content with picking up commissions from actor-managers and country gents who wanted a Tudor house remodelled or a new one built. He wanted more.

Inigo Jones's importance in the history of British architecture cannot be overstated. He changed the nation's architectural landscape, introducing a rational, methodical code of humanism from beyond the Alps. During two trips to Italy he fell under the spell of the ancients, and also fell for the distillations from the ancients made by Renaissance humanist architects such as Alberti and later theoretical works by Andrea Palladio. The latter's writings harked back five hundred years to the Roman architectural writer Vitruvius, from whom future luminaries such as Michelangelo Buonarroti and Leonardo da Vinci learned much. Jones was not alone in having noticed some of these correspondences, nor in having read Vitruvius or Palladio, but he was the first person to bring these ideas back to England, determined to put them into practice. Importantly, he had the ability to do so. In essence, what Jones realised was that when the great fifteenth-century architect and engineer Filippo Brunelleschi planted an octagonal dome on top of Florence's cathedral he had firmly put the lid on Gothic architecture.

The first building designed by Jones in the Italian manner was at Greenwich, on the site of a royal palace and castle dating back to the thirteenth century. This revolutionary building, designed by Jones for Queen Anne (the wife of James I), would be called the House of Delight, harking back perhaps to the 'Palace of Pleasaunce', or Placentia, built for Margaret of Anjou, wife of Henry VI. Jones's new building was designed as a lodge attached to the old palace. When the queen fell ill work ceased; it was not resumed until the reign of Charles I, when the lodge was completed for Queen Henrietta Maria. The new building, afterwards known as the Queen's House, exhibited a smooth, mathematical restraint quite different from anything seen before in England.

The Queen's House was quickly followed by another royal commission, the Banqueting House, built for James I. With its enormous double-cube reception hall, it was a radical departure from the medieval great room, replacing its typical mullioned, latticed windows and heavy beamed ceiling with large, clear windows and rood beams hidden above a flat plaster ceiling, decorated in a stately Italian classical manner. Jones designed not only the hall but the sets, costumes and special effects for many of the masques staged there, until the installation of the famous ceiling paintings by Peter Paul Rubens put paid to theatrical events for fear of candle smoke damaging Rubens's images of a transcendent and divinely appointed James I.

Jones had hoped – as had James – that the Banqueting House would be the first section of a glorious new palace on the banks of the Thames. Like so many of the building plans of the House of Stuart, it was not to be; in this case it was stymied when a not-so-transcendent Charles I was led out from under the scenes of divine providence to his execution.

When Jones died, three years after the King's execution, his enormous collection of drawings and books, including those gathered during his travels in Italy, was left to Webb. Most importantly, Webb also inherited Jones's ideas, skills and love of Italian architecture. While Webb received the great man's library, his wife, Jones's first cousin once removed, inherited his wealth. Webb was therefore fully equipped to continue his mentor's work without financial worries. He had worked with Jones on royal buildings, including Somerset House, set by the Thames about half a mile downriver from Whitehall Palace, as well as the plans for the proposed new palace at Whitehall itself. He also worked with Jones on domestic buildings, including Wilton House in Wiltshire, where the double-cube room echoes that at the Banqueting House.

Webb was at the cutting edge of the new vogue for the classical in architecture. He designed the first classical portico on an English house, at The Vyne, near the village of Sherborne St John. This was a not altogether happy marriage of Gothic and Palladian, the portico being placed on a house with crenellations or false battlements across the roofline. It was an early mismatch, caused by the 25-year-old architect's youthful ambition. The design may have been fumbled, but Webb would not make many more mistakes.

Given the theoretical and practical training he received from his mentor, it was not unreasonable for Webb to think that with the monarchy restored he would be appointed to his old master's position. With his advanced thinking, Webb saw himself as the pre-eminent choice as surveyor to the returned King. It was not to be.

Making sure he described the work he had done so speedily at Whitehall, Webb wrote a petition to Charles, asking for the job of Surveyor of the King's Works, which he said he had in effect carried out for some time for the King's father. In this role he had worked on designs for a new palace at Whitehall, which he discussed with Charles I while the King was a prisoner at Hampton Court, and then at Carisbrooke Castle on the Isle of Wight, in 1647–8, during the months leading up to Charles's trial and execution. Charles's desire for a new palace, designed all of a piece, to replace the hodgepodge at Whitehall dated back to his time in Spain in 1623 when he saw the Escorial, the palace of Philip IV.[8]

The old Whitehall Palace was to be pulled down and a new one – intended to rival Versailles – built in the garden of St James's, leaving the waterside open.[9] The evidence of the collections of drawings now held at Worcester College, Oxford, and in the collections of the Cavendish family, the Dukes of Devonshire, at Chatsworth House, shows a vast neoclassical palace set around a series of symmetrical courtyards. The plans, initially drawn up by Jones, were worked up into finished drawings by Webb shortly before Charles I's untimely death put an end to the project.[10] It was to these thwarted dreams that Webb referred in his application to the new King.

Webb's petition fell on deaf ears. Unknown to him, Charles had made his choice of surveyor before sailing from Holland. Webb was sidelined in favour of the courtier Sir John Denham. Although described by John Evelyn as 'a better poet than architect', Denham had the advantage of being a royal favourite. In 1649, following the execution of his father, Charles II had offered Denham the post of Royal Surveyor if and when he regained the throne. Eleven years later he made good the promise.

Denham was born into a family of high-ranking royalist lawyers in Ireland in 1614. His father was chief justice of the King's Bench in Dublin and his mother daughter of Garret Moore, 1st Viscount Drogheda. Denham attended Trinity College, Oxford, and qualified as a lawyer from Lincoln's Inn, being called to the bar in 1639. With the death of his father, he inherited ten estates; moreover, his wife, Anne Cotton, brought a Buckinghamshire manor to the family. They had two sons and two daughters.

So far, so good, but Denham was a gambling addict. Although his estates provided an income of above £10,000 per annum, in one year he was reported to have run up debts of £4500 and signed away several estates owing to his love of cards and dice. He seems to have developed this taste for reckless gambling while still at Oxford, where he was reprimanded for not repaying a debt to the city's recorder.[11]

According to those who knew him as a student, Denham gave no inkling of wit or poetic abilities. But on the eve of the Civil War in 1642, he published anonymously both a verse play that was performed and a poem that was to become famous. The poem, *Cooper's Hill*, took the form of a bucolic reverie in which a description of the Thames from a famous viewpoint at Egham became a metaphor for the virtues of monarchy at a crucial point in history. John Dryden declared it 'the exact standard of good writing'.[12] Today it seems florid and laboured, but for many years it was much admired. During the Civil War Denham wrote anti-Parliamentary ballads and continued to run up gambling debts.

The odd thing about Denham was that although consistently tormented by creditors, he proved expert at raising money for the royal cause. On one occasion he brought £10,000 from Poland to the exiled royal court at Breda. Denham, therefore, was a man with faults but also with real strengths, particularly powers of persuasion. When not combing northern Europe for money, he resided at the exiled royal court.

When weighing up Denham's suitability for the position as surveyor versus that of Webb, there arose the problem of Webb's political reputation. During the interregnum he had not devoted himself purely to work for royalists. He had worked for Lord Fairfax, the former head of the Parliamentary army, drawing up designs for the rebuilding of the Fairfax seat at Nun Appleton in Yorkshire, and had worked for another prominent Parliamentarian sympathiser, the 4th Earl of Pembroke, whose seat was at Wilton.

Webb, however, had also done good service for the royal cause, having once been imprisoned during the Civil War for his undercover work as a courier and spy. When he heard of Denham's appointment he was so incredulous that he wrote a second petition rather rashly suggesting that the King change his mind, 'that Mr Denham may possibly as most gentry in England at this day have some knowledge in the Theory of Architecture but nothing of ye practique soe that he must have of necessity have another at his Maties charge to doe his businesse ... His Matie may please grant some other place more proper for Mr Denham's abilitye and confirm Mr Webb the Surveyors place ...'[13]

Charles was not about to begin his reign by allowing a commoner to persuade him to change his mind. Webb would have to be content with the position of Denham's assistant. Denham proved himself to be an able administrator, leaving Webb to carry out architectural design and oversee building work. With the King's blessing, Denham and the Lord Chancellor, Edward Hyde, convened a royal commission to do something about the congested and dilapidated state of the capital, 'for reforming the buildings, ways, streets, and incumbrances, and regulating the hackney coaches in the City of London'.[14]

John Evelyn, always with the wellbeing of London in mind, praised Denham for paving the streets of Holborn.[15] Denham's new paving meant that carriages could move more quickly and efficiently, while new gutters improved drainage to such an extent that he saved life, 'so many of the fair sex and their offspring having perished by mischances ... from the ruggedness of the unequal street'. Unencumbered by remedial works, Webb was free to rebuild Somerset House, as well as producing more new plans for a proposed Whitehall Palace designed along classical lines. Under Webb, classicism would signify the country's return to monarchy and Charles Stuart's grandeur as a rightful king, and set the tone for a nation led by hereditary kings, not commoners. But all that was yet to come.

Webb's new role as Denham's assistant surveyor promised much. He knew the long history of the various attempts by the House of Stuart to build a new royal palace at Westminster. He had seen Jones's early designs prepared for James I, followed by those for Charles I in the 1630s and late 1640s, largely drawn up by Webb himself in the years before the King's death. Charles II renewed the Stuart interest in a new palace and Webb was soon at work preparing new plans and reworking the drawings from the 1640s.

There were also ambitions for a new palace at Greenwich. When Charles first visited Greenwich he was surprised at the state of dilapidation into which the venerable Tudor palace had fallen. The house in which Henry VIII was born had lain vacant during the Commonwealth before being turned into a biscuit factory for the navy. Charles ordered it to be pulled down: only Inigo Jones's House of Delight was spared.

Webb was soon at work on plans for a new palace. But whereas the Whitehall scheme foundered on the financial rock that shattered so many Stuart building plans, the palace at Greenwich actually got under way. Webb's designs, based on drawings by Jones, abandoned the plain front of Jones's Queen's House and substituted a palace with all the exuberant ornament of the baroque. Inevitably, the money soon ran out. One wing was built, now known as the King Charles Building and part of the Royal Hospital. That was all. Charles never used it as a residence. The complex we see today was completed after Webb's death, when others took up the challenge to fill the largely derelict site.

Webb had other outlets for his prodigious skills. His knowledge of theatre design and production, honed under Inigo Jones, came to the fore. Soon after the Restoration, William Davenant approached him to design his revolutionary new theatre inside the disused Lisle's tennis court at Lincoln's Inn Fields.

The 54-year-old theatre professional, Davenant, and the 49-year-old architect, Webb, knew they had to make their mark now or never – and they trusted one another to succeed. They would make history and change theatre in Britain. Davenant's intention was to give the public something of the concealed wizardry previously reserved for the eyes of royalty, while offering the players a platform on which they would be free to move among their audience. Webb and Davenant knew they were on to a good thing. But it would take time to design and build.

To the problem of adapting a building that had been designed for a different purpose, Webb came up with an ingenious solution. His idea was to erect a building within a building. He designed a wooden structure to sit inside the masonry walls of the former tennis court. A wooden skeleton would support the raised stage, the wings, the proscenium arch, the flies for machinery, the seating and all the rest. Behind the arch, to the sides and in front of the wings were doors of the type via which a medieval actor would have been comfortable making entrances and exits. To the sides and at the back, the auditorium was flanked by raised galleries. The proscenium arch fronted a deep stage with wings sufficiently wide to allow for scenery flats that could be moved on and off from the sides. The flats could be arranged one behind the other from the front to the back of the stage, giving the illusion of great depth via receding planes. The English theatre as we would know it for the next three hundred years was born.

The theatre's patron, the Duke of York, was so pleased with the designs concocted by Davenant and Webb that he showed them off to visitors. The representative of the city of Florence, Giovanni Salvetti, wrote home that the Duke showed him 'the design of a large room he has begun to build in the Italian style in which they intend to put on shows . . . with scenes and machines'.[16]

Salvetti's dispatch pointed out that these innovations for the London public stage copied what was already the norm in Italy, where moveable scenery and machines for moving clouds and deities about were already the least that opera goers could expect. He might have added that Inigo Jones, thanks to his travels in Italy with the Earl of Arundel, had long since brought these ideas to England for use in court masques. As has been pointed out by others, Lisle's court theatre was the most important new playhouse in the history of the Restoration stage.[17]

While Webb was engaged in his many differing projects, the man whose name was later to overshadow his own was working in disciplines unrelated to architecture, with no inkling of his own future crucial role in shaping the nation's capital city. At the time of the Restoration, Christopher Wren was twenty-seven and spending his time between Gresham College in London, where he was professor of astronomy, and All Souls College,

Oxford, where he was a Fellow and bursar. As befitted a young virtuoso,* Wren was interested in several fields of empirical philosophy. He carried out experiments and observations in many areas, including medicine, but his primary interest at this time was in mathematics. In this he allied himself with the small but increasing number of natural philosophers who believed mathematics essential for understanding the observable world; even to be the foundation of God's creation. Mathematical demonstrations were, Wren said, the 'only truths that can sink into the mind of Man void of all uncertainty'.[18]

There is only one small clue to Wren's passing interest in architecture – a note in his papers that prior to 1660 he made some drawings of designs exhibiting 'strength, convenience and beauty in building'. This tripartite recipe revealed that, like Jones and Webb, Wren had read the works of Vitruvius, whose 'strength, utility and beauty' became the motto of the neoclassical revolution. But it was his mathematical interest that was to change Wren's life, for mathematics was seen not only as the core of the new empirical science but as the bedrock of architecture. Within a year Wren would be asked to offer his advice on repairing the crumbling fabric of St Paul's Cathedral.

---

* In the mid-seventeenth century a virtuoso was someone who, after the Latin *virtu*, had virtue, especially by being a skilled experimenter in the field of natural philosophy, or science. Only later did it come to be applied specifically to a talented musician.

CHAPTER 5
RIVALS

Sir William Davenant was not alone in his pursuit of the King's warrant to build a theatre. He had several rivals, chief among them the veteran producer and actor Michael Mohun, the bookseller William Rhodes, and the courtier and playwright Thomas Killigrew. Killigrew had the advantage over Davenant of being close to the King, as a companion and confidant. When Charles sailed home from Holland on board the *Royal Charles*, Killigrew was among those who accompanied him. Pepys, also on board, described Killigrew as being in 'very high esteem with the King'.

Killigrew had little formal education but made up for the deficiency with his natural wit and intelligence. His high good spirits and fondness for the stage were exhibited early on. According to Pepys, young Thomas frequented the theatre in his boyhood and when a request was made for a boy to go on stage and play a 'demon', as extras were known, Thomas would quickly volunteer. Unlike his brothers, Thomas did not attend university but went into service at the royal court, where he became a page to Charles I. He travelled widely on the continent and at the age of twenty-three was present in Loudun, France, during the notorious witchcraft trial, on which he reported.[1] In the same year, he wrote his first play, a tragicomedy entitled *The Prisoners*, performed at the Phoenix Theatre in Covent Garden by the Queen's Servants, a troop named in honour of their patron, Queen Henrietta Maria.

Though Killigrew has been portrayed as a libertine, in Anthony van Dyck's portrait, painted at the time Killigrew wrote *The Prisoners*, he appears as anything but. He has the sensitive face of a young man likely to be concerned by what others thought of him, rather than that of a rake. He was put down by Pepys as a 'court jester', employed to make Charles laugh. While that is certainly true, there was more to Killigrew than that. He was a well-read man from a cultured family that had been in royal service for generations. Upon the Restoration, his interest in theatre extended to becoming a manager. This was hardly surprising; like all the returning Cavaliers, he was financially hard up. His writing didn't help much. He probably received nothing at all for his plays performed while in exile. Even in England, playwrights were traditionally given the box office receipts for the third performance of each play, after which the theatre companies were deemed to own them. Only if the play were a tremendous hit would the playwright receive any further money. So, if a playhouse had 400 seats and charged five shillings to see a play, then the playwright's take was £100. This was not a pittance but nor was it a fortune, being about six times what a skilled provincial tradesman earned in a year. To live well, a playwright had to be prolific or have a share in the business. Early in his career, Killigrew had made efforts to open a theatre of his own but had been thwarted by the outbreak of the Civil War.

When the young Prince of Wales went into exile, Killigrew

went abroad in his service. In 1650 he was given an important role as royal representative in Venice. His task was to extol the royal cause and extract money to help restore Charles to the throne, much as Denham was expected to do elsewhere. While in Venice, Killigrew finished a play titled *Cecilia and Clorinda* which he had begun before his appointment, and wrote another, *Bellamira her Dream*, in its entirety.

Killigrew's mission to Venice did not go smoothly. Anxious not to inflame relations with the Commonwealth, in 1652 the Venetian government expelled him on the pretext of a charge that he ran a smuggling racket. According to a Venetian politician, the underhand method of his expulsion had a deeply unsettling effect on the young diplomat.[2] He was afterwards given the uncomfortable nickname 'Ambassador Tom'.

As fundraiser, diplomat and occasional spy, Killigrew travelled widely across Europe in search of money and support. While in Madrid he wrote his most successful play, *Thomaso, or The Wanderer*, with a plot based upon the foreign adventures of exiled Cavaliers. By 1655 Killigrew was in The Hague, where he met and married Charlotte van Hesse-Piershil, the daughter of a member of the court of the Prince of Orange. By now Killigrew had command of a regiment in the Dutch army, as was so often the way for impecunious Cavaliers.

At the Restoration, Killigrew's services were not immediately rewarded. He applied for, and failed to be awarded, various offices or sums of money, including a position suited to his military background as the keeper of the Greenwich armoury. When nothing materialised, Killigrew changed tack. On 9 July 1660, only five weeks after Charles's arrival in London, he applied for a royal warrant to start a theatre company named the King's Company of Players. Charles gave the project his blessing. With the advantage of the King's patronage, Killigrew's troupe was seen as being the direct successor to the King's Men of the Jacobean era. This was important, for it meant the company had exclusive rights to many of the older plays, including all of Ben Jonson's works and preferential rights over those of Shakespeare.

Killigrew's warrant was a blow for Davenant. He had waited twenty-one years to stage a play once again for a king, only to see his opportunity slipping away. For a playwright whose own plays had been produced by the original King's Men, the awarding of the warrant to another must have been personally grating and commercially daunting. Davenant was very different in character from Killigrew, being both more serious minded and more practised in the theatrical arts. He was also very determined. Desperate to salvage something from the situation, he suggested to the King that he and Killigrew should both hold warrants and run two separate theatres in London. Charles agreed, and so was born the Duke's Company, sponsored by the King's brother, the Duke of York. In July 1660 Davenant and Killigrew were rewarded with licences to run a joint monopoly, to 'erect two playhouses ... and absolutely suppressing all other playhouses'.[3]

The licences given to Davenant and Killigrew were hereditary, with the warrant holders able to assign their patents to their relatives or others they appointed. The peculiar notion of an inheritable monopoly on the stage dated back twenty years or more, to an attempt by Davenant to take hold of the theatre in Dublin.[4] Now the idea returned with the creation of a monopoly designed to squeeze smaller companies out of business. More importantly, Charles's granting of a monopoly meant that two trusted monarchists had absolute control over the theatre in London.

By the late autumn, both theatre companies were ready to begin production, helped by enlisting personnel from other companies who had little choice but to join them or starve. Davenant elected to form his company out of William Rhodes's young players from the Cockpit Theatre, while Killigrew chose the older players from Michael Mohun's company. Initially both companies had similar repertoires, comprised of Renaissance plays by Shakespeare, Webster, Fletcher, Middleton and the like, along with some new works by Davenant and others.

Killigrew was ready first, and his new company opened in the venerable Red Bull theatre in St John Street, Clerkenwell, on 5 November, before moving to a much more central site between Lincoln's Inn Fields and the Strand three days later. One of his first productions was a play by Davenant. Whether or not this was produced as a friendly nose-thumbing to the author is not recorded. Davenant would open a week later at the Salisbury Court Theatre, his revolutionary theatre at Lisle's tennis court being still under construction.

When Londoners entered Killigrew's new theatre, what they saw looked little different from a public theatre in the Elizabethan age. A stone's throw from Davenant's, Killigrew's playhouse was built in Gibbons's former tennis court in Vere Street, next to Clare Market, a small marketplace developed in the late sixteenth century, its tightly packed streets and Elizabethan buildings now housing a swarm of food stalls and shops.* Gibbons's tennis court was so narrow there was no space for wings or scenery, if Killigrew had wanted them, and actors made their entrances through doors at the back of the stage.

Though undoubtedly put at a disadvantage by the King's Men opening before him, Davenant banked on playing a long game. His new playhouse was far from ready, but his temporary

---

* Today, the site of Clare Market is largely covered by the buildings of the London School of Economics.

venue already had some innovations. Davenant also trusted his shrewd judgement of the ability of his players. He had the benefit of a leading actor of great talent and drawing power. Just as Shakespeare had written for the star of his day, Richard Burbage, Davenant had the star actor of his era, 25-year-old Thomas Betterton, who had gained early experience and training in illegal performances put on by William Rhodes at the Cockpit Theatre.

Lacking Davenant's technically advanced facilities, Killigrew planned his own crowd-pleasing novelty. On 8 December, one month after their first production, the King's Men produced Shakespeare's *Othello*. A prologue written by the actor, playwright and panegyrist Thomas Jordan announced to the audience that they were about to see something fresh, something that would correct a long-standing theatrical defect:

> Our women are defective, and so sized
> You'd think they were some of the guard disguised;
> For, to speak truth, men act, that are between
> Forty and fifty, wenches of fifteen:
> With bones so large and nerve so incompliant,
> When you call Desdemona, *enter* giant.

But, said the prologue, this would not be the case tonight:

> I come, unknown to any of the rest.
> To tell the news; I saw the lady drest –
> The woman plays to-day; mistake me not,
> No man in gown or page in petticoat.

And so the audience saw a woman play the main female role. The name of the actress who played Desdemona is unknown, but it was probably either Ann Marshall or Margaret Hughes, Killigrew's new female talents.

Before 1660, adolescent boys or young men had played female roles on the English stage. This did not mean that women were never seen on any stage. The private masques of the royal court were often graced by the participation of female members of the court and occasionally by the Queen. As we have seen, on at least one occasion in 1657 a woman acted in one of Davenant's semi-underground opera productions. Yet the skill of the female impersonator was in general accepted and lauded. With the Restoration, the sexually ambiguous Edward Kynaston was still young enough at twenty to play female roles, in which he was highly praised for his loveliness and ability to evoke emotion in the audience – 'a compleat stage beauty' according to the Duke's Company prompter John Downes.[5]

Since female members of visiting French companies had previously been seen on the London stage, the move away from an all-male cast was not quite revolutionary. Nor did female impersonation vanish with Killigrew's innovation: actors like the androgynous Kynaston continued to dress up and play the opposite sex for a few years yet. But from Killigrew's *Othello* onwards their days in drag were numbered. With his introduction of female actors into the mainstream theatre, Killigrew gambled that in his rivalry with Davenant, he who won the race would win all.

Various reasons have been put forward for the innovation in the autumn of 1660. One was that after the eighteen-year ban on theatres in London there were insufficient numbers of adolescent boys trained to play female roles, while the young adult leads who had played such parts had become middle-aged. Another was that the presence of women on the stage would help to refine the otherwise bawdy aspects of the theatre. There was even a clause written into the royal warrants awarded to Davenant and Killigrew stating they had the right to put women on the stage for this purpose. The real reason, however, seems to be more earthy. Charles had seen female actors in France and he wanted to see them in London. Women were put on the stage to provide the explicit ingredient of sexuality. Apart from enjoying the actresses' professional art, theatregoers developed considerable interest in their private lives.

Davenant's new theatre at Lisle's Court, fitted out with its elaborate wings and shutters, was months away from readiness. In the meantime, his players continued to perform at the pre-Civil War theatre in Salisbury Court. When his new theatre in Lincoln's Inn Fields opened eight months after his rival's, his instinct for providing spectacle was proved right – his theatre was an instant success. The theatre itself was a blend of two types, combining the thrust stage of the public Jacobean playhouse and the proscenium arch stage invented by Inigo Jones for court masques. Given that Davenant had little money and was stepping into untested territory, it is to his great credit that he took such pains to give the London crowd a novel multi-sensory experience. From the start it was clear that the older man was more ambitious, seeking to move the art of theatre forward. This was hardly surprising, for Killigrew played little part in the running of his theatre, leaving his business largely in the hands of his players and stage managers.

With the reopening of the playhouses, Londoners – or at least the tiny proportion of the city's population the two new theatres could cater for – rediscovered the delights of theatre. Of course, some of the belle monde had experience during the interregnum of playhouses and opera houses on the continent, but for the majority of even the most fashionable, this was a pleasure to be learned, or learned anew.

There has been a good deal of discussion about which sections of society actually frequented the theatre in the years following the Restoration. Some theatre historians see it as having been essentially a court audience. Pepys, however, makes several references to rowdy audiences made up of apprentices. Even allowing for a good cross-section of society, few could ever have seen the performances either at Lincoln's Inn or Vere Street and their subsequent replacement houses. It has been estimated that these early houses each seated somewhere between 400 and 600.[6] With a population of 385,000 in the city, this meant that between one in a thousand and one in six hundred Londoners could see any one performance. Yet from this small base, Davenant and Killigrew, vying with one another for the best plays, the latest theatrical innovations, the most fashionable audiences, the fullest houses, and, of course, the greatest profit, were to change the history of the English stage. The rivalry between the companies would colour London life during the first two decades of the King's reign.

In an era before the duopoly of Killigrew and Davenant, London had boasted nine or ten theatres at any one time. The writing talent to sustain this number of playhouses had long since retired or died, so their plays were dusted down and rewritten for the new era. The comedies of Fletcher and Beaumont became favourites. The works of Shakespeare did not escape being rewritten; they were often given new endings and, almost invariably, musical interludes. Soon, the new theatres attracted a new generation of writing talent, but the works from the high point of the English Renaissance provided the major part of the repertoire.

Although the general population of London would never have set foot in either theatre, thanks to the city's gossip sheets they knew who the stars of the playhouses were, and could follow their careers.* A star system was thus born. Killigrew's company featured the veteran actors Charles Hart and Major Michael Mohun, soon to be joined by the new wave of female actors including Elizabeth Knepp and Nell Gwyn. Davenant had to begin with lesser lights but, along with the early services of Thomas Betterton, was soon able to offer Mary Saunderson (after the pair's marriage, she was often referred to as Betterton), and later again the talented dancer Mary, or Moll, Davies.

Restoration theatre was set to become an expression of Caroline culture, with the theatre a form of public relations platform for the kind of society Charles encouraged to flourish inside and outside the court. Charles wanted his court to mirror that of France, with style, licentiousness and wit taking centre stage. So completely did the theatre become enmeshed with high society that many aristocratic wits – those who Marvell called 'the Merry Gang' – took up writing. Soon the professional writers had to compete with the likes of the Duke of Buckingham, the King's childhood friend, the irrepressible rake Charles Sedley and others. The loose morals soon to be displayed on the stage would reflect of those of the royal court itself. The theatres sent out a clear signal that the days of Puritanism were over.

As the rivalry between Davenant and Killigrew settled into a peculiar relationship foisted on them by the King, another, far more serious rivalry encouraged by Charles was about to enter a new phase. This was the old rivalry between the English and

---

* The general population did attend plays, often of a rough and bawdy nature. Usually these were performed at London's various annual fairs, chief among which were St Bartholomew's Fair, which took place in Smithfield over two weeks in August around the international cloth sales fair, and Southwark Fair, held in September. The latter was notorious for its debauchery, being situated in one of London's main brothel districts.

the Dutch for the riches of international trade. As 1660 drew to a close, the Company of Royal Adventurers made preparations for its first exploratory voyage to West Africa. The Duke of York made good his promise of help from the Royal Navy. He loaned the company not only five ships but also one of its most capable captains, Robert Holmes. At the age of thirty-eight, Holmes was vastly experienced and had a reputation for brilliance and troublemaking in equal measure. He was just the sort of man to lead a force to Africa with the intention of taking on the Dutch and relieving them of some of their profitable trading.

Holmes, born in Mallow, West County Cork in Ireland, was a professional soldier and a close confederate of Prince Rupert. Having fought with the Prince in the civil war and later on the continent, Holmes switched to seafaring when Rupert took command of a Royalist fleet during the Civil War, and demonstrated an ability to command warships. He had served under Rupert during his piratical campaigns off Africa in the early 1650s. Quarrelsome and abrasive, but also charismatic and capable, Holmes was the epitome of the Cavalier officer – brave and adventurous but difficult and ill-disciplined. Rupert planned to accompany Holmes on the African voyage – a last hurrah for the old comrades and a final adventure for a military prince without a war to fight. The Duke of York put his foot down; his able cousin was not going to go careering off to Africa and possibly get himself killed.

In early January 1661, Holmes's squadron sailed from the Thames. Much of England's foreign policy at this time was bound up with London's view of international trade. There had long been a view in England that the Dutch had too great a slice of world trade. Cromwell had proposed in 1651 that the Dutch should have rights to Africa and Asia, in return for helping England to conquer all of the Americas by taking on the Spanish. The Dutch view was that free trade was the best way forward. This was precisely what England did not want. The Dutch had flourished under free trade to the detriment of England, and so negotiations broke down. Shortly afterwards Cromwell declared war and a bruising encounter in 1652 ended with the collapse of the Dutch economy, although the trade dispute between the two nations was no nearer to resolution. The two countries had remained at loggerheads over trade rights ever since.

When Charles II took over the reins at Whitehall, relations were no better, owing both to his animosity to the Dutch Protestant ruling elite and to his support for London's craving for trade supremacy. Charles's policy was to revisit the trade impasse. Though the Dutch economy had recovered since the previous war and the navy had been rebuilt, Charles's aim was to take on the Dutch with a direct assault on one specific part of their trade – their long-established trading system in West Africa, from where they dealt in commodities and slaves.

This was not to say that England had no experience of trading in West Africa. Since Tudor times, the gold that had gone into English coinage had come from Guinea.* The intention now, though, was not to trade for small quantities to make golden guineas, but to search for the source and take as much gold as possible. Holmes's instructions, dictated to him before he left London by the Duke of York's secretary, William Coventry, were to find the mountain of gold described so vividly by Rupert and to assist the new Company of Royal Adventurers' agents in the region. What this latter instruction meant was not spelled out. Holmes took it to mean he could take a tough approach to the Dutch presence in Gambia.

---

* Hence the coin known as a golden guinea.

The fleet was supplied with barrels and sacks to fill with gold or 'the richest sands' (presumably sand bearing gold dust). As an afterthought, the instructions stipulated that if there was any room left for extra freight they should bring back 'such negroes . . . you possibly can'. This was the first reference to slavery in the history of the company. It was an augury for the future.

Having made good speed, Holmes's flotilla reached the Dutch-held island of Goree in the Cape Verde Isles, off the African coast, by the end of January. Holmes appears to have bristled with aggression. According to the Dutch governor, the English commander told him curtly that the King of England claimed the exclusive right of trade and navigation all the way from Cape Verde to the Cape of Good Hope. The Dutch, who had operated in this immense stretch of territory for in excess of two hundred years, had six months to pack up and be gone.

Over the next four weeks the flotilla anchored off the Guinea coast while Holmes harassed and intimidated Dutch traders, forcing the surrender of the Dutch fort of St Andreas on the Gambia River, and ferreting out potential allies for England among the local figures of power. His journal speaks of 'caressing and presenting the natives whose friendship we had almost lost' because of the Dutch.

Despite the best efforts of the expedition, no gold was found. The climate proved inhospitable and it is unlikely that Holmes carried out any mining. Having failed to discover (or, as some suspected, to look for) any gold, Holmes headed back to London, bringing what produce he could, along with a large ape. (Samuel Pepys wondered if the ape might be the product of a female baboon and a man, and might therefore be open to instruction.) Admiralty papers record that on one of the returning ships, the *Amity*, thirty-eight of its crew died while they were in Gambia or en route home. We do not know the mortality rate on board the other vessels. On return to London the expedition landed goods including ivory and hides that were sold for £1567.8s;[7] the cost of the voyage has been estimated at between £4000 and £4500.[8] Pepys, always a man for a reckoning, noted that Holmes afterwards had a lavish lifestyle. Perhaps more goods were brought back than were accounted for.

Further voyages to West Africa proved an additional drain on the company's finances, without any new income. The company had not made a great start. Its charter, granted by Charles, stipulated that he was to receive two-thirds of any gold discovered. The other third, minus expenses, was to be divided between the remaining shareholders. As things stood after Holmes's first expedition, such fractions hardly mattered.

Amazingly, the voyage made Holmes's name. While failing to make any money, he had demonstrated that the Dutch could be taken on in their established trading grounds. This was exactly what Charles wished to know. Holmes was presented to the King and soon boasted to Pepys about how well he got on in palace circles. 'He seems to be very well acquainted with the King's mind and with all the several factions at court,' wrote Pepys in his diary. 'Being a cunning fellow, and one (by his own confession to me) that can put on two several faces and look his enemies in the face with as much love as his friends. But good God, what an age is this, that a man cannot live without playing the knave.'[9]

Holmes's first voyage appears to have caused a rethink on how West Africa might be made to turn a profit. Gold became a secondary consideration. Taking a leaf from the Dutch traders' book, it was decided that slave trading was the way forward. The English had been carrying on slavery for many years, though on a small scale. Now it would become the major policy of the monopoly company, rather than a matter for individual ship owners, traders and merchants trading illegally outside the company's monopoly.

The point had been a long time coming. From the time that sugar was introduced into Barbados around 1640 it had been recognised that slavery was the means by which it might be exploited. The economic basis for sugar planting became a matter of debate and discussion. At least one book published in the mid-1640s on Barbados was part travelogue and part self-help manual for the would-be sugar planter, explaining everything from how to buy a plantation, to how many slaves would be required per acre and what profits could be made.[10]

Sugar spread rapidly to Jamaica and the Leeward Islands. By the time of the Restoration it was outpacing tobacco in terms of value as the chief commodity from the colonies. Slave trading provided a growing flow of labour for the sugar industry. London merchants and gentlemen with money to invest were now anxious to support the sugar industry in the West Indies. New plantations were opening up and long-established ones increasing in size. A slave workforce was the way forward, copying the tested Dutch model in Brazil. Slavery was not new for the English, but the trade had not been run in any orderly or large-scale manner.

Statistics recently compiled on slave voyages give some idea of the rate at which the trade was increasing. According to the ambitious Trans-Atlantic Slave Trade Database at Emory University, the numbers of slaves shipped from England increased sharply during the middle of the seventeenth century. The database records the transporting of no slaves from England between 1646 and 1650. Yet during this period slave ownership grew quickly in Barbados and other islands in order to keep up with the market for sugar. It is hard to believe that all the slaves arriving in the West Indies during this period of rapid expansion landed only from Dutch or Portuguese vessels. Many of the planters were known to import their own work-forces. For this reason, the statistics in the Slave Trade Database must be viewed as incomplete, omitting at least some voyages commencing in England but not at the time listed as primarily slave voyages.

Bearing that in mind, the figures for the next five-year period, from 1651 to 1655, still show a remarkable increase from zero African slaves shipped to 1755 embarked on ships whose voyages originated in London. The reason for this rapid growth was the British takeover of Jamaica in 1650, with its attendant stress on slave-produced sugar. In the following five years (1656–60) the number of African slaves embarked on ships out of London jumped to 3625.[11]

This then was the situation when Charles II came to the throne. He and those around him could see that there was room for growth in the slave trade allied to the growth in overseas colonies.

Outside London the Company of Royal Adventurers' new monopoly was unwelcome. Many attempts were made to break it, some successfully. A ship from Exeter took on thirty-five slaves in West Africa. Another 315 were loaded onto a ship from Bristol, while 335 were embarked on ships from other English ports. The fact that these numbers were so low signified that London's monopoly held remarkably well. During this time, Dutch opposition remained an impediment to English trade in Africa. This would soon change as London became a slave-trading city to rival the Spanish and Portuguese. Over the next five years, 1661–5, the English and the Dutch fought campaigns against one another off West Africa, and London-based ships carried 10,049 African slaves across the Atlantic.[12] In fifteen years, therefore, London's slave trade increased almost sixfold, and in the first five years of Charles's reign by two-thirds. This next stage in opening up the African slave trade to English ships would again involve the irrepressible Captain Holmes.

CHAPTER 6

THE CROWNING OF A KING

While Holmes made mischief in Africa, London prepared for the coronation of Charles II, King of Great Britain and Ireland. The ceremony was scheduled to take place on St George's Day 1661 in Westminster Abbey. The organisers, though, had a major problem to overcome before the coronation could take place: there were no coronation regalia. The regalia had been destroyed on the orders of Cromwell; the crown and orb, along with many other pieces, were melted down, and the gold and precious stones sold off. They were, Cromwell had said, a reminder of 'the detestable rule of kings'.

For goldsmith and banker Robert Viner, now twenty-nine years old, the lack of a crown was an opportunity not to be missed. He would seize the moment and ensure that his workshops made replacement regalia. By so doing, he would position those workshops at the zenith of London's goldsmiths and create for himself a lasting personal relationship with the King. Viner secured this vital commission by spending £30,000 of his own money, buying precious stones and gold and paying for the labour of his finest craftsmen. His new crown was a replica of the one that had been destroyed, the eleventh-century crown of St Edward the Confessor, used in coronations for six hundred years. Reputedly, William the Conqueror wore it at his coronation, and subsequently so did William II, Henry I, Henry II, Richard I and King John. All this history Cromwell had dismantled, turned into ingots of gold and a clutch of precious stones sold for a total of £2647 18s 4d.

Using detailed accounts of the venerable crown of the saintly King Edward, Viner fashioned a magnificent recreation. The new crown had a frame of purest gold set with 444 gemstones including rubies, amethysts and sapphires. Inside the frame sat a cap of royal purple, trimmed around its base with ermine.

Robert Viner had come to London from Warwick as a boy apprentice to his uncle Sir Thomas Viner, a well-established goldsmith and important banker. Although Sir Thomas was Presbyterian, his nephew grew up in the Anglican faith. Robert's unusual brilliance both in shaping precious metals and designing ornaments and jewellery, and more particularly in business, was quickly recognised. Sir Thomas taught Robert the arcane banker's knowledge that would enable him to take in money at one rate and lend at another, ensuring the balance was always in his favour. Gaining such knowledge placed Robert among the favoured elite of London's wealthiest.

It was therefore not surprising that apprenticeships to the top London guilds were expensive. Those joining the Guild of Goldsmiths had to pay an entrance fee, running costs and a fee to a master. The total could be anything from £500 to £3000.[1] Its new members therefore tended to be sons of well-established merchants, tradesmen or craftsmen, or the younger sons of the gentry. A third of all trainees came from the higher social classes, and the proportion was nearly the same for those entering all the merchant and other trade guilds. Surprisingly, only a small proportion (4 to 6 per cent) were the sons of London goldsmiths. A third of apprentices came from outside London, indicating both the desire of wealthy families around the country to ensure their sons got a start in London business, and the extent to which London drew in people to fulfil its need for extra skills.[2] Out of the hundreds of London goldsmiths, several dozen – perhaps as many as ninety – acted as bankers.[3]

The city would have to be prettified for the coronation, but how? Seen from across the Thames, its medieval streetscape rising up from the river presented a charming view, but a traveller taking a wherry across the river and walking up from the quays into its ancient heart would be assailed by smells too terrible to analyse and forced to breathe air mixed with soot and toxic fumes.

The city fathers marshalled their plans for a major spring clean, to be followed by the erection of elaborate decorations. John Evelyn seized the moment to publish a book setting out practical proposals on how to cleanse the city's noxious air. He wrote what was in essence an environmentalist's handbook.[4] But his book was more than that; it was a royalist broadside, the cleansing of the capital's air a metaphor for ridding the city of the corrupt air of the Commonwealth and letting in the refreshing zephyrs of monarchy.[5] London's 'otherwise wholesome and excellent Aer', he wrote, was mixed with 'an impure and thick mist, accompanied by a fuliginous and filthy vapour' that corrupted the lungs of the inhabitants. London, said Evelyn, resembled the 'face of Mount Aetna, the Court of Vulcan, Stromboli or' – his best and most English invention – 'the Suburbs of Hell'.[6]

Evelyn was a man of independent means, whose money allowed him to indulge his curiosity about many subjects, including the quality of London's air, a matter about which he strongly felt something should be done. He had what today would be called a social conscience. His solution involved the moving of all major coal-burning factories downwind of London to north Kent, a location that would happily also be safely downwind of the Evelyn estate at Deptford. To replace the burning of coal, he advocated a return to wood and charcoal, supplied by planting great forests on private estates throughout England.

Evelyn envisaged a return to the clean airs London was reputed to have enjoyed long before Cromwell and coal polluted them; a time when the city air was scarcely contaminated, and wood and charcoal were burned by all. This happy state of affairs had changed towards the end of the thirteenth century when brewers, dyers and other trades introduced sea-coal, a fuel that burned at a higher temperature than charcoal, giving off dark smoke. Coal burning produced such a nuisance in London that Edward I prohibited its use, not once but twice. His proclamations had little effect.[7] By the middle of the fourteenth century, other measures were taken to help cure London's polluted air and noxious smells. Edward III ordered the Lord Mayor and sheriffs to banish slaughter yards from the city. No cattle were to be killed closer than Knightsbridge in the west and Stratford in the east.[8] By the seventeenth century Edward's edict was observed merely in the breach.

For his pains, Evelyn gained an introduction to the King, but was satirised in the press. London was a hive of lampooners and humourists, commentators who had honed the edge of their quills during the political upheavals of the 1640s and 50s.

Any pretension to superior knowledge, such as Evelyn's plans to cleanse the air, was open to ridicule. Even the group of distinguished professors who met at Gresham College were merrily targeted for fun. Their many proposals for enhancing the quality of life, along with Evelyn's proposition for London, gave rise to the following lines:

> Oh, blessed witt that thus contrives
> By new found out but fertill arts,
> In pleasure to lengthen our lives.
> To teach us next to perfume farts
> And without fuell or coal make fire
> Some other member will aspire.[9]

Evelyn's plans came to nothing; cleansing London's air remained a long-term goal.* For now, the Corporation of London cleaned the streets as best as it could and put up decorations. Triumphal arches were built and theatrical tableaux designed. Not to be outdone, London's guilds and merchant companies planned their contributions. People passing up and down Leadenhall Street in the spring weather watched as a remarkable wooden structure rose up on the façade of an Elizabethan mansion named Craven House. When the superstructure was finished, an artist went to work, painting a mural of a flotilla of merchant ships in full sail. Above the mural stood a larger than life-size figure of a merchant seaman saluting all who walked beneath him. This wonderful piece of bombastic illustration was London's first advertising hoarding. It marked the headquarters of

* Evelyn's dream of a city without smog would not come true until the Clean Air Act of 1956.

the East India Company, London's most powerful trading organisation.

The company had its beginnings in early English voyages to establish trade in the Indian Ocean and beyond. Queen Elizabeth granted a royal charter in 1600 to the group of investors and merchants who put together the fleets of ships sent out to explore the possibility of developing trade on a long-term basis. This was an exceptionally risky business. Ships could be lost due to pirates, storms, illness or hostile locals, or to strenuous competition from the Spanish or the Dutch East India Company. Hence the London merchants, and their aristocratic backers, spread the risk, emulating the Dutch and other continental trading groups by setting up a joint stock company.

At first, the company imported spices, quickly expanding into exports of English cloth and metalwork. In time, it took on the saltpetre trade, essential for the manufacture of gunpowder. But what really made the company a success in the early 1600s was its business importing and exporting pepper. Fortunes were made selling it onward into the European market. The company looked set to be a continuing success until rivalry with other English traders and then with the Dutch almost caused it to go under. Competition between English and Dutch spice traders in Indonesia led to an agreement enforced by the governments of England and the Dutch United Provinces that they would share trading posts. Thus began an uneasy coexistence of the EIC and its Dutch rival, the United East India Company.* This arrangement broke down in 1623 when the Dutch accused the English of plotting against them in Indonesia. In what came to be known as the

* Vereenigde Oost-Indische Compagnie, or VOC for short.

Amboina Massacre, the Dutch authorities tortured English merchants to reveal details of the plot, before executing several of them. The event caused a sensation in London and repercussions continued for decades.

With the Dutch firmly established in Indonesia, the English looked for other foreign trading centres. Madras in India appeared to provide the answer. But with the outbreak in hostilities between the House of Stuart and Parliament in 1642, all organisations connected with the Crown came under suspicion. It took Cromwell to reaffirm the company's place as a central tool of the nation's trade with the East, giving it a new warrant in 1657. The death of the Protector the following year plunged the company back into uncertainty.

The situation was resolved during Charles II's coronation year. Granting the EIC a new royal charter, Charles gave it astonishing powers. The company's colossal new entablature atop Craven House announced more than its resurgence – it announced the confidence that came with its new charter. Charles had no say in the running of the EIC, but he made sure he had a financial interest to match his imperial ambitions. The country had few resources: some coal and wool, some tin and lead, a very little gold and silver. But since the defeat of the Spanish Armada in 1588 there had existed a collective desire to become a major sea power reaching out into the world to take what could be taken.[10] Under the reign of Charles II, this ambition was prosecuted as never before. The playboy king became the adventurer king.

The rejuvenation of the venerable EIC was symbolic of Charles's ambition to top up the insufficient income granted by Parliament. The royal guarantee of a monopoly was so advantageous that the company promised Charles a colossal 70 per cent of all profits (though it's most unlikely he ever received anything like this amount). In return, the new royal charter granted the company judicial authority over all persons living within its territory (i.e. its trading posts and factories) in India and elsewhere and the power to imprison any rogue traders who did not wish to operate under its jurisdiction (a continuing problem). By granting these powers the King was ensuring that the company had the ability to concentrate on increasing trade.*

As preparations gathered pace for the coronation, Charles honoured those who helped the national effort in some way. Knighthoods were handed out to merchants and officials as rewards, or to keep them on side. Among those to receive such favour were several members of the EIC. In March, a month before the coronation, the merchant William Rider was among those honoured. A major investor in the company who over a long and successful career had imported everything from tobacco to pilchards, he was knighted for services to the King in recognition of his role in supplying the navy with many of its most important basic needs, including timber and tar.

It would eventually be discovered that Rider was not above sharp practice, selling cheap hemp from Scandinavia at a substantial premium and making up a story that the tar warehouse in Stockholm had burned down so that he could inflate the price he charged the navy. Navy Office stalwart Samuel Pepys called Rider 'false'. True or false, the navy needed Rider – and his star continued to rise.

*

---

* By 1665 the company would pay its members a dividend of 40 per cent.

On 22 April, the day before the coronation, the King paraded through London in a grand procession based on those undertaken by his father and by Elizabeth I. The participants – who included trumpeters, the King's bodyguards, known as the Gentlemen Pensioners, Knights of the Garter, his brother the Duke of York, heir to the throne, and dignitaries including aristocratic office-bearers and the Lord Mayor – set out from London Bridge and wended slowly through the city to Whitehall. Fountains poured out wine at intervals along the route, and there were bands, dancers and various tableaux vivants. The route went through four triumphal arches of great size and magnificence. The first of these, in Leadenhall, represented the triumph of monarchy over rebellion. The female figure of Rebellion was 'mounted on a Hydra in a crimson robe, torn, snakes crawling on her habit, and begirt with serpents'. Her companion Confusion was a 'deformed shape'.[11]

Not to be outdone, at nearby Craven House the council of the EIC had set up a live tableau of its wealth and largesse. Two Indian youths were positioned outside, one mounted on a camel, the other attended by two 'blackamoors'. The camel carried two panniers, filled with silks, spices and jewels, which the youths flung out among the spectators. In Cornhill the King was met with the sight of eight nymphs cavorting in the ancient water cistern, while at the Royal Exchange was an arch with scenes depicting the River Thames and one of His Majesty's warships. At the junction of Wood Street and Cheapside a grand arch represented Concord. In Fleet Street, the final triumphal arch represented the Garden of Plenty. As the King exited the city at Temple Bar he was greeted by a cage containing a variety of wild animals.

The coronation itself took place on 23 April. London was decorated from end to end; gallants and their ladies dressed in opulent finery. At the King's insistence, the streets again ran with wine, an outward sign of profligate luxury which probably had the added attraction of masking the city's more noxious smells. At the crowning ceremony in Westminster Abbey, Viner's replica crown was a fabulous success. A near contemporary of the King (he was younger than Charles by a year), Viner became a royal favourite. He was as close to being a friend to the King as any commoner was likely to be.

Indeed, Viner, like other merchants before him, became indispensable to the King. He was not only the royal goldsmith but, like his uncle and father before him, a banker. Though usury was still frowned upon by many, London's bankers charged interest on loans and so were vital in greasing the wheels of commerce. To carry out their business in the city the goldsmith bankers had to become members of their guild, part of the elite group among guilds along with the mercers and grocers. The apprenticeships served by these trainee merchants were rigorous. Mathematical ability was necessary to master the many facets of business. Bookkeeping in its many forms was taught according to well-understood and established principles. The application of credit, commission on sales and so on, had to be mastered along with the means of accurately recording transactions, and computing likely and actual outcomes. Records had to be kept of orders taken, goods dispatched, payment received. For the elite among merchants, business was international; therefore exchange rates had to be understood and factored in. Interest charged on loans was tied to risk and there were rules on how to gauge it. This world of money provided those given entry to it the means to become part of an aristocracy separate from but parallel to that of inherited titles and land.

Viner was not alone in thinking that lending money to the restored monarchy was as secure as any other business loan, and as his fame and fortune grew, he lent increasingly large sums to the Crown. Samuel Pepys visited Viner at his grand home, Swakeleys House at Twickenham, to collect loans for the King. Charles, who had an insatiable need for money, made Viner first a knight, and then a baronet.

The coronation had been a huge propaganda success for the House of Stuart. All of London had turned out and cheered. In the spring of the palindromic year of 1661, all could surely look back to a tormented past and forward to a glorious future.

CHAPTER 7

'TOO GREAT AN HONOUR FOR A TRIFLE'

Science came to London via a number of scholars who shared an interest in an emerging idea: that the nature of the world was best investigated through experiment. From among their ranks in the preceding years had grown a loosely defined assemblage which became known as the 'invisible college' or the 'experimental philosophical clubbe'. Several of these scholars were professors at Gresham College, the institution of public learning in Bishopsgate, close to London's Roman walls. The college's grand headquarters were located in the former home of Sir Thomas Gresham, the founder of the Royal Exchange. In 1597 Gresham had bequeathed his home and the revenues from the shops lining the exchange in order to found the college and pay the stipends of seven professors, namely of astronomy, divinity, geometry, music, law, physic and rhetoric.*

---

* Today, free public lectures are still given by the current holders of the original seven chairs, which have been augmented by professorships in commerce, technology and the environment.

On the evening of 28 November 1660, Christopher Wren, Gresham's 27-year-old professor of astronomy, gave a lecture at the college, after which he was among a group which gathered in the college rooms of Dr Lawrence Rooke, the professor of geometry, to discuss the formation of a new society. It would be something entirely new: a national body to promote science – natural philosophy, as it was then known. Nothing like it existed anywhere in the world.

Among others present were the wealthy experimentalist Robert Boyle, the influential clergyman and polymath John Wilkins, the mathematician Viscount Brouncker and Sir Robert Moray, a soldier and statesman with an interest in natural philosophy and, importantly, a friend of Charles II. These founding fathers, as it were, of what became the Royal Society were therefore not solely experimentalists, but included Anglican clergy and well-connected royalists and grandees. The mix was no accident; it was undoubtedly designed to ensure that the society would appeal to the King and receive royal approval. In this way, from its inception the society was a highly political act.

Sir Robert Moray undertook the task of obtaining approval from the King in the form of a royal warrant. At the committee's next meeting on 5 December he reported he had secured the King's approval. Charles, who had an enquiring if easily distracted mind, was eager to support a society to explore astronomy, navigation, trade, alchemy, medicine and the rest. The Royal Society of London for Improving Natural Knowledge was born, though it would be more than a year before it would be granted its royal warrant and be entitled to use its full title.

John Evelyn suggested the name, saying it was 'too great an honour for a trifle'. Evelyn is also credited with the society's motto, *Nullius in Verba*, or 'take nobody's word for it', emphasising the society's aim of verifying all theories by observation and experimentation. The society's formation was a key moment in the early development of what became known as the Age of Reason, the Enlightenment. Under the roof of the Royal Society, scientific discoveries would henceforth be presented in public, tested in public and disseminated freely for the public good.

The society's origins dated back to well before the Restoration, to at least 1645. Learned virtuosi also met in other places, especially in Oxford. In his correspondence, Robert Boyle used the term 'our invisible college' for an informal group of like-minded men with whom he was associated in 1646. There was, it appears, no one single group that acted as a precursor to the society; rather, there were many who had considered new forms of education and of the collection and dissemination of the new ideas. The Anglican priest and distinguished mathematician John Wallis wrote about the origins of the society:

> About the year 1645, while I lived in London (at a time when, by our civil wars, academical studies were much interrupted in both our Universities) . . . I had the opportunity of being acquainted with divers worthy persons, inquisitive natural philosophy, and other parts of human learning; and particularly of what hath been called the New Philosophy or Experimental Philosophy. We did by agreements, divers of us, meet weekly in London on a certain day and hour, under a certain penalty, and a weekly contribution for the charge of experiments, with certain rules agreed amongst us, to treat and discourse of such affairs . . .
>
> About the year 1648–49, some of our company being removed to Oxford . . . our company divided. Those in London continued to meet there as before (and we with them, when we had occasion to be there), and those of us

> at Oxford ... and divers others, continued such meetings in Oxford, and brought those Studies into fashion there ...[1]

The group at Oxford was led by men of extraordinary merit, including Boyle, later of world renown, and Wallis himself, an exemplar of the renaissance man. By the time he left school, Wallis had mastered Latin, Greek, French, Hebrew and logic, going on at Emmanuel College, Cambridge, to study anatomy and medicine along with mathematics. He contributed substantially to the development of calculus before Isaac Newton's decisive work and introduced the ∞ symbol to represent infinity.

The group required a meeting place conducive to informal debate. Somehow, an apothecary named Arthur Tillyard was persuaded to open a coffee house around 1655 in which the group of friends regularly met. They became known as the Oxford Coffee House Group.

Those who gathered in London had fluctuating luck with their regular meeting place, as Wallis explained:

> The London group continued to meet at Gresham College until the year 1658 when they had to disband in fear of their lives as soldiers took over their meeting rooms and London underwent a period of terror. In February 1660 Monck's army entered London and restored order. King Charles returned to London at the end of May 1660 and the meetings at Gresham College resumed.

Thus the idea of a college had been around for many years and had taken several forms. In September 1659 John Evelyn, a religiously devout individual, had written to Robert Boyle putting forward a proposal for a monastic college, with its members taking a vow of chastity. Those members who, like

Evelyn, were married would be furnished with separate rooms for their wives to avert temptation. Unsurprisingly, the idea was not universally applauded. Evelyn persevered, writing to Boyle three weeks later, 'Might not some gentlemen whose geniuses are greatly suitable, and who desire nothing more than to give a good example, preserve science, and cultivate themselves, join together in society . . .'[2]

A letter written by Evelyn to John Wilkins, the Warden of Wadham College, Oxford, on 17 February 1660 provides further evidence that the notion of a learned society or college was well advanced. Evelyn hailed Wilkins, a noted polymath, as the 'President of our Society at Gresham's College', and indicated that a group had been meeting there for some time with the aim of forming themselves into some new society. Despite his central role in uniting the Oxford and Gresham groups, Wilkins felt that in the post-Restoration era it was better for him to stay out of the limelight. Though an Anglican priest, his politics were Cromwellian. Not only that, he was married to Cromwell's sister Robina.

Thanks to the persuasive power of high-level courtiers Sir Robert Moray and Sir Paul Niele, the King visited Gresham College in October to see for himself what was afoot. The star of the show appears to have been Christopher Wren, who set up a telescope for the King to view the stars. The Anglo-Polish intelligencer Samuel Hartlib* wrote of the meeting: 'His Majesty was lately, in an evening, at Gresham College, where he was entertained with the admiral long tube, with which he viewed the heavens, to his very great satisfaction.'[3]

---

* In the seventeenth century an intelligencer was someone who collected and imparted information. The term could equally apply to a spy or one who assembled academic knowledge.

The tube was long indeed – thirty-five feet long. It had been donated to the college by Sir Paul Neile, an astronomer of some renown. Neile thought highly of Wren and commended him to the King for 'greater preferment'.[4]

A few weeks later, the mission undertaken by Moray at the request of his colleagues proved successful, as recorded in the minutes for the meeting of 5 December 1660: 'the King had been acquainted with the design of this Meeting. And he did well approve of it, and would be ready to give encouragement to it. It was ordered that Mr Wren be desired to prepare against the next meeting for the pendulum experiment . . .'

The reference to Wren preparing a demonstration of a pendulum indicated how highly valued the youngest member of the group was from the outset. Wren had a wide-ranging knowledge in many fields, including anatomy, mathematics and astronomy. He had the ability to design instruments and the mechanical understanding to ensure instrument-makers accurately followed his instructions. He was therefore the most practically minded of the founding Fellows and was very active in society meetings.

Interest in pendulums had increased since the success of Dutch scientist Christiaan Huygens in building a pendulum clock in 1656, so putting into practice an idea first proposed by Galileo Galilei in 1641, the year before he died.* The pendulum clock was much more accurate than any previous timepiece, reducing the device's inaccuracy from around

* Galileo (1564–1642) was arguably the central figure in the scientific revolution of the seventeenth century, producing evidence to support the Copernican system of the universe, declaring that the 'book of nature' was written in mathematics and becoming the first genuine experimentalist. He worked at Padua and Pisa and his work was known internationally in his lifetime.

fifteen minutes a day to as little as fifteen seconds. With the pendulum's many fascinating characteristics now coming under scrutiny, it was natural for a man with Wren's varied interests to wish to demonstrate some of the pendulum's properties to the new society.

Wren's usefulness to the society was not limited to his broad experimental interests. He was from a family that was close to the Stuarts. His father had been not only Dean of the chapel at Windsor Castle but also register (registrar) of England's oldest chivalric order, the Order of the Garter.[5] During the Civil War and after, Wren's father took great care to gather up all the records of the order, which could have perished during the interregnum. It fell to Christopher to fulfil his father's intentions (his father died in 1658) and present the precious records to the returned King. From that moment on, Charles took a personal interest in the career of the young virtuoso.[6]

If Wren was the ideal Fellow of a society dedicated to natural philosophy, Charles II was the ideal patron. He was fascinated by all things new, loved architecture and chemistry and was especially attracted by alchemical experiments whereby lead might be turned into gold. Like his cousin Prince Rupert, Charles set up a laboratory in which to pursue alchemical investigations. But Charles's interests went beyond the hermetic; he was essentially a practical man, whose love of sailing fuelled his interest in the latest developments in shipbuilding and navigation, advances that might help England open up new trade routes and expand her influence abroad.

Charles's interest in the advancement of the city's trade was not entirely that of a benevolent father figure. Thanks to the royal warrants given to monopolistic trading companies, the King was rewarded with a portion of their profits. Charles saw the new experimental society as a practical tool to help trade and shipping, rather than as a society of learning for its own sake. He was quick to request that the society turn its mind to such things. On 19 December Petty and Wren would be asked 'to consider the philosophy of shipping and to bring their thoughts about it to the society'.[7]

As was the nature of the times, women could not become members of the new society. Thus Edward, 1st Earl of Conway, joined while his wife Anne, one of the most eminent philosophers of the day, did not. Viscountess Conway was her own woman: she ran a centre for Quakerism, though membership of this oppressed group opened her to much mistrust. She studied philosophy under the Platonist Henry More and, as he said himself, became his equal. A sufferer from migraine headaches, she was treated by the physician Thomas Willis, one of the society's founders. Despite his eminence in understanding the brain – it was Willis who coined the word neurology – he failed to cure Anne. They did, however, have an affair.

From the beginning, the members discussed grand ideas of forming a physical college, a grand building with rooms for researchers and staff, laboratories and lecture theatres. This was based to some extent on ideas put forward by Francis Bacon more than thirty years before in his *New Atlantis*, describing an ideal college he named Solomon's House.[8] Owing to a lack of funds, the society would never build its great research institute. It continued to meet at Gresham College, where it would remain for several years. Despite its financial limitations, however, the society got off to a flying start with the presentation of a historic scientific breakthrough.

Peter Lely's former pupil Robert Hooke, now Boyle's scientific assistant, recorded the Gresham College meetings in a diary he labelled *Dr Hooke's Extracts out of the Journal-Books of the RS* [Royal Society] *for his private use*. The very first entry reads:

> 1661 April 3. Mr Boyle brought in his book concerning glasse tubes ordered that every member of the Society should have one of Mr Boyle's books to Discourse against this day sevenight[9]

With this simple entry Hooke recorded one of the wonders of the age. The book referred to was nothing less than Boyle's seminal work on the relationship between pressure and the volume of air, which would culminate in the establishment of Boyle's Law, one of the basic laws of the behaviour of gases.[10] Boyle was an aristocrat, born in County Cork, Ireland. He owned an estate in Dorset but lived chiefly in Oxford, where he lodged with a learned apothecary. Aided by Hooke, his paid scientific assistant, he carried out his experiments in a laboratory at the apothecary's house.

Boyle was not alone in investigating the phenomenon of the relationship between pressure and volume. His most notable contemporary in the field was Richard Towneley, an independent enthusiast for empiricism who, like others around the kingdom, had little or no connection to London, carrying out his investigations at his home near Burnley in Lancashire. Towneley was a Catholic and so was excluded from English universities, which were then controlled by the Church of England. He seems to have been educated in Europe and carried on his mathematical and scientific work thanks to a private income from family estates.

Towneley cleverly designed a simple experiment in which he and his friend and fellow experimental enthusiast, the physician Henry Power of Halifax, carried a barometer up Pendle Hill in Lancashire. As they went, they recorded the changes in the level of the mercury column.[11] From this they recognised the relationship between the density of air and its pressure. Towneley published little, but he corresponded with many contemporary figures; Boyle certainly saw an early account of his work, written by Power, and discussed the experiment with Towneley when the latter made a rare visit to London. In the history of the discovery of a mathematical relationship between pressure and volume Towneley is, however, almost forgotten.

Boyle's great advance in this sphere of experimentation was to be the first to carry out a series of controlled, repeatable and measurable experiments on what he called 'Mr Towneley's hypothesis'. With Hooke's help, he sealed a quantity of air in a J-shaped tube by introducing a quantity of mercury at either end, and noted that the volume of air in the tube decreased as he increased the pressure on the mercury. Air, he deduced, had a 'spring' in it, what we call today elasticity. Boyle's insistence that everything should be verified by experiment was a breakthrough in an age when even Galileo was wont to describe an experiment but not actually carry it out. Boyle and Hooke not only carried out their experiment, but repeated it with improved apparatus until they could test the hypothesis that supposed the 'pressures and expansions to be in reciprocal proportion'.

A week after Boyle came to talk about his work on the 'spring' in air, Hooke wrote that the society would debate what he called only his own 'little booke'. This was Hooke's report on what is now called capillary action. Hooke had had made for him several very thin glass tubes by which he demonstrated that the water rose up in accordance with the bore of the pipe. From this it is clear that by dint of being a mere employee, Hooke had to fit his own experiments around those he was involved in with Boyle or others – a fact that was to have serious repercussions upon his career.

On 15 May, Boyle was back at Gresham College, this time to 'present the Society with his Engin'. This was his famous vacuum pump, designed and made by Hooke. The pump was a large and delicate apparatus, which had to be transported to London from Boyle's lodgings in Oxford. Hooke was in charge of all arrangements, including the actual operation of the 'engine'. As an aristocrat, it would have been unseemly for Boyle to operate a machine – even one of his own invention.

At the core of Boyle's elaborate vacuum pump was a large glass sphere fifteen inches in diameter; he and Hooke had wanted it to be larger, but the glass blowers were unable to create a larger bowl that retained sufficient strength to withstand the stress put on it by the vacuum the experimenters planned to create within. Objects could be inserted into the vessel through an aperture at the top measuring four inches across, while below the receptacle was a vertical metal shaft in which a piston was cranked up and down using a rack and pinion attached to a winding handle. When the piston was cranked down, a valve was opened so air could be drawn out of the vessel then closed again, while another valve opened at the end of the shaft to expel the evacuated air. Boyle recognised that owing to the constraints of the apparatus, achieving a total vacuum was impossible; Hooke would simply wind away until something approaching a vacuum was arrived at.

Boyle and Hooke had been developing the air pump for some time; its earliest form had existed in 1659. The design of the pump was described at length over nineteen pages in Boyle's groundbreaking book *New Experiments Physico-Mechanicall, touching the Spring of the Air*;[12] he had taken such trouble in describing the construction of the pump because he wanted people to be certain that he had built such a machine.

He also wanted other experimenters, if they so wished, to copy and validate his work. In the current philosophical climate, it was generally held that those who dwelt in the realm of thought should not become involved in mechanical operations. Such operations were, according to the prevalent ideology, likely to muddy the pure waters of philosophical truth. Critics of the Royal Society's endeavours went so far as to say that by its very experimental nature, the society was moving away from the superiority of thought into an arena into which natural philosophy was not meant to go. The reasoning was that God had not intended apparatus to be employed in philosophical endeavours and to do so was unnatural. It was firmly felt that mechanical things got in the way of logic.

All of these arguments weighed on Boyle, who was a religious man, but ultimately the desire fully to understand the nature of God's creation overcame any constraints. He was clearly setting himself apart from the philosophical theorists who considered such experiments unnecessary. There was a further departure; the book was published both in an English edition and in Latin, the common language of the intelligentsia of Europe, so that it could be read by experimenters abroad.

Hooke and Boyle carried out many experiments using the vacuum pump. They made observations on the change in levels of mercury in a barometer according to the amount of air withdrawn. They observed what happened when various flammable materials were inserted into the sphere and set alight; Hooke recorded his surprise when the flames were ultimately extinguished. He thought the vacuum should have allowed more space for what he termed – in relation to an experiment involving burning coal – 'the stifling steams' to expand into. Hooke's surprise was understandable, for it would be more than a hundred years before Joseph Priestley discovered oxygen.

Boyle's vacuum pump had the ability to demonstrate several of the characteristics of air. The fact that sound could not travel through a vacuum was demonstrated by placing a striking clock inside the vacuum glass. As the air was extracted the chimes became inaudible. The pump was also used to demonstrate categorically that air was necessary for life. A cat was placed in the jar, the air sucked out and the cat died. This experiment gave rise to two of the most deliciously cruel lines ever written about empirical science:

> Out of the glass the air being screw'd,
> Pus died and never so much as mew'd.[13]

The vacuum pump lent itself to other macabre experiments. Inserting insects, a lark, a sparrow, a mouse and so on, Boyle and Hooke recorded how the animals would drop down and cease activity as the air was extracted, only to revive when it was readmitted. When a creature was subjected to the withdrawal of air a second time, it did not revive. Hooke reached the conclusion that the creatures required air to breathe. These experiments were all demonstrated in the medieval surroundings of Gresham's old house, the hunched and contorted Hooke dextrously operating the machine as the tall, aristocratic Boyle provided a running commentary. Their presentations held the distinguished members of the society in a state of wonder.

To explain the springiness in the air, Boyle explained that it was like fleece – when compressed and then released, it bounced back. Based on the work of others as well as his own observations, he also explained that air had weight and pressure. In 1662, partially egged on by criticisms of his 1660 publication of his experiments using the vacuum pump, Boyle published a further work which contained his groundbreaking law on gases – Boyle's Law. This revolutionary work demonstrated how the pressure of a gas decreased as its volume increased. Today,

Boyle's law is expressed by the statement 'the absolute pressure exerted by a given mass of an ideal gas is inversely proportional to the volume it occupies if the temperature and amount of gas remain unchanged within a closed system'; this can be expressed in the formula $PV = k$, where P is the pressure of the gas, V is the volume and k is a constant.

Helped by the mathematically superior Hooke, Boyle's work created a great stir. Without Hooke, it is unlikely that he could have directed the manufacture of the pump, let alone have done the mathematics to formulate his eponymous law.

There was no doubting the society had got off to a fine start. Inspired by Boyle, other members of the society, with perhaps more enthusiasm than understanding, began to suggest myriad experiments they would like to see. It became obvious that the society would require a permanent employee to oversee its programme of experiments and demonstrations. It also became clear that this man was Hooke, if his patron Boyle could be persuaded to release him.

In the terms agreed by the twelve who had gathered in Dr Rooke's rooms, the society had first been known as a 'college for the promotion of physic-mathematical experimental learning'. Since the summer of 1661 the members had discussed a new name for the society and how they might obtain a royal charter. After further petitions to the King, a charter of incorporation gained the Great Seal on 15 July 1662 and the Royal Society of London officially came into existence. The King presented the new society with a silver mace on which were engraved the emblems of England, Ireland, Scotland and France (for the English monarchy still quaintly made claim to the French throne). As a sign of its potential importance to Charles, the courtier Lord Brouncker was appointed the society's first president.

Charles had little interest in the more arcane experiments that interested most of the empiricists; he hoped the society would apply natural philosophy to questions of commerce and navigation, vital for the expansion of trade and foreign territory. And at the same time that Boyle published his famous law, just such a development was made by one of the Fellows. Sir William Petty invented a dual-hulled ship, or catamaran, which he claimed would prove to be a huge advance over traditional ships in speed, stability and carrying abilities. The King, who knew a great deal about ship design, disagreed. Samuel Pepys was present at the Duke of York's apartments when the King entered into a long discussion with Petty about his recently launched double-hulled ship. When he began teasing Petty about the novel design of the new vessel, Petty offered to place odds in a bet that his boat could outpace any ship the King liked to offer for comparison. Charles refused the bet but continued to tease Petty. Then, turning his attention to the activities of Petty's fellow members of the Royal Society, he made fun of their failure to come up with anything more interesting than 'weighting of ayre', a reference to the experiments of Boyle and Hooke.

Later in the year, the activities of the society were placed on a firm empirical footing. On 12 November, at one of its weekly meetings, the society unanimously voted for Robert Hooke to become its curator of experiments. Boyle was thanked for letting Hooke go and the society ordered that Hooke 'should come and sit amongst them'.

The arrangement was hardly to Hooke's advantage: his brief was such that he would soon find himself overloaded with work. He was instructed to 'bring in every day of the meeting 3 or 4 experiments of his own and take care of such others as should be mentioned to him by the Society.'[14] On the same day, the aristocratic virtuosi Lord Brouncker and Sir Robert Moray proposed an experiment to measure the velocity of different falling bodies. The gentlemen would do none of the measuring themselves. Ever helpful, and keen as mustard, Hooke would carry out the work.

And so it would be from then on. In return for his industry, Hooke earned a stipend of £30 a year, and was given rooms in Gresham College, where he was made a professor on a stipend of £50 a year for life, thanks to the beneficence of Sir John Cutler, who earned for himself an honorary fellowship of the Royal Society. Further on the debit side, Cutler rarely paid Hooke his money; the great scientist had to plead for it on many occasions. On the plus side, however, Hooke was now a resident of London, a 27-year-old bachelor with a salary (albeit small), his own lodgings and the world of science at his feet. He set about making the most of the city that was now his home.

For a young man with Hooke's intelligence and genius for devising experiments, there was no better place to be. From his diaries we see that he was a gregarious individual, regularly meeting friends and colleagues, daily frequenting the city's ordinaries (dining rooms), taverns and coffee houses. On his rounds he gossiped and exchanged philosophical and scientific ideas with the Fellows of the Royal Society and anyone else who was interested. Hooke's life was perhaps as sociable as that of the equally gregarious Pepys. They both moved daily around the city in a way that put them at the centre of its activity. Where Hooke and Pepys differed was in their preoccupations. Hooke led an intellectual life of the kind that his friend the administrator never did. Pepys, with his complicated sexual exploits, had a personal life separate from his professional one; Hooke, without a wife, was married to the coffee house and the Royal Society. Within a year he would be elected a Fellow himself.

The year 1662 saw great changes not only in science, but in the royal household. In May, Charles married Catherine of Braganza, the daughter of the King of Portugal. The choice of consort had not been easy. Many in the royal court had favoured a marriage connecting England with a northern European Protestant power. In the end, no suitable partner could be found. Portugal, though Catholic, was an old ally and promised an enormous dowry, while the King's daughter was available. As part of the Queen's dowry, Portugal gave Charles Tangiers in North Africa near the mouth of the Mediterranean Sea, and Bombay on the west coast of India. The ambitious merchant Sir William Rider, with his experience of trading in the Mediterranean, was appointed to the committee tasked with developing Tangiers as a trading port. Yet in the long run it was the apparently strategically insignificant Bombay that was to play a decisive role in expanding London's foreign influence.

Charles and Catherine married in both Catholic and Anglican ceremonies at Southampton and honeymooned at Hampton Court. The new Queen quickly learned that she was far from the only woman in her husband's life. The King's mistress Barbara Palmer had already ensconced herself at the palace and was pregnant. With a callous disregard for his new Queen's feelings, Charles insisted that Barbara become one of Catherine's ladies-in-waiting.

Charles was to exhibit a similar cold disregard for others in his dealings with two of his political enemies. Two formerly influential adversaries, Harry Vane and John Lambert, had been imprisoned since the Restoration, Vane on the island of St Mary in the Scilly Isles and Lambert in Guernsey. Neither had been involved as judges in the trial of Charles I, so both should have been subject to the general pardon promised by Charles in the Declaration of Breda in 1660. Later that same year, Charles had stated in Parliament that if either man were subsequently accused of treason he would pardon him.[15]

In 1662, when both men were accused of treason, Charles failed to keep his word. Vane, an unabashed republican, was falsely accused of 'compassing and imagining the King's death' – in other words, plotting to murder the King – and Lambert was accused of having rebelled against the King by leading troops into battle against the forces of George Monck the year before Charles came home. As at that time Charles was still in exile, the charge of treason was fatuous.

Charles did finally keep his word regarding Lambert. After undergoing a trial for his life Lambert was returned to exile on Guernsey. With Parliament and the courts anxious to settle old scores, however, he buckled and lost his resolve to pardon Vane. Famously, he told his chancellor that Vane was 'Too dangerous a man to let live'. Vane was spared the grisly death of a traitor by hanging, drawing and torturing and was instead beheaded. The death of Vane was the second time Charles had broken the promises made in the Declaration of Breda. It would not be the last.

CHAPTER 8
FOREIGN ADVENTURES

Slavery was the most baleful of London's overseas trades. To create wealth from the new territories across the Atlantic, a cheap – or preferably free – labour force was required. That labour force farmed the new cash crops of tobacco, sugarcane, cotton and indigo.

To begin with, London's underclasses made up the bulk of it. In the early 1600s, prostitutes were shipped, along with criminals and orphaned children. This 'cleansing' operation was not enough. A new breed of trader grew up – the 'spirits', men and women who kidnapped the unwary and spirited them away into slavery. To begin with they were dispatched to the sugarcane farms of Barbados. Later they were sent to other islands and to the American mainland. The spirits loitered in and around the docks, waiting to entice unwary boys, girls and young men and women into locked rooms or ships about to sail.

In Restoration London, working men and even children had to beware not only of spirits, but of navy press gangs. These were the bane of London. Naïve young men who lingered too long around the docksides found themselves plied with drink and put on board a warship bound for battle or on a long voyage to India. At the Navy Office, Samuel Pepys was involved with the administration of the press gangs, though privately he was against them, calling them 'a great tyranny'. He described 'labouring men and housekeepers leaving poor wives and families, taken up on a sudden by strangers'.[1] Given the constant threat to English shipping from the better-equipped Dutch navy, the press gang was seen as a necessary evil. The transportation of foreigners from their own lands was not even remarked upon.

As the plantations grew in size and number, insufficient numbers of enslaved fellow Britons could be persuaded or compelled to make up the workforce. The planters and traders therefore turned to the Spanish for inspiration and began to transport enslaved Africans. Though for the most part the trade was run from London, the slaves never set foot in the city, let alone on British soil, being shipped directly across the Atlantic on the arduous Middle Passage of the triangular slave trade between England, Africa and America or the sugar islands such as Barbados.

The ever-aggressive East India Company wanted a part of the growing African slave trade. It tried to bribe James, Duke of York, in order to procure a monopoly of the trade along the east coast of Africa. A 'present' of £1000 of silver plate was given to him to secure his support. As seen earlier, James, however, had gone into business with his cousin Prince Rupert to secure the African monopoly with the Company of Royal Adventurers Trading to Africa. Virtually every member of the royal family had shares in it, the King included.

For the King to be involved in private enterprise was unheard of, yet here was Charles set up as the major beneficiary of a joint stock company. Something unusual must have led to such a financial novelty – and so it had. When Parliament arranged the King's income it did so by reintroducing the income stream his father had enjoyed before the civil wars broke out, primarily based on customs and excise tax and estimated at £1.2 million per annum. The actual income generated turned out to be well short of the expected sum. Charles and his family were therefore keen to procure some private income. The commercial structure that had served the City of London so well for generations – the joint stock company – seemed the perfect vehicle for a royal family in need of cash.

Charles did not stop there. In 1662 he successfully entreated Parliament for more income. Parliament responded with a new tax. The hearth tax was a tax levied on most households in the kingdom, at a rate of two shillings a year for each fireplace or stove in the building, with some allowance for those living in properties below a certain value. It was estimated to generate £300,000 a year, the estimated shortfall in the King's income. In practice, the new tax, like the other components of Charles's income, did not deliver the expected amount.

The purpose of the Company of Royal Adventurers was, therefore, not only to fulfil Charles's wish to make England a major world trading and political power, but also to a great extent to provide the Stuarts with a private income stream. Charles was to take half the profits from the cargoes of any ships seized, whether English or foreign, deemed to have broken the company's monopoly.

The success of the Company of Royal Adventurers' trade in slaves would depend on three things: a need for slave labour in the expanding agricultural economies of the new semi-tropical colonies; a stable source of slaves from accessible territory where slavery was already culturally acceptable and whose inhabitants could withstand the rigours of manual labour in a hot climate; and a means of connecting need and supply, not only between the parties involved but with a market for the resulting produce in Europe. This last link in the chain was provided by the Atlantic weather system, which north of the equator provided winds circulating in a clockwise direction. Ships were thus able to sail with relative ease south to Africa, then west to the Caribbean, finally completing the voyage in front of the winds – now westerlies – home again to England. In this way, the northern trade winds favoured the English, the Dutch and the French, while the southern trade winds, which circulated anticlockwise, favoured the Spanish and Portuguese, who had therefore historically traded and set up colonies in Central and South America.

Long-distance trading voyages took a great deal of planning. First, the cost of the voyage had to be ascertained by calculating the cost of acquiring a ship, fitting it out, hiring a captain and crew and buying the victuals for the journey. Next, the cost of the cargo at its point of acquisition had to be estimated, to offset against its price at sale. In the case of a trading voyage dealing in cloths, metals and spices, this could be worked out quite easily by the known prices the goods currently fetched, multiplied by the quantities carried and traded. When the cargo was human, the sums became more variable. A European ship trading in West Africa depended upon the abilities of its local agents and traders along the coast. A certain quantity of slaves might be required, but it was up to the local traders to find them. These traders acted as middlemen, negotiating between tribal chiefs and the visiting Europeans. There were many hurdles to overcome. There was no guarantee that the desired number of slaves could always be provided.

It is unlikely that the Duke of York, the chairman of the

Company of Royal Adventurers, spent much time on such details, but his secretary, Sir William Coventry, would have been closely involved – as would the city merchants who bought shares in the company. Thanks to the tradition of long training apprenticeships within London's great trading houses, the many considerations for estimating risk in international trade were well understood. For James, the joint efforts of London's merchants inside the monopolies granted by the Crown were only one facet of what was also intended as an imperial project.

There was one other enquiring mind that must not be forgotten: that of Prince Rupert of the Rhine. Rupert, like Charles and James, was a man with a keen interest in seafaring matters. Living in Whitehall Palace on the charity of his cousins, Rupert had become a sardonic and embittered man who tried to keep himself engaged in as many pursuits as his station permitted. Planning such an enterprise undoubtedly suited him.

Charles had awarded the company charter in 1660 but it had taken two years to bring together the finance, planning, ships and manpower for the company to launch its first commercial voyage. Finally, with everything ready, on 26 September 1662 the *Mary*, owned by the Royal Adventurers and captained by John Denne, put out from London and followed the trade winds south to the Gold Coast. Once there, Denne traded goods for a cargo of 224 men, women and children. On the infamous Middle Passage west across the Atlantic, forty-nine of Captain Denne's enforced passengers died – 22 per cent of the total. That left 175 men, women and children to be sold when the ship arrived in Barbados.

From the point of view of the traders, a human attrition rate of around twenty per cent was not ideal but it was acceptable. For the slaves, it was hellish. Such were the perils of the trade that the death rate could be very much higher. Adverse weather could mean that voyages outlasted water and rations. Bad or inadequate supplies at the outset, harsh or cruel treatment during the voyage, the spread of disease on board the ship – all of these might contribute to a high death rate among the slaves. In December 1662 a Captain Bowles sailed out of the Thames in command of the Royal Adventurers' ship *Blackamore*, bound for the Bight of Benin. The ship reached Africa safely and 373 Africans embarked. Two-thirds of them were women and one-third were men. There were no children. During the Middle Passage things went very badly wrong. When the *Blackamore* came to the dockside in Barbados only 150 Africans remained alive. A total of 223 had died, a mortality rate of almost sixty per cent.*

The day after the *Blackamore* moored up in Barbados, the *William*, another company ship, arrived under the command of John Wayward. The planters and traders at the quayside must have wondered what possible horrors lay on board. A total of 125 men, women and children survived – sixty per cent of the original cargo of 180. The next company ship to arrive in the West Indies from Calabar in the Bight of Benin was the *Hope*, commanded by Captain Nicholas Pepperell. Of its original cargo of 229 Africans, 156 survived the crossing, an attrition rate of just below 32 per cent. The day after, the *Zebulon* arrived. It landed a cargo of 197 men, women and children from the Bight of Benin, having lost 24 per cent of its original human cargo. Three days later, the *Amity* docked with only eight slaves for sale. The original size of the cargo had been just nine, indicating that something – most probably a Dutch warship – had prevented the

* The *Blackamore* had been involved in a notorious incident the previous year when George Downing kidnapped three regicides in Delft, one of them his former friend and mentor John Oakey, and shipped them back to England to be executed.

Amity from taking on more. The *Katherine*, another company ship, under the command of Joshua Tidde, landed 145 men, women and children out of an initial cargo of 209 bought at New Calabar, Benin. The death rate was 32 per cent.

Such mortality figures were inordinately high for what should have been a voyage which, shipwreck aside, most would hope to survive. The death toll indicates that the conditions in which the human cargo was transported were very much worse than those in which any person should reasonably have been kept. One must conclude that the company either did not provide individual captains with sufficient funds for rations, or allowed them to skimp on rations in order to subsidise their own pay. Either way, given the consistently high level of mortality seen on these early voyages, we can deduce that the company did nothing to prevent the deaths of Africans.[2] We may surmise that the company had computed that despite the loss of a high proportion of its cargo, profits could still be made. The operating ethos of the merchants of the City of London was a hard-hearted one. As for profits on these voyages, up to £20 a head was the going rate for a slave delivered from Africa to the quayside in Barbados. This could make a voyage very lucrative. A cargo of 200 slaves was worth £4000. One Barbados sugar planter complained when he had to pay the company £6000 for a consignment of 300 new slaves.[3]

The trade in humans from Africa took place out of sight of Londoners, registering only as figures of the Company of Royal Adventurers. Nevertheless, physical manifestations of the trade would make an occasional appearance. These were young African boys and girls brought into England to make picturesque house servants for lords and ladies of fashion. Such children, their dark features handsomely set off by well-made clothes, acted as visual foils for their mistresses, whose skin tended to be as fair as that of their slaves was dusky. Sometimes these child slaves appeared in paintings, as in Pierre Mignard's fine portrait of Louise de Kérouaille, the Breton noblewoman who became Charles's mistress. In the painting, a cute African girl dressed in silk offers her mistress a cornucopia of pearls.[4] The portrait provided proof that Charles and other members of the royal household came into contact with African slaves, although it was usually held that none existed in England.

Now and again these children felt the need to run away from their fine surroundings, seeking freedom in whatever way they could. Their adventures were recorded in advertisements: 'An East-Indian tawny-black boy', went one. 'Long-haired and slender, a mark burned in his forehead and chest, his name Peter, in a purple suit and coat, ran away.'[5] It seems Peter did not much care for his life in fine clothes, waiting upon fine people. The mark on his chest was a brand showing that he had run away once; that on his forehead indicating he had run away a second time. When caught again – as he almost certainly would be – his reward for running away a third time would be a voyage back across the Atlantic. On the sugar plantations of Barbados there would be nowhere for Peter to run.

The following year, 1663, Charles took a decisive step in widening his imperial interests by creating a new North American colony called Carolina. The colony was enormous, in theory if not in practice, reaching from Virginia at 36 degrees north all the way south to Florida at 31 degrees north, and right across the continent to 'the south seas'. It therefore comprised twelve of today's states (including the greater part of Texas and southern California), encompassing 'parts of America not yet cultivate or planted, and only inhabited by some Barbarous people who have no knowledge of Almighty God'.[6] According to its royal charter, eight Englishmen, its proprietors, now owned this vast land. They were the Lord Chancellor, the Earl of Clarendon; the head of the army, the Duke of Albemarle (George Monck); the Chancellor of the Exchequer, Anthony Ashley Cooper (Lord Ashley, later Lord Shaftesbury); Lord Craven; Lord John Berkeley; Sir George Carteret; Sir John Colleton; and Sir William Berkeley.

What was created was a new feudal territory ruled by a cabal of eight aristocrats of the king's choosing. It was notable that all these men lived outside the old walled city, close to the seat of royal power at Whitehall Palace. Cooper, for example, lived on the Strand, while Clarendon lived near St James's Palace. This was part of a deliberate design to move the nexus of economic power closer to the Crown. No matter that Clarendon and Cooper disliked one another; the goal was economic enrichment for the Crown and its closest adherents.

The structure of a proprietary colony meant that the proprietors ruled everyone and everything within their land, in direct line of control from the King. Something like it had been tried before. Charles's father, Charles I, had given the same huge territory to his attorney general, Sir Robert Heath, who failed to establish a colony. Before that, Sir Walter Raleigh had made five attempts at establishing settlements, all of which failed. In the spirit of colonialism and state-sponsored enterprise surging through Restoration London, there was a strong impulse to make Carolina a success this time round.*

While the Carolina and Africa companies busily set about increasing the population of England's western colonies, a

* Carolina's cotton industry, powered by slavery, would go on to play a major part in Britain's industrial revolution.

different sort of mind set about calculating the population of London. In the spring of 1663 John Graunt, the haberdasher-cum-demographer, published his groundbreaking work on London's mortality and population. Its typically unwieldy seventeenth-century title was *Natural and Political Observations made upon the Bills of Mortality*. It was an instant success, running to five editions.

The bills of mortality were the parish records of the numbers of people who died each week, classified according to the cause of death; their purpose was to warn of the onset of plague epidemics so that wealthy people, and anyone else who was able, could escape to the hopefully healthier countryside. The information was collected by 'searchers', women categorised by Graunt as 'ancient matrons'. Earlier in the century, London had set up what was intended as an early-warning system to alert the city to the onset of a plague epidemic. Each parish had to compile a weekly record of deaths and the possible causes. These were then sent to the Guildhall, where administrators compiled a complete tally in order to see when the number of deaths by plague in the city was on the rise. Such knowledge would allow the city's inhabitants to flee before they were infected. By analysing these lists, Graunt realised that the figures for instances of plague were greatly underestimated. Diagnosis was a very inexact art at the time. Several recorded causes of death, such as convulsions, might be due to plague, he reasoned – particularly if such cases occurred when plague deaths took place in the same parish. Graunt reached the alarming conclusion that instances of death by plague could be four or even six times the numbers reported. Graunt hoped his analysis would be taken note of – for the great benefit to Londoners, particularly those willing to pay for the information.

The publication of Graunt's epidemiological work coincided

with reports of an outbreak of plague in Holland. The risk of plague travelling long distances was well known even if the mechanism of transmission was misunderstood. Charles therefore instigated a temporary ban on trade with Holland to prevent ships bringing the plague to England. It was a shrewd and necessary decision, though unpopular with the City of London, which carried on a great deal of its business either with Holland or through Dutch ports into Europe.

According to the biographer John Aubrey, Graunt researched and wrote his book by rising early and working on it before going into the family shop for the day's business. His book presented the first known tables of life and death based on real mortality data. Graunt observed that about one-third of all deaths occurred from childish ailments and guessed that some of the other illnesses also caused deaths among children. From this he estimated that about thirty-six out of every 100 deaths in London related to children under six years old. Hence he argued that, of every 100 children conceived, only sixty-four would reach the age of six. He then used a mathematical projection to obtain the numbers of the original 100 who would reach the ages of sixteen, twenty-six, thirty-six, and so on. Since he now had the numbers of births and deaths, Graunt was able to work out the approximate population of London, which, as we've seen, he put at 384,000. It was an ingenious piece of work, which brought Graunt to the attention of the King.

Always interested to hear of new ideas, Charles saw the benefit of Graunt's work and commended him to the Royal Society. As a tradesman, Graunt was not of the right social class to be a member of a society composed of gentlemen. However, the society could not refuse the King's command and so Graunt was made a Fellow, an unlikely figure among the moneyed, university-educated members of the society. Charles saw what the society failed to see; that a man from a lower social order but with the right intellectual equipment was probably as suitable a member of an organisation for promoting knowledge as any other. After all, Graunt's friend Sir William Petty had started off as little higher than a servant.

With so much happening during the opening years of Charles's reign in so many fields, social, artistic and commercial, it must have looked to most as if London and the realm were well set for a peaceful and prosperous future, at odds with the recent past. But questions over religion still bedevilled the country. Charles was uneasy about Presbyterianism, having felt himself let down and belittled by the Scots when negotiating with them after his father's death. Yet his identity was not especially allied to Anglicanism in the way that it was for the English upper classes. He wanted a tolerant approach to other religions, largely because of the continuing influence of his own Catholic mother. As for the many schisms in Protestantism that had appeared during the interregnum, his views on them were very much less severe than the majority of those in the church hierarchy or in politics.

His naturally relaxed views regarding religion caused constant strain between Charles and his own government, the Anglican Church and Parliament. A series of Parliamentary Acts, known collectively as the Clarendon Code after the Lord Chancellor, sought to tighten the grip of the high Anglican establishment on religious observance and church governance, while restricting public office to those who abided by the new Anglican prayer book. In London, where nonconformism was rife among clerics and laity alike, the tightening of the religious screw did not play well. Under pressure from Presbyterians, assorted nonconformist

Anglicans and his mother, Charles attempted to bring in an Act of Indulgence, softening the line against those of differing religious persuasions. The political roof fell in. A move was made in the House of Lords to have Clarendon impeached. In the end, Charles had to back down.

The King had completely misread the strength of feeling among his own supporters, the Anglican bedrock in the Church and Parliament. Rumours spread in London about his true religious allegiances and his reputation took a further battering because of his sex life. As Pepys wryly commented, the King 'doth mind nothing but pleasures'.

Pepys was not entirely correct. Charles had an overriding obsession with pleasure and sex, it was true, but he had several other interests. Some of these, including sailing and horse racing, were also pursued purely for personal pleasure, but he had other long-term goals. One of these was that his reign should be marked by great buildings. In this he was supported by the hierarchy of the Anglican Church. Both King and clergy saw that all great times were marked by their architecture, which would live on after the actors had left the stage, as with ancient Rome. The partially ruined St Paul's Cathedral was an early target of their ambition. They had discussed its future in 1661, with some input from Wren, and now, two years later, the subject came up again. Charles instructed the commission set up to oversee and repair the church to restore it 'unto the ancient Beauty and Glory of it'.[7] The commissioners reported that the structure was in a dreadful state. A further report recommended patching up what was there. The church's future would remain a talking point for King and commissioners for years to come.

At the same time as Charles was attempting and failing to promote religious tolerance, he endeavoured to promote a new woman to his bed. This was Frances Stuart, a teenage beauty and a new lady-in-waiting to the Queen. Charles had received advance intelligence of her arrival from France, where she had lived for some time at the French court with her mother. The news came from that impeccable source, Charles's sister Henrietta, who informed her brother that Frances was 'the prettiest girl in the world'. When she arrived in early 1663, aged fourteen, Charles was smitten. His official mistress, Barbara Palmer, was a beautiful 22-year-old, but Frances was said to outshine her.

Charles made a laughing stock of himself chasing the noncompliant new girl around the palace. His affair with Barbara – who had borne him two children, with a third on the way – had already become public knowledge and was the talk of London. She ran a very grand salon at her house in King Street, next to the palace, where she entertained in grand style as one with royal influence. The King's new infatuation was soon the talk of the court, and beyond. Unusually for Charles, this time he found his advances endlessly rebuffed. La Belle Stuart made a fool of him.

Henrietta was responsible for much more than casual intrigues over her brother's sexual desires; she was an important conduit of communication between Charles and her brother-in-law, Louis XIV of France. In October 1662, Henrietta was the go-between for a controversial deal in which England sold its military outpost Dunkirk to France. The deal gave Charles a great deal of money (five million French livres). But he also gained the animosity of many of his subjects, who believed any deal with the French was foolhardy. Louis was perceived as a more significant long-term threat to England than the Dutch. For most, a deal with Catholic France was to be viewed with suspicion.

It had been an unfulfilling period for Charles. Not only had his amorous advances been rebuffed, he had found his influence with Parliament limited too. There were to be greater difficulties ahead.

PART 2

1664–1667:
THE YEARS OF DISASTER

CHAPTER 9

TRADE WARS

In 1664 the King gave his consent to one of the most audacious plans ever conceived to enrich his inner circle. If successful, the plan would coincidentally make a great deal of money for those of London's merchants who traded in Africa.

The Company of Royal Adventurers Trading to Africa was underfunded, badly led and underachieving. What was required was what we now call a relaunch. New shares were issued. The reformed company was once more a joint venture between the royal family and London merchants, with the Duke of York taking control. Along with the injection of funds, meanwhile, the company's goals changed. Trading for gold along the Gambia River was still an aim, but the company's major activity was now to be slave trading.

The reformed company's royal charter was breathtaking in its cold ambition, its monopoly extended to include all of West Africa, from the coast of Morocco to the Cape of Good Hope. To the company was consigned 'the whole, entire and only trade for the buying and selling bartering and exchanging of, for or with any Negroes, goods, wares and merchandises whatsoever to be vented or found at or with any of the Cities on the west coast of Africa'. The reconstituted company would launch a concerted effort to extract wealth from West Africa in the form of human cargo. New investment was raised from stockholders and a new fleet bought to drive the enterprise to financial success.

European slave trading in Africa had a long and complex history. The Spanish and Portuguese began running African slaves to their extensive colonies in South America around 1500. It is thought that some English privateers may have participated soon after, though in a desultory way. The first organised English trading took place in the 1550s, when a London merchant named John Lock imported ninety-four Africans from the Gold Coast for sale to the Spanish. After that, the trade really took off in London. From 1561 to 1570 the number of African slaves sent to foreign colonies increased to 1591. During the next decade no slaves were transported, but in the 1580s a total of 237 were taken.[1]

Following that there was a hiatus until 1626, when the trade from England began once more. African slaves, possibly provided by Dutch traders, had first been reported in the English territory of Bermuda in 1617. In 1619 the first African slaves were landed at Jamestown in the Chesapeake Bay area of Virginia, the first successful English colony on mainland America; they were sold by John Colwyn Jupe, a Cornish Calvinist minister turned privateer. There followed another lull in English slave trading in the early 1630s, for the trade was still in an early, spasmodic phase. It began again in earnest in 1638 when the English built Fort Cormantin, also known as Fort Koromantine, on the Gold Coast, in modern-day Ghana. The fort was among the first European buildings in Africa to incorporate a slave hold – a prison in which to incarcerate the human cargo bartered from the local Ashanti people while waiting for the next slave ship to arrive.*

The growth of the slave trade did not go entirely unopposed. In 1657, the Quaker leader George Fox wrote 'To Friends beyond the Sea, that have Blacks and Indian Slaves'. Some took this vaguely worded epistle to question the ownership of slaves, while others understood it only to mean that as the gospel was 'the power that giveth liberty and freedom', slaves should be converted to Christianity.[2] In general, Quakers were either for slavery or ambivalent about it.

On 7 July 1664, the *Hopewell*, owned by the Company of Royal Adventurers and commanded by a Captain North, set sail from London bound for the Gulf of Guinea. The *Hopewell* was the first ship sent out by the reformed company to be tasked with loading slaves for sale in the colonies of Barbados and Jamaica. En route for Africa, Captain North had to keep a lookout not only for the Dutch but for Barbary pirates operating out of Salé in Morocco. The Sallee Rovers, as the pirates were known, were the scourge of European shipping. If captured by them, North and his crew could find themselves taken as slaves.

Five days after the *Hopewell* set out, Captain Thornborough on board the *Martha* ordered his crew to haul in the anchors and set course for the Gulf of Guinea. Four days after the *Martha*, Captain John Newman and his crew hoisted sail on the *Spy*, setting the same course. On 22 July, the *Victory* set sail under the captaincy of Isaac Taylor. Between them, the five ships were

---

* Ashanti were chiefly taken to Jamaica. To avoid feuding, their neighbours and traditional enemies the Fante, from present-day Ghana and Ivory Coast, were taken to Barbados.

expected to load more than 1500 Africans to sell on the quay-sides of the West Indies. If they made £20 a head on the sale, the London merchants, aristocrats and royalty investing in the voyage stood to make a gross profit of £30,000.

They never got their money. The ships successfully evaded the Barbary pirates but once off Africa all were intercepted by the Dutch and taken as prizes before they could load so much as a single slave.[3]

While the Dutch inflicted such damage upon the fortunes of the Company of Royal Adventurers, in London Sir William Davenant did his utmost to rouse in his audience the strongest possible pro-Stuart sentiments. He put on a production of Shakespeare's *Macbeth*, heavily rewritten and revised by Davenant himself, making the language clearer and ridding it of much poetic complexity. Thanks to the backstage effects department of Davenant's theatre, the witches were able to fly through the air. And thanks to the vogue he had created for operatic touches, there were many songs and much dancing – quite a striking departure in a tragedy. Davenant must have thought his additions were in danger of unbalancing the play, so he decided to edit Shakespeare's comic interludes, cutting the famous night watchman scene in its entirety. Besides the crowd-pleasing antics, Davenant rewrote many lines to heighten the play's theme of regicide, one that was sure to resonate with his audience and with the royal family:

> Usurpers lives have but a short extent
> Nothing lives long in a strange element[4]

It's not known what the King thought of Davenant's version, but Evelyn thought it excellent and Pepys considered it 'pretty good' on first seeing it on 5 November. Davenant's *Macbeth* remained the default version well into the eighteenth century.

News of the fiasco off Africa reached London on 22 December, the very day the King, accompanied by the Duke of York, watched a new and larger version of William Petty's dual-hulled ship launched at Rotherhithe. It was named *The Experiment.* Pepys, who was among those present, recorded his feelings on the news from Africa, saying the English fleet had been 'beaten to dirt . . . to the utter ruin of our Royall Company'. The Duke of York and the company stockholders decided immediate retaliatory action should be taken. A new military voyage to West Africa was commissioned. Originally it was to be commanded by Prince Rupert. Again, Rupert's hopes of adventure and glory were dashed. Due to the losses he had encountered as a Royalist privateer, he had a bad reputation among many seamen. According to Pepys, at the news of Rupert's appointment to head the fleet, crewmen were displeased as 'he is accounted an unhappy [i.e. unlucky] man'. The Prince's reputation threatened to scupper the fleet before it had hoisted a sail.

Once more, the Duke of York told him to step aside; once more Captain Holmes, now appointed the African Company's de facto admiral, would go instead. While the plans were finalised for a new raid, Charles must have kept a firm hand on events from behind the scenes; after all, it now looked like war.

With the trade war heating up, a book appeared on London bookstalls on the very subject of overseas trade. It was by a man now dead for more than twenty years. Thomas Mun, a successful London cloth merchant and trader in the Mediterranean, had written *England's Treasure from Foreign Trade* in 1628 for his son John, who now thought to publish it. The book contained advice on trade far removed from the smash-and-grab tactics advocated by the Stuart family's African Company. Mun's guidance concentrated on the skills necessary to be a good merchant, rather than a predatory agent of a rapacious monarchy. He set out twelve key areas of knowledge, ranging from learning 'the Latin tongue' to knowledge of international taxes, from understanding how ships were built, outfitted and navigated, to knowing what goods each country made and 'what be the wares they want'.[5] According to Mun, a good merchant was a polymath for whom religious observance went hand in hand with love of one's country and an ability to serve it through trade. His creed was distilled Puritanism expressed in an era of absolute monarchy.*

Thomas Mun was born into a well-to-do London family. His father was a successful mercer, his grandfather a provost of the Royal Mint. Mun made his money trading in the Mediterranean, in particular with Turkey, before settling in London and becoming a senior figure in the East India Company. At the age of forty-one he married Ursula Malcott and they set up home in the old city in the parish of St Helen's Bishopsgate, an area fashionable among wealthy families. They had three children, of whom John was the eldest. Thomas was a religious man with a strong sense of duty to Crown and country. His parish church, the medieval St Helen's, had been William Shakespeare's church; it was also where Sir Thomas Gresham worshipped and was buried.

England's Treasure did not confine itself to advice from a father to his son. It offered advice on how all of England might be enriched. This was what convinced John Mun he should

---

* For Mun's twelve-point plan on how to be a good London merchant, see Appendix I.

publish his father's work – 'for the common good', as he put it. The book's appearance in 1664 was no happenstance; Mun's decision coincided with a new and dangerous phase in the trade battle between London and Amsterdam for supremacy in foreign trade. The prize for winning that battle was the unhindered ability to export more goods.*

England's Treasure spelt out how London's merchants could make the kingdom rich by exporting more to create a surplus of the value of exports over imports. It was a clear expression of mercantile capitalism. Mun explained how the use of many different factors, including carefully set import taxes, would help ensure a healthy balance of trade so that the country could flourish.

The debate over how to increase trade had been going on since the beginning of the century. In 1622 the merchant Edward Misselden wrote an influential treatise in support of free trade as practised by the Dutch, unhindered by tariffs and duties, while still ensuring a positive balance of trade. His work was still read long after the Restoration. Misselden outlined what he saw as the reasons for a perceived 'decrease in trade' in English woollen goods in both the domestic market and for export. Among the reasons he gave for poor trade was the cost of borrowing money, as high as 100 per cent per year:

> it is not an Usury of ten in the hundred only, that wringeth this Common-wealth, but an extorsion also of 20-30-40, nay of Cento per Cento per Anno, as the Italians speake, given and taken on pledges and pawnes, and that on poore peoples

---

* If every country strives for it, free trade becomes the serpent that devours its own tail. As no one has yet succeeded in working out what to do about this cannibalistic phenomenon, it is hardly surprising it was a hot issue in the seventeenth century.

> labours, in London especially: which is a biting Usury indeed, and a fearefull crying sinne before God.[6]

Mun and Misselden agreed that high interest rates caused harm to business. 'Trade decreaseth as Usury increaseth, for they rise and fall together,' said Mun. In 1660s London the cost of money was still an issue. As the decade progressed it would become of ever greater importance.

According to Mun, English trade was impeded by taxes on the importation of English cloth into neighbouring countries, together with the low value of English money. Mun saw that the balance of trade deficit led to a shortage of silver bullion. A good supply of silver was necessary to fund more trade. This was a key tenet of mercantilism. If the silver, or 'plate' as it was called, was used to buy goods in countries outside 'Christendom' the money supply dwindled even more. Once plate was spent outside Europe it was likely never to return, whereas at least some of the silver spent in Europe was likely to come back home again sooner or later due to the cyclical nature of trade. Misselden, however, thought that the export of bullion did not matter, as long as the goods bought with it were re-exported and so created more wealth.

Given Charles II's keen advocacy of joint stock monopolies such as the East India Company and the Royal Adventurers, Misselden made interesting reading in the 1660s. Monopolies, he said, were impediments to trade, being vehicles by which 'this Common-wealth is deprived of that true liberty of Trade, which belongeth to all the subjects: when the Commodity of some few, is preferred to the publique good.'

As an investor in the East India Company, Mun had written in its favour, arguing that in the long term its goals and practices were for the best.[7] However, by 1628 he had changed his mind.

In *England's Treasure* he agreed with Misselden that monopolies restricted trade. A positive balance of trade was crucial: 'We must ever observe this rule; to sell more to strangers than we consume in value of theirs.'[8]

Mun and Misselden were particularly clear-sighted in recognising the need for the government to collate trade figures so that it was possible to keep track of the balance of imports and exports. Without such information, the ideas behind mercantile capitalism could not be practised with accuracy. For example, tariffs on foreign goods might be seen to work, but did they also hinder the business of domestic merchants who sold them? Where the recommendation for measuring the balance of trade fell down was that there was as yet no clear mechanism for doing so.*

There were several defects in the ideas expressed by Mun. The main one was that striving for dominance in trade and in profit would almost inevitably lead to war between trading partners as each tried to better the other. Mercantilism inevitably caused instability. And this is exactly what it did with regard to London's greatest rivals, Holland and France. The balance of trade with Amsterdam was unfavourable, but that with the French was worse, because of what Mun identified as an English love of French lace, wines and other luxury goods. After the return of Charles II, this love of all things French intensified thanks to the royal court taking on French manners and fashion and encouraging others to do the same. Of course, London's merchants did not see this imbalance of trade as a defect. For them, if the mercantile system were to thrive, then international

---

* Debate on what to measure and how to measure it goes on among economists today. Adam Smith in *The Wealth of Nations*, 1776, argued that it was unnecessary to worry about the balance of payments as in the long term it did not matter, a view that would have horrified many both in seventeenth-century London and today.

trade must be ensured at all costs. This line of reasoning rendered it natural that there should be agitation between London, emerging as the largest city in the world, and Amsterdam, the leading trading port in the world.

Amsterdam had long been the pre-eminent European trading port. In the trade battles of the mid-seventeenth century the Dutch had an advantage: their goods were traded freely, without import restrictions, in an early expression of what today is known as free trade, whereas goods coming into British ports were subject to customs duty. The British Exchequer was heavily reliant on duty and customs taxes. Therefore Britain had long been at a trading disadvantage with the Dutch States, which relied on domestic taxes levied through local government.

To counter this imbalance in trade, the British Parliament passed a series of Navigation Acts, encouraged by the diplomat and politician George Downing. His hand was behind almost every piece of legislation regarding shipping and trade during the Restoration, despite his fellow committeeman John Evelyn thinking him 'not worth a groat'.[9]

The Navigation Acts had their basis in a sense of the national interest that went back centuries. Many European countries had at various times introduced some form or other of legislation designed to give an advantage to home trade or manufacturing. For example, in the fourteenth century England had forbidden the importation of iron. Whatever its nature, the central purpose of such legislation was the same: to create a trading advantage for the home state by restricting the trade of other countries.

England introduced its first Navigation Act in 1651. The impetus was an economy that was suffering a downturn.[10] Primarily, the act was aimed at international Dutch trade. It stated that only British ships could bring in goods from 'Asia, Africa, or America', with a similar embargo being imposed on goods from Europe.[11] This meant that only English ships could trade with British colonies and only English ships could import goods to England. The new rules meant that Dutch ships could no longer bring goods from Dutch colonies to England. Dutch ships could trade in English ports, but only if they brought goods made in home territories. Hence a Dutch ship could bring gin, but not pepper from the Indies. This trade advantage created the instability that led the following year to the First Anglo-Dutch War.

By the 1660s, as the trade war between the rivals continued to heat up, London cared little for the political dangers of restricting international trade, for there was money to be made. The Navigation Act passed a decade before by a republican administration now deemed to have been illegal was renewed in 1660 and amended the following year, under direct guidance from Charles, and passed by Parliament.[12] The trade embargoes stipulated were so strict that had they been fully observed in all territories affected by them, wealth creation would have ground to a halt. The mercantilist creed, however, dictated that protectionism was necessary to stop wealth flowing outwards rather than in.*

The time came for the new expedition to Africa to set sail. This time Holmes led a larger fleet. The reason was simple: he was to start a war. It was an enormous gamble by the King, based on the debatable premise that the Dutch were a greater threat to England than the French. If one man can be identified as the architect of this policy, warning against Dutch trade expansionism and arguing for an aggressive policy against it, that man was George Downing. A successful diplomat under the

* For the partial text of the Navigation Act of 1660, see Appendix II.

Commonwealth and Protectorate, Downing had switched sides so quickly at the first whiff of the Restoration that afterwards any man who violently betrayed his principles was known as 'an arrant George Downing'. It was true that Downing was a nasty piece of work, successfully plotting the downfall of several of his former friends and colleagues, but, as Charles recognised, he got things done.

While his character was not the most appealing, Downing was brilliant, first as a diplomat and spy, then as a politician and financial expert. His financial planning was an important factor in Britain's adoption of a modern fiscal system. His diplomatic missions to The Hague, first under Cromwell and subsequently under Charles II, had given him first-hand knowledge of Dutch ambitions and of the financial policies that supported them. Downing thought Charles should combat the Dutch with some of their own financial policies and, if that failed, should take them on militarily.

It is worth noting that Charles viewed England's place in international politics through the prism of a personal desire to place Britain firmly on the European stage, a view held by monarchs since the end of Saxon times.* This was reinforced by the great antipathy he had long nursed for the Dutch United Provinces.[13] To some extent this stemmed from events following the execution of Charles's father in January 1649. At that time the Prince was staying in The Hague as a guest of William II. Relations began to deteriorate when Charles planned to wrest back the throne with the help of the Irish Confederacy, a coalition of pro-Royalist Catholics in Ireland. The Dutch were unimpressed by the prospect of an alliance with Catholic forces.

---

* This view held at the centre of British politics until Britain voted in the referendum of 23 June 2016 to withdraw from membership of the European Union.

As a result, Charles was forced to leave The Hague and return to his mother in France.

Moreover, following the death of his sister's husband, William II, in 1650 Charles saw the subsequent removal of power from the House of Orange, to be ceded to a regime based on elected regional authorities, as an attack on royalty itself. His view worked against any viable, long-term alliance between two countries that might – given their Protestantism and similar mercantile histories – have seemed natural allies.

During his time abroad, Charles had had an opportunity to study the forms of government in several countries, and especially to compare the Dutch United Provinces and France. Contemporary commentators later pointed out that Charles spoke favourably of France, where the king, his cousin, ruled with absolute power. Charles's mother, Henrietta Maria, was the daughter of a French king, and had professed her religion and culture in a very open way, processing publicly to her private chapel on the Strand. When the English Civil War turned against the Crown, it was with his mother that the young Prince had initially gone to live near Paris. Charles had grown up learning the habits of the French court.

While some in Whitehall thought France, with its expansionist ambitions, was England's real adversary, Charles kept up cordial relations with the French through his younger sister Henrietta Anne, wife of the French king's brother, Philippe. This familial connection was of genuine importance, for Henrietta was party to French state secrets and was Charles's lifelong confidante. Charles's only connection to the Dutch stadtholder, or prime minister, Johan de Witt was through Downing, who as English ambassador maintained a hostile front. Charles's personal experiences and preferences thus helped colour a foreign policy that was now moving somewhat recklessly towards war.

As Downing's anti-Dutch policies took hold, the English put pressure on the Dutch, raiding their ships and attacking their trading ports. This scheme, run in tandem with Holmes's exploits in Africa, was designed to goad the Dutch into declaring war. In August a squadron of Royal Navy ships arrived off the Dutch colony of New Amsterdam in North America and demanded the colony be surrendered. The governor, Peter Stuyvesant, was made of stern stuff and at first resisted. But with ammunition and gunpowder low and the population fearful, he had no alternative but to surrender. New Amsterdam was renamed New York after the heir to the throne.

Downing's arguments in favour of war proved persuasive for the King's brother James and the current royal favourite, the politician Henry Bennet, 1st Earl of Arlington, whom Charles had appointed – largely because of his success in procuring young women for the royal bed – to replace the elderly Sir Edward Nicholas as Secretary of State two years earlier. York and Bennet in turn won the argument with the King. In October, the Commons voted the enormous sum of £2.5 million to prepare the navy for war.

Holmes was the agent by which the conflict would be engineered. His written orders, drafted by the Duke of York's secretary William Coventry and signed by James himself, were to 'promote the Interests of the Royall Company' and to 'kill, take, sink or destroy such as shall oppose you'.[14] The Duke's unwritten orders were to foment as much trouble as possible for the Dutch, forcing them to retaliate and enabling the English to claim Dutch aggression as an act of war.

With a flotilla numbering twenty-two warships, Holmes appeared off Cape Verde on 25 December 1664. In a lightning campaign he captured or sank two dozen Dutch ships and wreaked havoc at Dutch forts and other strongholds along swathes of the continental coastline. By the time Holmes reached London with news of the strongholds he had taken, a Dutch fleet under Admiral Michiel de Ruyter had recaptured all but one. The fact that the English held on to that one fortress nevertheless provided them with a foothold they would go on to exploit in future years.

Astonishingly, the military reverses had no great immediate effect on the British slave trade in West Africa. The numbers of slaves exported remained fairly constant. Perhaps the Dutch could not afford to maintain a strong naval presence for long so far from home. But the political damage was done. Full-scale war between the English and the Dutch was not far off.

CHAPTER 10
A NEW WORLD OF SCIENCE

Around the end of 1664, two Frenchmen died in Covent Garden of suspected plague. There had already been a few cases in London during the year, perhaps twelve in all, but in seventeenth-century London this was little to panic about. Plague never completely went away; it ebbed and flowed, changing with the seasons and occasionally building up to an epidemic.

Common at the time in England and other European countries, bubonic plague is caused by a bacterium carried by fleas that live off rats. There had been many epidemics. In the fourteenth century plague had wiped out between 30 and 60 per cent of the population of Europe. More recently, during 1663–4, an epidemic had taken hold in Holland. The English authorities were therefore wary. A period of quarantine was imposed on shipping coming up the Thames from Holland in case it carried the infection. The winter of 1664–5 was particularly cold, and it was known that plague did not spread much, if at all, in cold weather. Nevertheless, throughout the winter, vigilance was the watchword. Meanwhile, London continued about its business.

The royal household was not immune to such diseases. Another scourge of the time, smallpox, had nearly carried off the Queen late in 1663 and by the following year she was still recovering. By the time of her illness Catherine and Charles both knew she was most unlikely to carry a child to full term; to add to the Queen's sorrow, Barbara had given Charles four children. Then, in a fever, Catherine had imagined giving birth to a baby boy, an heir to the throne. Charles was reported to have comforted her in her delirium, tenderly going along with her fantasy.

With ill-health circling London and the royal family, it might have been a timely moment for the Royal Society or the Royal College of Physicians to make some breakthrough in medicine, but that did not happen. Medical science was insufficiently developed to find remedies for most ailments, a fact that was soon to become all too clear. However, two books which appeared in London bookshops that winter, and which could not have been more different in appearance, were both of great and lasting importance. One was large, with imposing leather binding; the other was a slight thing of only a few pages, like a newsletter. The small publication was the first edition of *Philosophical Transactions*, a journal recording developments in the field of natural philosophy, or science, in which medicine markedly played almost no part. The larger book bore the odd title *Micrographia*. It was written by the Royal Society's curator of experiments, Robert Hooke, and was published by the society in January 1665, when the Thames was still frozen over.

It was not the first book to be published under the imprimatur of the Royal Society. That honour had gone the previous year to *Sylva*, John Evelyn's learned discourse on the properties and propagation of forest trees. Evelyn was born in Surrey and had grown up in the family home of Southover Grange in Lewes, Sussex, where he developed a lifelong love of trees; he was, he later said, 'wood born', which accounted for his interest in plants. His book was a call to arms, asserting that a rigorous programme of replanting was necessary. According to Evelyn, Britain was in danger of running out of suitable wood with which to manufacture ships – 'our floating castles' – and to make charcoal for the key manufacturing industries of iron and glass.

English forests truly were being depleted at an unsustainable rate. One cause was the burden the shipbuilding industry put on the stock of oak trees. A first-rate warship required the felling of a hundred acres of oak forest, or up to 2000 oak trees, each of which had taken on average 150 years to grow to maturity.[1] Another reason, according to Evelyn, was that during the interregnum Cromwellians had taken over estates owned by royalists and wantonly grubbed up the forests.[2] The chief reason for the depletion of the forests was both prosaic and irreversible: during the previous hundred years England's population had doubled. Forests were being ripped out to make way for agricultural land. The enormous growth of London had gone hand-in-hand with that of the entire population. The expansion of agriculture, however, had outstripped that of the population, for food production had to sustain not only the agrarian population and connected rural communities but London itself, which was essentially non-productive in terms of food, except for the baking of its daily bread.

Unfortunately, *Sylva* was a dry read – a fact accidentally acknowledged by the author in his florid introduction to the reader – 'if these dry sticks afford him any sap ...' *Sylva* had but one illustration, a dull diagram of how to pile wood to burn for charcoal. Possibly because of its worthy subject, and worthier prose, it was received with no great enthusiasm by the book-buying public, nor did the navy's shipbuilding programme expand, as Evelyn had hoped, via a national oak forest planting scheme.

While *Sylva* failed to excite, the Royal Society's second publication caused a sensation and become an instant best seller. Unlike *Sylva*, Robert Hooke's *Micrographia, or some Physiological Descriptions of Minute Bodies made by Magnifying Glasses*, was not only revolutionary but lavishly illustrated. Thirty-eight full-page copperplate engravings contained dozens of illustrations such as its readers would never have seen before – the grid-like eye of a fly in extreme close-up, the cell-like structure of vegetation, those scourges of domestic London life, the flea and the louse, both reproduced at over a foot long, and even frozen human urine, all seen under the microscope.

Hooke was twenty-seven when he began the observations for *Micrographia*. He realised that this had to be *his* work, *his* book, his moment to show what he could achieve in many different fields of study. He even included a section at the end about observations that could be made with a very different type of optic tube from the microscope – the telescope – with a description of 'the different types of stars' one could see. The final plate, no. 38, is a beautiful engraving of craters on the moon.

The idea behind the work was not Hooke's, however, but that of the King. It had come to Charles's attention that Christopher Wren had observed several small creatures though a microscope and made drawings of them, including a louse and a flea. The King was so amused by the drawings that he asked for more. A collection of illustrations would make a worthy book for the King's cabinet of curiosities. Wren was engaged in so many other projects that he had to decline the commission. The task was passed to Hooke, who dedicated his work to the King and gave generous acknowledgement to Wren's prior work in his introduction, describing his friend's drawings as 'one of the ornaments of that great Collection of Rarities in the King's Closet'.[3]

Hooke's book was a triumph for the Royal Society. Although it did not set out to do so, it advertised to the world that the society had great ambition; its extraordinary goal being no less than the exploration of almost everything. Yet the Fellows had few tools to aid them in their explorations. New experiments generally required the manufacture of new apparatus. Hooke was alone among the virtuosi in having the technical ability to make such equipment. Having been elected a full Fellow of the society in 1663, he remained its key employee. He was a busy man with too many different calls on his time. As curator of experiments he had to do everything from conducting experiments and overseeing the manufacture of equipment, to recording results, meanwhile coming up with presentations of newly observed phenomena with which to amuse the Fellows at their weekly meetings. All this put Hooke in the unusual position of being at once the society's resident scientific genius and its performing seal.

From his apparently idyllic childhood in a parsonage in the Isle of Wight, Hooke had developed a lasting interest in the world about him, together with a natural aptitude for careful observation, excellent ability as a draughtsman and skill at making things. He once replicated a brass clock in wood, and it worked. As a boy, Hooke was fascinated by the fossils he found in the rocks on the southern shores of his home island, and he remained so as an adult. He explored the beautiful rock strata and lines of sedimentation at Carbis Bay in Cornwall and other beauty spots. From his observations, he began to think about the age of the earth, leading him to question Archbishop Ussher's strict edict of five and a half thousand years.* Hooke came to the conclusion that the earth was much older, though he was to discover something much trickier than science: the difficulty

* Archbishop Ussher (1581–1656) deduced from biblical studies that the world had begun at 9 a.m. on 26 October 4004 BCE.

of putting such an idea across to people unused to hearing the Church's official line questioned. He knew that if he publicly posited a world of almost unimaginable age, he would be guilty of heresy. This matter of the age of the earth illustrated concisely the social and religious constraints with which the new experimentalists had to grapple in their quest to reveal the secrets of the physical world. On the one hand, they felt duty bound to explore and reveal God's work; on the other, the evidence could sometimes point to a reality that, if not beyond the work of a supreme being, was at least outside the strictures of religion.

Following encouragement at Westminster School, where he became a lifelong friend of John Locke, and further education at Balliol College, Oxford, where he developed a further lifelong friendship with Christopher Wren, Hooke became involved with the scientific circle in Oxford, employed as a technician who could design the various experiments the virtuosi desired. It was at Oxford that he became chief scientific assistant to Robert Boyle, who became his patron. Hooke lived in Boyle's house; only with his appointment to the Royal Society would he gain his own home – his rooms at Gresham College. By this time, Boyle and Hooke had become close friends. When Boyle finally moved to London to live with his sister, he and Hooke usually dined together once a week.

While labouring as the Royal Society's curator of experiments, Hooke continued to work with Boyle. In 1663, he was asked by the society to set in motion a series of observations using microscopes. As requested, he diligently worked away while carrying out his duties for the various Fellows of the society and his primary patron. Fortunately, Hooke was in the prime of his abilities and was a willing workhorse for his various employers.

By late 1664 Hooke had presented so many images produced

from observations under the microscope that on 23 November 1664 the president of the society, Lord Brouncker, ordered a book to be printed. It was ready by January. The first customer appears to have been the ever-inquisitive Samuel Pepys, who recorded that on 20 January he bought Hooke's book, 'of which I am very proud'. He would most likely have bought it from James Allestry's bookshop in Duck Lane. Allestry and his partner John Martyn were printers to the Royal Society.

The book made Hooke's reputation. He was already moving among the scientific and philosophical elite of his day, easily crossing social divides, and was on good terms with a vast array of people, most of whom, owing to his gregarious and engaging nature, he could count on as friends. He opened his great work by explaining his methods, keeping his game-changing illustrations for later. He explained that he generally used a microscope made with a tube between six and seven inches long, with an object lens at one end and an eye glass at the other, with a middle glass between them which could be removed to change the magnification and so aid the observation of different types of subject. Hooke did not necessarily know exactly what magnification his different microscopes would afford, so beside the object under the microscope he placed another object of the same type and size, beside which he kept a ruler marked with very small intervals. By this method he could work out the magnification of his images.

Hooke's first plate was an engraving of the very tip of a needle, one-twentieth of an inch in length, blown up to span six inches on the page, giving a magnification of object to printed image of around 120:1. 'As with nature,' he wrote, 'the most natural way of beginning is from a Mathematical point.' The result of this magnification was that the needle's point was revealed to be rounded, with a rough surface, studded with cavities and with innumerable imperfections. From this very first illustration Hooke made his own point clear about man-made objects as compared with those in nature: 'the Microscope can afford us hundreds of instances of points many thousand times sharper: such as those of the hairs, and bristles, and claws of multitudes of insects.'

To ram his lesson home, Hooke followed the needle with an engraving of a printed full stop. Under the same magnification it appeared like an irregular splodge, or an ink blot. Similarly, the edge of a razor became an uneven, wavy line with many indentations and gouges. In the next plate, Hooke moved on to illustrate exceptionally thin hollow glass tubes he had had made – no thicker than a spider's web, he said – with which to examine the upward capillary movement of liquid. From these experiments he deduced that this could be the same means by which sap moved through plants.

Every plate illustrated new marvels. *Micrographia* included plates of everything from plants to the head of a drone fly reproduced twelve inches high, via such wonders as the jawbone and teeth of a snail and the eerie beauty of the feather-winged moth. Plate 5 showed how urine that was beginning to freeze took on crystalline star shapes. Hooke said of these that they were 'extremely curious and wonderful' and that they deserved the 'attention of all diligent observers of nature'.

Looking back at his work from our own age, one of the most remarkable illustrations was Plate 8, a piece of cork, which when viewed either straight on or obliquely was revealed to be composed of a regular pattern of pockets, giving it its springy, buoyant quality. From the extraordinary divided structure he observed, Hooke was reminded of the structure of a beehive and coined the word 'cell' for the individual building blocks he saw. From his observations, he estimated that one cubic inch of cork contained more than 1.2 million cells.

No less astonishing to the eye were the images in Plate 9, of mould on the leather cover of a book. Under Hooke's microscope, a small white spot measuring 1/32 of an inch was revealed to be composed of a forest of elegant stems at the head of which were frothy, broken heads, for all the world like miniature chrysanthemums. His illustration of a stinging nettle revealed spikes with points much sharper than that of the man-made needle in his first illustration, attached to a cucumber-like bladder which fed stinging liquid up the hollow needle. Equally marvellous was the image of a bee's sting, very long and hollow like the nettle's points but armed with barbs. A drawing of a fish scale (from the skin of a sole) is surprisingly beautiful, aided in no small part by Hooke's prowess with a pen and his engraver's skill with a burin.

One of the last images in this encyclopaedic book of the author's many interests is of a little creature that, in the author's words, 'fears not to trample on the best; and affects nothing so much as a Crown; feeds and lives very high, and that makes it saucy, as to pull any one by the ears that comes in its way'. He is referring to the louse. In seventeenth-century London, the louse was a pest to all. Hooke pictured it in glorious fold-out enormity, with a monstrous, conical, alien head and six multi-jointed legs. In his drawing, the louse appears to be clutching the stem of a plant but Hooke informs us this sturdy bough is in fact a human hair. He tells us he kept several lice in a box until they were very hungry, then took one out and put it on his hand where it began sucking his blood through a snout that was not so much a mouth as a feeding tube. Under his microscope, Hooke could see his blood entering the translucent creature and being taken up into a sac in its body. He marvelled at how the insect could draw up blood without penetrating beyond the outermost layer of his skin, so proving, he said, that human blood vessels were dispersed into every part of the skin – even, as he put it, 'into the Cuticula'.[4]

To draw detailed descriptions of his insects, Hooke had to keep them still. This was more difficult than might be imagined. At first he simply killed the insect. He discovered that when he did so he invariably crushed some part of the animal, rendering it useless to observe. Next, he tried sticking the creature's feet in some sticky substance such as honey or glue. He described how an ant twisted and wriggled so much in attempts to break free that he abandoned the idea. His solution was as ingenious as one might expect from so questing a mind. He discovered that if he dipped an ant in brandy before putting it under his microscope it lay stunned for thirty minutes or more, before reviving and going on its way.

Two months after *Micrographia* appeared in print, the small journal entitled *Philosophical Transactions* was published for the first time. Appearing on 6 March, priced at one shilling, this was the world's first journal devoted to science – although, as with so many great things, the momentousness of the event was not initially apparent. The *Transactions*, as it would come to be simply known, introduced to the world the process whereby scientists reviewed one another's work, allowing particular experiments or theories to be evaluated by the emerging scientific community. From the beginning, the little journal was an international platform for the dissemination of scientific knowledge.

The journal was the idea of one man, a 46-year-old German émigré named Heinrich Oldenburg. A former diplomat and teacher with a fondness for discovering the latest ideas in all areas of knowledge, Oldenburg had met many of the foremost theologians, scientists and scholars in Europe during a peripatetic life as a tutor to the sons of wealthy families. Among those he had tutored was the scientifically minded seventh son of the 1st Earl of Cork. Robert Boyle would go on to become Oldenburg's patron, keeping him afloat financially through thin times in the 1650s and later.

Over much of his life, Oldenburg maintained an incomparable network of correspondents throughout European intellectual circles. He kept up a voluminous correspondence with leading philosophers, experimenters, theologians and political theorists, conversing with each about their particular fields of interest with apparent ease. Among his circle of correspondents were Leibniz, Spinoza, Milton, Boyle, and Boyle's sister, Katherine, Lady Ranelagh, a woman whose place in London's intellectual circles was long overlooked. So great were Oldenburg's interests and so widespread his contacts that in his own time he was widely recognised as a leading virtuoso and intelligencer.

At the end of his career Oldenburg settled in London, where he became known as Henry rather than Heinrich. Thanks to his diplomatic status, he lived in the exclusive upmarket street of Pall Mall, by the walls of Whitehall Palace gardens, where he was a neighbour of the esteemed physician Thomas Sydenham and of Countess Ranelagh.* An excellent linguist, his perfect English was commented upon by all with whom he had dealings, among them Joseph Glanvill, a clergyman and a leading member of the newly emerging virtuosi.[5] Oldenburg's interests ranged from the trivial to the global. He was as interested in fanciful musings as he was in actual breakthroughs. His friend

---

* Oldenburg had one rocky moment during his long sojourn in England. During the second Anglo-Dutch war he was suspected of being a spy, but was exonerated. He would die at his home in Pall Mall in 1677, aged fifty-eight.

Glanvill made one such prediction, saying the time would come when mankind would be able to communicate with people around the world by means of 'magnetic waves that permeate the ether'.

Although Glanvill showed an eerie degree of prescience, such predictions were not in themselves unusual in philosophical circles of the time. The Fellows of the Royal Society loved making wish lists of developments they would like to see become reality. In this, as in other things, they took their cue from Francis Bacon, who had seen such lists – desiderata, he called them – as part of the method by which mankind stretched itself and advances were made.[6] Oldenburg's patron Robert Boyle compiled a 24-part list beginning with his hope for 'The Prolongation of Life', continuing with 'The Recovery of Youth' and on to the 'Art of Flying', making it the most famous of all such lists.*

Through his close connection to Boyle and so many of the founders of the Royal Society, it was not surprising that Oldenburg was asked to become one of the society's two founding secretaries, before being appointed as a Fellow in 1664. Oldenburg immediately saw the need for a journal in which the flow of ideas between scholars and experimenters could be aired and discussed. At first, he funded the journal entirely out of his own meagre funds. He dedicated it to the Royal Society: 'In these rude collections, which are only the gleanings of my private diversions in broken hours, it may appear that many minds and hands are in many places industriously employed . . . in pursuit of those excellent ends, which belong to your heroical undertakings.'[7] The introduction to his first newsletter set out his plan:

---

* For Boyle's complete list, see Appendix III.

> Whereas there is nothing more necessary for promoting the improvement of Philosophical Matters, than the communicating to such . . . it is therefore thought fit to employ the *Press*, as the most proper way to gratifie those, whose engagement in such Studies, and delight in the advancement of Learning and profitable Discoveries, doth entitle them to the knowledge of what this Kingdom, or other parts of the World, do, from time to time, afford . . .

The first edition of the *Transactions* opened a window into the connected world of Mr Oldenburg. It began with a report from Paris on improvements in 'Optick Glasses' for use in telescopes. Another account, also from France, concerned the mathematics necessary to predict the movements of a comet. These writings were translated by Oldenburg into English, as were all those originally written in Latin or another language. There was an account of whaling off Bermuda and a report on lead ores found in Germany and Hungary, followed by one from a military officer on a British naval ship on duty in the Leeward Islands on the superior accuracy of pendulum watches in determining longitude. The death was reported of Pierre de Fermat, the French lawyer and mathematician who would earn lasting posthumous fame for a piece of marginalia he had jotted down in a book of ancient Greek mathematics, and which would become known as Fermat's Last Theorem. Oldenburg described Fermat as a universal genius, excelling in mathematical science and other activities: 'That, which is most of all surprizing to many . . . he composed Latin, French and Spanish verses with the same elegancy as if he had lived in the time of Augustus, and passed the greatest part of his life at the courts of France and Spain.'[8]

To complete the contents of his first edition, Oldenburg turned to work from two of his fellow members of the Royal

Society. The first was an account of Robert Boyle's latest book, entitled *New Observations and Experiments in order to a History of Cold*. Boyle also gave an odd report of a deformed calf discovered in Lymington, and there was a report from Robert Hooke on how he had recently used a twelve-foot telescope to observe one of Jupiter's belts moving from east to west about half the length of the planet's diameter in the space of two hours.

The mere dissemination of knowledge was not enough for Oldenburg. He indicated from the start that he hoped his publication would play an active role in the advancement of new discoveries. Those who were 'addicted to and conversant in such matters, may be invited and encouraged to search, try, and find out new things, impart their knowledge to one another, and contribute what they can to the Grand design of improving Natural knowledge, and perfecting all *Philosophical Arts*, and *Sciences*'.

By the fourth edition of the *Transactions*, published in June 1665, debate among Oldenburg's acquaintances was well established – even to a vitriolic degree. The first reported row involved Hooke, a man not afraid of a spirited discussion. A French correspondent, M. Auzout, took exception to some of the claims Hooke had made about his mechanism for grinding optical glass. One can surmise that the Frenchman did not realise just what – or who – he was taking on. Nor did Hooke and Oldenburg see eye to eye. This was awkward for the society, for they were its chief working office holders. The pair were eventually to fall out.

From the moment his journal was under way, Oldenburg reported on significant moments in the history of observational science. The sixth edition of the *Transactions* carried a review of *Micrographia*. The book's most famous image is Plate 32, the huge, two-page fold-out engraving of a flea, described by Hooke as 'adorned with a curiously polished suit of sable armour' and equipped with the most ingenious legs, which it could fold up and then spring out, all six together, to allow it to jump with its whole strength. This insignificant creature was already making its mark on London.

CHAPTER II

THE YEAR OF THE FLEA

In the spring of 1665 plague broke out in the parish of St-Giles-in-the-Fields, outside the old city, to the north of Covent Garden. At first it affected just a few people in one family, then a neighbouring family, then another. Although London had been through it before, most recently in 1636, what was to grow from these small beginnings was truly terrible.

Bubonic plague is a bacterial infection of the body's lymphatic system. When a plague-carrying flea bites its victim, the bacteria enter the system and travel to the nearest lymph node. These nodes are distributed throughout the body with clusters around the groin, the abdomen, the armpits and neck. Among the first symptoms is a swelling of the lymph nodes. With plague infection these nodes become enlarged and can even break open. Along with the swelling, the patient usually suffers a variety of flu-like symptoms including a temperature, headaches and vomiting. The infection in most cases progresses rapidly, with the patient suffering great pain, gangrene in extremities such as the toes, fingers and nose, and necrosis of other parts of the body, causing black spots to appear as the skin dies – hence the term Black Death. In the ultimate stages there is vomiting of blood, delirium and finally death. The disease is very contagious and only a small number of those who contract it survive.

As the plague took hold in the slums of outer London, relations with the Dutch reached crisis point. The sporadic maritime skirmishing between the two nations had escalated since the previous year. English privateers harried Dutch shipping, capturing many vessels and taking them to English ports. War was now inevitable. Many factors were involved, including interference by the House of Stuart in Dutch domestic affairs in order to support the political ambitions of Charles's nephew, William, Prince of Orange. There were the individual ambitions of the Duke of York and the Earl of Arlington, both of whom hoped to benefit from the annexation of Dutch colonies. There was the desire for war among naval commanders hoping to grow rich on prize money. All of these had to be measured against the outcome of the First Anglo-Dutch war, fought during the Commonwealth era, when the English were victorious but failed to destroy the Dutch fleet. Since then, the Dutch had been building new warships at a furious rate.

The loss of New Amsterdam to the English led the Dutch to retaliate. They retook their erstwhile outposts in West Africa and seized the economically important English colony of Barbados. On 4 March the Dutch fleet was issued with orders to fire at will when threatened by English ships. Charles took this as a provocation and declared war. Both sides now prepared their fleets for the set-piece naval battles they hoped would settle the matter.

While England and Holland headed into a naval war, a

single shipping tragedy took place in the Bay of Biscay. In April 1665 *The Experiment*, Sir William Petty's double-hulled ship, sank in a storm on its way home from Portugal with all hands lost. The ship was a further development of the one the King had mocked three years before. Many in the shipbuilding industry were pleased the revolutionary boat had failed. *The Experiment* had been described as 'dangerous'; it was argued that if the Dutch copied its shallow draught and impressive carrying capacity they might be able to transport an army right up the Thames to London and invade. The failure of the ship in heavy weather was the most serious setback for any practical project by the Royal Society to date. Petty had put at least £1500 of his own money into the venture, while other investors had put in £3000, and Petty's close friend and supporter Wren had contributed not money but his opinions and judgements.[1] For Charles, the Royal Society's patron, hopes for the society were pinned on practical advances in shipping and navigation. The society's prestige undoubtedly took a beating from the sinking of *The Experiment*. It is fair to say that Charles lost some interest in his pet scientific brains trust.

As England plunged into another war, the plague stealthily established itself throughout the closely packed houses of the shipbuilding community on the marshy riverside at Deptford. From there it spread west and north, entering the crowded ancient city. By April the death rate was rising rapidly. The authorities had no accurate records to tell them the increasing death toll was caused by plague, but they knew the signs from previous epidemics. Parish authorities responded by quarantining suspected households. Those who read John Graunt's tables could see for themselves the growing numbers of cases and decide whether or not to remain in the city. In truth, his tables mattered little. Despite his success three years before, when the results of his study of the bills of mortality had been published to royal enthusiasm, no one thought much about them now, though they had been republished in a second and a third edition.

The chief problem with Graunt's system was that it was still in an embryonic form. For his early warning method to work adequately he would need to publish regular data, perhaps every week, with very fine changes tabulated for the whole of London and outlying areas. This was beyond Graunt's resources. To collect and work on the mortality figures as they came in weekly from all 122 parishes throughout London, taking in the area inside the walls, Westminster, the liberties and suburbs, would have been a tremendous task. It could probably not have been done at all well with the methodology and bureaucracy available in the mid-1660s.

In the early summer of 1665, moreover, people could see for themselves what was happening. Those as yet unaffected by the outbreak heard quickly enough once word began to spread. Houses were boarded up in the parish of St Giles, often with their families inside, an almost certain death sentence. Riots broke out and crowds forced open some of the boarded-up houses.

The King and the Privy Council met to consider how to contain the plague, which had now appeared in several towns across England. They had the experience of previous outbreaks to draw on. A list of fifteen 'Rules and Orders' was quickly drawn up to be sent to local officials in towns and cities around the country.[2] Under the rules, public gatherings were banned and free movement into and out of towns was restricted to those with certificates of health signed by a physician. As the burning of herbs was believed to cleanse the air from the contagion, fires were to be lit during church services. Searchers were to be appointed to seek out the infected. The houses of those infected were to be shut up for forty days, with the ill incarcerated inside. Town officials were to care for and feed the poor, if necessary raising a local rate (tax) to do so. Cats and dogs, thought to carry the contagion, were to be banned from the streets. Pest houses in which the infected could be isolated were to be built outside the town. Those who died of the plague were not to be buried in churchyards or graveyards, but in isolated graves away from towns and villages.

In London, during the week ending 6 June, deaths from suspected plague rose from seventeen to forty-three. The following week the death toll rose to 112. Panic set in and people began to leave the city.[3] Samuel Pepys walked down to the river above London Bridge and took a wherry for Whitehall. At the palace he discovered 'the court full of waggons and people ready to go out of towne'. The King left for Hampton Court three days later. London's well-heeled joined the exodus, making for their country estates. Among them, the Earl of Craven closed up his town house in Drury Lane and made for his Berkshire estates. William Craven, a commoner who had washed the taint of trade from his skin by joining the army and affecting the manners of a military gentleman, had been elevated to the peerage by Charles II and made a privy councillor. It is said that after fleeing London, Craven felt so ashamed that he returned to the city, assisted in the relief of the ill and donated land for burials.

Four days after the royal party arrived in Hampton Court, the English fleet, commanded by the Duke of York, scored a considerable victory over the Dutch in the Battle of Lowestoft. The English sank seventeen enemy ships for the loss of one, the worst defeat in Dutch naval history. But James, in an error of judgement, failed to pursue the fleeing Dutch and so missed out on pressing home an advantage. It was to be the key decision in the war.

By July London was in the middle of a heatwave. What should have been a summer of ease turned life in the city into a waking nightmare. The rats carrying the disease flourished in the warm weather, and with them the numbers of fleas, spreading the plague more rapidly to humans. With the disease rampant, people died in huge numbers. Commercial life faltered and the theatres closed. Soon, even Hampton Court was considered unsafe for the royal family. King and court departed for Salisbury, and then on to Oxford, a city connected with royal exodus ever since Charles I had decamped from London at the beginning of the Civil War. For the court of Charles II, Oxford was a congenial setting, providing better facilities for effective rule than Salisbury. Never one to do without his pleasures, Charles was accompanied by his chief mistress, Barbara Palmer, Countess of Castlemaine, as well as his theatre group, the King's Players, including the young Nell Gwyn, yet to attain her fame and place in English history.

In London, conditions continued to deteriorate. Ships stopped sailing up the Thames. Coal became scarce. Vessels carrying goods out of London were prevented from docking in foreign ports. London became almost a ghost city; few among the remaining population ventured out except to fetch water and food and go to church and pray. Charles had not forgotten the struggling city; he merely preferred not to be near it. At his instructions, a central bureaucracy comprised of the Lord Mayor, the sheriffs and aldermen remained to keep public order.

Having a senior post in the Navy Office while hostilities were still a major concern, Pepys was one of those who stayed. He sent his gold for safekeeping to the house of William Rider in Bethnal Green – Rider's estate would become a treasure house of gold and valuables from friends and business acquaintances alike – and moved his household from Seething Lane to Greenwich. It says a great deal for the fortitude of the people of London that the administration stayed and carried out the King's orders and rules to the letter.

The onset of the plague gave a window into the state of practical medicine. Strange theories old and new abounded and quacks of all sorts were on hand to take money from the ill, the worried well and the dying. As the plague spread, so the terrified population became more open to suggestion, their terror driving a desire to believe there was a cure to be bought. Daniel Defoe, who much later carried out journalistic interviews with survivors, described people wearing 'Charms, Philters, Exorcisms, Amulets and I know not what Preparations'.* On every street, physicians of all degrees and none stuck up their advertising posters: 'Doctors' Bills, and Papers of ignorant fellows; quacking and tampering in physic'.[4] For both patient and physician these were difficult times. While many thought that quackery was to be deplored, others thought it was every man's duty, whether an amateur or not, to do what he could in extreme circumstances to find a cure. This well-meaning approach led to all sorts of abuses.

The clergy fled in large numbers – as did most members of the Royal College of Physicians, including its president, Sir Edward Alston – leaving the people to their fate. John Graunt

---

* Though his exact date of birth is unknown, Defoe was probably about five when the plague broke out. He published A *Journal of the Plague Year* in 1722.

was shocked, recording the hope that 'neither the Physicians of our souls or bodies may hereafter in such great numbers forsake us'.[5] Among the doctors who stayed, Nathaniel Hodges was one of the most notable. Born in Kensington, then a village south-west of London, where his father was the vicar, Hodges gained a scholarship to Trinity College, Cambridge, but switched to Oxford, attracted like Wren and others to the experimental philosophy group led by John Wallis. After gaining a degree in medicine he became a member of the College of Physicians in 1659 at the age of thirty. He carried on his medical practice from his home in the parish of Walbrook, a few minutes' walk north-west of London Bridge, and named after the subterranean, culverted watercourse which rose in Moorfields Commons, outside the walls, and flowed south to the Thames.

When the plague started, Hodges stayed to treat his patients, never flinching in the face of the disease. He saw patients at his house and visited them at their homes, both risky businesses. Hodges did not remain in London for purely altruistic reasons – he wanted to conduct a medical trial on as large a scale as his patient list would allow, and saw the plague as providing an opportunity to test the standard remedies set out by the College of Physicians. While aware of the risks, he also saw that such opportunities to study plague came round only at intervals of ten to twenty years or more. The last great outbreak of plague in London having been in 1636, another chance for a large-scale empirical study might not come around for some time. Hodges was in his mid-thirties and he wanted to make his mark.*

Contemporary pictures exist of the elaborate ways in which

---

* He succeeded: the year following the epidemic Hodges published a book denouncing quacks and in 1672, after he had published an account of the plague, he was elected a Fellow of the Royal College of Physicians. He later became an examiner, or censor, of the college, and gave it a fire engine.

'plague doctors' protected themselves from the disease. Since plague was believed to travel in the air, long gowns covered the entire body to the feet, gloves were worn, a wide hat was pulled well down over the head and, most impressively, a mask was worn with a long proboscis shaped more like that of an anteater than a human nose. Inside this comic protuberance the wearer would stuff various herbs and unguents thought to offer protection from becoming infected. Oddly, modern research has shown that plague can, to an extent, travel in the air, borne in water droplets from an infected person's breath.

Hodges wore no fanciful clothes. He took a few simple precautions believed to stop the disease from entering the body; before starting work he ate a ball of herbs and other medicines considered to ward off illness. This was known as an electuary; the dose Hodges took was, he said, as 'big as a nutmeg'. He was then ready to see his patients. If making a house call, he would ask the family of the patient to burn some disinfectant herbs on hot coals, pop a prophylactic lozenge in his mouth and enter. Hodges was a thorough man with a belief in an empirical approach. He carefully recorded his patients' symptoms, dividing them into two classes according to severity. Symptoms of the second class included 'a fever . . . palpitation of the heart, bleeding at nose and a great heat about the precordia' (or pericardium, the sac surrounding the heart). Pericarditis – inflammation of the pericardium – may be caused by bacterial infection. Quite feasibly, Hodges had identified the symptoms of infection. Symptoms of the first class were 'horror, vomiting, delirium, dizziness, headache and stupefaction'. First-class symptoms indicated death was not far away.[6]

Anxious to work to a scientific method, Hodges carefully tried the remedies that were available to him at the time. These included such venerable cures as ground unicorn's horn. The horn proved ineffective. Hodges registered its failure in his records, noting his doubts about whether such a creature actually existed. Some of his patients, he wrote, were sick only of 'fear'. He himself twice felt he had contracted the plague, but after drinking more sack than usual he felt well again.

He also tried the ancient and expensive remedy of bezoar stones. Formed in the stomachs of ruminants such as cows and goats, these were thought to have healing properties, particularly if they were a particular earthy yellow in colour. Small quantities of stone were pulverised, made into a paste and washed down by the patient with some liquid. Hodges noted politely that his trials proved bezoar was useless: 'without having an Inclination to contradict a received Opinion, I have been so convinced by a Multitude of Trials, that the Truth will speak for itself, which manifestly denies its Virtues to be at all equivalent to its value: And I have truly given it in Powder many times to 40 or 50 Grains,* without any manner of Effect: and I dare affirm that the Bezoar with which I made these trials was genuine.'[7] He did report some remedies as useful, including hartshorn (exactly what its name implied – deer antler, ground and calcinated) and *Aristolochia serpentaria*, or Virginia snakeroot.

In due course, Hodges published his account of the plague, discounting many of the medical approaches passed down from the Greek physician Galen, 1500 years before. Galen's theory that the body was regulated by four humours – blood, black bile, yellow bile and phlegm – led physicians to attempt to restore its balance by methods that included sweating, purging and bloodletting, all of which were likely to hasten the patient's

---

* A grain is a measurement of weight equivalent to that of a single grain of barley, or today 64.79891 milligrams.

death. The idea that the body needed to be in balance, as first posited by Hippocrates some 300 years BC, was essentially sound. What was disastrous was the subsequent understanding of what balance actually entailed, and how it could be achieved when there were no scientific methods of measuring the physical state of the patient, including body temperature. The seventeenth-century doctor faced one central dilemma: almost all treatments didn't work.

Hodges took careful note of what happened when various interventions were tried. From this he drew some definite conclusions. 'Opening the pores', or sweating the patient, was out. Bloodletting was to be avoided; as Hodges laconically said, 'I should pass it by as fatal.' By saying so, he stepped onto contentious ground. Bloodletting was one of the main means by which medicine, as practised in the seventeenth century, sought to restore the patient's inner balance and so his or her health. It was particularly entwined with astrology, a major influence in seventeenth-century life, including the practice of medicine. The historical centrality of astrology to the intellectual life of the early modern age was overlooked until Keith Thomas's 1971 work, *Religion and the Decline of Magic*, broke new ground. A surprising measure of just how integrated astrology was with the practice of medicine is the statistic that of all astrological almanacs published between 1485 and 1700, a third were written by physicians.[8]

In his rules for bloodletting, the eminent Oxford physician Peter Levens had written in his popular guide to practical medicine, first published in 1587 and republished six times until 1664, that the physician should 'let no blood, nor open no vein, except the moon be in Aries, Cancer, the first half of Libra, the last part of Scorpio, Sagittarius, Aquarius, or Pisces'.[9] Such ideas based on astrology would not be called into question until later in the century. By then the theory that the solar system revolved around the sun, propounded by Nicholas Copernicus in the middle of the preceding century and by others dating back to antiquity, had become more widely accepted. After that, astrology began to lose its validity among the scientifically minded. To its credit, the College of Physicians of London, to which Hodges belonged, put a good deal of effort into stamping out astrology in medicine, trying to identify astrological physicians with a view to having them barred from practice.

The College of Physicians was a body created to regulate the practice of medicine in the monarchical era, long before the civil wars of the seventeenth century.* This meant neither that its members were all monarchists, nor that they were all Anglicans; during the period immediately before and including the civil wars, the college was predominantly Puritan. In line with the fate of other institutions, its pre-eminent position as the regulating medical body in London declined sharply with the upheavals of the middle of the century. With the return of Charles II, the college hoped its central position would be restored. It was disappointed; two other organisations grew in importance to be recognised by Parliament – the Barber-Surgeons' Company and the Society of Apothecaries.†

Most importantly for its own self-view, the College of Physicians was a bastion of traditional medicine learned via Latin at universities, with many of its senior members having been educated not only at Oxford or Cambridge but at the pre-eminent medical schools in Leiden and Padua, where groundbreaking anatomical explorations had been carried out

---

* Its charter was granted in 1518.

† Both of these survive to the present day, with the College of Physicians continuing as the most important as it still administers professional medical qualifications.

in the previous century. As has been noted by many historians, the primary philosophical debate in the seventeenth century concerned what was known, how it was known and what was the best way to learn more in the future. This debate, between the revealed wisdom of the ancients, or of religion, and of the new thinkers, was carried out in fits and starts. For the medical profession, what was known was steeped in handed-down knowledge closely allied to the status of the universities from which the ancient ideas originated. The comparison has often been made between religion and the university-based received wisdom of medicine.[10] The practices of religion and medicine tended to become linked according to an individual's particular worldview.[11]

Hodges' empirical approach to studying the plague indicated a strong inclination to enter the enemy camp, deserting the views of both the college and the universities. He was prepared to take long-held theories instilled through generations of European university teaching and hold them up to practical scrutiny.

Hodges was not alone in staying in London to fight the plague. To their credit, some other members of the College of Physicians also stayed. A core of other practitioners, very different from the members of the elite of the college who remained in the city, formed a small group who could be seen as representing a changing of the medical ways. They followed the path of Francis Bacon, Paracelsus and others, although the traditionalist old guard lambasted them for being 'the dross of the earth'.[12] In the ferment of thinking in mid-seventeenth century England, the empiricists were often lumped in with 'enthusiasts' like Calvinists and other nonconformist religious sects. This was not without reason, for followers of the alchemist Paracelsus were often allied to the more extreme forms of Protestantism.

During the plague outbreak, among the new groups of empiricists arose those known as Helmontians. Named after the chemist Jan Baptist van Helmont, these physicians believed in creating medicines through the new chemical processes developed largely thanks to alchemy. Among the most eminent was George Thomson, who made close observations of the plague and its victims and administered his own chemically derived medicines. At great personal risk, he carried out a dissection of a plague victim. He was reported to have cured some patients. In all probability, his palliative care in some cases helped his patients recover, for the infection was not always fatal: the survival rate could be 10 per cent or more.

The reasoning behind claims that plague victims might be cured was made clear in the works of Thomson's fellow Helmontian, Thomas Sydenham. Later to become known as the 'father of English medicine', Sydenham chose not to stay in London during the plague. In the wide streets and comparatively hygienic environs of St James's, he and his Pall Mall neighbours would have been relatively safe, had they remained. Nonetheless, Sydenham took to the country. He may have done so for self-preservation, or simply because he realised there was little or nothing he could do to help. At any rate, he later updated his well-regarded textbook on fevers with a chapter on the outbreak. In an age of few definitive remedies, Sydenham – following in the footsteps of Hippocrates – observed that, given a helping hand, the body could often regulate itself and allow illness to subside.

In the case of fevers, Sydenham recommended that his patients should not receive the standard treatments of bleeding, purging and so on, but be given cooling compresses and lotions to help them survive fevers such as smallpox. Famously, Sydenham said that often he had done best by his patients by doing nothing. Given the degree of medical knowledge available at the time, and the often bizarre and even harmful remedies employed, Sydenham helped patients to rally and, if they could, fight their illnesses with their body's natural defences. Here he is in characteristic form on scarlet fever:

> I hold it, then, sufficient for the patient to abstain wholly from animal food and from fermented liquors; to keep always indoors, and not to keep always in his bed. When the desquamation [peeling off of scaly skin] is complete, and when the symptoms are departing, I consider it proper to purge the patient with some mild laxative, accommodated to his age and strength. By treatment thus simple and natural, this ailment – we can hardly call it more – is dispelled without either trouble or danger: whereas, if, on the other hand, we overtreat the patient by confining him to his bed, or by throwing in cordials, and other superfluous and over-learned medicines, the disease is aggravated, and the sick man dies of his doctor.[13]

The sick men, women and children of London were not going to die of this doctor. Perhaps Sydenham's greatest contribution to medicine was the realisation that fever was not itself illness but was a symptom of the body's reaction to illness, perhaps in an effort to combat infection.

Sydenham's methods came to be advocated by others – including, perhaps a little surprisingly, Dr Millington, a member of the Royal Society who was also president of the conservative College of Physicians. It had been recognised for some time that certain ailments were just not curable by any methods known to current medical practitioners and that others simply got better. Often, the observed symptoms of disorders followed patterns mimicked by the prescribed treatments: fevers subsided after the patient's temperature rose or when they were artificially sweated. Gastric ailments subsided following natural diarrhoea or when patients were given emetics, and so on.

As the plague was recognised as largely fatal, physicians concentrated on preventatives. Like the preparations of Dr Hodges, a variety of concoctions thought to ward off infection were to be eaten, drunk, stuffed up the nose – or, in the case of tobacco, smoked. Most herbal mixtures involved plants common in England, as outlined in Culpeper's *Herbal*.[14] Other herbs were brought from Europe along with exotic plants from America, the Far East and elsewhere. The most potent of oral remedies was Venice Treacle, an expensive cure-all known from ancient times, made from many herbs and often containing opium and the flesh of snakes. Galen made his own version. By the seventeenth century it was mainly imported from Venice, where it was manufactured and matured for many years, hence its great cost.

As the plague moved through London's population, little could be done except quarantine the city and wait for the epidemic to burn itself out. Those wishing to travel out of the city had to receive a warrant from the Lord Mayor certifying they were healthy. Surrounding towns and villages were wary of anyone not bearing such a certificate. The summer remained exceptionally warm and dry, the smell of death hanging in the narrow streets. John Evelyn observed the rising death toll from his home in Deptford. He sent his wife and family to the safety of Wotton House in Surrey, the home of his older brother George, and where he himself had been born in 1620. On 1 July, the Lord Mayor took the drastic step of enforcing the government's emergency 'Rules and Orders' and ordered all houses in which inhabitants were infected to be boarded up, thus imprisoning the healthy with the ill. Watchmen were hired to ensure no one left the quarantined houses and to bring food and drink to the inhabitants. Evelyn recorded that in the second week of July 1100 died in London. In the following week the death toll almost doubled to 2000.[15] On Sunday 2 August a fast was held throughout the nation 'to deprecate God's displeasure against the land by pestilence and war'.[16]

On 12 August, in an act of kindness, the Lord Mayor issued an order for a curfew to be observed throughout London. At nine o'clock in the evening all healthy people were ordered to stay at home so that the infected and those who had been boarded up with them might leave their homes for one evening to take the air. With the death rate rising, the initiative was not repeated. By September, the death toll rose to its highest point, 7165 in one week. Mass graves were dug around the city fringes. They filled faster than they could be dug. As a description of the horror at this time, Nathaniel Hodges' words speak more eloquently than most:

> Who can express the calamities of such times? The whole British nation wept for the miseries of her metropolis. In some houses carcasses lay waiting for burial, and in others persons in their last agonies; in one room might be heard dying groans, in another the raving of delirium, and not far off relations and friends bewailing both their loss and the dismal prospect of their own sudden departure. Death was the sure midwife to all children, and infants passed immediately from the womb to the grave. Who would not burst with grief to see the stock for a future generation hanging upon the breasts of a dead mother? Or the marriage-bed changed the first night into a sepulchre, and the unhappy pair meet with death in their first embraces? Some of the infected ran about staggering like drunken men, and fell

> and expired in the streets; while others lie half-dead and comatose, but never to be waked but by the last trumpet; some lie vomiting as if they had drunk poison; and others fell dead in the market, while they were buying necessaries for the support of life.[17]

One of the reasons the plague was so virulent was that London gave it the opportunity to spread with ease. Households typically included large numbers of people. The poor lived in multiple-occupancy tenements, while even the 'middling sort' of people had large households. A shopkeeper or merchant of modest means could have ten or more people under his roof. A family with four children might have two maids and two or three apprentices living in the house with them. When the plague struck one member of a household, everyone who lived under the same roof was in danger.

In the parish of St Giles, where the plague had first been reported, the death toll was devastating. The parish had fewer than 2000 households, yet by the end of the year its graveyard held the bodies of 3216 victims. When the plague was raging at its height, Evelyn drove through the city in his coach to see the situation for himself. He wrote in his diary, 'I went all along the city and suburbs from Kent Street to St James's, a dismal passage, and dangerous to see so many coffins exposed in the streets, now thin of people; the shops shut up and all in mournful silence, not knowing whose turn might be next.'[18]

Despite the danger, Evelyn continued to travel about the city and up and down the Thames on his wartime business. Conscious as always of his public duty, he had undertaken the work of Commissioner for Sick and Wounded Seamen, a difficult enough task during the war, and now exacerbated by the numbers of seamen who contracted the plague in the docklands, where rats and infection multiplied. On a later journey through the city Evelyn was obliged on several occasions to alight from his coach to transact business. He found himself surrounded by 'multitudes of poor, pestiferous creatures begging alms; the shops universally shut up, a dreadful prospect!'[19]

With whole families wiped out, fear gripped the living. People behaved abominably to one another. Families threw their infected relatives and servants into the street. People fought over scraps of food. Pepys observed that the plague was 'making us cruel as dogs to one another'.[20] Boarded-up houses condemned those within to probable death. Nathaniel Hodges thought the boarding up of the well together with the sick contributed to the death toll. He also condemned the actions of some of those assigned to help the afflicted: 'what greatly contributed to the loss of people thus shut up, was the wicked practices of nurses (for they are not to be mentioned but in the most bitter terms): these wretches, out of greediness to plunder the dead, would strangle their patients, and charge it to the dis-temper in their throats . . . '[21]

Life was difficult not only for those inside the city but also for the majority of ordinary people who had fled on foot into the country, often reduced to sleeping rough and foraging off the land. Nevertheless, few were left in the city except for those who could not afford to leave for fear of their businesses being ransacked, or for love of their afflicted relatives. The only familiar figures on the streets were the drivers of death wagons, the watchmen, various city officials, some apothecaries and physicians, a few clergy, and poor wretches denied shelter and condemned to die. The only types of person to flourish amidst the chaos were preachers of doom.

Sermonisers of the apocalyptic sort raved against mankind for having brought the catastrophe upon itself. The Old Testament was quoted from pulpits and street corners: 'The wrath of the Lord was kindled against the people, and the Lord smote the people with very great plague;' 'And I will smite the inhabitants of this city, both man and beast; they shall die of a great pestilence.'[22]

The city was eerily quiet. Grass grew in the streets. Yet although commercial life ground to a stop, the people did not starve. This was thanks to the sharp-witted reaction of the Lord Mayor, the sheriffs and aldermen. The aldermen, a breed of independently minded men who had mostly either fought in Cromwell's army or supported the Parliamentary cause, were used to difficult situations and not averse to standing up to their duty. The mayor, Sir John Lawrence, was a former Master of the Haberdashers' Company. His house stood in Queenhithe ward, on the ground sloping from St Paul's Cathedral to the river. He was a former colonel in the White Regiment, one of the Parliamentary trained bands. At the Reformation he relinquished his colonelcy and was knighted by the King. A strong-willed man, Lawrence continued to keep a coterie of former White Regiment men about him as a band of persuaders or dissuaders, according to the situation.

Among a raft of plans to keep the city from disintegrating, Sir John put in place a system for the provision of food. Daniel Defoe, with his businessman's interest in all things commercial allied to a journalist's interest in people, later explained how the city authorities decreed that the bakers had to keep their ovens going on pain of losing their privileges as Freemen of the city. To supply the bakers, country vendors came into the city along major streets that were kept clear of dead bodies or other possible carriers of disease. The mayor and his lieutenants maintained a daily patrol to ensure the flow of food continued through the various gates.[23] To buy provisions, physical interaction between buyer and seller was unnecessary. The buyer surveyed what was on offer in the vendor's baskets, said what he wanted, and the seller dropped the goods in the offered bag or on the ground. The buyer then put his or her money in a pail of vinegar to disinfect it. When all trading was done, the seller took the money from the pail and returned through the appointed gate. The work of Sir John and the other representatives illustrated the extent to which the city was well organised and run.

A more complicated form of food transaction was instituted to supply the many seamen, their families and friends who had taken to living on board ships moored on the river all the way from the Pool of London down to Limehouse and beyond. Watermen whose normal trade had ceased could earn a small income by rowing supplies out to the ships.[24] Coal had to be discharged from ships lying in the river, a slow and backbreaking task if performed without cranes.

Several of the physicians who stayed to help died. Among them was George Thomson's friend George Starkey, who, seeing he was infected, hung a dead toad around his neck in the belief that 'atoms' from its putrefaction would counteract the plague, a remedy widely held to be effective. Similar reasoning advocated the use of snake parts as remedies for poisoning – a little poison could counteract the greater threat, it was thought. This thinking was little more than a form of the sympathetic magic to be found in many supposedly much less advanced societies. As the symptoms spread, Starkey noted that after he drank a large quantity of 'small beer' his pores closed, preventing the atoms from the toad from entering his body. In other words, the alcohol had made him dehydrated. Thomson looked after his friend as best he could, but to no avail. Starkey soon followed the toad to oblivion.

So how did Hodges and Thomson survive? The answer is, undoubtedly, down to luck. Unlike the fleas that usually feed off humans, rat fleas like to hitch a ride in clothing, helping the disease to be spread through social interaction. Whereas the primary cause of plague infection is via a bite from a flea, we now know that infection may be caused by close or direct contact – skin to infected skin, mouth to mouth, from the spittle in sneezes, and so on. Therefore, bubonic plague is not simply spread by infected fleas jumping from one host to another and biting the skin of the new host. Hodges, Thomson and their fellow doctors could therefore easily have been infected while examining their patients.

Some prophylactic measures taken by Londoners helped, if not in the way expected. The smoke from burning herbs would not have prevented infection through the air, as was thought, but might have simply kept fleas at bay. Smoke may similarly have worked for the men who brought the death wagons around to pick up the corpses, as they puffed on their prophylactic tobacco pipes while they manhandled bodies into their carts. Another factor at work was that the dead bodies no longer offered a blood supply, and so corpses were likely to be free of infected fleas, though the tissues of the dead could still have been deadly to the touch.

One school of seventeenth-century thought held that cats and dogs might carry the plague. They were therefore exterminated in great numbers. According to Defoe, tens of thousands of dogs were killed. An attempt was made to cull mice and rats in case they carried the infection. Of course, killing rats in any quantity without terriers trained for the job was hopeless. Little did the people of London know that by killing their pets they were indeed protecting themselves, for modern research has shown that many species of animal – including domestic cats and dogs – may carry the disease or become infested with the plague flea.

Towards the end of September, the tide turned. It has been said that because of the dry summer, the rat and flea population decreased, leading to a decline in the death rate. But the weather is unlikely to have been the cause of the improving situation. If anything, rat fleas, like their hosts, are more likely to thrive in warmer weather. It is much more probable that the disease began to subside because the rat fleas ran out of live flesh to feed off. A bubonic plague epidemic kills off the black rat population quite quickly; the hungry fleas then look for a substitute host. Since humans live in close proximity to black rats, they become the species most likely to be chosen. Once the human host begins to dwindle, the flea population also dies off.

The flea might have been master of events in London during 1665 but it was not infallible in its powers. Indeed, the fleas that carried the bubonic plague bacillus were not clever enough to realise that by killing off such a large proportion of their host population they were effectively committing suicide. This may explain the characteristically sharp rises and falls in plague epidemics throughout Europe and why they finally ceased altogether, although another theory has it that the rat population began to develop a level of immunity to the plague.

The plague had a profound effect, both upon the survivors and those who watched from the comparative safety of surrounding towns or their country estates. It may well have helped to nudge young William Penn towards the Quakers, a sect he was to join soon afterwards. He wrote that the ravages of the plague gave him 'a deep sense of the vanity of this world, and of the irreligiousness of the Religions in it'.[25] The rather vain young man had possibly learned some self-scrutiny as he saw so many of the clergy abandon the poor to their fate.

In October, Charles convened Parliament at Oxford to discuss the continuing conflict with the Dutch. A further sum of £1.25 million was agreed to fund the fleet. For the relief of London nothing was forthcoming. In retrospect, the priorities of the Crown would be seen as a political blunder. Economic strain, allied to existential dread, took its toll in the capital both physically and politically.

The vast communal graves dug in a ring around the capital held thousands of Londoners. With them lay the hopes of many of those who had supported the return of the King. Along with hope lay the decomposing body of medieval medicine. Physicians – with a few honourable exceptions – had refused to treat the victims, leaving them to their own devices: to follow the physicians out of London if they could afford it, to stay if they could not, and to seek what help they could from nurses and other low-paid carers.[26] The old medical remedies, based on theory rather than empirical evidence, had been tested and found to be mostly useless.[27] The plague left more than the physical fabric of London in ruins. The world of medicine would never be quite the same again. If the old ideas hung on it was because there was little to replace them in terms of treatment. After all, the practice of medicine has always been to some extent about the delivery of hope.

By December, London was declared safe, though the plague carried on claiming victims well into the following year. At a terrible cost, the city had survived. On New Year's Eve John Evelyn wrote, 'Now blessed be God for his extraordinary mercies and preservation of me this year, when thousands, and tens thousands, perished and were swept away on each side of me.' *The Intelligencer*, the official government newspaper published during the plague, reported that not one person of substance or authority had died. The plague was a disease of the poor.

CHAPTER 12

PESTILENCE, WAR AND FIRE

In the new year of 1666, with the plague dying out, London's residents began to return to their city. By February, it was considered safe for the royal family to take up residence in Whitehall once more. Merchants and city grandees returned with their riches. Great houses were reopened. Ships sailed up the Thames into the Pool of London and offloaded vital food and supplies. The storehouses along the Thames were replenished. Drovers brought their sheep and cattle to Smithfield to be slaughtered. A few survivors emerged from their homes, emaciated and blinking. Refugees who had endured the hardship of the countryside walked ragged but relieved back into the city. New migrants came from around the country, sensing an opportunity. In the seventeenth century, life in a hazardous city was preferable to that of an agricultural labourer.

According to parish records the plague had killed 68,596 Londoners. If we take the total population of the city, including surrounding liberties and suburbs, at John Graunt's 1662 estimation of 384,000, then the dead numbered 17.8 per cent of the population. Lord Clarendon thought the true figure was maybe twice that, or 35.6 per cent. If one took Sir William Petty's 1665 estimation of the population as being up to 460,000, then the death rate as a proportion was considerably lower.

Today it is generally agreed that around 20 per cent of London's population died. This would make the true number somewhere around 92,000, though many now accept a figure closer to 100,000. The contemporary official estimate of plague deaths in the whole country was put at 200,000.

Economic and social life gradually returned to the city – how could it not? Before the plague London had been en route to becoming the epicentre of trade and commerce for north-west Europe. Those who had been dispersed from it knew nothing of the world of crops and animal husbandry. They were anxious to return to what they knew, to making and buying and selling. London, with its workshops and factories, its shops and stalls, its guilds and storehouses, its great trading houses, was their home.

One enterprise that was slow to pick up was tax collecting, specifically of the hearth tax, the proceeds of which went directly to the King. By the spring, Charles was feeling the financial pinch so badly that he decided to scrap the current system of collecting the tax and introduce another, hopefully more efficient. Responsibility was taken away from local officials and put out to tender to private tax collectors, known as tax farmers. A consortium of London merchants bought the right to collect the tax. They would be allowed a profit, to be taken from each shilling raised. The tax was thereby privatised. Charles's belief that he would do better through a farmed tax leads one to suspect that he was badly advised, for tax farming was a notorious racket.

While London returned to work, cases of plague continued, particularly in outlying areas. Evelyn reported plague at

Deptford as late as April 1666 and cases were reported elsewhere into the autumn.

Intellectual life also resumed. On 22 March the Royal Society met again for the first time since the suspension of its meetings the previous spring. Among those at the meeting was Christopher Wren, newly returned from Paris.

Unlike so many others, Wren had not left London to flee the plague. He had for some time been planning a foreign trip to study architecture. Although Wren had no official position as an architect, John Denham, the King's surveyor, had directed him to go to Paris to study the latest ideas.[1] There could be only one purpose behind Wren's visit – to look for ideas to use in the preservation or rebuilding of St Paul's Cathedral. It could be seen as a snub for John Webb, who was after all the King's surveyor in all but name, but he was busy on various royal projects. Wren was a young man brimming with ideas and waiting for a position in life.

The man behind the decision to send Wren to Paris was not Denham, but the King himself, for Charles had followed Wren's career and wished to enhance it. The strength of Charles's admiration could be measured by the fact that in 1661 he had offered Wren the important post of surveying and building a new harbour at Tangiers. The offer came via the familial and court connections so vital to a career in London during the Restoration. Wren's cousin Matthew Wren was Bishop of Ely and wielded considerable influence, having been chaplain to Charles I. He recommended his cousin for the post as an individual of known mathematical ability. However, on the advice of William Petty, whose colonial service enabled him to see that this particular job would lead only to headaches, and because of his health, which was always frail, Wren turned the King's offer down. He did so with reluctance, for with the commission came the promise of the post of Surveyor-General of the Royal Works once Sir John Denham died. Luckily for Wren, Charles did not take the refusal as an insult.

Wren probably wished to go to Italy to see ancient Rome and the architecture of the Renaissance at Florence and elsewhere. He did not have the money, however. But he knew that if he wished to expand his knowledge of the neoclassical architectural ideas sweeping into northern Europe, he needed to see some of it for himself. The books of plans he consulted at home were insufficient. Of all the possible destinations within his means and with sufficient architecture of interest, there was only one choice: Paris. Armed with an invitation to stay with the British ambassador, Wren set off just as the plague was taking hold in June 1665.

It was possibly his second visit to Paris.* While there, he was thrilled by the churches surmounted by domes rather than by traditional English towers and spires. He met the ageing François Mansart, the venerable architect who had introduced symmetrical classicism to France. He also met the great Italian architect and sculptor Gian Lorenzo Bernini, who had been invited to Paris to consult on the rebuilding of the Louvre Palace. Bernini was so famous throughout Europe that crowds stopped to stare whenever he walked by. Wren was lucky to meet Bernini, who was not given to indulging young upstarts, no matter how polite and cultured they might be. In the end, Wren gained a few minutes of Bernini's time, during which he was given a fleeting glance of the great man's drawings for the

* According to Liza Jardine in her biography of Wren, he had probably visited Paris once before, on his way back from a trip to Heidelberg. Previously, it was thought the 1665–6 visit was his first. Jardine argues persuasively that for Wren to have begun building as he had, he must already have seen the new European ideas in person.

important commission to revive the east front of the Louvre. For possession of these drawings, Wren said, he 'would give my skin'.[2] Louis XIV and his court gave rather less: after laying a foundation stone, they rejected Bernini's plans.

Wren's enthusiasm for Bernini's architecture revealed much about the direction of the young man's thinking. Bernini had, along with Francesco Borromini, created the extravagant baroque architecture that expressed the Catholic Church's anti-Protestant counter-Reformation. It was not so much the counter-Reformation that interested Wren, for he was as firm an Anglican as could be, but the imaginative verve of its architecture.

Once Wren returned to London, the question of what to do with the crumbling St Paul's was as fresh as ever. Conservative architectural voices gave their opinion, as before, that the old church should be patched up. Wren saw how the ancient nave leant away from the vertical owing to its weak foundations and the heaviness of the roof. The old church was falling down under its own weight. No amount of shoring up could mend it for long. Fresh from his Paris experiences, Wren was ready with new proposals. Backed by his friends John Evelyn and William Sancroft, the Dean of St Paul's, he suggested a solution – tear it down and start again. Patching it up would only mean delaying matters 'to ye next Posterity as a further object of Charity'.[3]

For Wren, only a revolutionary approach not seen before in England could fulfil the need of creating a cathedral that would be the pride of London while satisfying the needs of the new Anglican liturgy. With the reforms that led up to the Savoy Conference of 1661, the Church no longer had need for a long nave from which the people would watch the mystery of the Eucharist. But the Anglican Church hung onto its orthodox views. The new inclusive idea, which Wren supported, of a congregation participating in the religious service and listening to readings and a sermon in a basilica was to run into trouble. What Wren wished for was a less hierarchical space, in which the nave would widen out and shorten under a great dome until to all intents and purposes it disappeared altogether to become a square, a fat stubby cross, or even a circle.

Wren wrote to the commission for the rebuilding of St Paul's that the traditional crossing, the meeting point of nave, choir and transepts, should be transformed into something else: 'a spacious dome or rotunda with a cupolo [cupola] or hemispherical roof and upon ye cupolo for ye outward ornament, a lantern with a spire to rise proportionally'. (This last detail showed that Wren was conscious that the church hierarchy would, no matter what, still want an English Gothic spire.) He went on to point out the major advantage of his new space: 'Ye church which is much too narrow for its height rendered spacious in ye middle which may be a proper place for a Vast Auditory.'[4]

Wren's revolutionary ideas had their supporters, including his longstanding friend John Evelyn. For his ideas to prevail, however, they would have to be discussed at a full meeting of the commission and its advisors.

Before such a meeting could be called, there occurred a major turning point in the war with the Dutch. Despite some victories at sea in the preceding year, the British still faced the prospect of Dutch supremacy over trade routes. A great Dutch fleet laden with spices had returned from the East Indies unchecked by the British. To make matters worse, because of their expansionist ambitions in Europe, the French declared war against the English on the Dutch side. Charles's ambitions regarding international expansion were seen by his cousin Louis XIV as interfering with French interests. The Royal Navy faced the prospect of having to fight two fleets. A French fleet took control of English colonies in the Caribbean and Suriname, with the intention to sail against Virginia, although an English fleet dispatched in June retook Suriname and destroyed much of the French fleet's capability.

Before matters could escalate any further, Charles decided the Royal Navy urgently needed to inflict a serious blow against the Dutch. A fleet under the command of George Monck, Duke of Albemarle, opened the action by attacking the Dutch fleet at anchor off Dunkirk. The Four Days' War, as it came to be called, lasted from 11 to 14 June, and was the longest sea battle in history. Both sides claimed victory, but in the final tally the British fleet suffered much heavier losses than the Dutch, losing some twenty ships, with 1000 men killed and 2000 taken prisoner. The Dutch lost six or seven ships with 1500 men killed. The English losses resulted in a withdrawal of the fleet to the safety of the Thames Estuary. According to an eyewitness account, hundreds of bedraggled and wounded sailors were to be seen struggling along the road from the navy town of Rochester, heading towards London, looking as if they were unlikely to return to active service.[5] The Dutch mounted a blockade on the Thames Estuary, hoping to prevent the English from putting out into the Channel or North Sea.

Anxious to force home their naval advantage and prevent another fiasco like the surprise attack on their merchant fleet, the Dutch decided to put into effect a scheme they had been hatching for more than a year. The plan was to wait until the English fleet put into Chatham dockyard for repairs, then attack and utterly destroy it. Despite its merits, this plan had one major drawback: it was dependent upon the English for its timing. At the end of July a large Dutch fleet commanded by their best admiral, Michiel de Ruyter, set sail to carry out the plan, hoping to find the blockaded English fleet bottled up in Chatham. The weather was against the Dutch, and an expected supporting fleet from their new French allies failed to show up. De Ruyter had to postpone his plan. On the morning of 25 July he discovered the full English fleet at sea off North Foreland, under the command of Prince Rupert and the Duke of Albemarle. The ensuing engagement would be known as the Battle of St James's Day.* Although both sides lost few ships, the Dutch lost many more men in the fighting. At one time the Dutch position became so desperate that de Ruyter stood on the deck of his flagship crying out to be martyred by English gunfire.

Two days of fierce fighting resulted in a narrow English victory. Three hundred English seamen died and 1200 Dutch. The following month, a fleet commanded by that unswerving scourge of the Dutch, Admiral Robert Holmes, raided the Dutch town of West-Terschelling, finding 160 Dutch merchant ships at anchor and destroying most of them. In what became known as Holmes's Bonfire, he also sacked and burned the town. The Dutch took this attack on a town as a great provocation, reinforcing their desire to deal the English a knockout punch. Thanks to their superior shipbuilding industry and economic backing, the Dutch navy could be restored to full capability sooner than the English.

During the conflict, some London merchants made fortunes. If they could find crews willing to take the risk, merchants could bring supplies across sea lanes patrolled by enemy warships to sell the goods at a premium. William Rider continued to supply the Royal Navy with tar, pitch and timber from Scandinavia.

* In the then current Julian calendar the date was 25 July, St James's Day.

Now rich, he enjoyed showing off his country house to friends and business acquaintances, including Samuel Pepys, a key contact who administered Rider's naval contracts.

Though both London and the King had been all for the war only a year or two earlier, opinion was now divided. The war had started out well enough, but as it dragged on it showed up some severe discrepancies between English and Dutch sea power. Although England was much more populous than Holland, its population was comprised mainly of rural peasantry who paid little or no taxes. Holland was chiefly urban, with a strong tax base, and so could spend proportionately higher sums on its navy. The English ambassador to The Hague, George Downing, reported that in order to have a strong navy the Dutch were prepared to pay high taxes. During the war, for every warship the English built, the Dutch built seven. For any proud Englishman taking a ferry down the Thames past the Royal Navy dockyards at Southwark and Rotherhithe this would have come as a surprise, for London prided itself on having been a shipbuilding city since Tudor times. Amsterdam, however, was everything London was in shipbuilding and more.* In the 1660s, with the Exchequer empty, the question of whether the English fleet was capable of delivering a victory against the enemy was earnestly debated in Parliament.

In such financially straitened circumstances, the matter of repairs to St Paul's Cathedral became tiresome, a thorn in the side of the church authorities and of the government. A decision had to be made. On 27 August the Dean of St Paul's, William

---

* The discrepancy between seventeenth-century English and Dutch sea power led directly to Britain later spending much more on its navy and becoming the greatest sea power in the world.

Sancroft, left his deanery on the south side of the cathedral and walked the two hundred yards up a narrow lane to the cathedral's west front, before ascending the steps to Inigo Jones's great classical portico over the west door. A clutter of shops and stalls now lined the steps and porch, designed to award Italian gravitas to the ailing Gothic building. Sancroft went in, to chair yet another meeting on the future of the cathedral.

The church Sancroft held in his care was the largest in England and the third largest in Europe. St Paul's had sat above London on Ludgate Hill since its foundation stone was laid during the reign of William the Conqueror in the late eleventh century. A previous church on the site had been destroyed by fire. The construction of the current building had been delayed when a serious fire broke out in the city in 1135, and another in 1212.* The Norman church was not consecrated until 1240. Since the fourteenth century, its fabric had gradually decayed. The graceful spire, among the tallest anywhere in the world, was damaged by fire after being struck by a lightning bolt in 1444. In 1561, when lightning struck again, the spire caught fire and fell. During the civil wars, Parliamentary soldiers used the nave as a barracks. This was no new desecration; in Elizabethan times the nave had been London's public promenade and was known as Paul's Walk. People of all classes gathered to walk up and down, exchanging information and gossip, making conversation and business deals twice a day, morning and evening, as if called to matins and evensong.

Dean Sancroft was joining his fellow commissioners for the repair of St Paul's, who were gathering along with various invited experts to see matters for themselves. John Evelyn was present

---

* After the fire of 1212 thatched roofs were banned in London, in favour of shingles or tiles.

to lend his omniscient grandeur. Wren was there, as were the fashionable architect Roger Platt and the master mason Joshua Strong. Wren expressed his view that the nave walls were leaning dangerously outwards owing to the weight of the roof. Platt disagreed. His opinion could not be dismissed; having studied the architecture of Rome, he had more recently designed Lord Clarendon's house, currently going up on Piccadilly. One of the first private houses to be built in England in the classical style, its design was already influential.

Plumb lines were deployed to test Wren's theory. The walls were found to be leaning – the why was debated. The party moved on to the crossing. Here, Platt said the old, unsafe steeple could be repaired or replaced. Wren, supported by Evelyn, argued that it would be best to pull it down and build anew. One can speculate that Evelyn and Wren had agreed beforehand on their joint submission. Unanimity among the commissioners was impossible, but Wren was asked to prepare plans and costs for a dome to replace the steeple. This arrangement received general acceptance, suggesting prior support from Wren's close friend and patron, Dean Sancroft.

While the St Paul's commissioners continued their deliberations, tax inspectors went out on their twice-yearly rounds of London to ascertain the amount of hearth tax due to the King. In August, an inspector went down a small street near London Bridge inhabited by skilled working men and women. Pudding Lane was a typical medieval street, built mainly of wood and plaster, with jettied upper storeys jutting out over the road. The inspector moved from house to house, noting down the number of stoves and fireplaces in each building. Mary Whittacre, a widow, had two; George Porter, a plasterer, three; the Widow Gander one. Thomas Knight, as befitted his trade as a glass maker, had four; William Ludford, another plasterer, also had four, one of which was stopped up to avoid paying tax on it. And so on down the street. The twenty-one households in Pudding Lane had between them sixty-eight hearths, making a total in taxes owed to the King for the half-year of £3 8s. The household paying the most tax was that of Thomas Farriner, a baker who made hard tack, or ships' biscuits. Farriner's house and shop had five hearths and one oven.[6]

On the evening of Saturday 1 September, Farriner, together with his family and maid, raked out the oven and fires and went to bed, looking forward to a restful Sunday. But by one o'clock in the morning his home was on fire. It is not known exactly what happened, but it appears that sparks escaped from the oven and set fire to the bakery. By the time the family was roused, the bakery was well alight. Unable to go downstairs and exit through the bakery to the street, the family opened a top floor window and escaped across the roof to an adjoining house. The maid froze in fear and died in the flames.

The fire spread quickly along the congested street. By the time the constable was roused and the church bells rung to call out the yeomanry, which doubled as a part-time fire brigade, several houses were blazing. Flames leapt from building to building across the narrow street. A strong east wind – dubbed by John Dryden 'a Belgian wind' – whipped up the flames and caused the fire to spread rapidly.

London's fire hazard had been obvious for many years and was periodically discussed. John Evelyn had warned of it as lately as 1659. Despite the constant risk, little was done about it. Though outbreaks of fire occurred regularly, they were generally contained. The last serious London fire had been in 1638. London's firefighting consisted of three basic components: spraying water, pulling down buildings, and blowing them up.

Taking water first; it was either passed hand-to-hand in buckets, squirted from heavy and ungainly hand-held water squirts that looked something like giant water pistols, or pumped from a number of wheeled fire engines that took time to manoeuvre through the narrow streets and had very limited range. Water was obtained from the Thames and there was a water wheel beside the northern end of London Bridge. In extreme cases, the wooden water mains could be hacked open; but this usually resulted in the water merely draining away.

The second weapon employed was the fire hook, a pole eight to ten feet or more in length with an iron hook on the end. These were used to pull down buildings or sections of buildings that were already on fire. Third was the demolition of buildings not yet touched by the fire, either manually using fire hooks or by gunpowder, to create firebreaks, spaces across which the flames could not reach.

In the case of the fire in Pudding Lane, the first method was late in deployment because the fire began in the middle of the night. As was usual in case of fire, the mayor, Sir Thomas Bloodworth, was roused from his bed. Sir Thomas had recently taken over the post from Sir John Lawrence, who had acquitted himself so admirably during the plague. Now it was Sir Thomas's turn to be tested. If property needed to be destroyed to create firebreaks, his permission was required first. In major cases, the King's permission needed to be sought. Bleary-eyed from his bed, Bloodworth was not impressed by what he saw. Inspecting the fire, he famously offered the opinion that 'a woman could piss it out' and returned to his bed.[7] Pleas to pull down houses to create a firebreak were ignored.

In his home in Seething Lane, under the walls of the Tower, Samuel Pepys was roused from his bed with news of the fire. At first his reaction was much like that of the mayor. Fires were a frequent occurrence – and anyhow, Pepys felt his home was safe as the fire was to the south-west of his house and the wind in the east. He went back to bed. At dawn, with his head clear, Pepys had second thoughts and climbed the battlements of the Tower to look west towards the fire. What he saw shocked him. The fire was out of control, spreading out from Pudding Lane in a V-formation, south towards London Bridge and north towards the centre of the city. From what Pepys could see, no one had issued orders to make a firebreak.

Pepys had little time for the Lord Mayor, having previously encountered him on Admiralty business. On those occasions Pepys had been concerned by the numbers of London men being press-ganged for the navy, a major cause of dispute between the city and the navy. At meetings with Bloodworth, Pepys got little response from the mayor; he recorded Bloodworth as being 'a mean man of understanding and despatch of any public business'. They were prophetic words.

When Pepys went to the front line of the fire, he found his assessment to be correct. Bloodworth was dithering and indecisive. Pepys then went to the river, took a boat to Whitehall and informed the King of the situation. It was not yet midday. Knowing that Pepys was an able man, Charles listened to his assessment and realised instant action was necessary. He dispatched the Earl of Craven to the city with orders for the mayor to tear down houses. Craven, who had acquitted himself with honour during the plague, was an ideal choice, being both an able soldier and a privy councillor. He therefore had the capacity to assess the situation for the King and the ability to organise firefighting, as well as having previously demonstrated his love of London.

Pepys returned to the city. There he found Bloodworth in Cannon Street crying that people would not obey him, that the fire was spreading faster than it could be contained and that he was off to 'refresh himself' as he had been up all night. The King had sent an offer of troops via Lord Craven to back up the men at the mayor's disposal. Bloodworth turned them down. Pride might have been at the heart of his refusal, but there was also the longstanding desire within London's governance to be seen to be able to manage its own affairs. An historic independence of spirit meant that royal troops were generally unwelcome. Despite Bloodworth's refusal of help, the King dispatched a troop from the royal barracks.[8]

As the fight to save something of medieval London continued, looting took place across the wider city. Thieves pillaged parts of the palaces of St James and Whitehall. The fire grew so fierce that it created vacuums and surged in eddies, sometimes swirling back against the wind and consuming buildings not directly in its path. The majority of London's population flooded out through the medieval gates or took to the river to escape the unpredictable course of the fire. They made for the outlying villages and countryside to sleep in makeshift dwellings. Along the quays, spices stored in the great warehouses vaporised in the heat, sending a heavy aroma over the city. The water wheel at the end of London Bridge burnt down, as did some of the bridge itself. Parish church spires erupted into fiery candles pointing to the sky, the lead from their roofs flowing down their flanks like grey rain. Stone disintegrated in the extreme heat and turned to cinders. The flames spread west along Cornhill, taking with them the rows of goldsmiths' workshops and houses, and along Cheapside, consuming the grand bankers' houses. Sir Robert Viner's great house in Lombard Street, The Vine, from which he ran his banking and goldsmith's business, was destroyed (but not before he had rescued his gold), as were the house and surgery belonging to the doctor Nathaniel Hodges. John Graunt's haberdasher's shop and home were destroyed.*

Finally the flames reached the eastern flanks of St Paul's. The great east windows shattered in the heat, and the flames illuminated the altar, the choir and the nave. The conflagration swept through it all. The ancient cathedral, no stranger to fire, was set alight once more. Flames raced through the choir and up the nave to Inigo Jones's west front. Under the ferocious heat, the classical stonework crumbled and fell. Somehow, the medieval nave was left standing, hollow and open to the sky.

On Tuesday, the King instructed the Duke of York to take charge. Despite Bloodworth's refusal of the deployment of troops, the Duke gathered more men from the palace barracks and rode up the Strand and into the burning city through Ludgate. He quickly deployed his men to protect property against looting. With the fire raging, the King joined his brother and soon they were both involved in organising the struggle against the fire. James ordered troops into eight firefighting bases, each with thirty soldiers and a hundred volunteers. Ordering fire hooks to be used to create firebreaks, James rode between bases to coordinate their actions. Charles took it upon himself to ride through the streets, cajoling Londoners to join the firefighting crews, doling out money from a bag in encouragement. This was the sort of situation in which the King was at his best. Charles had not had a chance to show his personal bravery since his heroic but futile stand among his men at the Battle of Worcester fourteen years before. Now, in the midst of physical hazard, he became a man of action once more, rather

---

* Graunt never recovered financially from the disaster. The fire, along with other business disasters, some of which were to do with his conversion to Catholicism, reduced him to penury and he would die eight years later in poverty.

than one of mere administration. Dismounting from his horse, he joined a crew operating a fire engine for hours at a time.

In the west, the fire had leapt the city walls and was heading towards Whitehall and Westminster. James commanded that gunpowder be used to create more firebreaks, ordering streets of houses blown up to stop the fire spreading north out of the walled city and west towards Whitehall. The fierce wind carried burning embers as far as Whitehall and the Banqueting House was thought to be at risk. In the east of the city, troops stationed in the Tower, said to be acting on their own initiative, but possibly on the orders of the Duke of York, blew up more houses, preventing the fire from entering the fortress, where huge supplies of gunpowder were kept.

By Wednesday the fire was under control thanks to the combined efforts of troops, aldermen, yeomanry, the King and the Duke, and many ordinary Londoners who finally tore down and blew up houses to stop the flames. The fire came to a stop in an arc that ranged from the Middle Temple in the west, then north and east to Holborn Bridge, through Cripplegate, Aldersgate, the northern end of the great thoroughfare of Bishopsgate, the end of the once beautiful Leadenhall Street, to the medieval church of St Dionis Backchurch at Fenchurch Street, and down to Tower Basin in the east. It had been brought to a halt with gunpowder and fire hooks. The *London Gazette* reported, 'On Thursday by the grace of God it was wholely beat down and extinguished.'[9]

At least sixty-five thousand people were displaced from the city. In all, five-sixths of the buildings inside the city walls were destroyed, along with many outside the walls to the west – some 13,500 houses in all. Along with St Paul's Cathedral, eighty-nine of the ninety-seven parish churches inside the walls were destroyed. The Guildhall was ruined, reduced to a shell. The Exchequer, the Royal Exchange, the Custom House and Goldsmith's Row, the city's financial centre, had all gone, reduced to rubble. The great merchants' warehouses along Thames Street had been incinerated, along with their contents, tar and tallow providing the kindling. Workshops and factories were wiped out, destroying London as a working city. Near the Tower, Aldersgate had perished, its buildings reduced to smoking ruins; they included the grand home of Sir Thomas Bloodworth, the man knighted by a king but who failed to save his city.

Astonishingly, few people died in the fire. An old woman, one of the hundreds who had sought refuge in St Paul's before the fire surrounded it, was unable to move further and perished by the west door along with scores of dogs. Including Farriner's maid, the official death toll was put at six. In all, fewer than twenty died inside the city.[10]

These figures did not take account of the many who died after fleeing the city. Untold numbers of those made homeless died of exposure, hunger or poverty. The winter of 1666–7 was exceedingly cold, as would be the following one. Evelyn recorded that he saw 200,000 people of all ranks lying among their few belongings along the roads and ditches of Islington and Highgate. A programme of aid to the homeless was put in train. The government issued a series of orders for the relief of the homeless and hungry. The Corporation of London had to dig deep into its resources, as did the guilds, to provide shelter and food for the stricken. With many bivouacked outside the walls in the open fields and commons, and many more in hastily erected makeshift camps in Lincoln's Inn Fields, Covent Garden and Moorfields, the suffering was great. In the confusion no record of deaths was kept.

It was the end of medieval London. On 6 September John

Evelyn took a wherry up the Thames to see what was left. His aesthete's eye was hurt by what it saw. Gone were 'the exquisitely wrought Mercer's Chapel, the sumptuous Exchange, the august fabric of Christ's Church, all the rest of the Companies' Halls, splendid buildings, arches, entries, all in dust'.

Scapegoats were sought, and found: it had all been a Catholic plot, with even John Graunt suspected; or the Dutch had started it. The latter theory was much favoured, seen as an act of revenge for Admiral Holmes's raid on the Dutch coast two weeks before, during which the entire town of West-Terschelling was burned down during an attempt to destroy most of the Dutch merchant fleet. Neither of these theories was correct. There remained one other possibility: that God had chosen to punish London for the sins of its inhabitants. On Friday 7 September, the King ordered soldiers to be withdrawn from the city. He then rode around the makeshift camps to give heart to the homeless. At Moorfields, Charles visited the huge encampment containing many thousands who had lost their homes. In a speech to give the people heart, he told them the fire had been created by 'the Hand of God' and there had been 'no plot'.

Sir Thomas Bloodworth, now a figure of scorn, was placed on a committee to buy new equipment for firefighters. With commendable gallows humour and a nod to Bloodworth's already infamous remark on how the fire might be quenched, the committee ordered the purchase of 'receptacles', suggesting chamber pots as much as buckets.

CHAPTER 13
THE AFTERMATH

Much of old London had gone, and with it many important administrative buildings, including the Navy Office, the tax office and the Royal Exchange. But the country was still at war. Buildings in the wider city were requisitioned so that government could continue. The Dutch and French were anxious to know what effect the fire would have on England's ability or desire to wage war. The answer soon came. Both ambassadors reported that Londoners rose in fury over their destroyed city and wished for retribution against the enemy who had done this terrible thing to them. The Venetian ambassador reported that despair might drive the people of London to invade Holland.[1]

The wish for revenge was one thing; the ability to carry it out quite another. The Royal Navy's fighting power was severely hampered by both fire and plague. The Navy Board's great victualling yards to the north-east of the Tower had survived the fire, but the ability to fill them with supplies had been harshly affected by the plague. Livestock were scarce, as was flour to make bread. Beer was in short supply because so many of the coopers who made the barrels were dead. In the vast sprawl of the sailor-town downstream of the Tower, huge numbers of those able seamen not on board their ships when the plague hit had been struck by the contagion. Mercantile trade also suffered. There was neither the money nor the men to send as many ships out into the world as there had been before the twin disasters. In the five years following the plague and fire, the numbers of slaves shipped across the Atlantic by London vessels almost halved, from 10,049 to 5947.[2]

Looking back over 1666, the last thing Londoners would have thought of describing it as was an *annus mirabilis*, or year of miracles. Yet this is just what John Dryden called it in a poem he wrote at the beginning of 1667. Dryden was driven by a desire to be cheerleader for the stricken city, and to express his feelings about what had passed. As in all ages, there were many who looked for portents that gave meaning to what had happened. The very number of the year of the plague – 666 – was seen as a reference to the beast in the Book of Genesis. Many thought the comet sightings during the winter of 1664 and the spring of 1665 were portents of dreadful events. Dryden would have none of it:

> The utmost malice of their stars is past,
> And two dire comets, which have scourged the town,
> In their own plague and fire have breathed the last,
> Or dimly in their sinking sockets frown.[3]

Dryden's ode to London looked to the past and to the future, both to victories against the Dutch at sea and to the opportunity to build a glorious, resurgent city:

Methinks already from this chemic flame,
I see a city of more precious mould:
Rich as the town which gives the Indies name,
With silver paved, and all divine with gold.

Metaphorically, Dryden's vision would come to pass, but before that could happen there was much work to be done and great hardship to be endured. Charles and his government recognised that order had to be imposed on the rebuilding of the city. On 13 September, Denham, the Surveyor-General, sent out an instruction that no one could rebuild his or her house until a survey had been carried out and a master plan devised. On 10 October, the King and the Privy Council met to decide how to measure the damage. They appointed a group of four experienced surveyors and draughtsmen to survey and draw up a plan of London, showing the scale of the devastation. Along with this, a Rebuilding Commission was set up under the combined authority of the King and the city's Corporation. Among those appointed were the two old friends and collaborators Christopher Wren and Robert Hooke.[4] Wren was appointed by the King, and Hooke by the Corporation. Now they would use their combined ingenuity to restore London – although Wren would have to wait several years before the full realisation of his fortunes under the patronage of Charles II.

The winter was severe. The Thames froze over. Homeless people froze to death. In Chatham, the sailors starved, paid by neither Parliament nor the King. Thanks to the fall in tax revenue following the plague and the fire, both were broke. There was also an increasing realisation that public funds were habitually diverted into the extravagant royal household. While the king's mistress Barbara Palmer craved and was given ever greater gifts, there was no money to feed the navy's sailors or send the fleet to sea.[5] The mood of Londoners turned from hostility to foreigners to hostility towards the Stuarts.

The keenest minds had known for years that something had to be done about London's ancient fabric. The King and the city corporation called the most imaginative minds to come up with plans to rebuild the city. All agreed that a more salubrious city should be built, with houses made of brick rather than timber, and with wider streets and better sewerage, as had already been built in Lincoln's Inn Fields and parts of Covent Garden.

There was no shortage of designs. As John Evelyn put it, 'Everybody brings in his idea.' Among those who offered their plans was Richard Newcourt, a cartographer who knew London intimately. His detailed map, made in 1658, is the only remaining representation of the city as it was before the fire. Newcourt suggested a city on a Roman grid pattern. It would be extended to the north and east as far as 'the windmills on Finsbury Fields' so that it would end up 'a handsome oblong square'.[6] On the southern edge of the city, following the line of the river, would run a continuous row of elegant buildings elevated on arches. Behind the arches, streets would run northwards into the city. Access to the Thames would be through the arches. Beyond this line of buildings was to be erected a great dockside, 'sixty yards long to the water's side', which would not be 'pestered with any buildings or other impediments to obscure the beauty of the arched work'.[7]

Newcourt's oblong city was traversed from east to west by seven grand, equidistant thoroughfares, each eighty yards wide. A further seven major streets led from north to south. In this way the city was to be divided into sixty-four square units, or 'parcels' as Newcourt termed them. Each unit would constitute a parish with a church at its centre. For major public spaces, four of the basic units would be combined. In the case of St Paul's, the rebuilt church would sit at the centre of a grand piazza, somewhat like Covent Garden. This radical plan, whose implementation would have required the destruction of all of the remaining part of London, was unsurprisingly turned down. It became instead an inspiration for William Penn's utopian dream of Philadelphia, advertised sixteen years later.*

A radical plan of a different form was put forward by Valentine Knight, a military officer. Knight suggested a canal should be dug leading from the Thames beside the Tower, north through the old city, then west across the metropolis to join up with the Fleet River outside the walls at the western side of the city. Knight's suggestion was a brilliant solution to travel around the congested city. Where it fell down was in the method of payment. Knight not unreasonably thought the King could charge a toll to travel by canal to help pay for rebuilding. Sensitive to his public image, Charles felt he would be seen to be benefiting from the disaster. He had Knight put in gaol.

Robert Hooke, always keen to take on another scheme no matter how busy, put in his plan. His home, Gresham College, had escaped the fire. With the Guildhall gone, the mayor and Corporation had no offices, so they sequestered the college until such time as a new Guildhall could be built. The Royal Exchange had also moved its activities into the college. The Royal Society now occupied the great palace of Arundel House on the Strand, next door to Somerset House, having been invited by Henry Howard, the 6th Duke of Arundel. Since everyone knew Hooke had no other home, he alone among all the professors was allowed to stay in his rooms.

---

* Any reader who wishes to understand the repetitive grid patterns of so many American cities need look no further than Newcourt's Roman folly of a design, preserved at the London Metropolitan Archives, 40 Northampton Road, London EC1R 0HB.

From there, right inside the ruined city, he concocted his ideas on how best to carry out its rebuilding. Like Newcourt, he came up with a geometric grid in which the key buildings, such as churches and commercial halls, could be sited as if on a chessboard.

The aldermen newly installed at Gresham College liked his design sufficiently to give it their approval, going so far as to turn down the plan offered by the city's official surveyor, Peter Mills. As Mills's plan has not survived we do not know what form it took. Another member of the Royal Society who was keen to enter into the discussion was Sir William Petty, eager to lend his views on organisation gleaned from his time in government administration in Ireland. He did not produce a city plan, but offered his thoughts on how the rebuilt one should be administrated.

Two more members of the Royal Society lent their minds to the task. John Evelyn and Christopher Wren both suggested a rational, classical city. Their plans were remarkably similar. This was not surprising, for they had discussed how to rebuild the city. Wren, always hyperactive, quickly drew up some initial plans, which no doubt Evelyn would have seen. At any rate, both men's plans had a key feature: the incorporation of Westminster and the West End into the overall design, so that a rebuilt city east of the Fleet River was linked to the newer city to the west. In Wren's plan, a huge new piazza was sited north of the Temple with eight roads radiating from it. A ring of outer connecting roads joined them to form an octagon. One of the radiating roads led to the Palace of Whitehall, and others into the old walled city. In this feature, the plans were strikingly similar. If that were not enough, both plans included major arteries running east from St Paul's, Evelyn's plan featuring three routes fanning out whereas Wren's had only two. Where the two plans differed substantially was in the area of the eastern walled city that had been saved from the flames. Here, Evelyn proposed wholesale redevelopment, including another grand octagonal piazza, where Wren left well alone.

Exhibiting the capacity for work that those who knew him remarked upon, Wren completed his fully worked-up plan eleven days after the fire, two days before Denham sent out his emergency measures. As a sign of how his mind was working, he did not present his plans to the Royal Society but to the King. (Evelyn, to his equal credit, presented his own plans two days later.) Thanks to Wren's marvellous skills as a draughtsman, his plan was beautifully drawn and presented. Not only that, but the plan itself was elegant and rational, laying out a modern city built around several key points, chiefly St Paul's in the western section of the old city, linked by the northern arm of his major east–west routes to the Royal Exchange, which became the focal point of the entire city. The symbolic link between God and Mammon could not have been plainer. Wren, evidently, had not only scrutinised architecture while he had been in France, but had taken on new ideas in planning, most notably Andre Le Notre's 1661 designs for the gardens and parklands of Versailles, laid out in grids and triumphant diagonals. It is perhaps little wonder that Wren did not present his plans to the Royal Society for discussion, for what he had created was a triumphal city for an absolutist monarch.

While Richard Newcourt's vision was for a religious city, designed around a grid of parishes, Wren's vision was more practical. Around the Royal Exchange were to be positioned the Post Office, the Excise Office, the goldsmiths' premises and, most interestingly, a space for something simply labelled 'Bank'. This last was a marker of the long-running debate over the launching of a national bank to replace the current hydra-headed system whereby multiple city goldsmith/bankers made loans to the Exchequer, which in turn was located not in or near the city but inside Whitehall Palace, placing it symbolically in the King's immediate domain rather than at the service of the nation.

Charles, always with an eye for the French way of doing things, favoured a massive rebuilding scheme that would create major boulevards and triumphant vistas. To this the city corporation perceived two impediments: the first was cost, the second the frenchified design favoured by the King. A meeting of Parliament reached no conclusion either way. Long after Wren's and everyone else's drawings were rolled up for good, the debate over the general needs of the city continued. Its economic revival was at stake. Merchants and shopkeepers did not want to wait for years to move back into a beautiful, triumphant city designed on classical Roman lines: they wanted to resume business right away, or as quickly as the ruins could be cleared and new houses of commerce erected.

Under Wren's friend Robert Hooke, a team surveyed the outlines of the destroyed city, making a map of the roads and alleys. From this, a plan was formed for widening the roads and working out how to compensate those whose properties would suffer. The new roads were to have different widths according to their function. At the dockside they were to be one hundred feet wide, major streets seventy feet, others fifty, forty-two, and so on down to alleys at sixteen feet; where possible, the latter would be dispensed with altogether. Building in wood with rubble or mortar infill was banned. All new edifices were to be built in stone or brick. No overhanging upper storeys or windows or galleries were allowed. All these stipulations were formed into a Rebuilding Act in 1667, by which time around 650 houses had been rebuilt. Compensation for those who lost land due to road widening was to be paid from a new tax of twelve pence per ton of coal landed in London for the following ten years.

While Hooke forged on urgently with laying out the surveyed city, its key organisations and entities had their own headaches. Most of the city's ancient livery companies had been obliterated, as had its churches. Nevertheless, some elements of London life revived with astonishing rapidity. Major functions of government carried on in their temporary accommodation. In Gresham College, the city corporation met more or less non-stop. Despite being dislodged and having several of its members involved in vital work surveying and redesigning the damaged city, the Royal Society swiftly recommenced its meetings. At a session held on 30 October 1667, Dr Wilkins suggested that the time was right for the society to build its own college. By the time of the next meeting, on 5 November, the idea had taken flight. Several of the society's wealthier members promised money. Letters were to be sent out to the whole membership asking for subscriptions.

By the following May, £1000 had been promised and the society voted that work should begin on its new home as soon as possible. The building was to be erected between the Strand and the river on land to be provided by the Duke of Norfolk. Both Christopher Wren and Robert Hooke – as if they were not busy enough – were asked to make draft plans. Wren's estimated cost was £2000. The cost Hooke arrived at is unknown, though both plans were put forward for a decision on 13 July 1668. In the meantime, Hooke was ordered, as usual, to shoulder the work, to make models, estimate costs, engage workmen, and make yet more drawings based on changes the society wished to make to the original plans. It all came to nothing. On 10 August, a meeting decided that work on building the new college should be put off until the following spring.[8] After that, all mention of the great scheme lapsed.

The Royal Society's failure to build itself a college was a deciding factor in its future fortunes. It is not recorded why the work did not go ahead but it is reasonable to surmise that sufficient money was not raised. Many of the members failed to pay their subs, and some were too poor to do so. It might also be the case that the Duke of Norfolk withdrew his offer of the land.[9] Whatever the case, the college went into a period of gradual decline and did not recover its prestige until Sir Isaac Newton became its president in 1703, bringing with him his international reputation.

But that was in the future; for now the society's usual flurry of events and publications continued, providing a sounding board for the new empirical ideas. During 1667 it was visited by one of its most remarkable critics, the aristocratic writer, thinker and philosopher Margaret Cavendish, Duchess of Newcastle-upon-Tyne. For Cavendish, experimentalism obstructed the working of pure reason. The crux of the matter was this: how could the introduction of mechanical instruments help in understanding God's world? God had designed the world so that those who lived in it were meant to understand it by the powers God had given to mankind – analytical deduction and so on. The anti-experimentalists argued that the use of machines such as microscopes intervened between mankind on the one hand and the rest of God's creation on the other.

Margaret Cavendish was not entirely opposed to the Royal Society's experimental work. She valued the role of observation in understanding the natural world and thought people should be trained to do so. But she shared Robert Boyle's belief that no theory or observation could be proposed as 'truth'; all one could do was put forward one's finding as a probability.[10] As Boyle expressed it, 'not to Dogmatize, but only to make an Enquiry'.[11]

Cavendish read *Micrographia* and was not convinced by all of Hooke's conclusions. Commenting on his observation that in various lights a fly's eye appeared to be constructed in different ways – a perforated lattice, cones, pyramids, etc. – Cavendish thought the microscope provided 'inconsistent and uncertain ground' and questioned how the experimenter could judge the 'truest light, position or medium that doth present the object naturally as it is'.[12] This was a fair point, based not entirely on hostility to the idea behind the observation but on the *quality* of the observation.

The Duchess was not alone in her criticism of the use of microscopes. Thomas Sydenham shared some of her reservations, adding his own feeling that the augmentation of human senses bestowed by God might even be sinful. He discussed his criticism of microscopy with a new acquaintance, fellow physician John Locke, who was to play such an important role in the Enlightenment as a philosopher and political theorist.

Locke was born in Somerset in 1632 into a Puritan family that supported the Parliamentary cause during the civil wars. Thanks to the patronage of his father's former commanding officer, Locke went to Westminster School and Christchurch, Oxford. In 1667 he was invited to London by Anthony Ashley Cooper, the Chancellor of the Exchequer and later 1st Earl of Shaftesbury, as his personal doctor. Following a successful operation overseen by Locke to remove a cyst on Cooper's liver the two men became friends. Cooper credited Locke with saving his life. And so two of the most important political minds of the age came together.

Locke lived at Ashley Cooper's home, Exeter House, next door to the Duke of Arundel's palace on the Strand. Here, probably at the suggestion of Cooper, who greatly influenced the younger man, he began his work on theories of government and the state. Like John Milton, and Cicero long before him, Locke concluded that the only just society was one in which there was a contract between government and people. If the ruler or rulers broke the contract the people could select a new government. Though the work could not be published during Charles's reign, it was secretly disseminated among those who, like Ashley Cooper, grew disenchanted with Charles's rule.

Locke continued his medical studies with Sydenham, who had a successful practice in Pall Mall, not far from Exeter House. He particularly admired Sydenham's insistence on keen clinical observation rather than 'indulging in idle speculations'. Sydenham also played an important role in the development of modern British philosophy. Along with Ashley Cooper, he is credited with planting the seed for what would become Locke's hugely influential work on the empirical basis of knowledge, later published as *An Essay on Human Understanding*. Long before that, however, Locke and Sydenham wrote a treatise on the use of the microscope in studying anatomy. Their combined assessment was that such unnatural aids reinforced the view that there were God-given limits to what mankind might observe and know. They argued that by examining the contents of the human body under a microscope all that was done was to aid the observation of the surface of more and more things, 'creating a new superficies for ourselves to stare at'.[13] It was an elegant argument. As scientific methodology improved, however, it was one that would become redundant.

The criticism of experimentalism that it tended to look only at the surface of things was linked in the seventeenth-century mind to the metaphysical idea of vitalism. This was the idea that animate and inanimate objects differed because of a 'vitalising' spark within things judged to be alive that was absent from those judged not to have life. Given the limited knowledge of biology available in the mid-seventeenth century, vitalism was a highly regarded philosophical position.

Desirous of seeing the Royal Society's experiments for herself, on 23 May Margaret Cavendish journeyed south from her ducal seat, Welbeck Abbey in Northamptonshire, accompanied by her husband William Cavendish, 1st Duke of Newcastle and grandson of the famous Bess of Hardwick. The Duke, who had fought in the Civil Wars on the Royalist side, was the immensely wealthy patron of several writers, including Jonson, Davenant, Dryden and Thomas Shadwell. But his greatest passion was the breeding and training of horses, and he hoped London would greet his new book on the subject with enthusiasm.

London was much more interested in Margaret. By virtue of her 'antic' dress and her wide-ranging interests in intellectual pursuits, such as poetry and natural philosophy, widely considered best left to men, she was seen as unconventional. In the male circles of literature and science her attainments were largely dismissed, though she was universally acknowledged to be very fine looking.[14] We are left a reasoned if partial portrait of this remarkable woman in the lines written by her husband as a poetic foreword to her extraordinary utopian novel *The Blazing World*, published the year before she visited the academicians:

> Her Beauty's found beyond the Skill
> Of the best Paynter, to Imbrace
> These lovely Lines within her face.
> View her Soul's Picture, Judgment, witt,
> Then read those Lines which Shee hath writ[15]

The attitude of the London virtuosi to this highly intelligent and astute student of the arts and sciences can be gleaned from Robert Hooke's diary entry for the day she visited the Royal Society. Several experiments, he wrote, were put on 'for entertain Duchess of Newcastle'. It seems not to have occurred to Hooke or the other members of the society that the Duchess might find in their experiments something more than mere entertainment. At any rate, Hooke and Boyle performed a series of experiments including the use of magnets, microscopes and their now famous vacuum pump in order to demonstrate 'weighing air in a receiver by Rarefying engine'.[16] What the Duchess made of these demonstrations is sadly unknown. We do know that she held to her belief in the superiority of pure reason over experimentalism. Royal Society Fellow Joseph Glanvill felt the need to apologise to the Duchess for what the society had been able to show her, writing to her that:

> all that we can hope for, as yet, is but the History of things as they are, but to say how they are, to raise general Axioms, and to make Hypotheses, must, I think, be the happy priviledge of succeeding Ages; when they shall have gained a larger account of the Phaenomena, which yet are too scant and defective to raise Theories upon . . .[17]

Just as he had been strangely far-sighted in his prediction of communication via magnetic waves, Glanvill could see that where the society currently fell down was that its knowledge was at an early stage. Once more was known, nature's secrets would become amenable to explanation. In the middle of the seventeenth century it took quite a leap of the imagination – one most were unable to make – to realise this.

By far the greatest voice raised against the experimentalists was that of Thomas Hobbes, who argued that 'sense' should not stand in the way of 'reason', and that no number of devices such as a telescope or Boyle's vacuum pump could make up for the application of reason by the pure natural philosopher, who should not be some mere designer or maker of engines. He wrote scathingly that the practitioner might

> get Engines made, and apply them to the Stars; Recipients made, and try Conclusions; but they are never the more Philosophers for all this ... not every one that brings from beyond Seas a new Gin, or other jaunty device, is therefore a philosopher. For if you reckon that way, not only Apothecaries and Gardeners, but many other sorts of Workmen, will put in for, and get the Prize.[18]

There was little doubt that class played some part in the debate; the genteel classes were liable to sneer at those who made or operated any kind of apparatus. And so the man without a machine was a superior thinker to the man with one. This distinction would remain an impediment to the advancement of the Royal Society for some years to come.

There was another field of exploration in which the past overlapped with the new thinking. This was the discipline of alchemy, the meeting place of mysticism and chemistry.

In the seventeenth century, the terms alchemy and chemistry (*alchemia* and *chemia*) were interchangeable. Many important figures practised alchemy in some form – Charles II, his cousin Prince Rupert, Isaac Newton, Robert Boyle and Nicholas Culpeper the herbalist. Alchemy was not only about the attempt to achieve the transmutation of metals – lead into gold and so on – but had a spiritual side. Robert Boyle, the father of modern chemistry, thought that the fabulous material known as the philosopher's stone, famed for its ability to transmute metals, was also an elixir of life which could enable men to talk to angels. When Boyle moved from Oxford to live with his sister, Katherine Jones, Countess Ranelagh, in her house in Pall Mall, she had a laboratory built for them to work together on alchemical experiments.

Another devoted alchemist was Isaac Newton. Newton had taken the premise of vitalism and expanded it until it became a theory of a central animating spirit of the universe that had little to do with the Christian Holy Trinity. He wisely kept some of his more heretical ideas under his hat. Unknown to the Stuarts, he was not only a heretic, denying the existence of the Trinity, but rejected the idea of a God-anointed king. To him, such notions stood in the way of his own theories on the central animating spirit that controlled the cosmos. Newton stated in public that his ideas on planetary orbits, gravity and the rest were a rediscovery of the known works of the ancients, the Babylonians and Pythagoreans. He was therefore not given to orthodox Christian views.

Newton's writings on alchemy, meanwhile, were more voluminous than those on his scientific observations or on mathematics. John Maynard Keynes said of Newton that 'he was not the first of the age of reason, he was the last of the magicians.' During the height of his alchemical researches, Newton suffered some form of mental breakdown. At the time this was put down as a manifestation of the physical and psychological changes alchemy was supposed to induce. One wonders whether the breakdown might instead have been caused by a physiological reaction to some of the materials he was using, such as lead and mercury.

This interest in the spiritual among proto-scientists grew from a belief that their researches were inquiries into the working of God's universe, and as such were a form of ordained or godly works. Newton and his friends were for the most part deeply religious men; either they had taken holy orders, or like Newton and Hooke, they had almost done so. Newton believed himself chosen by God to interpret Holy Scripture. Indeed, during his lifetime, he was known as a major theologian, corresponding widely on matters of biblical interpretation.

At least some of the virtuosi, among them Newton and Joseph Glanvill, believed in the existence of witchcraft. Glanvill argued that the world could not be understood by pure reason alone. Though experimentalism was required to examine the true nature of natural phenomena, among these phenomena, according to Glanvill, were those of the supernatural; he considered reports of supernatural activity to be sufficient evidence of their existence, as long as interviews with witnesses were carried out with sufficient rigour and the circumstances carefully examined. He thought the existence of supernatural spirits was documented in the Bible and wrote at length on how to deny the existence of spirits and witches was to fly in the face of evidence.[19] Glanvill's writings were later cited by the New England Puritan minister Cotton Mather as a justification of the witch trials in Salem, Massachusetts, in 1692–3, as a result of which twenty people were executed for witchcraft.

The city in which this fervour of debate and experimentation took place was still a building site. It would remain so for many years. Rebuilding the city took many heroic feats of labour and instances of hard-headed acumen. No contributions were greater than the efforts of Robert Hooke and Peter Mills, the city surveyor, who together organised the surveying and staking out of the new, wider streets. In little more than two months they measured out and put down stakes and ropes that effectively laid out the new city. With a team of labourers they covered eleven miles of streets, encompassing an area of 436 acres – an astonishing achievement.[20] Not only that, but Hooke spent the next five years tramping out every morning to view the plots of new foundations so they could be signed off and building begin. It would take six years for the city to be restored to a working entity with a reasonable number of businesses and residences replacing those that had been lost.

Even then there remained major projects such as the Mansion House, the parish churches and the hall of the Mercers' Company, the most venerable of the city's guilds. When Charles ordered a monument to be erected in memory of the fire, Wren and Hooke collaborated to design a column to stand in Fish Street near London Bridge, barely two hundred yards from where the fire started in Pudding Lane. The old experimentalists could not resist adding a special feature of their own. In its lower levels they designed a high room with an aperture in its domed ceiling from which a shaft went all the way to the top of the tower, and around which wound the staircase. The shaft was designed for the conduct of experiments involving gravity and pendulums, as well as allowing an observer to see the stars.

Before London was completely rebuilt thirty years or more would elapse. But that city would be nothing like the one it replaced. The classically inspired architecture of Wren, Hooke and others would announce London as a modern city.

CHAPTER 14

A STAR IS BORN

On 2 March 1667 Samuel and Elizabeth Pepys went to the Theatre Royal in Drury Lane. It was the first night of a new play and both the King and his brother the Duke of York were present. What they saw that night was the creation of a new star of the London stage. Pepys recorded his reaction in his diary:

> After dinner, with my wife to the King's House to see 'The Mayden Queene', a new play of Dryden's, mightily commended for the regularity of it, and the strain and wit; and, the truth is, there is a comical part done by Nell which is Florimell, that I never can hope ever to see the like done again, by man or woman.

The play was a smash hit and Nell Gwyn was its shining star. One of the attractions of her role was that in some scenes she had to roll about the stage in a flurry of petticoats. There was also a scene for which she was required to don male breeches. This was always popular with male audiences, as Pepys recorded:

> But so great performance of a comical part was never, I believe, in the world before as Nell do this, both as a mad girle, then most and best of all when she comes in like a young gallant; and hath the notions and carriage of a spark the most that ever I saw any man have. It makes me, I confess, admire her.

The Maiden Queen was the biggest hit either the playwright or the actress ever enjoyed. It propelled Nell to the level of a true theatrical star in the eyes of fashionable London – and especially in those of Charles II, who, according to Dryden, graced it with the title 'His Play'. Given the nature of the characters portrayed, the play's subject matter was, as Sir Walter Scott was subsequently laconically to remark, something in which the King had considerable expertise.[1]

Pepys developed quite a crush on Nell, just as he previously had on the King's mistress, Barbara Palmer. Unknown to him, the King would also develop a crush on the actress. Within a year he would make her his mistress.

Three weeks after its premiere the play was still being performed. Pepys went again, this time accompanied by Sir William Penn, a Commissioner of the Navy. Pepys's pleasure was unabated: 'saw "The Queene" again; which indeed the more I see the more I like, and is an excellent play, and so done by Nell, her merry part, as cannot be better done in nature, I think.'

For such an acclaimed star, Nell's early life had not augured well. There are many mysteries: where she was born and when, the identity of her father and, not least, since she was possibly illiterate, how she managed to become a successful actress. All we know is that she succeeded to overcome the problems arising from an obscure, impoverished background to become a star.

Her only advantage early on seems to have been that the brothel kept by her mother in Coal Yard Alley was close to Killigrew's new theatre, the Theatre Royal in Drury Lane. This was the first purpose-built theatre in the fashionable West End. At its opening in May 1663, Nell Gwyn had been an orange girl, one of the theatre's sexily dressed teenagers who sold fruit, interacted coquettishly with the male audience and acted as messengers, carrying billets-doux between flirting young bloods and ladies of the audience. Nell's good looks and ebullient character brought her to the attention of Charles Hart, the theatre's most established actor.

Thanks to collaboration between Killigrew and Davenant, London's first theatre school had also opened in 1663.* Nell was an early pupil, enrolled at the age of fourteen, probably by Hart who tutored her in theatrical craft with the aid of comedian and dancer John Lacy. Not only had Nell to learn the skills necessary for the stage, she had to learn an ever-changing repertoire. With a small audience base, the London stage depended upon novelty. A theatre would perform sometimes two, or even three, plays a week. If the theory is true that Nell was illiterate, she must have depended upon learning her roles by rote, repeating them after a prompter.[2]

In all this, Nell – or Nelly as she was invariably known – had the help not only of the much older Hart, who became her lover, but also, it has been suggested, of the literary libertine John Wilmot, 2nd Earl of Rochester. In his biography of Gwyn, her descendant Charles Beauclerk argues persuasively that Rochester became Gwyn's lover before she was fifteen. If that were so, he suggests, might not Rochester have given her

---

* LAMDA (the London Academy of Music and Dramatic Arts), founded in 1861, claims to be the oldest *continuous* acting school in London.

acting lessons? Rochester, after all, possibly tutored the initially unpromising Elizabeth Barry, helping to turn her into one of the finest actors of her time.[3]

Nell graduated to become a member of the repertory company of the King's Men sometime in 1665. Her career was very uneven. Thanks to the lowly circumstances of her upbringing, she had a ready and bawdy wit that audiences liked.[4] She had a narrow professional range, unable to cope with dramatic or tragic roles, but in playing herself she had no equal. The place of women on the Restoration stage allowed theatre managers to give a new depth to the rendering of past classics, but also allowed new writers to reflect London's sexual temptations and the amoral behaviour of many well-born men and women. In such a milieu, Nell's earthy sexuality was bound to appeal.

Whatever advantages the young actress had, in her first recorded appearance all did not go well. She was meant to be in what was intended to be an unabashed crowd-pleaser with an all-female cast due to open in November 1664. This was Killigrew's own play *Thomaso, or The Wanderer*, written ten years before while he was in exile in Madrid. *Thomaso* was semi-autobiographical and partially based on earlier sources. The cast included the ingénue Nelly Gwyn, and the more established Mrs Knepp and Anne Marshall, the latter one of the most accomplished actresses of the time.*

Killigrew had successfully produced an all-female play, his own *Parson's Wedding*, in October 1664. The production of *Thomaso* was meant to follow a few weeks later. All-female ensembles were cast purely for box office receipts. The use of women on the Restoration stage was not a sign of a sudden flowering of feelings of emancipation or liberalism towards the

---

* Not to be confused with her younger sister Rebecca, also an actress.

female sex; it was, rather, exactly the opposite. Women were mainly cast in roles in which their sexuality could be exploited. They would be the tragic heroines of plays set in exotic lands so that their clothing could be as revealing as decency allowed; or they would be cast in 'breeches' roles in which they were required to wear men's trousers, so allowing them to show as much leg as possible. The popularity of the latter was strongly referred to in the epilogue to Dryden's *Maiden Queen* when acted by an all-female cast:

> Here we presume, our Legs are no ill Sight,
> And they will give you no ill Dreams at Night.[5]

Excepting the most accomplished of them, such as Elizabeth Barry or Mary Saunderson, actresses were not expected to have a great deal of skill in acting. They were more in the line of comediennes or song-and-dance girls, delivering prologues and epilogues frequently quite unrelated to the plays to which they were attached, during which they were expected to play up the most engaging side of their personalities. They would regularly be required to sing songs and dance numbers equally at odds with the action or subject of the play – these were even, as with Davenant's *Macbeth*, placed in the middle of Shakespeare's tragedies. Actresses were used unabashedly to get the punters in.

Rehearsals of *Thomaso* were troubled. For a start, the play had been written not to be performed but to be read – what was then known as a closet drama. Its extraordinary number of scenes (seventy-three in ten acts) was daunting even for the most accomplished modern company. Before the play could be performed it was abandoned.

Nell's first appearance, therefore, was postponed to March 1665, when she was cast in the strong, dramatic role of Aztec princess Cydaria, the daughter of Moctezuma, in Dryden's *The Indian Emperor*. Among Dryden's sources for the play was a masque by the owner of the Theatre Royal's rival playhouse, Davenant. This work, *The Cruelty of the Spaniards in Peru*, had been staged publicly in 1658 and encouraged by Oliver Cromwell as a piece of anti-Spanish propaganda. There is no record of Nell's first performance, but we do know what the inveterate theatregoer Pepys thought of her performance in the same role two years later, when he wrote that he was 'most infinitely displeased with her being put to act the Emperour's daughter; which is a great and serious part which she do most basely'.[6]

The play's theme was the conflict between love and honour, a subject much admired by the members of the royal court, with Cydaria involved in a love triangle with the Spanish invader Cortez. Hart, by then Nell's real-life lover, had doubtless schooled her in the part, but it made no difference; Nell was temperamentally unsuited to intense or tragic roles.

Rochester's fellow theatre lover and rake the Duke of Richmond wrote an epilogue for Nell to speak at the end of a play by his friend Robert Howard: 'I know you in your hearts/ Hate serious plays as I do serious parts.' Moments such as this, when the player addressed the audience, or let the audience into their feelings not as characters but as their real selves, were a regular trope in Restoration plays. Thus Nell's character in James Howard's *The English Monsieur* could say, 'This life of mine can last no longer than my beauty . . . I might e'en sell oranges for my living.' Those connected to Nell were obviously paying close attention to the young actress's ability. That they did so indicates that whatever her shortcomings as a dramatic actress, her good-natured, freewheeling character, allied to a most engaging personality, had already marked her out as having star quality. Such quality was good not only for the star but for those around her.

Accordingly, a close political, personal, theatrical 'and even financial' connection was forged between Gwyn, Killigrew, Buckingham and Robert Howard.[7] Soon, the faith of Killigrew and others would be rewarded. In the spring of 1665 Nell played opposite Hart in *All Mistaken, or the Mad Couple* by Robert Howard's brother James.

The play was a tragicomedy, composed of two plots, one a tragedy, the other a comedy. By most assessments, the tragic part was not fully developed, and had many lumpen lines. However, the comic part was a triumph of sparky dialogue of the type London audiences loved. Among the first-night audience were the King, the Duke of York and Samuel Pepys. Nell and Hart shone as the 'gay couple' a standard conceit London's theatre audiences had come to expect; it entailed a witty rake or man about town and the beautiful female object of his desire engaging in verbal sparring before finally admitting their mutual attraction. Ultimately, the role would become Nell's speciality.

As a device, the sparring couple owed quite a lot to Shakespeare's characters Benedick and Beatrice in *Much Ado About Nothing*. As a result of the fashion for what the Duke of Richmond, with his cynic's ear for weakness, called 'prize fight' repartee, the momentum of a play often ground to a halt while the warring couple engaged in a long display of verbal fisticuffs.

Two years later, in *Secret Love, or The Maiden Queen*, Dryden got the balance right, placing the battle of the sexes at the centre of the action. The work was the quintessence of Restoration theatre. From the play's beginning, Dryden wasted no time in introducing the sparring partners, together with their bawdy conversation. After a brief first scene in which the courtier Celadon chats to his sister and we learn that he is a philanderer, we cut to the second scene in which he encounters two women he has not met before, Flavia and Florimel, both maids of honour to the queen. They wear masks and refuse to allow Celadon to see their faces. Celadon can only judge them by their wit.

From Celadon's opening salvo Dryden draws the audience immediately into the louche world of Restoration comedy:

> *Cel.* Cannot I serve you in the gentleman's room, ladies?
> *Fla.* Which of us would you serve?
> *Cel.* Either of you, or both of you.
> *Fla.* Why, could you not be constant to one?
> *Cel.* Constant to one! – I have been a courtier, a soldier, and a traveller, to good purpose, if I must be constant to one: Give me some twenty, some forty, some a hundred mistresses! I have more love than any woman can turn her to.
> *Flo.* Bless us! Let us be gone, cousin: We two are nothing in his hands.
> *Cel.* Yet, for my part, I can live with as few mistresses as any man. I desire no superfluities; only for necessary change or so, as I shift my linen.[8]

At this point, Florimel says in an aside that Celadon is 'a rare sort of fellow' who fits her humour 'exactly'. Within a few more lines of sparring, Celadon says much the same of Florimel and the audience knows it is about to be taken along on a wave of wit and pleasure before the two finally admit they are made for one another.

By the end of the play Celadon and Florimel have agreed a truce; they will be married – but it will be a marriage born from the cool, knowing style of Restoration wit.

> *Flo.* But this marriage is such a bugbear to me! Much might be if we could invent but any way to make it easy.
>
> *Cel.* Some foolish people have made it uneasy, by drawing the knot faster than they need; but we that are wiser will loosen it a little.
>
> *Flo.* Tis true, indeed, there's some difference betwixt a girdle and a halter.

Thus, at the very close of the play the characters reveal they will not stay true inside their marriage. With cynical dialogue like this from an artist of Dryden's ability, it is hardly surprising the contemporary theatre was the window to the age. In the words of one modern critic, 'The strongest case for regarding this as an especially dissolute age must . . . rest on taste in the theatre.'[9]

The play was so popular that Killigrew included it regularly in the repertory, staging it many times in the ensuing years – and this at a period when plays might fold in a day or two, very seldom lasting more than a week before giving way to new material. A measure of its triumph was that Pepys and Sir William went again in May, and Pepys with his wife in August. The following January the play was published. Pepys bought a copy, complaining that in the preface Dryden 'seems to brag' although it was 'a good play'. Later that month, the Pepyses went a third time. Nell became London's Cinderella. According to a bishop she was 'the indiscreetest and wildest creature that ever was in court'.[10]

The Maiden Queen propelled the young woman brought up in a brothel to the equally louche circles of the court aristocracy. When the theatres closed for the summer, the aristocratic poet and playboy Charles Sackville whisked Nell off to a love nest in Epsom along with his friend Charles Sedley. The threesome became public knowledge and the satirists had a field day.

It provided a moment of frivolity before London was threatened once more. As was so often the case during Charles's reign, gravity had been masked by levity.

PART 3

1667–1685: THE YEARS OF TURMOIL

CHAPTER 15

THE THREAT FROM ABROAD

While London struggled back to normality, the government grappled with a serious problem it had yet to make public: the Exchequer was empty. Among the state offices drained of finance was the biggest and most important, the Navy Board. With no money coming from the Exchequer, the board ran out of cash to pay the fleet. By early 1667 it was obvious that the war, begun in 1665, simply could not go on.

Keeping one of its first-rate 100-gun warships at sea cost the Admiralty £3500 every month, which helped explain why the fleet tended to sail for short periods at a time and naval wars were fought in brief encounters.[1] To put this huge sum in perspective, Robert Hooke's salary from Gresham College was £50 per annum plus lodgings. Sir Peter Lely earned £200 a year as royal painter (augmented by private commissions), while the King's personal friend of long standing, Thomas Killigrew, earned £500 a year as a gentleman of the bedchamber – and this only after years of exile and penury. The sum of £3500 was therefore a very considerable one.

Various issues were to blame for the catastrophic lack of money. The plague had hit tax revenues badly, and just when it looked as if the economic life of London was returning and tax revenues increasing, the Great Fire cut the economic heart out of the city. The public purse was further strained by the cost of Charles's expensive court, not least by the avaricious demands of his mistress Barbara, Countess Castlemaine.

When the government needed money, the normal course of action was either to ask Parliament to raise taxes, or to borrow from the city bankers and gold merchants. Unfortunately, Parliament had lost much of its enthusiasm for banking a king whose dislike of the institution was proving to echo that of his father. The cataclysms of the preceding years meant moreover that there was little money to be had among the bankers who lent money to the Crown. The goldsmith-banker Thomas Viner said it was hard to find a goldsmith in the city, let alone one who had money to lend.[2] London's bankers had removed their money from town. Now they were leery about lending what they had to fund a war that was running on and going badly.

To make matters worse, even if the money could be found to pay the men and provide the victuals, it was as difficult to find unemployed men to crew the warships as it was to find a compliant banker. The naval towns stretching along the Thames Estuary from London into Kent had been hard hit by the plague. Seafaring families had been wiped out or had moved away. The Crown's negotiations with Parliament over money had become turgid and fractious. Miscalculations about the state of hostilities, plus Charles's domestic financial problems, were also to blame. The chief issue was simply the enormous cost of the war. The shortfall in revenue to the Exchequer caused by the plague was more than £500,000, while the total cost of the war was approaching £5 million.[3]

Following the major sea battles of the previous summer, the King and his admirals had taken the view that hostilities for the foreseeable future were at an end. Both sides had suffered severe blows. Owing to fluctuating fortunes, the war had subsided into a ceasefire. Erroneously believing they had the upper hand, the English began peace talks at Breda, feeling the Dutch were unlikely to retaliate during negotiations. The English had not taken into account the fact that they had not succeeded in destroying Dutch military sea power. Peace talks dragged on for over a year. In the face of multiple problems at home and drawn-out talks in Breda, Charles decided to take a gamble.[4]

In the winter of 1666–7, Charles instructed the fleet to be laid up in Chatham dockyard, securely situated miles inland up the Medway River, and dismissed the crews. Charles assumed that military defences on the river would ward off any Dutch attack. Much store was laid on the effectiveness of a hefty chain stretching from bank to bank in order to prevent warships getting through to the dockyard. The Dutch had other ideas.

In June 1667, a huge Dutch battle fleet set sail for England. News from coastal shipping and garrisons in Kent quickly spread towards London. Among those watching the Dutch fleet gather at the mouth of the Thames was John Evelyn. He saw the fleet manoeuvre for several days, testing for a response, then, seeing none, sail up the Medway. On 10 June the Dutch blasted past the few shore batteries in service and severed the chain across the Medway with ease.

Between 10 and 13 June the invaders set fire to Chatham dockyard and everything in it. They blew up or burned thirteen English ships before towing two major vessels back to Amsterdam. Their most important prize was the *Royal Charles*, pride of the English navy, first under Cromwell (when it was called the *Naseby*) and then under Charles – the very ship that had brought the King home from exile.

On the first evening of the attack, Charles, instead of directing defences, was partying with Barbara Palmer. According to one account, they made a game out of searching for a moth.

News of the enemy destruction caused panic in London. Rumours spread that it was a full-scale Dutch invasion, backed up by a French army. What if the Dutch sailed up the Thames and took the city? With the best of the English fleet destroyed there was little to stop them. Panic turned to terror. Andrew Marvell, an astute onlooker, recorded:

> Up to the Bridge contagious terror struck:
> The Tower itself with the near danger shook.'[5]

Anti-monarchist crowds gathered in London shouting 'Parliament!' Some courtiers, thinking the King would be deposed, fled the city. Barbara Palmer shouted hysterically that she would be first to be lynched. If there had been any lynching she might well have been first; her public position as the King's mistress, allied to her Catholicism, made her a hate figure to the determinedly Protestant London mob.

With an invasion seemingly imminent, the King and his brother snapped out of their complacency. They called for a barge and took themselves downstream to the waterfront of the old city. Once there they ordered the sinking of ships downstream from the Tower to block the river. Marvell, forever unimpressed by monarchy, watched as London was protected by nothing more than scuttled ships:

> Once a deep river, now with timber floored,
> And shrunk, least navigable, to a ford.'[6]

Then, as if by a miracle, the Dutch turned back. The Dutch admiral de Ruyter later admitted that had he known the state of England's defences he would have carried on to London. So the capital was saved, as was the Crown – but not Charles's reputation. Lampoons appeared, making a great deal of the true story of the King and his mistress playing at hunting a moth while the Dutch burned the fleet. The name of the Emperor Nero was invoked. Charles hurriedly arranged further peace talks to be held at Breda. Such was the power of the East India Company that it had its own representative at the talks. Peace was agreed, on terms unfavourable to England.

After the triple disasters of fire, war and pestilence, London had little to be proud of. In Holland, the Dutch put the *Royal Charles* on show at Hellevoetsluis as a tourist attraction and outraged the court at Whitehall and the navy by showing foreign dignitaries around it. Charles complained that his royal dignity was besmirched. The Dutch stopped the tours.

Scapegoats were sought, and found. One of the unfortunates was Peter Pett, the only Commissioner of the Navy with any knowledge of ship design or building – ironically, Pett had been the architect and builder of the *Royal Charles*. Having also designed the first frigate, a type that would become a mainstay of the navy for many years to come, thanks to his vast knowledge he had been given responsibility for the Royal Dockyards at Chatham. Pett's apparent crime was to have failed to protect the fleet more strongly. He assured all who enquired that the chain across the Medway would hold against a Dutch raid: it did not. It was said that Pett should also have brought the major ships further up the river, where the Dutch would have found it difficult to reach them.

Pett's final crime was that once the raid had begun and the British fleet set on fire, he had been more anxious to save models of the endangered ships than the ships themselves. He suffered a good deal of comic abuse when he told an official inquiry that he had saved the models because they were more valuable. There was method in his actions. He understood that plans alone were insufficient to build a warship – scale models were required so that the carpenters could see exactly how the ship was put together. Models were therefore an essential part of the shipbuilding process. As for the charges directed at Pett for not being prepared, they could equally have been directed at senior officers of the army and navy. They were not. Andrew Marvell wrote:

> After this loss, to relish discontent
> Someone must be accused by punishment
> All our miscarriages on Pett must fall:
> His name alone seems fit to answer all.[7]

Charles's sacking of Pett was particularly cruel. The Petts were an illustrious family of shipbuilders and designers who had been associated with the Stuarts and the Royal Navy for generations. Peter's father, Phineas, First Commissioner for Chatham before his son took up the post, was one of England's finest ship designers. His skills had brought him to the personal attention of Charles I. In 1634 he made a toy ship on wheels for the four-year-old Prince Charles to trundle up and down the long gallery at St James's Palace. Before that he made for Charles's elder brother Henry a scale model of a ship of the line that was twenty-eight feet long. Since the sixteenth century the Pett family had harvested their own forest in Kent to supply the oak necessary for hewing into ships' keels.* They had sufficient surplus cash to invest in the slave trade.

---

* Today, Petts Wood is a suburb in the south-eastern London borough of Bromley.

Phineas and Peter were among those instrumental in creating the modern warship that fought the Dutch wars. In 1637 they had built the vast *Sovereign of the Seas* for Charles I at their dockyard at Woolwich. By then, the principal warships were growing so large that London became the chief provider of manpower, money and resources to build them.[8] Merchant ships were still built at dockyards all around England, Scotland and Ireland, but only the yards on the Thames or at Portsmouth were capable of constructing the new, super-large warships designed to deliver a devastating broadside to knock out enemy vessels without the messy business of having to board them first.

The scale of the new ships pioneered by the Petts was impressive. The *Sovereign of the Seas* weighed 2072 tons and her keel – from which sprouted a skeleton hewn from hundreds of mature English oak trees – measured 127 feet. Her main mast was 113 feet of Scandinavian spruce, with a main yard 105 feet long. Her guns were all forged of brass, arranged in three tiers to bring maximum firepower to bear on the enemy. On the top tier were forty-four guns, on the second tier thirty-four and on the lower tier twenty-two, making a hundred guns in all. To enable this great war machine to work required a complement of 850 mariners, officers and marines. Her stern was so richly carved and gilded, and her firepower so great, she was known to Dutch sailors as the Golden Devil.

Peter Pett went on to build the next generation of ships of the line, including the *Royal Charles*, then named the *Naseby*, at the family dockyard at Woolwich for the Parliamentary navy in 1655. Not only had the *Royal Charles* carried Charles II home from Holland in 1660, it took part in three actions against the Dutch in 1665–6. What must have truly irked the King was that this of all vessels was towed away by the Dutch and turned into a tourist attraction.* Pett, who had taken no part in the disastrous decision to mothball the fleet, but who had been involved in designing the hijacked flagship, was singled out to be made an example of.

A much more important figure than Pett was also forced to resign. The Lord Chancellor, the Earl of Clarendon, Charles's longest-serving and most senior courtier and statesman, was a much more prominent target than Pett. Though Clarendon had been against the war from the beginning, he was vulnerable. His view of the Crown was based on an Elizabethan model of monarchy advised by a close cabinet and moderated by Parliament. From the point of view of the absolutist Stuarts this was not an ideal model.[9] Indeed, Charles had expressed his disdain for it.[10] Clarendon had been Charles's advisor since the civil wars; he had developed a propensity to lecture, and Charles now found him irritating. For all his abilities as a politician, Clarendon had little social finesse and even less desire to bend with the wind. His final gaffe was to make public his animosity towards Barbara Palmer. From the moment Charles returned from Europe with Barbara in tow in 1660, Clarendon had made his feelings towards the courtesan clear, cutting her in court and instructing his wife to do the same. He underestimated the King's feelings towards Barbara, and when the opportunity presented itself to Charles, Clarendon discovered he was out in the cold. Within weeks of the Medway disaster, he was forced to resign. Facing impeachment on trumped-up charges in Parliament, he fled to France and wrote his memoirs.

Shortly afterwards, Nell Gwyn opened at the Theatre Royal in Sir Robert Howard's *The Duke of Lerma*. Howard was a

---

* The ship's ornate stern plate, bearing the British Royal emblem flanked by a gilded lion and unicorn, is today on display at the Rijksmuseum, Amsterdam.

member of the Country Party, the newly emergent anti-court faction later known as the Whigs. They were opposed to the pro-monarchist Court Party, later known as the Tories, and especially to the Duke of York. Nell played Maria, the put-upon daughter of the Duke, a 'Renaissance overreacher . . . unscrupulous'.[11] The King, as usual, went on opening night, accompanied by Samuel Pepys, marking the latter's rapid social rise.

Pepys thought the play could be conceived as a critique of the King and his relationship with the royal mistress. A more particular interpretation was that it was a veiled attack on the already disgraced Clarendon. In real life, the Duke of Lerma (1553–1625) had been a favourite of King Philip III of Spain who fell from grace and was stripped of his power. In the background to the power struggle lay Spain's bankruptcy during a war with the Dutch. There was one other odd contrast to be drawn: although Philip III was as religious as Charles was irreligious, both were seen as being discreditably detached from the day-to-day business of government.

If such parallels were intended, Charles overlooked them. He loved Nell and the play.

By the following year, 1668, the charred skeleton of St Paul's Cathedral still sat mouldering on Ludgate Hill. The intense activity as London was rebuilt around it sounded a reproof to the church authorities, who could not agree what to do with their ruined cathedral. Downstream, that reproof was echoed in the royal shipyards at Deptford and Woolwich as they resounded with the din of shipwrights working non-stop. Thanks to lessons belatedly learned after the disaster at Chatham, a naval rebuilding programme was instigated to make good the destruction. The King, passionate about all things nautical, took a personal interest.

A replacement for the *Royal Charles* was ordered and

launched. The *Charles II* exemplified the pinnacle of contemporary English naval design and firepower. With ninety-six guns, she was a first-rate ship of the line. A first-rater had the greatest number of guns the current state of naval architecture could accommodate. These huge ships, with their awesome firepower, were designed to take part in battles in which opposing fleets sailed in line astern towards one another until they formed two parallel lines. The theory was that at this moment the maximum number of cannons on each fleet could be trained on the enemy line. If tactics and luck were removed from the equation, the fleet with the greater firepower should win. Hence, English ships of the line became bigger and bigger.

London's shipyards had a lot of catching up to do. Although Dutch ships were smaller in size, the number of ships in the Dutch navy outnumbered that in the English fleet. The frenetic rebuilding programme would continue for several years.

Together with shipping losses following Dutch marauding, the war was costing London as well as the Exchequer dear. London merchant ships had to face the threat of interception by the Dutch navy in the North Sea and the Channel, as well as an explosion of Dutch and French piracy in the Caribbean. Merchants lost heavily and went bust. The Company of Royal Adventurers Trading to Africa collapsed. This was no small matter for the Stuarts. A great deal of the Duke of York's prestige rode on the company's ships, not to mention his reputation as a player in the world of London business. The trade in slaves continued, carried out by freelance captains and merchants prepared to carry individual risk and dodge Dutch warships on their way around Africa and up to Europe.

Meanwhile, the cathedral chapter made up its slow collective mind. A new cathedral should be built. Its design would be entrusted to the man they considered best equipped for the job. Dean Sancroft summoned his friend Christopher Wren to give him the news that he had permission to tear down and rebuild St Paul's. In his habitual way, Wren set to immediately to draw up plans.

Wren was instantly at loggerheads with the church hierarchy. The Dean, together with the chapter of St Paul's, wanted a recognisably English church with a Gothic spire. Wren wanted to build something never before seen in England, something echoing the architecture of ancient Rome.

If any of the church authorities wished to see what was in the mind of the man they had hired to rebuild their great church, they had only to travel sixty miles to Oxford, where Wren's first major building was nearing completion. The university had commissioned the Sheldonian Theatre for the express purpose of hosting its graduation ceremonies. It was like no other building in all England. It was U-shaped in plan, reminiscent of an ancient Roman theatre. From one angle it appeared akin to a mannerist Italian church designed by the sixteenth-century star Italian architect Sebastiano Serlio, from another it was a polygonal frenchified baroque confection topped by nine huge oval roof lights arranged in a semicircle around a cupola. It was as un-English as it was possible to be.

On 19 March 1669, Sir John Denham, Surveyor-General of the Royal Works, died at home, in his official residence in Scotland Yard at Whitehall Palace. He was fifty-four. John Webb, his able assistant, now aged fifty-eight, saw this as his long-awaited opportunity. He applied for the job he had in essence been doing for nine years. He had worked on designs for Somerset House, for a new palace at Whitehall, for another at Greenwich, and on various other royal works.

Again, Webb's hopes were dashed. This time he was beaten to the post not by a poet and courtier friendly with the King but by Wren, a man who had not so much chosen architecture as his profession but had it thrust upon him by the King. For Webb, who considered his life's work to be a continuation of the tradition of classical architecture stretching back through his patron and teacher Inigo Jones to Palladio and beyond, it must have been galling to see another younger man moving into the surveyor's apartments in Scotland Yard, though at thirty-seven Wren was hardly youthful. Within three years, Webb would follow Denham to the grave.

As surveyor, Wren's first royal commission was to design and build a replacement Custom House in the City. The new cathedral would have to wait a little longer. The Custom House was an important commission, for it was imperative to have a new home for this key provider for the Exchequer. With its site by the river inside the old walled city, it was also intended as a symbol of Charles's authority in the heart of the merchants' domain. Situated midway between London Bridge and the Tower, Wren's new classical Custom House would dominate the quayside where London's shipping was at its busiest. Its elegant eleven-bay central block, surmounted by the royal crest and flanked by two wings jutting forward towards the river, symbolised to anyone arriving in London by sea the power of the throne over all that took place in the city. And still the question about what to do with St Paul's hung over the city in the form of its burnt-out shell.

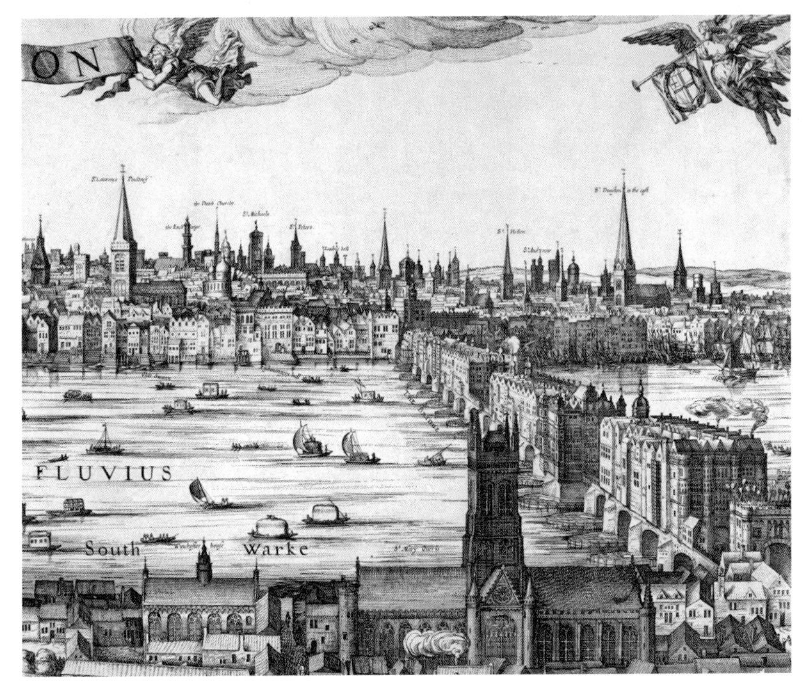

When Charles II returned to London on his thirtieth birthday, after an absence of eighteen years, he entered the ancient city by crossing London Bridge, begun in the twelfth century and partially financed by the sale of building plots on the bridge itself.

(© Heritage Images/Getty Images)

The Royal Exchange symbolised the financial strength of seventeenth-century London. Built in the sixteenth century, it was the city's centre of trade and commerce. Twice a day a bell summoned men of business to made deals, socialise and gossip.
(© British Library, London, UK/© British Library Board. All Rights Reserved/Bridgeman Images)

Samuel Pepys exemplified Restoration success: through patronage and skill he rose from the position of private secretary to become one of the most important figures in England, creating a modern navy and, as the guitar in this painting indicates, enjoying the many delights London had to offer. (© Getty Images)

Sir William Davenant was the foremost theatrical impresario of Restoration London. Running a theatre under a licence from Charles II, he helped restore theatre to London, brought opera to England, introduced the proscenium arch and developed innovative moveable scenery and effects – and all within eight years between the King returning and Davenant's own death in 1668.

(© Kean Collection/Getty Images)

The Duke of York's Theatre, also known as the Dorset Gardens Theatre, was London's first tailor-made theatre in the Restoration period. Although built after William Davenant's death, it contained all the innovations of stage machinery he wished for. The building itself was an example of the new fashion for baroque architecture, based on early classical Roman and Greek architecture. (© Mary Evans Picture Library)

One of the grandest streets in seventeenth-century London was Cheapside, lined by multi-storied medieval merchants' houses with their gables facing the street and filled with shops offering luxury goods from around the world. Foreign visitors remarked upon its grandeur. Along with most of old London, it would be destroyed in the fire of 1666. (© Mary Evans Picture Library)

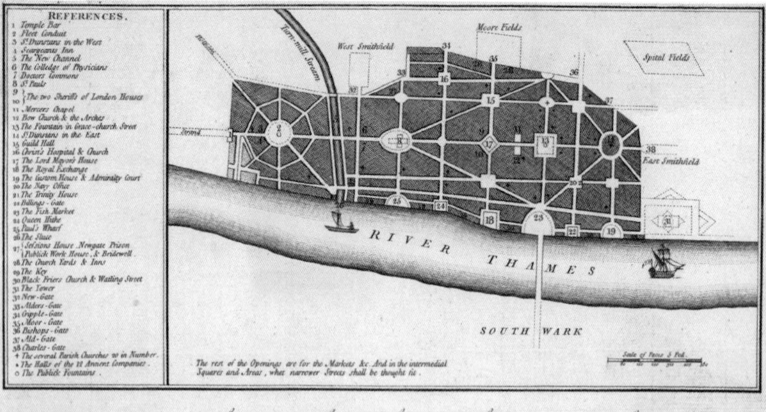

After the Great Fire of 1666, several plans were put forward to create an entirely new shape for London, built along rational, geometric lines. This plan was developed by Sir John Evelyn, a founding member of the Royal Society and a friend of the King. It bore a striking similarity to that proposed by his friend Sir Christopher Wren. Commercial and financial constraints meant that none of the new plans were implemented. (© Mary Evans Picture Library)

Nell Gwyn was not the first woman to grace the London stage after Charles relaxed the Puritan ban, but she was certainly the most famous. Her personality and wit allowed her to overcome many shortcomings as an actor, to the extent that the premier playwright John Dryden wrote parts expressly for her. Here she is seen with her two children, Charles and James, both fathered by the King, whose mistress she was for many years.
(© Mary Evans Picture Library)

What skills Nell Gwyn lacked, Elizabeth Barry, the foremost female actor of the Restoration stage, had in abundance. She was not only a talented comic actor but excelled in tragic parts. The actor-manager Thomas Betterton said of her that she could make a success of a play that would 'disgust the most patient reader'. (© Getty Images)

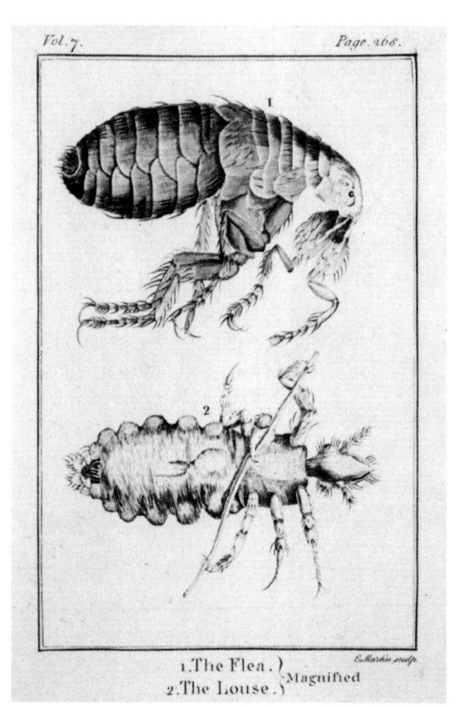

When the Royal Society published *Micrographia* by Robert Hooke in 1665, it caused a sensation. Its engravings of observations made under a microscope revealed a new world of discovery for Londoners. The illustration of a flea attracted particular attention. Little did Londoners know that this little creature was even then already carrying bubonic plague into the city. (© Mary Evans Picture Library)

Robert Boyle, a member of an aristocratic family in Ireland, was the first notable scientist of the Restoration. He formulated a law on the behaviour of gases and demonstrated the properties of a vacuum to the Royal Society, using his famous vacuum pump, made in collaboration with Robert Hooke and seen here in the background.
(© Mary Evans Picture Library)

Anthony Ashley Cooper seemed to have it all – an aristocratic lineage, a mansion by the Thames, a seat in the government and the foremost philosopher of the age, John Locke, as his in-house savant. But he fell out with Charles over the succession, founded the opposition Whig party and finally had to flee the country, accused of treason.
(© Universal Images Group/Getty Images)

Sir William Petty is the forgotten genius of the age. He rose from cabin boy to academic star, founder member of the Royal Society and man of wealth. He was a proto-economist and political philosopher of note who worked out how to estimate the wealth of a nation, creating GDP – gross domestic product – that rod for the backs of politicians ever since.
(© Mary Evans Picture Library)

Sir Christopher Wren's rebuilt St Paul's Cathedral was the finest building erected in England in the seventeenth century. Entirely alien to traditional English church architecture, it resembled not an Anglican cathedral but a great European Catholic basilica. The fact that Wren got away with it owed much to the patronage of Charles II.

CHAPTER 16

NEW TERRITORIES

While Wren worked up his plans for a Custom House that looked like a royal palace, an inconspicuous little ketch named the *Nonsuch* sailed up the Thames in October 1669, and anchored at Deptford. Its captain, Zachariah Gillam, and his most important passenger, a Frenchman named Médard Chouart des Groseilliers, had completed a remarkable assignment which would further enrich London and change the history of a huge expanse of the North American continent. Gillam and des Groseilliers brought a valuable cargo of furs, together with news that there was a vast sea in northern Canada surrounded by lands untrammelled by Europeans. The inhabitants, the Algonquin Indians, were friendly and eager to trade. The proof of des Groseilliers' claims was soon on the quayside for all to see: a cargo of fine beaver skins for which a London furrier paid the impressive sum of £1300.

The origins of the *Nonsuch*'s voyage lay in events years before, when des Groseilliers and his brother-in-law, Pierre-Esprit Radisson, fell out with French colonial officialdom in

Quebec. Des Groseilliers, a truly remarkable figure in the history of exploration, was piqued by official refusal to allow him to explore further north and west of French-controlled territory around Lake Superior. He went anyway, accompanied by Radisson, who was some twenty years his junior. During the winter of 1660–1 they endured great hardships, almost dying of starvation in particularly harsh conditions when heavy snow prevented even the Algonquin from hunting.

They returned to Quebec carrying a large quantity of furs and the knowledge from Cree traders of vast hunting grounds to the north-west of Hudson's Bay. For their pains, their furs were confiscated and, when they complained to colonial officialdom in France, found the official ear was deaf to both their discoveries and their complaints.

Dissatisfied with their reception in Paris, where their project was described as 'chimerical', the brothers-in-law decided to pursue British help. They went to Boston, where they hoped to receive backing for a further expedition into the Hudson's Bay area. Their plans were greeted with enthusiasm, but a voyage was aborted because of another unusually cold winter in which the bay was blocked with ice early in the season.

They obtained an introduction to Colonel George Cartwright, one of the King's commissioners sent to New England to resolve various colonial disputes. Cartwright saw what the French had been unable to appreciate: if new fur-hunting grounds were to be found west of Hudson's Bay and if – a big if – the bay offered a channel through to the Pacific, this was a project worth pursuing. He suggested that des Groseilliers and Radisson sail for London.

En route, Radisson began to write an account of his adventures, designed to persuade Charles II that he and his companion were men worth taking seriously. Radisson had an extensive knowledge of the vast region of Canada. He had spent many years travelling through it, ten of them with des Groseilliers, each journey taking two to three years, during which the pair endured extremes of hardship and danger. Radisson was an adroit linguist and spoke several native American languages. Among the great events he witnessed were the French-Iroquois war and the almost complete destruction of the Huron nation by the Iroquois. The most shocking of his personal experiences happened while he was out shooting duck with two friends. Surprised by an Iroquois raiding party, Radisson was taken prisoner. His friends were killed and beheaded. 'They shewed me their heads all bloody', he wrote. For over a year he remained a slave before escaping, being recaptured, suffering dreadful torture, finally escaping once more and making his way to a Dutch outpost and freedom. If such details were included in the account he proposed to present to Charles, they made a strange opening gambit from a man hoping for financial backing.*

The ship bearing Radisson and des Groseilliers arrived on the Thames in October 1665, at the height of the plague epidemic. The royal court had moved from Oxford to Hampton Court, and it was probably there that the travellers were introduced to the royal circle. Their account of untapped wealth in uncharted territory brought them introductions to Prince Rupert, the Duke of York and finally the King. The explorers were put up at the expense of the Crown and, with the support of the royal family, plans were drawn up for an expedition.

Hostilities with the Dutch forestalled any voyage until 1668. The first, exploratory voyage was a modest affair with two ships,

---

* It is not known how much of this Radisson wrote down in the first version of his memoirs given to Charles II, for the King's copy was lost long ago. What we have today is mainly compiled from a handwritten version owned by Samuel Pepys and discovered among the Pepys papers at Oxford in the nineteenth century.

the *Nonsuch* carrying des Groseilliers and the *Eaglet* carrying Radisson. The captain of the *Nonsuch*, Zachariah Gillam, was handpicked for the task. He came from a well-known family of New England shipbuilders. During a career at sea he had gained an excellent knowledge of the eastern American seaboard. Gillam was entrusted to represent the interests of the Crown, sailing with French adventurers who had demonstrated they could change sides at will.

In a storm off Ireland, Radisson's ship suffered damage and had to turn back. At a loose end in England, he continued writing about his expeditions and experiences among the indigenous peoples of North America, including accounts of battles between the French and their allies the Huron and Algonquin against the Iroquois.[1] As it has come down to us, his account does not have the air of a sales document designed to make the reader long for the discovery of the North-West Passage. It is much more than that: a gripping first-hand account of a key period in the history of European expansion into the New World and of great personal hardship and endurance. Radisson's account was very possibly extended at Charles's behest, for as we have seen the King had a keen interest in foreign adventures and exploration. Charles would have read Richard Hakluyt's celebrated *Voyages*, compiled the previous century. Now he had the opportunity to hold in his hands an account of exploration written by someone who, unlike Hakluyt, had actually been there.

The *Nonsuch* successfully completed its voyage across the Atlantic and sailed into the vastness of Hudson's Bay, all 1.5 million square miles of it. Des Groseilliers and Gillam made contact with the natives and explained their desire to trade. The winter was spent at the mouth of a river draining into the southern edge of Hudson's Bay, which they named the Rupert River. There they built a house, grandly naming it Fort Charles.

In the spring, native trappers fulfilled their side of the bargain and reappeared bringing a rich harvest of beaver furs. Gillam and des Groseilliers set sail for London. The faith put in the two Frenchmen by the London court had paid off handsomely.

News of the success of the voyage caused jubilation among its backers, not least among them the Duke of York and Prince Rupert. The obvious way forward was to form a joint stock company under a royal charter guaranteeing a monopoly to the company. Rupert lost no time in drawing up a document setting out the company's objectives:

> To undertake an expedition into Hudson's Bay to discover a passage into the South Seas and find a trade for furs, minerals and other commodities. The Governor and Company of Merchant Adventurers Trading into Hudson's Bay has sole rights to trade, power to get warships, to erect forts, make reprisals, exercise a monopoly, send home any unlicensed traders, declare war and peace.

Under the patronage of the Duke of York, the company had eighteen stockholders. Several of these were also investors in the Company of Royal Adventurers Trading to Africa, including Prince Rupert, the Duke of Albemarle, Lord Arlington, Anthony Ashley Cooper, Sir Robert Viner and Sir John Robinson. Charles signed the royal charter in 1670, and a second voyage was planned. This time, Radisson would accompany his brother-in-law to the forests of Canada they both knew so well and in which they had both gained and lost fortunes. The French and Dutch colonists were surprised to see them turn up in the pay of the British. In comparison to other joint stock companies, such as the powerful East India Company or even the beleaguered Company of Royal Adventurers, the Hudson's Bay Company was, to begin with, a small affair. For London and for Britain its significance could not have been greater.

The colonisation of foreign lands was key to London's prosperity and to Charles's vision of colonial might. Early pioneers, including Sir Walter Raleigh, had failed to establish colonisation as much more than an aspiration. Under James I the first colony in Massachusetts had been established not as an instrument of royal patronage but as an act of religious defiance in the face of royal decree. The English settlement of Virginia was a financial enterprise run by a joint stock company with royal backing to create what Richard Hakluyt, an investor in the venture, called 'a prison without walls'.[2] Under Charles I, Barbados and other islands developed as slave colonies. Charles II was keen to make his mark on the New World. Under his patronage, Carolina had been developed into a slave economy, its low-lying grasslands and swamps turned into paddy fields for cotton production.

The right of colonists to take over the lands of indigenous people such as those in Carolina was at least in part based on biblical interpretations. Sir Robert Filmer argued in his *Observations upon the Original of Government* (and would do so again later in *Patriarcha*) that God had made Adam the father figure of all humanity and that by descent humanity had ownership of all of the world.[3] This ownership was manifested through the divine right of kings. When the early European explorers arrived in the New World they noted that the indigenous people had a very different notion of land ownership from that pertaining in Europe. To European eyes, the land they encountered was held in common ownership, or even left as wilderness, rather than being farmed or cultivated in a system of individual ownership. The Europeans could not see the patterns of tracks and trails that denoted a landscape well understood and sustainably harvested by countless generations of people, nor could they understand collectively tended cornrows as agriculture. A divinely appointed European king, they felt, surely had the right to such lands.

The transition from common to individual ownership came through labour. The point was ingeniously argued, not least by Ashley Cooper's in-house philosopher John Locke in his *Second Treatise on Government*, published posthumously in 1689 though begun twenty years earlier.[4] Locke claimed that when God gave the earth to all people this did not constitute ownership. Ownership only came to those who worked the land. Since the inhabitants of Carolina and elsewhere were largely hunter-gatherers they did not own the land. If one were to search for a thesis that defined the essence of Protestant colonialism it would be hard to do better.

It is interesting that the King chose this moment to have his portrait painted in full armour. Up to now, Charles had chosen to have himself represented in regal clothes, sitting on a throne and wearing the insignia of the Garter. The new court portrait was another in a long line commissioned from Peter Lely. Many of these were copied by mezzotint artists and turned out as prints for London's burgeoning art market. Samuel Pepys had one of them, a portrait of Barbara Palmer, over his mantelpiece at the Navy Office. Many of Lely's court portraits were undistinguished, being largely worked up by assistants. The same state of affairs applied to his portraits of the King, being produced as gifts for supporters, foreign dignitaries and rulers. For this royal portrait, Lely tried something new. He would paint the King dressed as a soldier.

Anthony van Dyck had painted Charles I in full armour on horseback. Even though Charles II was more of a horseman than his father, Lely did not attempt such a feat. He knew he was no van Dyck. He painted the King three-quarter length, standing, bareheaded, wearing exquisite burnished black armour; the pose harks back to a portrait by William Dobson of the King as a boy wearing part of a suit of armour, with a page holding his helmet, probably at the beginning of the civil wars in 1642.

In the Lely portrait, Charles wears around his neck a gold chain and medallion, while around his waist a golden chain holds a ceremonial sword. In his right hand he bears a rod of office. His left hand rests on top of a helmet sitting on a plinth. Behind the helmet sits the King's coronation crown. The message is clear: here is a powerful king who will support his growing empire with arms if necessary. It is a shame that Lely diminished the effect by painting the King with an oddly lowered left shoulder, giving him a short upper arm. The hand on the helmet is therefore not so firmly planted. Perhaps it is well that this hand was not depicted resting on the crown.

For the indigenous peoples of Carolina the march of colonialism and mercantilism was a disaster. They resisted, in vain, what became a flood of migrants supposedly blessed by God. Far away, London-based investors including Ashley Cooper obtained an income from their colonial investments in Carolina, adding to London's mercantile wealth. Locke's ideas on labour, which became known as the labour theory of property, were to have a major influence on capitalist thinking.[5]

The Arab scholar Ibn Kaldun had done similar work in the fourteenth century, but his theories were unlikely to be known to London merchants in the seventeenth. Londoners may, however, have known of Thomas Aquinas's writings on the subject. Aquinas thought that value came from 'the amount of labour which has been expended in the improvement of commodities'.[6] A problem with the labour theory was that it concentrated on the value of goods, omitting the value of work done by those who, like doctors, administrators and official functionaries of all types, were not themselves goods, and whose services could not be so measured. It would be some time until a new breed of social researchers named economists put these theories to more rigorous testing.

As profits were made and capital accrued, questions were posited about how value actually came about. Without labour, it was argued, no profits were made. Labour could take many forms as long as it took account of the activity necessary to obtain, create or acquire goods and sell them. Thus labour came to be seen as the basis of profit. One of those who argued for this view of how wealth accrued was Sir William Petty, in work he published in the early 1660s.[7] His work was built upon by Locke and accorded Petty the right to be known as one of the many fathers of economics. Indeed, the value of land, measured by the cost of working it and selling the produce, became the comparative basis by which to measure the value of other things. In this way, a value could be put upon assets and the labour cost of setting them to work.[8] If Sir William had examined his own career more closely he would have recalled that another way to make money was to undervalue other people's land and sell it off at knockdown prices to others – and to oneself. This was what he had done with the expropriated land of Irish Catholics he surveyed in order that it could be sold to Protestant planters.

In general, Londoners were doing well. The city still smelt of sewers but peacocks strutted above the mire. John Evelyn described a gentleman of fashion he spotted at Westminster:

> It was a fine silken thing which I spied walking the other day through Westminster Hall, that had as much Ribbon on him that would have plundered six shops, and set up twenty

> country pedlars: all his body was dres't like a May-Pole ... the motion was wonderful to behold, and the colours were Red, orange and Blew, of well-gum'd satin.[9]

According to the brewer, importer and East India Company panjandrum Josiah Child, the lot of Londoners had improved greatly over the preceding fifty to sixty years:

> Gentlewomen in those dayes would not esteeme themselves well cloathed in a Searge Gown, which a Chamber-Maid will now be ashamed to be seen in: Whether our Citizens and middle sort of Gentry now are not more rich in Cloaths, Plate, Jewels, and Household Goods, etc. then the best sort of Knights and Gentry were in those dayes. And whether our best sort of Knights and Gentry now, do not exceed by much in those things the Nobility of England sixty Years past: Many of whom then would not go to the price of a whole Sattin Doublet.[10]

Child had made his fortune selling beer to the navy. John Evelyn described him as 'most sordidly avaricious' (this from a man whose family owed its fortune to gunpowder). Like many of those who had done well in London, Child lived outside the city, having built a huge hubristic estate at Wanstead Manor in Essex. Evelyn was most sniffy about it, though he was complimentary about an avenue of trees Child had planted. Child was intellectually capable and rose to be president of the EIC, running it as if it were his own.

The maintenance and expansion of trade, Child saw, depended upon the supply of money and the creation of conditions in which trade could prosper. He wrote widely on economic matters, relating in one pamphlet how all the ills of English trade could be ameliorated if only they copied their enemies, the

Dutch: 'The prodigious increase of the Netherlanders in their Domestic and Foreign trade, Riches and multitude of shipping, is the envy of the present, and may be the wonder of all future Generations.' He set out fifteen areas in which the Dutch might be imitated, taking in everything from the cost of shipbuilding to the sums charged by lawyers in commercial legal fees. Child thought it important for the good of business that wives should be as well educated in mathematics as their husbands, that the English should be thriftier, that inventors should be properly rewarded, and that merchants with experience in foreign trade should be brought into the government, rather than leaving it all to professional politicians.

Child had one specific message – that the cost of money was paramount in ensuring a nation thrived. Interest rates had declined during the preceding century or more, with the result that England was wealthier. But more was to be done. The Dutch, he said, lent money at 3 per cent, the rate rising to four in times of war. In England the rate stood at 6 per cent, with the King having to pay much more when hostilities began. If these rates could be lowered to match the Dutch rate, England's trade and wealth would increase. Child's opinions went beyond the narrow ambit of commercial interests to encompass some acute views on the nature of English society, marking him out as a keen social observer. Several of his observations remain valid today.*

As a major benefactor, Charles took a close interest in the East India Company. In 1670 he gave the company a new charter with many new rights. The company would be permitted to act

* For an excerpt from Child's fascinating pamphlet, containing a list of his observations and proposals, see Appendix IV.

like a sovereign state with its own army. It could acquire foreign territory, mint its own money, form alliances, make war, raise armies and exercise criminal and civil justice over its territories. This meant that foreign rulers had to deal directly with the company rather than with the Crown. It had become the first multinational, theoretically answerable to the Crown but in reality answerable to no one but itself. The company was to use these new powers with profound consequences for India.

As part of his dowry when he married Catherine of Braganza, Charles had received the Portuguese territory of Bombay. He now rented it to the EIC for £10 a year. It would become the most important property England had in the entire continent.

The EIC enforced its monopoly with fervour. Company agents dealt ruthlessly with 'interlopers' – merchants who tried to operate independently in the vast stretches of territory covered by the company's monopoly. The case of one particular merchant who fell foul of the monopoly rules became famous because it was fought through the courts and Parliament for so many years. London merchant Thomas Skinner began trading off Bengal in 1657. The following year, Skinner's ship, cargo and property were seized by EIC agents, his trading post was gutted and the merchant himself badly beaten and left destitute thousands of miles from home.

A few years later, Skinner reappeared in London and began a battle for restitution. In 1668 he seemed to have won when the House of Lords ordered the EIC to pay him £5000 in compensation. The Commons, which contained many EIC investors, promptly ordered Skinner to the Tower. In turn, the Lords, furious at the Commons' intervention, ordered the chairman of the EIC, Sir Samuel Barnardiston, to the Tower as well. A constitutional battle lasting years developed, the Lords arguing their prerogatives against those of the Commons. With neither side stepping down, the dispute reached the King. At first Charles seemed sympathetic to Skinner. But his sympathies ultimately lay with his financial interests in the EIC. In 1670 Charles ordered both houses to drop the case completely. One of the reasons given was that the case was taking up parliamentary time that should have been spent voting the King's supply – his state income. Charles could not have that. As a result, Skinner appears never to have received his compensation. He had tried to take on the might of the EIC and had learned that the company was not only a sovereign state abroad, but had friends in high places at home.*

* In 1694 an Act of Parliament would finally deregulate trade to India, meaning that any company could set up in business there. In practice the EIC continued to have almost total control, except for a parallel company briefly set up in opposition, which the EIC soon gobbled up by buying shares in it.

CHAPTER 17

LAW AND ORDER

In 1670, Parliament made two violent crimes punishable by death, neither of which up to then had been subject to serious punishment. The first was that of stealing people. People theft, or 'spiriting', remained a major form of organised crime in London, particularly around Thames Street and the docklands downstream. Although this aspect of London's underworld has been mentioned earlier, a description of this fascinating and pernicious trade is necessary here to fill out a proper description of London life.[1]

Spiriting began soon after the first colonies were established around the Chesapeake Bay area of America in the early seventeenth century. By 1645 the practice had become such a menace that Parliament ordered law officers to keep a watch for 'those stealing, selling, buying, inveigling, purloining, conveying or receiving children'. London's port officials were instructed to search all vessels 'in the river and the Downs for such children'.[2] These measures, and others that came after, made little difference.

The problem facing those who wished to stamp out spiriting was that it was no ordinary crime, carried out purely for the benefit of one or two lowly perpetrators. Spiriting was a shady low-life business with major benefits for the colonial project that had the patronage of the royal family. One authority has pointed out that spirits had an important function within the economic system of colonialism: 'instead of being deplorable outlaws in the servant trade they were faithful and indispensable adjuncts of its most respected merchants.'[3]

The stock-in-trade of the spirit was a plausible manner and a connection to the shipping business. The unwary would be tricked in one of several ways. They might be plied with drink and then locked up by the spirit's associate, who had access to a secure room in a dockside house or tavern. From there the poor victim would be taken by force to a ship and sold into slavery in the colonies. Other ruses involved a stranger striking up a conversation with the intended victim, who was then invited to look around a ship. Before they knew it, the ship was at sea and they were on their way to a new and brutal life. Some spirits used persuasion to get gullible people to sign up as indentured servants, in the belief that they were going to a better life rather than one of unremitting drudgery and possible death.

All ages and all types became prey for the spirits. An undated broadsheet told of the arrest and commitment to Newgate prison of 'The Grand Kidnapper', Captain Azariah Daniel. Under questioning, Daniel admitted to the spiriting of two missing twelve-year-old children who were found in his house, hidden in an attic. A second case, related in the same broadsheet, told of the disappearance of the son of a Mr Vernon of Stepney. Asking around, Vernon learned that a boy looking like his son had been seen in the company of a mariner called Edward Harrison. Having obtained a warrant from a magistrate, Vernon and a constable went to Harrison's house. No boy having been found, the suspect was questioned by the magistrate and confessed to having put him on board a ship bound for Barbados. He made the further sensational claim that besides the Vernon boy there were 'above a hundred and fifty more aboard several other ships in the said river [the Thames] bound to His Majesty's Plantations'.[4] The satirist Ned Ward, who visited the West Indies, painted a far from rosy picture of life in a sugar colony, describing Jamaica as 'The Receptacle of Vagabonds, the Sanctuary of Bankrupts, and a Close-stool for the Purges of our Prisons . . . as Hot as Hell, and as Wicked as the Devil'.[5]

Spiriting became progressively more widespread until attempts were made to try to stamp out the spirit trade. To no avail, a group of London merchants and aldermen petitioned Parliament to pass laws against the trade. In 1664 a plan was put forward to interview every emigrant for the colonies to ensure they were going of their free will. Nothing came of it. Finally, in 1670, Parliament made spiriting – 'any deceit or force to steal any person or persons with intent to sell or transport them into ports beyond the sea' – punishable by death.

The Act would not be applied. For example, a London spirit named Ann Servant was fined thirteen shillings and sixpence for putting a young woman named Alice Flax aboard a ship and selling her in Virginia. A horse thief would have been hanged. Four years later, two spirits who kidnapped a sixteen-year-old girl were fined twelve pence. The horrible fact was that spiriting had become an integral part of the plantation enterprise; too many London merchants, sea captains, plantation owners and others had too much at stake to effectively clamp down on the practice. Spirits were simply a fact of London life.

Ned Ward had gone to Jamaica because he was impoverished, unable to make a good living either by his humorous writing or as an occasional tavern keeper in London. He had arrived in the capital from Oxfordshire to find that without connections or an education of grammar-school level, life as a poet and satirist was hard. He soon joined the throng who felt the need to try their luck in the colonies. The necessity for, and eager supply of, new labour across the Atlantic gave rise to one of the first prolonged episodes of racketeering in British history. Those with the price of a one-way ticket could, like Ward, try their luck in the New World and either thrive – as he did – or not. Those without means could sign up to work their passage. In return for the price of their one-way ticket on a vessel to the West Indies or America, they would be sold to an estate owner as a labourer for a fixed period of four to seven years, after which they would be free to go their own way and make a living for themselves.

The system was open to abuse on an industrial scale. The trouble often began at the quayside in London's docklands. Those selling their labour for a passage to a new life could find themselves signed up with some very unsavoury people. This might only become apparent once the ship docked on the other side of the Atlantic. The poor immigrants would be lined up on the dockside to be bought and sold like cattle, and were often treated as such. They were owned life and soul by their master, who could sell them on, restrict their freedoms and mete out harsh punishments. Indentured servants could find themselves whipped and flogged, manacled, branded, starved, denied the right to time off, to marriage or even the company of the opposite sex, and punished for any misdemeanours by having their period of indenture lengthened. Freedom could become an unattainable abstraction. Servants, so-called, were often worked to death, their value reckoned as less than that of an African, for Africans cost more and had to be looked after for a lifetime of labour.[6]

The indentured servant racket spread out from London to Bristol and beyond, even reaching Ireland, so giving rise to the peculiar situation in which those who were already colonised might become part of the slave labour force for yet another new colony. The racket was only brought to a stop with the American War of Independence. Until then, it coexisted with the slave trade from West Africa.[7]

London's less lawful side extended into everyday life. Late on the night of 3 February 1664 Samuel Pepys was in his coach going up Ludgate Hill towards St Paul's Cathedral when he saw two men abduct a young female shopkeeper he knew by sight. He recorded the incident in the following terms: 'I saw two gallants and their footmen taking a pretty wench, which I have much eyed, lately set up shop upon the hill, a seller of riband and gloves. They seek to drag her by some force, but the wench went, and I believe had her turn served . . .'

In other words, Pepys watched two members of the upper classes, aided by their servants, abduct a female shopkeeper in order to rape her. Such was the attitude of upper-class men to lower-class women, Pepys did not feel shocked by the event. He was moved by it in an altogether different manner: 'and, God forgive me! what thoughts and wishes I had of being in their place.'[8] How telling was that phrase 'God forgive me!' – Pepys admitting his base envy of the men dragging off a woman he fancied.

The event does not reflect well on Pepys, who recorded no thought of intervening. In his defence, it is doubtful, should he have wished, that he could have materially changed the course of the assault. The problem lay not only with the prevalent attitude of men towards women, but also with the wider issue of law and order in seventeenth-century London. The upper classes were almost immune to censure by the law. There was no police force worthy of the name, only a few night watchmen, paid for by local parishes, and part-time parish constables, recruited from among the local population to serve on a rota system. The constables had power of arrest, but generally they played a passive role. The victim of a crime would have to go and find the constable to make a complaint. If the victim knew or could recognise the wrongdoer, the constable could act, either apprehending the alleged miscreant or reporting him or her to the magistrates, whose job it was to bring a charge and conduct a trial at court. One of the problems facing magistrates was that when it came to offences involving affray or violent disturbances, there was no Public Order Act.

When petty thieves were apprehended, it was often thanks to the 'hue and cry' whereby the victim and others would chase after the robber, shouting 'Stop, thief!' in the hope that other passers-by would catch the villain and hand him or her over to a constable. If the person involved was guilty of a petty offence such as pilfering, running away (by servants), begging, swearing in a public place or drunkenness, the constable would commit the perpetrator to the Bridewell prison. Every two or three weeks the Bridewell governors would meet and decide what to do with their new inmates. If their offence was minor they were often released, having already spent time in gaol.

The second Act of Parliament of 1670 to make a crime punishable by death was brought in specifically to prevent violent acts of revenge. Until then, such actions had not been seen as crimes at all. Hence, someone who had been publicly slighted or had their reputation damaged in some way could deliberately disfigure the offender, putting out an eye or cutting off an ear or nose, and get away with it. Until the notorious case of Sir John Coventry in December 1670, deliberate mutilation was not a felony. Coventry was an MP and the son of the wealthy politician and judge Sir Thomas Coventry of Croome Park, Worcestershire. On his way home to Suffolk Street, off Pall Mall, following a sitting of Parliament, Coventry was set upon by a group of royal guards officers who cut off his nose, apparently in revenge for a witty, derogatory remark he had made just a short time before in Parliament about the King.* The assailants escaped punishment. Enraged that one of its members had been assaulted, Parliament passed an Act making an assault that resulted in mutilation a felony, a capital offence punishable by execution. Once again, the law was seldom enforced.

A few weeks after the Coventry affair, in early 1671, an even greater public scandal erupted, involving the King's 21-year-old son, the Duke of Monmouth. The flashpoint was in Covent Garden, an area known for its brothels. Monmouth, accompanied by his friend the Duke of Albemarle and several other young aristocrats, tried to force entry to a brothel. It was said they wished to enact some form of revenge on a prostitute who had infected Monmouth and Albemarle with the pox (either gonorrhoea or syphilis). Perhaps they wanted to slit her nose, a common act of violence meted out to women accused of selling sex for money. The night watch was called. A fight broke out and most of the night watchmen fled, leaving one man pleading for mercy at sword point. The aristocrats ran him through.

The watchman's murder caused public uproar. Dryden penned some satirical lines:

---

* The debate, on a tax on the theatre, took place in December 1670. Sir John remarked that the King's only interest in the theatre was in actresses. The assault took place on 21 December. The King pardoned the assailants.

> T'was an injury beyond repair
> To clap a king's son and a great duke's heir.[9]

There was no question of punishing any of the perpetrators of this coldblooded crime. Charles called the watchman's death a 'sad accident' and issued a proclamation giving a 'gracious pardon' to Monmouth of 'all Murders, Homicides and Felonyes whatsoever . . .' To reassure the public that young aristocrats would not be allowed to run riot and kill ordinary people without redress, the King announced that the royal guard was ordered to help the watch in tackling wrongdoers 'whatsoever quality they be'.[10] This was a bit rich: it was the royal guard that had attacked Coventry.

There remained a general problem of energetic, often drink-fuelled, public misbehaviour or brawling by the upper orders. In such cases, the magistrates had limited powers. The pull of the aristocratic caste far outranked the magistrates' station, the latter usually being recruited from the gentry. The year before Pepys witnessed the abduction of the young shopkeeper, a less serious public disturbance illustrated the point. It took place in Bow Street in Covent Garden, a favoured haunt of those seeking a more easy-going and artistic form of life, a home to theatricals and poets, and because of its prostitutes a favoured night-time carousing spot for young bloods of the better families. Bow Street, so called because of its shape, curving in a bow in a north-westerly direction from Russell Street at its southern end, was developed on former estate lands of the Earls of Bedford. The west side was developed first in the early to mid-1630s, work carrying on at roughly the same time as the 4th Earl was developing his new Covent Garden piazza a hundred yards to the west. The east side was developed by 1640, three years after the completion of Inigo Jones's gracious piazza, making the area a desirable one in which to live.[11] But Bow Street never became the fashionable residential street for the upper classes it was designed to be. By the 1660s it was a street of mixed use and quality, comprising housing, shops and taverns. One of the watering holes frequented by the 'Wits', a band of well-born young men who considered themselves arbiters of manners with a licence to thrill, was the Cock Tavern.

One summer evening several young 'gallants' went drinking in the Cock. They included Charles Sackville and Sir Charles Sedley, the rakes we met earlier when they took Nell Gwyn off to Epsom. These men were no longer callow youths, Sedley and Sackville both being twenty-four years of age. Sedley was embarking upon an active political life, while Sackville was fully employed at the royal court as one of the 'Merry Gang', the King's unofficial jesters and entertainers. On this evening the friends, blind drunk, decided to entertain the people in the street. They went onto a balcony and mimed various positions of sexual intercourse. Then they took off their clothes and performed stark naked for the gathering crowd. Sedley dipped his penis in his glass and then drank the health of the King, whereupon rioting broke out.

Brought to court, Sedley was found guilty of lewd behaviour and bound over to keep the peace. Who knows what fate might have befallen a person of lesser rank – beheading or transportation for treasonous behaviour? Sackville and another pal were let off with cautions.

A more serious incident involving Sackville had occurred in Covent Garden a year before. Together with his brother Edward, he and several friends killed a working man by the name of Hoppy in a street fight, claiming afterwards they thought he was a robber. Given the rank of the assailants, they were found not guilty. Even the Earl of Rochester, no stranger to drunken escapades, wondered aloud to the King how Sackville was able to get away with so much. For a man who had spent time in the Tower because of his own bad behaviour, this was no idle musing.

One of the most notorious events of the 1660s involved Rochester's friend, fellow member of the 'Merry Gang' and de facto first minister of the government, George Villiers, Duke of Buckingham, who had been reconciled with the King since Charles snubbed him at Dover. Buckingham embarked upon an affair with Anna, Countess Shrewsbury in 1668. When her husband discovered the affair he challenged Buckingham to a duel. Word of the challenge reached the King, who made it clear that the duel should not go ahead. The duel was nevertheless held, discreetly, outside London on Barnes Common, across the River Thames from the Bishop of London's estates at Fulham.

Tempers ran so high that the duel developed into a general fight. Buckingham ran Shrewsbury through the chest, fatally wounding him.* One of Buckingham's seconds, a man named Jenkins, was killed. Another second, Captain Sir Robert Holmes (the naval commander and leader of expeditions to Africa), seriously wounded Sir John Talbot, one of Shrewsbury's men. Because of Buckingham's status and closeness to the King, the duel caused uproar in London. Samuel Pepys confided to his secret diary that the world would think less of the King 'when the Duke of Buckingham, the greatest man about him, is a fellow of no more sobriety than to fight about a whore' and hoped the duel would spell the end of Buckingham's political career.[12]

The King chose not to act against his friend. No censure was

---

* Twenty years later, Shrewsbury's second son was killed in a duel by Charles II's illegitimate son Henry Fitzroy.

brought to bear on Buckingham, and within weeks he appeared in public at the state opening of Parliament. Charles's only reaction was to issue a proclamation that in future no one who killed another person in a duel would be pardoned.

These few instances of crimes involving the uppermost layers of society illustrate how extremely lax was law and order in London. In a city of almost 400,000 inhabitants, where the influx of newcomers was fast outstripping its fearsome infant mortality rate, crime was a popular subject for gossip. Like city dwellers everywhere, Londoners loved to read about it in books and newssheets. In this way, crime paid. Among those it paid were Henry Marsh and Francis Kirkman, London-born booksellers, writers and publishers with a shop at the sign of the Prince's head in Chancery Lane. Within a few years of the Restoration they published a novel entitled *The English Rogue*. It was written by Richard Head, who was born in Ireland, possibly a parson's son, and educated at Oxford University.

Head had a weakness for gambling. It haunted his life. While dodging his creditors between Ireland and England, he took up writing satirical and humorous works.[13] When his writing did not pay sufficiently, he settled in London, where he became a bookseller. But with *The English Rogue*, Head finally attained the success he longed for. The censor Roger L'Estrange initially turned the book down for being too lewd for publication. With some revisions, it was licensed and published by Henry Marsh. What seemed a small event in the London book trade, the publishing of an amusing tale for popular enjoyment, was in fact no less important than concurrent developments taking place on the London stage.

In Richard Head's invention can be seen sprouting the early shoots of the English novel form. Indeed, *The English Rogue* has a very good claim to be the first English novel. It first appeared thirteen years before the more usual contender for the title, John Bunyan's *Pilgrim's Progress*, well before another contender, Aphra Behn's *Oroonoko* in the mid-1680s, and several decades before Daniel Defoe's *Robinson Crusoe* (1719).

Claims that earlier works, including the prologue to Chaucer's *Canterbury Tales*, or Thomas Malory's retelling of ancient fables in *Le Morte d'Arthur*, could be characterised as novels are surely fanciful. Quite why *The English Rogue* has been so regularly overlooked, however, is hard to fathom. Perhaps its bawdy, amoral content or the fact that its narrative form was rather slight, being essentially a collection of interlinked adventures, are to blame. There can be little doubt, however, that *The English Rogue* was an important progenitor to Defoe's much later runaway success, *Moll Flanders*.[14]

The book, told in the first person, purported to be the reminiscences of a highwayman and thief named Meriton Latroon.[15] It cannot in any way be claimed as a major work of literary fiction shaped as a memoir; London would have to wait for Defoe's *A Journal of the Plague Year* (1722) for that. But both books to some extent depended upon the claimed experiences of the narrator: in the case of Head, his experiences in Ireland during the uprising of 1641; in Defoe's, his childhood memories and those of his family during the plague. At any rate, *The English Rogue* was so successful that when Henry Marsh died shortly after publication Kirkman immediately republished the work. When the new edition sold well, a second volume of Meriton's memoirs appeared, the title page proclaiming that Head was still the author, along with Kirkman. Third and fourth volumes followed.

Head disowned his co-authorship of the later versions. He may have continued to be involved; we don't know. But the four books' racy style, allied to an endless sweep of outrageous escapades, amused an audience well used to the proximity of the darker side of city life. A major part of the books' attraction was that they contained many sexual encounters, exhibiting as much variety as the author could manage. Among tales of thievery and getting-away-with-it, the books included handy hints on how to evade robbery by highwaymen or mugging in the city. A few years later a sequel appeared in which the rogue was no longer English but French; it was written anonymously, though some scholars still see in it the hand of Richard Head.[16]

So many crimes were labelled a felony that the hangman was kept busy. The full application of the law in so populous a city meant large-scale executions of poor, hungry and mainly law-abiding people on a depressingly regular basis. There was one way of avoiding the death penalty. First-time offenders could claim 'benefit of clergy' so as to receive a lesser sentence, or none at all. This unofficial 'right' had developed out of an ancient dispensation for priests, who could be tried by an ecclesiastical court rather than a civil one. Over time, it had become adapted to the civil world, so that anyone charged with a first offence could ask for and expect leniency.

The law did not treat men and women equally in this matter. Though women were given the right to claim benefit of clergy in 1624 if they were accused of stealing goods valued at less than ten shillings, a man could claim the same right for goods up to forty shillings.* The distinction mattered a great deal, for in the mid-1600s there were no fewer than fifty crimes (including all types of theft, murder, witchcraft and treason) that merited the

---

* The law was changed to give parity to the sexes in 1691. Benefit of clergy was abolished in 1823.

death sentence, and benefit of clergy was available for most types excluding witchcraft and treason.

When it came to crimes of immorality, a healthy strain of hypocrisy characterised the treatment of the differing social classes. Men and women could be tried and sentenced for being a bawd (i.e. a pimp, or one who solicits sex from another to be sold to a customer) or a prostitute. Despite this, the King's servant William Chiffinch was widely known as the 'king's whoremaster', since among his many duties was that of soliciting girls for his master. Several members of the court also pimped for the King, among them his childhood friends the Duke of Buckingham and Baptist May. Charles was also widely rumoured to be a client of Madame Creswell's infamous brothel in the docklands, east of the City walls. It is unlikely that he frequented Madame Creswell's in person, the more likely scenario being that girls were sent for and brought up the river in a wherry to alight at night at a private jetty. From there they would be taken up a staircase that led directly into private rooms presided over by Chiffinch and adjoining those of the King. But to accuse Chiffinch – or Buckingham – of being a bawd would have been unthinkable.

For the petty criminal, meanwhile, London was a magnet. Shops displayed every conceivable kind of merchandise. Cornhill was lined with the premises of goldsmiths and silversmiths, Thames Street was lined with merchants' warehouses containing valuable goods from across the world, and the increasingly well-to-do merchant classes carried money, gold watches and jewellery. All this gave plentiful opportunity for the different varieties of thief to exercise their skills. A look through the records for the Middlesex Assizes and the Old Bailey shows that the majority of cases were of theft. For the Londoner with money in his or her purse, pickpockets were a constant curse.

But the most feared of all London's thieves were the footpads. These were armed robbers who worked mainly at night in the city's ill-lit streets and alleyways. If a victim proved slow to hand over money, the footpad would rarely hesitate to use extreme violence.

To deal with its crime, London had an assortment of law enforcement officers employed by the parishes. While primary enforcement was haphazard, the penalties were not. Almost any crime perpetrated by an ordinary person could result in the death penalty. Death in exchange for a silk handkerchief was not out of the question.

According to John Graunt, London's murder rate was surprisingly low. In one of the years whose bills of mortality he followed, 1632, there were just seven recorded murders in London. In an entire twenty-year period for which Graunt compiled figures, out of 229,500 deaths only eighty-six were due to murder, making an average of 4.3 per annum. Against this, Graunt compared London to Paris, where 'few nights scape without their Tragedie'.[17]

Graunt explained the low murder rate as being down to two factors. The main one was that Londoners policed themselves on a local level, with constables paid by the parishes. This, he said, led to 'no man settling into a trade for that employment' (i.e. murder). The second reason had more to do with Graunt's view of his own nature and that of his fellow-countrymen, who had 'a natural and customary abhorrence of that inhumane crime, and all bloodshed by most Englishmen'. There might possibly be other reasons, of course; among them that the murder rate was under-reported and that Graunt, like all good patriots, overestimated the pacific nature of his own tribe and the lawlessness of foreigners.

Hangings took place at Tyburn, a village to the west of

London where a permanent 'hanging tree' stood to remind anyone travelling in or out of the city, to or from Oxford, Bristol and all points west, of the penalty for an enormous range of crimes. Prisoners to be hanged would be taken from Newgate prison, next to the Old Bailey, west via the Oxford Road (today's Oxford Street) to Tyburn. Hence to be hanged was to have 'gone west'. Executions became a form of entertainment for the poor; on hanging days, huge crowds made their way out of London to Tyburn. Prisoners were taken from Newgate by cart and when they reached the gallows they would often make a speech before they died. The crowds expected it.*

There was one way of evading the noose: transportation to the colonies. In the 1600s the new colonies in the Leeward Islands and Virginia were voracious in their need for workers. The slave trade alone was not sufficient, even when augmented by the iniquitous indentured servant business and the quasi-legal spiriting trade. The cash crops of Virginia and of islands like Barbados required enormous numbers of new workers. The attrition rate in the harsh climate was heavy, abetted by the equally harsh treatment of the majority of the workforce, whether black or white. Working conditions were brutal. There was no health care for the workers, who were treated as chattels, bought and sold like animals. The transportation of criminals had the dual advantage of reducing the prison population at home and increasing the cheap labour force in the colonies.

Sometimes those sentenced to hang were offered the option of transportation. Thus in the Old Bailey records we find petty crimes rewarded with a harsh lifetime in the colonies, as in the case of a woman apprehended by a night watchman while

* So began the tradition of Speaker's Corner, at the north-east corner of Hyde Park.

stealing a silver tankard from a victualling house and sentenced to transportation.[18]

For the many Londoners who lived on the very margins of existence the experience of law and order was a brutal one. Minor offences could result in the offender spending several days in the stocks, where treatment by the elements and at the hand of their fellow citizens could be pitiless. Homelessness itself was a crime, which could send the offender to a foreign land. For those attracted to London's promise of better things but who somehow did not make the grade, forced into living life on the fringes, the gap between their fragile day-to-day existence and extinction at the end of the hangman's rope was a narrow one.

CHAPTER 18

A SPY IN THE FAMILY, THE COURT AND THE THEATRE

On 1 June 1670, a secret treaty was signed between Charles II and Louis XIV.

Even Anthony Ashley Cooper, Charles's Chancellor of the Exchequer, knew nothing about it. According to the secret terms, Charles agreed to help Louis's expansionism in Europe, to renounce the Anglican faith, to become a Catholic and make England a Catholic country. In return, Louis would bankroll Charles, enabling him to rule without having to recall Parliament to raise taxes for the Exchequer. Charles received an initial payment in excess of £100,000, scarcely enough to keep the coming war effort running for a month or two. As a cover, a second, public treaty was prepared and signed, leaving out the highly contentious clauses regarding Catholicism. The ever-willing Duke of Buckingham negotiated it, remarking afterwards how easy it had been to achieve agreement.

The go-between in negotiations for the treaty was Charles's

younger sister Henrietta Anne. Not only was Henrietta – known affectionately to Charles as Minette – so close to her brother that he had trusted her to channel money to the kidnappers and assassins sent out to track down his father's regicides; from her teenage years, she had been au fait with the ways of espionage and secret deals. With regard to the secret Anglo-French treaty she was the sole emissary between the two cousins, the kings of France and England.* This placed the 26-year-old princess at the heart of one of the most extraordinary secret deals ever transacted between two countries. If word of it had leaked out, it could have led to the end of the House of Stuart.

Apart from Minette, the only others who knew of the treaty on the English side were two government ministers, Henry Bennet, Lord Arlington, who had been bribed by Louis with a gift of 10,000 crowns to his wife, and Thomas, 1st Baron Clifford, a Roman Catholic. The deal was kept secret from other members of the government. That Charles was willing to gamble so much on such shaky foundations said a good deal about his character and state of mind. He was willing to be reckless at the prospect of freeing himself from Parliament's financial reins.

As for his promise to declare himself a Catholic and make England a Catholic country, the treaty specified no time frame. Charles could take his time over the former, while he knew the latter would be impossible. There has been much speculation regarding Charles's intentions regarding the provisions of the treaty. One interpretation is that Louis was prepared to allow him to backslide as long as he was firm on his support of French expansion in Europe – and that Charles was prepared to say anything in order to receive an income stream from France.

---

* Charles's mother Henrietta Maria was the daughter of Henry IV of France; Louis XIV was Henry's grandson.

When in England negotiating the treaty, Minette brought with her as a lady-in-waiting the beautiful young Breton noblewoman Louise de Kérouaille. She wrote to her brother about her, saying she would be an ornament to the court at Whitehall. Charles took the hint, and so arrived a woman whose role was not only to please the King of England but to report back to the King of France. Within a year, Charles and Louise would become lovers; at the same time, Louise kept the French ambassador informed of developments at court.[1]

On 20 September 1670, the autumn season opened at the King's Company with a play by a new, untested author. *The Forc'd Marriage* was a run-of-the-mill tragicomedy featuring the tried-and-tested formula in which lovers denied the objects of their true affections were finally united, after many hiccups, and all ended well. The play, though as flawed as any first effort by a new writer might be, was a success, playing to full houses and making money for both players and writer.

What was most noteworthy, though, was that its author was a woman, one of the first professional female writers for the English stage. Equally remarkable were the circumstances that led her to take up writing.

The author's name was Aphra Behn; today that name is of some renown but for centuries it lay in obscurity. Her early life is far from well understood. It is thought she was born in Harbledown, Kent, on 14 December 1640, the younger daughter of Bartholomew and Elizabeth Johnson, née Denham. She was christened Eaffrey.[2] Around 1663 Johnson, his wife and two daughters set sail for the English colony of Suriname, on the north-eastern coast of South America. The reason for this journey to a small and insignificant colony is unknown, though it is thought Johnson may have been given some minor appointment. At any event, he seems to have died during the voyage.

English settlers had founded the little agricultural settlement in Suriname only ten years before. The executive force behind the enterprise was one Captain Marshall, who founded a colony on a river that became known as Marshall's Creek. The planning and money for the settlement came from Francis Willoughby, 5th Baron Willoughby of Parham, a professional colonial administrator and adventurer who became governor of Barbados. Suriname was sometimes known as Willoughby Land. The settlers depended upon cash crops such as tobacco, sugar and cotton that could be shipped back to England via other colonies around the West Indies.

At some stage, possibly as early as 1663, Aphra, now a young woman of twenty-three, had a relationship with William Scot, an English sugar planter and anti-monarchist who had fought on the Parliamentarian side during the Civil War. Their relationship was mentioned in letters from a colonial official. It has been suggested that Behn was engaged in Suriname on espionage for the Crown, having previously met Thomas Killigrew, who did intelligence work for Charles II before the Restoration.[3] Whatever the truth of the matter, Behn left the colony the following year, accompanied by her mother and elder sister.

Back in England, possibly in London, life was equally difficult for the independently minded young woman. She seems (for all details of her early life are sketchy) to have married a merchant of German extraction named Johann Behn, but either the marriage did not last or she merely took on the title as protection in a cruel and cynical city. Almost all doors were closed for a woman without means except for those of drudgery in domestic service, or of prostitution, either of the basest type in a brothel or in its more elegant form of being kept by a wealthy man. Prospects did not look good for Aphra Behn. She turned once more to spying.

In 1666 the King's spymaster, Joseph Williamson, instructed Behn to go to Antwerp. Her orders were to rekindle her affair with William Scot, the exiled Cromwellian officer who was now serving in an English regiment of the Dutch army. Scot was the son of an executed regicide, Cromwell's spymaster, Thomas Scot, and as such had considerable status among expatriate anti-monarchists living on the continent. If Scot could be persuaded to spy for the King, it would be a huge advantage for the London government, which was in fear of an invasion launched by the many Cromwellians at large in Europe. Scot had been ordered home under the dubious terms of the King's amnesty for enemies of the Crown living abroad. Other parliamentarians had returned and been executed. Scot wisely ignored the invitation. Behn, codenamed Astrea (after a Greek goddess of goodness and virginity), was under orders to ensure Scot complied with the order to return, or at least to persuade him to become an agent for the King.

Behn was an efficient agent and seducer. In August she reported that Celadon (Scot's codename, possibly after the river mentioned in Homer's *Odyssey*) was 'extremely willing to undertake the service'.[4] Scot subsequently provided intelligence on the Parliamentary and anti-royalist officers in Holland. He wrote reports not only for Behn, but also directly to Charles's spymaster Joseph Williamson, ultimately reporting that the chances of an invasion were fizzling out.

Scot was rewarded for his work, pardoned and allowed to return to England. Behn was not so lucky. From Holland she wrote to the Secretary of State, Lord Arlington, informing him she was broke and required money to pay her debts and travel home. Arlington abandoned her to her fate. After borrowing money from a moneylender in London, Behn managed to return there, to discover the King was not inclined to pay her any time soon. Unable to repay her loan, and threatened with imprisonment for her debts, she turned to her old friend Thomas Killigrew, imploring him to find the money to save her, writing, 'Sir, if I have not the money tonight you must send me something for I will not starve.'[5] Whether she spent any time in prison is unknown. She may have been saved by court connections such as Killigrew, though he himself was always scrounging for money and favours from the King.

And so, shortly after, began the professional playwriting career of Aphra Behn, one of the most colourful characters of the Restoration, her writing born out of necessity. She used the pen name Astrea – what else? – producing poetry and prose of variable quality, along with an acclaimed semi-autobiographical novel, *Oroonoko*, set in Suriname. The novel's main protagonist, the eponymous Oroonoko, is an enslaved African prince of the Fon people from West Africa, as a result of which the book has been lauded as an early anti-slavery text. In fact, the text reveals an attitude that, far from opposing slavery, deplores the enslavement of Oroonoko solely because he is of royal blood. Indeed, Behn depicted Oroonoko as a member of a slave-trading nation, which in historical fact traded slaves to the Dutch and then the English.* The work thereby reinforced prevalent attitudes regarding slavery while extolling the merits of monarchy. The descriptions of Oroonoko's male perfection, meanwhile, were designed to ensnare a female readership. An openly female point of view was groundbreaking in the history of English literature.

Whatever the merits of Behn's poetical and prose writings, the

* The Fon were the majority group of the ancient kingdom of Dahomey, modern-day Benin.

only kind of writing that could provide a living wage in the 1600s was that for the theatre. Dryden had been forced by necessity to turn away from his great love of epic poetry to writing for the stage. Now Behn also turned to the theatre for a living.

So when Thomas Killigrew entrusted the opening of his new season to *The Forc'd Marriage* by an unknown playwright he was taking a risk – but one which, if it came off, would repay him handsomely. The play's prologue played up its novelty value, proclaiming the pseudonymous writer not only to be a woman, but one with wit as well as beauty to charm the male audience in this, her first play. The prologue warned the gallants in the audience to beware the new armaments and stratagems women would wield, along with beauty and charm, in order to their 'lives invade':

> Today one of their party ventures out,
> Not with design to conquer, but to scout.
> Discourage but this first attempt, and then
> They'll hardly dare to sally out again.[6]

The prologue went on to give a clue to the writer's past profession:

> The poetess too, they say, has spies abroad
> Which have dispersed themselves in every road,
> I'th' upper box, pit, galleries, every face
> You'll find disguis'd in a Black Velvet Case.*

There had been other female Restoration dramatists before Behn. Frances Boothby was the very first woman whose work

* A reference to the fashion for women to attend the theatre wearing masks.

was produced on the London stage, her *Marcelia, or, the Treacherous Friend* having been put on by the King's Company the year before, in 1669. Even earlier, the renowned poet Katherine Philips's translation from the French of Corneille's *Pompée* appeared in published form in London, though it was only ever performed at the Smock Alley Theatre in Dublin. Behn, however, was to have a much more serious and prolonged career writing for the theatre. Over a period of seventeen years, nineteen of her plays were performed and she probably had a hand in many more. Only Dryden would have as many plays produced. Behn became a renowned writer, though as was the way with the financial ups and downs of stage writing, she never made much money. She did, however, become part of the racy set that included court wits and society rakes, most notably John Wilmot, 2nd Earl of Rochester, together with notable figures of the theatre including Nell Gwyn.

Of the many stories surrounding Gwyn, there is one that includes Behn. It was said that Gwyn, anxious to sabotage Moll Davies, her actress rival for the ardour of the King, obtained a laxative from Behn. Gwyn then baked the laxative into cakes which she fed to Davies before the latter's tryst in the royal bedchamber. According to the anonymous wits reporting royal scandal in the city's chapbooks, the cakes did their work. Davies was ejected from the royal bed in favour of Gwyn.

Behn credited the Earl of Rochester with helping her with her poetry. Rochester had all the credentials. He was witty and occasionally capable of excellent versifying himself; moreover, like many of his class and predilections, he had an ardent interest in the theatre. When Behn created a successful line in sexually explicit poetry and drama, the guiding hand of Rochester might be discerned, for he wrote some of the most outrageously bawdy verse ever conceived. Several of Behn's risqué poems were at first attributed to Rochester, including one in which a tree comments on the love-making taking place beneath its boughs. Behn's plays contained character studies of rakes of a type exemplified by Rochester. In one of her poems, Behn described Rochester as 'sweet' and 'gentle', perhaps revealing her feelings towards him, and incidentally revealing also something of the notorious rake's amorous technique.[7] When he died, she wrote his eulogy.

Behn believed the individual should be permitted to express him- or herself, free of conventional restraint. The hedonists of London were often boorish, but some were serious proselytisers for a new way of life. Among them were exponents of the dramatic arts sufficiently skilled to bring a vision of glittering, amoral existence, unconstrained by the Church, into life on the stage. But the presence there of female players brought something more to the theatre than their sex: it offered playwrights the chance to develop and create female characters who could exhibit emotional depth, something that had been lacking before. With this came the opportunity for playwrights to introduce major characters from lowly walks of life – harlots, orphans and even rape victims – whose representation would have been unthinkable before.

No one exemplified this new acting talent better than Elizabeth Barry. After several so-so performances, she learned her craft, becoming to tragic acting what Nell Gwyn was to comedy (though Barry could also do comedy). When she first appeared for the Duke's Company, aged seventeen, Barry had been so bad she was fired. Then something happened to turn her into the finest actress of the age. As recounted earlier, it has been said she was coached by Rochester; at all events, they had an affair lasting five years, resulting in a child. (Barry had another child by the playwright 'Gentle George' Etherege, feted following the great success of *Love in a Tub*, which had introduced that staple of Restoration comedy, the sparring repartee between would-be lovers, later to be refined by Dryden.)

Barry achieved the art of portraying pathos so realistically that audiences were deeply moved. 'In the Art of exciting Pity,' wrote the actor-manager Colley Cibber, 'She had a Power beyond all the Actresses I have yet seen, or what your Imagination can conceive.'[8] Unlike so many players of her time, Barry had a remarkably successful career, financially as well as artistically. She was one of the few actors of the period whose skill could rescue a bad play.

At this stage, still in the early flush of her career, having been acting professionally for two years, Barry starred in Behn's greatest success, *The Rover*, which was clearly an adaptation of Killigrew's earlier play *Thomaso, or The Wanderer*. Plays at this period were freely adapted from earlier works; nevertheless, Behn was accused in print of plagiarism. In an epilogue to the published version of *The Rover*, Behn admitted using Killigrew's story but insisted that the characters and dialogue were all her own.[9] Nor was Killigrew among the accusers – he had probably suggested to the young playwright that she take his successful play as a model.

The play was an enormous improvement on Behn's earlier work. It heralded her triumphant return to the theatre after a fallow period of three years following the failure of her play *The Dutch Lover*. Behn's standard contract with the King's Company allowed her the box office receipts every third night. The new play's success allowed her to gain a precarious and fleeting financial independence during a career that was by its episodic nature economically fragile.

The plot of *The Rover* revolved around the amorous exploits of several Englishmen and a group of young Spanish noblewomen in the kingdom of Naples. At the centre of the first group is a cynical, rakish sea captain named Willman. The name Willman sounded very like Wilmot, Rochester's family name.

At the heart of the other group is Hellena, determined to experience love before her brother puts her in a convent. The interplay between Willman and Hellena ensured that the play struck a chord with its audience in more ways than one. Restoration audiences had come to expect a rather monochrome cynical tone from their heroes and heroines; now it seemed they also had to expect whole sections of dialogue that were almost replicas of one another. While Behn admitted reworking a play by her mentor Killigrew, her central characters bore more than a passing resemblance to those in Dryden's *Maiden Queen* of three years earlier.

To a London society audience, none of this mattered very much. If the play's sentiment chimed with the tenor of the times, the audience would lap it up. In the final scene, Willman tells Hellena, 'Marriage is as certain a bane to love, as lending money is to friendship'. Given that divorce was almost impossible, and that marriages were made for monetary and dynastic reasons, there could be no escape from an unsuitable match. The play's sparring lovers conclude that if they wish to be together they have no other course. When Hellena seems about to rebuff Willman's advances, he asks for one kiss. She replies: 'One kiss! How like my page he speaks; I am resolved you should have none for asking such a sneaking sum.' To which Willman replies: 'I adore thy humour and will marry thee.'

The lovers do not agree to marry because they believe in the sanctity of the institution or that sex should occur only in marriage – they do so because they have no option. For Hellena to avoid being forced into a convent by her brother she must marry Willman. For Willman to be with Hellena he must marry her. Behn brought to the theatre the recurrent theme that the heroine should be free to choose for herself, to give free expression to her sexual desire and decide the course of her life.

Women who worked in Restoration theatre had a social licence not granted to other working people: they could lead a bohemian existence. Like Behn, they could have sex outside marriage, or, like Elizabeth Barry, they could have children out of wedlock and yet retain their reputation, if only of the professional kind; there was undoubtedly a personal price to pay. Women in the theatre attracted a great deal of critical attention from the (male) satirical writers in the newssheets. Actresses who played characters of easy morals or with a healthy interest in sex, so reasoned the anonymous commentators, must like those characters have the morals of alley cats. In contrast, Mary Saunderson, who married her fellow actor Thomas Betterton, was known to lead a blameless, rather gentle life.

Despite the hazards of the profession, Barry went on to have a very successful career as a single woman in seventeenth-century society, amassing fame and money, investing wisely, never marrying and retiring from the stage in 1709. Behn's career in the theatre survived several changes of monarch. Lauded by expert critics, she was nevertheless lambasted by those who saw not the skill of her writing but the unorthodoxy of her life. A product of her times, she was criticised both for copying and stealing from other writers (a common enough practice since Shakespeare's time and before), and for the bawdy nature of her plays. Given the circle in which she mixed and the audience for which she wrote, it is difficult to see how she could have survived without giving her audiences what they wanted. John Dryden defended Behn's professional reputation, though her private life was constantly picked over. Her long-term relationship with John Hoyle, a lawyer and rake who was tried and acquitted of sodomy in 1687, did not help her reputation, though it did help financially.

A passionate defender of the House of Stuart, Behn would die a few years after the accession of William and Mary. In the new strait-laced atmosphere her witty carnal plays were out of fashion and she herself in poverty. But from 1670, with the appearance of *The Forc'd Marriage*, until 1687, she had played a major role at the centre of the often rough and vulgar, yet supremely vibrant, artistic life of London.

Not everyone in London society was enamoured of the licentious nature of the stage. The same year *The Forc'd Marriage* was produced, John Evelyn – as good an example of religious rectitude as one could hope to find in Restoration London – accepted an invitation to see a play put on at court, *Mustapha*, written by Lord Broghill. Evelyn rarely went to the theatre 'for many reasons now, as they were abused to an atheistical liberty; foul and indecent women now (and never till now) permitted to appear and act, who inflaming several young noblemen and gallants, became their misses, and to some, their wives'.[10]

Evelyn went on to list those of noble birth who had been ensnared by women of the theatre, 'to the ruin of both body and soul'. They were the Earl of Oxford (ensnared by Davenant's wife), Sir Robert Howard (ditto Mrs Uphill), Prince Rupert (Mrs Margaret Hughes), the Earl of Dorset, and one who Evelyn coyly refers to as 'another greater person than any of them'. This, of course, was the King, seduced by Nell Gwyn. Not since its adoption of secular rather than religious themes in Elizabethan times had the theatre embraced so lustily the lubricious. Given the sexual politics of the times, it was not thought strange that women were seen always to be ensnaring men and not the other way round. The men were noble by birth and so could only be tarnished by the debased influence of women, who were still seen as a corrupt or corrupting force through their sexuality.

Samuel Pepys, who knew the theatre as well as any man in London, expressed the hold the actresses had over the young bloods who tried to woo them, when he called at the King's House for his friend Mrs Knepp:

> I did see Becky Marshall come dressed, off of the stage, and looks mighty fine, and pretty, and noble: and also Nell, in her boy's clothes, mighty pretty. But, Lord! their confidence! and how many men do hover about them as soon as they come off the stage, and how confident they are in their talk! Here I did kiss the pretty woman newly come, called Pegg [Hughes] that was Sir Charles Sidly's [Sedley's] mistress, a mighty pretty woman, and seems, but is not, modest.[11]

Women who worked in the theatre faced the double prejudice of being considered whores because of their profession and wanton sluts because of their sex. While some women employed in the playhouses, in particular the orange sellers, were often little more than prostitutes, availed of by rakes including the King and his brother, the same could not be said for the majority of female actors. The satirist Robert Gould, who made his reputation by writing particularly harsh satires, even by the standards of Carolinian invective, played on the prevalent misogyny in his verse on women and on the theatre:

> How oft, into their closets they retire,
> Where flaming Dildoe does inflame desire[12]

In early 1671, one of the most successful sirens of the London playhouses, a woman not unknown self-mockingly to revel in the title of whore, retired from the stage. Nell Gwyn's career had lasted a little more than six years, during which she acted in only ten plays. Yet in that short time and in a modest corpus of work, she had become a great star and captured a king. She had stopped acting once before, in 1669 when she became pregnant by the King. Charles put her up in a fine house in Lincoln's Inn Fields, where she gave birth to a boy she christened Charles. But Nell missed the adulation of London audiences and was determined to have one last hurrah in front of her crowd. She returned to the stage with *The Conquest of Granada*, written by John Dryden and Sir Robert Howard. The play, an overblown effort in two parts written in rhyming pentameter couplets, ran at the King's House between December 1670 and February 1671. With its heroic deeds and tragic tone, the play was not a successful vehicle for Nell's talents. It was probably her last outing on the stage.

To celebrate Nell's retirement, Charles leased a more imposing house for her at the western end of Pall Mall. No. 79 was very grand, as befitted a mistress of the King. It backed onto St James's Park, from where John Evelyn saw Nell leaning over her garden wall talking to Charles in a 'very familiar' manner.[13] Nell was soon pregnant again. On Christmas Day she gave birth to a second son, named James. Once settled into her new domestic arrangements, Nell transferred her comic talents to ridiculing her rival, the King's premier mistress Louise de Kérouaille. On one occasion she asked the French ambassador for a present from Louis XIV on the grounds that she served Charles II better than did Louise.

In Nell's absence the world of the London theatre did not stand still. In November 1671 the most revolutionary theatre in England opened on land that had once belonged to Dorset House, formerly the London mansion of the Bishop of Salisbury, and then of the Sackville family, Dukes of Dorset. The house was destroyed in the Great Fire and not rebuilt. The Duke's Men obtained part of the land beside the Thames on a 39-year lease. The company's plan was to fulfil Sir William Davenant's long-cherished dream to build London's finest playhouse. Davenant did not live to see his dream made real. He had died three years before at home at his theatre in Lincoln Inn's Fields. During his sixty-two years, Davenant had accomplished a great deal, moving with great professionalism through different literary periods, adapting as he went. He developed English opera and introduced moveable scenery to the English stage. He helped reintroduce serious drama by Shakespeare and others, even daring to abridge and rewrite works to fit with contemporary taste and his vision of the British monarchy, for which he was an ardent apologist. He was buried at Poets' Corner in Westminster Abbey on 9 April 1668. It was left to his widow and the company's actor-managers Thomas Betterton and Henry Harris to carry on. They raised £9000 and the Dorset Gardens Theatre, also known as the Duke of York's Theatre, was built.

The first remarkable thing about the new theatre was that it was beside the Thames. Patrons no longer had to make their way through London's grimy streets. Now they could take a boat and alight at the theatre's private jetty. From there they walked across a pleasant river-front terrace from which they could admire the theatre's imposing baroque front, its fashionable broken pediment holding the crest of the Duke of York. Then it was up a few steps into an entrance loggia created by an overhanging first floor supported on Tuscan columns. Finally, the patrons entered a grandly decorated interior. The carvings over the proscenium arch were by no less a figure than Grinling Gibbons.

The architect is unknown. Robert Hooke's name has been mentioned, though the swagger of the broken pediment and the participation of Gibbons point to Sir Christopher Wren. The theatre's real magic was hidden backstage, where all the apparatus Davenant could have dreamed of was in place to have clouds drift, thunderstorms crash and people fly through the air. Dorset Gardens was designed to bring to London theatre as spectacle. This it did; memorable early productions included a musical version of *The Tempest*, in which Ariel was able to break free of his imprisoning tree and fly.[14] The theatre was a fine memorial to an energetic, resourceful and inventive impresario.

Stepping into Davenant's shoes, Betterton and Harris saved the London theatre from oblivion, fulfilling his dreams of satisfying the audience's demand for magic. His productions might be frowned upon today but in their time they were looked upon as dazzling and daring. Betterton saw with Davenant's eyes how the proscenium arch provided a window through which the audience could view a world of illusion. As in Shakespeare's time, the actors had an apron stage on which to be close to the audience, but behind them were painted scenes which could be quickly changed to transport the London audience to fanciful and foreign places.

Within three years, the King's Men were to open a rival palace of wonders, a brand new Theatre Royal on Drury Lane, incorporating all the mechanical devices first introduced by Davenant to the London public at Lisle's tennis court. But it burned down the following year, leaving the Duke of York's Theatre as unquestionably the premier playhouse in London.

CHAPTER 19
TRADING IN PEOPLE AND MONEY

On 24 January 1672, John Dryden forsook his usual haunt, Will's House in Russell Street, Covent Garden, and went into the City to Garraway's Coffee House. What took him there was a novelty: an auction of furs from Canada.[1]

Usually, Hudson's Bay traders sold their products directly to London traders, who in turn sold them on to the continent, where there was a great demand for all varieties of pelts in cities such as Brussels and Paris. The trappers sent to Europe a wide range of small pelts ranging from beaver to Arctic and red fox, timber wolf and lynx. Demand in London was more modest than on the continent, beaver skins – from which were made winter coats, hats and rugs – being the sole commodity on offer. The lack of choice in the sale at Garraway's belied the central role played in the fur trade by the North American beaver pelt; while the European beaver was being hunted to extinction, the soft fur of the belly of the male beaver, caught in winter, was particularly prized in the making of felt. This single property made the North American beaver the mainstay of the trade.

Prince Rupert looked in on the auction. His patronage of French traders four years before had not led to the discovery of the fabled North-West Passage but at least it had paid off with the establishment of a lucrative trade. Unlike early attempts to establish the slave trade in Africa, in North America there was no adversary like the Dutch to contend with, for at this stage the English and French were yet to come into direct conflict on land.

While the Hudson's Bay Company flourished, a group of London merchants raised a large sum of money to refloat the Company of Royal Adventurers Trading to Africa, which had again gone bust, this time because of the failure of the war with the Dutch of 1665–7. Since then the Dutch had renewed their efforts to keep English trading at a minimum, imposing a greater naval presence off the African coast. The Company of Royal Adventurers felt the pinch so much that it subcontracted part of its trade to a new entity named the Gambia Company. Thanks to results that were far from encouraging, a decision was made to re-energise the original company with new shareholders and new capital. If the sugar and tobacco colonies across the Atlantic were to thrive, then so must the West African slave trade.

In the middle of the seventeenth century, London's population across the social classes comprised a consumer society. The new joint stock companies and the slave trade developed hand in hand with this new consumerism, and sugar and tobacco were the major cash crops driving London's prosperity. Tobacco had come first, growing in popularity from early in the century. In towns and villages across England, children were seen puffing on their pipes. The addiction grew throughout the century until campaigners complained about the habit. Sugar was introduced slightly later, with production on an industrial scale lifting off around 1640 in Barbados. Between 1600 and 1700 annual imports of sugar would more than double.[2] Sugar fed an increasingly sweet-toothed population, being used in coffee, tea, cakes, syllabubs, mulled wine and more.

In 1672, the reformed Company of Royal Adventurers Trading to Africa was named simply the Royal African Company. The new company merged the Royal Adventurers with the Gambia Company, and again its leading light and patron was the Duke of York. At first, the company assumed that its greatest profits would come from gold, but it was quickly recognised that the easier, more profitable, trade was in slavery.

The lure of profits from slavery transcended all social boundaries. From the start, royalty, aristocracy and the world of commerce invested in the Royal African Company. The governor and largest shareholder was James, Duke of York. The Duke literally left his mark on the slaves. Those not branded RAC, for Royal African Company, were branded DY, for Duke of York, on either the chest or the forehead. Many of the Company's investors also had a financial interest in the Hudson's Bay Company and the East India Company. As with its forerunners, a royal charter gave the Royal African Company monopoly rights to trade along the eastern coastline of Africa. Directors included premier London merchants John Portman and William Pettyman, and the aristocratic plantation owner Anthony Ashley Cooper, a senior member of Charles's government, promoted shortly before the reorganisation of the African Company to Lord Chancellor and made the 1st Earl of Shaftesbury.

Other investors included William Ashburnham MP, famous for investing in many different ventures including the theatre. Ashburnham had been born without a penny but thanks to family connections obtained the senior position of cofferer in the king's household.* In contrast to the courtier Ashburnham was George Cock, a high-living Newcastle-born merchant who had made his money as the agent of an English trading company in Danzig. Cock went on to supply the navy and was not averse to siphoning off prize money that should have gone to the Exchequer. Samuel Pepys and his benefactor Edward Montagu also invested. The most unlikely of all the investors was a dead man. Sir Martin Noell had been a colourful figure who had cornered a near monopoly on the salt market, had farmed taxes and made illicit profits from transporting Irish, Scots and English Royalist prisoners as slaves in Barbados during the Cromwellian era, and had even turned to piracy. His executors, holding his estate on behalf of his relatives, invested in the new company.[3] Sir William Coventry too was listed as a shareholder, though as the Duke of York's secretary, he may not have been investing his own money. In all, there were 120 founding shareholders. Many more invested later.

The honour of making the company's first voyage went to Captain Abraham Holditch, commander of the *Charles*. In 1672 he transported 149 Africans to Barbados. Thirty slaves died on the journey; the other 119 were safely delivered. Four more company ships made the voyage that year. They faced fierce competition: Dutch, French and Portuguese ships also made the journey to pick up slaves in Africa and take them across the Atlantic. The following year, trade picked up for the company. From then on, each year the company sent an average of twenty-three ships packed with Africans to the colonies.

There were other ways of making money in the slave trade

---

* The cofferer, named after a coffer or strong box, was one position below comptroller and ran and paid the staff.

apart from becoming a direct investor in the Royal African Company's voyages, or in the plantations worked by the slaves. John Eyles built up a successful London business based on the slave trade by doing neither. Along with his younger brother Francis, John ran the family business, Eyles and Co. The brothers came from Devizes in Wiltshire, where their father was a wealthy haberdasher. Once in London, they quickly made their mark. John became a collector of alnage (cloth) taxes, a position he bought for £9000. The buying and selling of such official positions was a deeply corrupt practice that bedevilled London's revenue collection, causing great difficulties for the Exchequer. Though the Eyles brothers were Baptists, they were in good standing with the monarchy. One reason for this was certainly that the Duke of York received a large proportion of the slavery profits the Eyleses helped to realise.

Eyles and Co. was essentially a service company, providing members of the Royal African Company with facilities and financial assistance. Planters often had to buy slaves and other provisions before they received payment for their sugar. The Eyles brothers provided the necessary credit. When the planters' sugar reached London, Eyles and Co. sold it, took their fee for the transaction, subtracted the money they had advanced, plus interest, and passed on the remainder to their clients. Servicing the sugar industry at each step of the way made the Eyles family very wealthy. Eyles and Co. was able to build grand headquarters on Leadenhall Street, close by those of the East India Company. John Eyles became Lord Mayor of London, founded a merchant dynasty and bought Southbroom House and its estates in his home town of Devizes.*

Like the Eyles family seat, many great country houses were

---

* The house is today the main building of Devizes School.

bought or built from the profits of the slave trade.* Paradoxically, some slave traders were philanthropists. The international cloth wholesaler Edward Colston used a fortune partially made in the London slave trade to renovate churches and build schools and almshouses in Bristol and London. Colston was born in Bristol and his family moved to London when he was still a child. Apprenticed to the Mercers' Company to learn the cloth trade, Colston later developed a successful trade with Spain, Portugal, Italy and Africa. In the mid-1600s his trade with Africa involved trading cloth for slaves; when his brother Thomas died, Colston inherited a sugar refinery in Bristol, giving him a further tie with the transatlantic slave trade.

The fortunes made by Colston and others were very considerable for their times. According to Richard Ligon, who visited Barbados in the late 1640s and wrote about the sugar business, the profit in relation to outlay was enormous.[4] The annual net profit from a 500-acre estate, after deducting costs of £1349, was £7500, launching the estate holder into the company of the super-rich. Some of these estate holders lived on their sugar plantations; others stayed at home and ran their enterprise from their London office.

While the newly reformed Royal African Company reinstated its slave business, conflict with the Dutch loomed once more. A large section of Parliament supported another war, believing it was the only way to attain the longed-for trade supremacy. The Earl of Shaftesbury, the Lord Chancellor, was in favour of renewed conflict, but only if the King agreed to a new Act of Parliament supporting religious toleration. Shaftesbury saw the Dutch as enemies in trade but as an exemplar in terms of

* The playwright Alan Bennett would much later dub these country seats 'houses of shame'.

religious tolerance. He wanted nonconformists to have the same rights as Anglicans. Charles agreed to the tradeoff.

There remained the problem of paying to re-equip the fleet, which had been mothballed for some time. Even with the secret French money, the problems facing the Exchequer had hardly changed in a decade: the country ran an expensive foreign policy predicated upon foreign wars, the King ran a spendthrift household and the economy suffered inflation owing to the South American gold that was flooding into European economies via Spain.

On top of this, the collection of taxes was inefficient. Over many years, a haphazard network of freelance collectors had developed that was not up to the job. Each collector, or farmer, was appointed directly by royal patronage, or else bought their position from someone who wished to retire from the post. The system provided income in an unpredictable way because of the temptation for dishonesty. There was also a clear conflict of interest: many tax farmers had a sideline as individual money-lenders to the Crown.

A start had been made on the problem by bringing the collection of customs duty under the control of Crown Commissioners in 1671. This went some way to plugging the vast hole in the Exchequer's finances. No move had yet been made on the lucrative field of excise duty, or tax on certain types of domestic consumption. It was little wonder the Crown consistently looked for loans from the city's bankers.

The following year, 1672, Charles sought new loans from the City, requesting £1.5 million from the Lombard Street merchant bankers and the Cheapside goldsmiths to equip eighty-two ships of the fleet to sail against the Dutch. But distrust had been building for some time between the Exchequer and the City. This partially arose from the fact that the City men were by nature mostly Parliamentarians, while the King's antipathy to Parliament had grown rather than abated. There was in addition constant friction between the needs of the Crown and the ability or willingness of the City to provide. In the background lay endless disputes over claimed discrepancies in goods supplied and the ability or willingness of the Exchequer or the Navy Board to pay up on time. As clerk at the Navy Board, Samuel Pepys – doubtless on the fiddle himself, for he amassed a fortune in gold – complained about the honesty or lack of it among his colleagues and their suppliers.[5]

With such a background, Crown and City were wary of one another. On top of this, the bankers had doubts about probity inside the highest levels of government. They were right to be suspicious. Charles had the habit of funding his mistresses out of customs and excise, from money earmarked for the navy or on occasion taken directly out of the Exchequer's strong rooms. He had already made Barbara Palmer a farmer of several taxes, thereby ensuring the money went straight to her rather than to the government.[6] As the King and his family – in particular his brother, the Duke of York – habitually lived beyond their means, bankers were able to charge extortionate rates of interest, as high as 20 or 30 per cent. Partly because of this, Charles had run up enormous debts.

When Charles wanted to take on new debt to fund the war, the question of the fate of previous loans was raised. The bankers, together with many in the House of Commons, wanted to know how loans totalling £5 million to date had been spent. A row ensued, during which the City asked to see the books. This was unheard of. The Exchequer refused. No wonder: according to Secretary Pepys, £2.3 million was unaccounted for. For the Crown, there was the feeling that the City was being neither flexible nor supportive, for was not the war being fought for the benefit of the merchants against their adversaries in the Dutch East India Company?

Five years had passed since the previous war had ended in humiliation on the Medway. Since then, opinion in London had shifted away from war with the Dutch. In the intervening years, lacking protection from a depleted navy, English overseas trade had greatly suffered. City merchants feeling the pinch were in no mood to bankroll a spendthrift king making war when it would have been advisable to steer a more pacific course. The City had no way of knowing about the provisions of the secret Treaty of Dover, under which Charles was bound to support Louis XIV in his war against the Dutch United Provinces.

The City refused the loan. The Exchequer went bust and the King defaulted on his loans. (He was not the first king to do so. In the previous century, Philip II of Spain had defaulted on his debts no fewer than four times, ruining many of his German bankers before finding new ones in Italy.) The caution and greed of the bankers had collided with the profligacy and bellicosity of the Crown. Charles cut payments to the City on some £1.4 million of outstanding loans held by the bankers and goldsmiths. This became known as the Great Stop.*

With the Great Stop, Charles's intention was to continue paying interest but cease all repayments on the principal sums for a year. The thinking was that during that time, the war would begin and, against previous experience, a quick, glorious victory would be won. Following that, financial pressure would ease and payments could resume. When the war became protracted, the Exchequer kept up interest payments for some months, after

* There would be further defaults: the United Kingdom defaulted on its loans three times in the nineteenth century, and did so again in 1932 as a result of the financial crash of 1929.

which it stopped paying anything at all. A year later, another stop was declared. The capital sum owed would finally be added to the national debt in 1705.

The Great Stop had a ruinous effect upon the City, bringing down many goldsmiths and bankers, including leading financiers. Bankers such as Sir Francis Child, founder of a famous banking dynasty, who did business solely with private clients, were unaffected. But Robert Viner's position was particularly parlous. His appointments as goldsmith to the King and banker to the Exchequer laid him open to especially large defaults. He had the greatest personal sum, at least £400,000, owed by the Exchequer. This colossal amount was one-third of the total owed to the City by the Crown, or, to put it differently, one-third of the total annual income settled by Parliament on the King at the beginning of his reign. Viner was paid some money immediately after the Stop, perhaps because of his personal friendship with Charles, and seems to have evaded out-and-out bankruptcy. He also had income from other sources, being a farmer of taxes. Nevertheless, he had to compound with his creditors (i.e. offer to settle by paying back a percentage of the money owed, at a certain amount in the pound). Ultimately, in recompense, the government awarded Viner an annuity of £25,000, a small sum in comparison to his losses. No doubt Charles was behind the deal.

It wasn't just bankers who were ruined; their depositors were, too, reducing many in the city, including numerous small investors, to bankruptcy. John Evelyn was incensed that widows and their children suffered from the Stop. The longstanding rift between Court and City widened into a chasm. The City now had reason to see the royal court as antithetical to its views and habits. Sir John Lawrence, London's hero during the plague, became very vocal on behalf of the ruined bankers, expressing the outrage felt in the City over the actions of the Exchequer. The City now feared some form of royal backlash, perhaps even a military takeover that would overthrow its self-government and impose rule directly from Whitehall.

Sir John, who was a leader of the Country Party, smelled a rat.* According to the anonymous compiler of the Account of the Aldermen, Sir John – anxious to forestall any move by Charles to clip the city's wings – put pressure on those in the City who supported the King, citing 'all the affronts and indignities imaginable upon all those persons that have been willing to venture their lives and estates in any military employment for His Majesty'.[7]

Referring to the Crown's refusal to pay its debts, Bishop Gilbert Burnet wrote of the Great Stop that 'the trade of bankers is totally destroyed' by 'this dishonourable and perfidious action'. The default on payment of capital, which was to last one year, was enough to take the major lenders under. But not all were ruined; their fate would depend on how disposable the Exchequer felt each creditor might be. Just as Viner was destroyed by his closeness to the Crown, the merchant and financier Sir John Banks was saved by his close connections with the Navy Board. During the Second Anglo-Dutch War, Banks had lent large sums of money to the Exchequer at what were said to be high rates of interest. As with other merchants-turned-financiers, Banks was heavily exposed to any default by the Exchequer, yet escaped ruin.

John Banks was the son of a wealthy Maidstone woollen

* The Country Party, which was expressly opposed to the Duke of York, later became known as the Whigs. It was in opposition to the pro-monarchist Court Party, which developed into the Tory party. 'Whig' was originally a pejorative term taken from the name for Scottish cattle raiders, while 'Tory' was a corruption of the Irish *tóraighe* for bandit.

draper and attended Emmanuel College, Cambridge. In 1652, at the age of twenty-five, he joined a London syndicate supplying rations to the navy. Two years later he married Elizabeth Dethick, the daughter of a leading London merchant, and soon after became a shareholder in both the East India Company and the Levant Company. He was so highly thought of in London circles that in 1668 he was elected a Fellow of the Royal Society. Banks was one of a number of merchants and goldsmith-bankers who saw that the current system of providing loans and credit was insufficient to fund the growing economy. In a chance remark to Pepys he revealed that he had been considering the need for a national bank, saying that the Exchequer, sited as it was inside the complex of Whitehall Palace, would never be

> a true bank to all intents, unless the Exchequer stood nearer the Exchange, where merchants might with ease, while they are going about their business, at all hours, and without trouble or loss of time, have their satisfaction, which they cannot have now without much trouble, and loss of half a day, and no certainty of having the offices open. By this he means a bank for common practice and use of merchants, and therein I do agree with him.[8]

Despite the need for a central bank, many competing interests prevented one being set up during Charles's lifetime. The main impediment was Parliament's fear that such a bank would allow the King to rule without Parliament, bypassing it to raise money in the form of city loans rather than taxes voted by Parliament.[9]

When the crash came, Banks was treated favourably. How could it be otherwise? After all, the navy depended upon men like him. Moreover, by the time of the crash, Banks and the Secretary to the Navy Board, Samuel Pepys, were firm friends.

Pepys was godfather to the Banks's eldest son, Caleb. The financier often had the Pepys family as guests in his fine town house in Lincoln's Inn Fields or at his country estate, a former abbey at Aylesford, Kent, described by Pepys as 'mighty finely placed by the river; and he keeps the grounds about it, and walls and the house, very handsome: I was mightily pleased with the sight of it.'[10] So quick had been Banks's climb to the top of the London merchant class that he had bought the estate in 1657, when he was barely thirty years of age. It was hardly surprising that he was paid where others were not.

However, once bitten twice shy: Banks was afterwards wary of doing business with the Stuart government, resuming his dealings only after the ascent of William III.[11] He was not alone in hesitating to deal with the Crown. The city bankers who rose in place of those ruined – men like Sir Francis Child and Sir Richard Hoare, who would later give their names to their private banks – avoided loans to the state.

Despite the financial crisis, the build-up to war went ahead, orchestrated by Charles in fulfilment of his pact with the French. Only four years before, Charles had entered into an alliance with Sweden and the Dutch Republic against France, in order to prevent the French from invading the Spanish Netherlands, which lay between north-west France and the southern borders of the Dutch Republic (the United Provinces). There were those who had wholeheartedly supported the triple alliance; they included the Treasurer to the Navy, Sir Thomas Osborne (afterwards Lord Danby), who was of the opinion that the major threat came not from the Dutch but from the French. It was a view shared by Shaftesbury and others.

Despite the contrary views in circulation, Charles set out to destabilise relations with the Dutch in order to create a pretext for war. He concocted a plot involving the diplomat Sir William Temple, who had helped to seal the triple alliance. Now Temple was instructed to antagonise the Dutch, with his wife Dorothy Osborne (Sir Thomas Osborne's cousin) as the unlikely agent. While the Dutch fleet lay at anchor off Brielle, the royal yacht *Merlyn*, with Dorothy on board, sailed through it on the pretext of having to put into port for repairs. Under the then current protocol, foreign warships were to salute another nation's royal vessel by lowering their flags and firing a fusillade of white smoke from their guns. Uncertain of the status of the *Merlyn*, the Dutch lowered their flags but did not fire a salute.

Charles now ordered the arch-schemer George Downing, ambassador to The Hague, to demand that senior Dutch admirals should be sacked for the insult visited upon the royal yacht. The Dutch refused. While French preparations for invasion went on apace, the diplomatic incident was used to cause a break with the Dutch and soften up public opinion in London. In April, using the *Merlyn* affair as an excuse, the British declared war. For the second time in seven years, Charles had used deceit to engineer conflict with the Dutch.

CHAPTER 20

WAR AND ENTERPRISE

War began again on 6 April 1672. The Third Anglo-Dutch War was part of a wider European conflict involving France and other states. Despite the reluctance of London banker-merchants to pay to equip the fleet, the eighty-two ships for which Charles had sought finance were fitted out and supplied to sail against the Dutch in support of a French invasion. Louis XIV assembled a vast army to march north in order to deliver a knockout blow against the Dutch.

On 7 June, a Dutch fleet of seventy-two ships, commanded by the brilliant Admiral Michiel de Ruyter, surprised the Anglo-French fleet of ninety-three ships, under command of James, Duke of York, at anchor off the Suffolk coast. As the Dutch came into view, the French made sail, moved away from the Dutch and did not fully engage in the action, leaving the English to go it alone. Vice-Admiral Edward Montagu's command the *Royal James* was so severely damaged that he and his crew had to take to several sloops. When one of them sank under the weight of escaping sailors, Montagu, Samuel Pepys's patron, drowned.

He would be given a hero's funeral and buried in Westminster Abbey. The Dutch Admiral van Ghent, who had executed the raid on the Medway, was killed by cannon fire. A battle of savage intensity continued, with great losses on both sides. Twice, James had to change ships when his vessels were disabled. Finally, with the wind turning, conditions began to favour the English and the Dutch withdrew.

The violent intensity of the battle was captured by the Dutch maritime artists the van de Veldes, a father and son team who went to sea to capture the action, becoming the first modern war reporters. In a painting by Willem van de Velde the Younger, we see ships enveloped in smoke and flames, men drowning in the foreground and a great ship of the line sinking with only its bow still visible. The entire scene is swathed in a dreadful, hellish orange light from the flames. The horror of seventeenth-century naval warfare is vividly captured in the painting; men of all positions from admirals to cabin boys could expect to be cut down by chainshot, blown to bits, burned to death or drowned. With the use of fireships and boarding parties, the wonder was that so many survived at all.

De Ruyter's plan to destroy the English and French fleets had been thwarted. In the meantime, a huge French army of 130,000 men led by Louis himself advanced with astonishing speed into Holland. The Dutch army fell back in disarray. To avert defeat they had to open a number of dykes and flood large areas of the country. With the French encamped on their soil, there was rioting as the Dutch blamed their prime minister, Johan de Witt, for the catastrophe.

As an English army waited to invade Holland, two further major sea battles went badly for the English. Admiral Edward Spragge drowned in similar circumstances to those in which Montagu had died. Aggressive, attacking tactics employed by the Dutch thwarted an English plan to intercept and destroy the returning Dutch spice fleet. With the English fleet having suffered severe damage, an invasion force waiting in Kent was never able to sail. For the English, the war was becoming expensive and fruitless.

On 9 December 1672 a young doctor named John Fryer set sail from Gravesend, bound for one of the foreign lands over which the war was being fought – India. The son of a London family of merchants, Fryer was educated at Trinity College, Cambridge, graduating in medicine. A year later he contracted as a surgeon for the East India Company. He was engaged at fifty shillings a month as a 'Chyrurgeon for Surat', in other words, a surgeon for the company's trading post at Surat, in western India, the first to be established in the subcontinent.[1] The company paid for the tools of his trade, his 'Chyrurgery Chest', and sent it ahead to India.

Fryer sailed on the *Unity*, a 34-gun frigate under the command of Captain William Cruft.* The *Unity* was part of the East India Company fleet which left the Thames at the beginning of winter each year to catch the most favourable winds for the voyage to Arabia, India and beyond to China. Fast fighting craft such as the *Unity* escorted large cargo ships known as East Indiamen, of anywhere between 600 and 1500 tons, which at an average speed of four to five knots could sail around 120 miles in a day. If all went well, the voyage to India would last six to eight months.

To sail each ship took a crew of 140 or so. On top of that there

---

* Captain Cruft and the *Unity* would take the young Edmund Halley to St Helena in the South Atlantic four years later to watch the transit of Mercury across the sun.

would be a handful of merchants and their clerks. Those who served on the ships, or merchants making the round trip, could reckon on being away from home for two to three years, a long and anxious wait for EIC investors in London to see a return on their investment. Those on a one-way ticket for a posting abroad knew they might not see England again for many years, if ever. Fryer himself was to be away for eight years.

The fleet carried a huge cargo of 'treasure', as cargoes of fine or valuable goods were called, destined for Madras, on the south-east coast of India. Once there, the treasure would be traded for other goods. When the fleet arrived off the Coromandel Coast in June 1673, they were faced by the unwelcome presence of a Dutch naval fleet blockading the coast and hampering English shipping. After some skirmishing with the Dutch, the EIC fleet determined it was unable to put into port at Madras and headed for its trading post at Masulipatnam further along the coast. Finally, the Dutch lifted their blockade and the fleet put into Madras.

Madras was the second trading post the EIC had set up in India. The city was built on uninhabited land purchased from the ruling Vijayanagara empire. Here the company built its first Indian fortress, naming it Fort St George. It was a square, stone fortress, with two concentric lines of walls, heavily defended by cannon. In the middle stood the governor's house, a fine building with a domed roof in the Indian manner. The city of Madras (present-day Chennai in Tamil Nadu) grew up around the fort. By the 1670s the population was around 50,000. Propelled by nothing more than the EIC's trading activities, a heterodox population expanded to cater for the needs of Europeans and their Indian middlemen. According to Fryer, there were 300 Englishmen and 3000 Portuguese. The 'Moors' had routed the latter from their stronghold at St Thomas and they now carried on their trade under English protection, paying duty of 4 per cent for goods in and out of the city.[2] The city boasted several Hindu temples and a mosque, but not yet a church, though there was a chapel inside the fort. Fryer noticed how the EIC's administration emulated the pomp and luxury of the Indian grandees they traded with. The governor of Madras was Sir William Langthorne, the son of a London merchant and investor in the East India Company. Emulating his father, Sir William had invested early in the company, becoming so successful that he was knighted in 1668.

In 1670, the company had asked Sir William to go to Madras to investigate charges of malpractice brought against its governor, Sir Edward Winter, who was caught up in a power struggle with his rival for the position, George Foxcroft. It seems Foxcroft was untrustworthy, while Winter was an honest man traduced by Foxcroft's agents, or factors. The result of Langthorne's investigations was that Winter and Foxcroft were both called home, and he himself was installed as governor.

By the time Fryer landed, Sir William had succumbed to the same pecuniary disease as had done for Winter. On top of his annual salary of £300, Sir William was said to be making £7000 a year by illegally trading on his own account. In the journal he kept of his travels, Fryer noted that that Sir William – 'a gentleman of Indefatigable Industry and Worth' – lived and travelled in grand style:

> His personal guard consists of three hundred or four hundred blacks, besides a band of fifteen hundred men ready on summons; he never goes abroad without fifes, drums, trumpets, and a flag with two bells in a red field, accompanied with his Council and Factors on horseback, with their ladies in palankeens [palanquins].[3]

The mention of 'three hundred or four hundred blacks' is telling. In 1620, the East India Company had begun importing slaves into India. At first they came from England's main slave supply zone on the Guinea Coast in West Africa, and later from East Africa, Mozambique and Madagascar. Later still, some slaves were imported from Indonesia. Sir William's 'blacks' were almost definitely West African slaves.

Under company rules, the governor had the power of life or death over his non-English employees and all others who resided in his territory. Though omnipotent in his own bailiwick, however, even minting his own money, Sir William still answered to London. In time the company read his reports, looked at the ledgers, caught up with Sir William's private trade and removed him. He returned to England, bought an estate in Kent, became a Justice of the Peace, and endowed almshouses and a school, gaining a reputation as a 'rich and beneficent nabob'[4] It is interesting to note that his replacement, Sir Streynsham Master – also sent to India as a reformer – was able upon his retirement to buy a castle and estate in Derbyshire and become High Sheriff of the county.

Fryer was finally able to sail for his posting in Surat, retracing his voyage round the Cape and heading up the west coast of India, arriving at his destination on 9 December 1673, a year to the day since he had left the Thames Estuary. Surat was founded in 1615 when Sir Thomas Roe gained from Mughal emperor Jahangir the right to establish a 'factory' in what is present-day Gujarat.* Surat nevertheless suffered from the insecurity that attended all European trading ports in India. The Dutch had arrived in India many years before the English, and

* A factory was a warehouse, usually protected like a fortress, with attached trading rights awarded by the current local administration or emperor.

the Portuguese long before that. More recently the French had established an interest. The hereditary rulers often quarrelled with the Europeans over land and trading concessions, sometimes favouring one country over another.

The climate also took its toll. Situated twenty-one degrees north of the equator, Surat had a tropical climate that was difficult for Europeans. For eight months of the year the temperature rose to above 90 degrees Fahrenheit and stayed there, sometimes hitting as much as 110 degrees or more. The monsoon lasted at least three of the hottest months, and the rest of the year remained hotter than any English summer. The climate was relieved only by occasional cooling breezes from the Arabian Sea.

So why did men like Fryer go? The answer was either the lure of the East or the hope of wealth. In Fryer's case, it was the former, for his company doctor's pay was never going to make him rich. While some who served with the EIC as senior merchants were able to return home with fortunes, most made it back, if at all, with little.

To begin with, Surat had been important to the EIC as a staging post on the spice run to Java. At its height, the city had a population of several hundred thousand and boasted the presence of the man said to be the world's richest merchant, Virji Vohra.[5] Vohra had become rich thanks to monopolistic trading and money lending, first within India's well-established proto-capitalist economy and later with Europeans. He was flexible, adapting his methods and spheres of business to the changing needs of local and European trade. He lent money to both the EIC and the Dutch East India Company at rates of between 1 and 1.5 per cent per month. According to EIC factory records, he regularly lent very large sums, often to English officials acting on their own behalf, in breach of company rules.[6]

Vohra controlled a trading network made up of a large, extended family, plus a web of associated merchants reaching from the Persian Gulf, across India to Hyderabad in the centre, down to the Coromandel Coast in the south-east, and as far as the Spice Islands of Indonesia. He specialised in buying up entire supplies of commodities and selling them on at inflated prices. Hence, he bought all the pepper brought into Surat by the Dutch from the Far East and sold it on to the English at a considerable profit. When EIC factors tried to buy pepper from other sources, Vohra's contacts enabled him to find out about their plans and swipe the pepper from under their noses.[7] It is hard not to believe that more than one EIC official might have seen a grim irony in the fact that one monopolistic entity forced another to trade at inflated prices. However, when the expensive pepper reached London it could still make a good return for EIC investors when sold on to other European countries without maritime trading systems of their own.

Vohra and his associates traded in anything from gold to opium, silk, spices and coral. He bought or exchanged lead, broadcloth, tin and copper imported by the EIC, selling in return the eastern commodities European consumers craved. London merchants travelling across India soon became aware that a sophisticated banking system was in operation, far in advance of anything London had to offer, with transferable loans available across the continent. In this way, a merchant like Vohra could buy in one region on locally arranged credit, sell on in another, buy again in a third with the credit passed on to another local banker, and so on until the merchant chose to bring the chain to an end and settle up.

The world Fryer had sailed into might not have had a climate suitable for Europeans, but it was one of power and wealth Londoners could only marvel at. The rulers of India ran empires of enormous mercantile wealth, trading goods in quantities and at values London could never match. To English eyes it must have seemed like a veritable paradise of luxury and capitalism. The effect on EIC officials of coming into contact with such a powerful and wealthy Indian merchant class does not have to be imagined: as we have seen, temptation among officials to grow rich by taking part in unofficial personal trading was often too much to bear.

When Fryer arrived at Surat, he discovered the port's EIC trade beginning to decline. The reason was that the company had recently opened up a trading post further down the coast at Bombay, ceded to the English as part of Queen Catherine's dowry and given by the King to the EIC at a rent of £10 a year. The Portuguese had cheated Charles over the dowry, failing to fulfil all its terms. But Bombay would prove to be the unexpected jewel in the English colonial crown, becoming the most important EIC outpost in India. Thanks to its topographical spread over several islands, Bombay offered a secure harbour and a base secure from land attack. In time, Bombay would replace Surat as the centre of EIC activities in India, controlling the company's far-reaching network of factories and staging posts.*

The EIC's extensive business in the subcontinent required a huge logistical effort. The company had its own locally based warships and garrisons in order to protect its shipping, warehouses and quaysides from pirates and foreign interventions. The enterprise was enormous – thousands were indirectly employed – and it was all controlled from the company's headquarters in the Elizabethan mansion on Leadenhall Street with a Jolly Jack Tar bestriding its rooftop.

*

* In 1687 the EIC transferred its Indian headquarters from Surat to Bombay.

While the English and Dutch vied for supremacy in the East, the war between them continued in the North Sea. What finally caused a dramatic turn of events was the power of the press. A Dutch propagandist used the might of the country's printing industry (the biggest in the world) to shower London with leaflets claiming that Charles's alliance with the French was part of a greater plan to make Britain into a Roman Catholic state. It was an unwitting bull's-eye. Opinion turned violently against the war.

As if to defy his critics, Charles conferred the titles of Baroness Petersfield, Countess Fareham and Duchess of Portsmouth on his French mistress Louise de Kérouaille. Previously, Louise had preferred to express her independence by being painted by the court painter to Louis XIV, Pierre Mignard; now Peter Lely, who by this time had established himself as the leading court painter, was commissioned to paint her. Various dates between 1671 and 1674 have been suggested for this portrait. By its composition and colouring it renders Louise as a duchess, formally seated in a classical landscape, wearing a loose-fitting antique gown of palest blue-grey silk. The tone of the portrait, together with the fact it is by Lely at all, leads one to conjecture that it was painted to mark Louise's elevation to several English titles. The portrait's cool tones and restrained style made a bold departure from the painter's usually overblown style of depicting women at court as languid, doe-eyed beauties in colourful gowns and elaborate hairdos. It marked a special moment for both sitter and painter, and also for the King, who was showing his disdain for those who questioned the real values and allegiances of the House of Stuart.

A month after Louise's elevation, on 20 September 1673, James, Duke of York, married Mary of Modena, a Catholic Italian princess chosen by Charles. A new Test Act passed through

Parliament, making it obligatory for all public servants to take the Anglican Eucharist and declare an abhorrence of the doctrine of transubstantiation. James refused, resigned from his position as Lord High Admiral, and was thereby publicly outed as a Catholic.

The reliably unreliable Duke of Buckingham, who was privy to the secret Anglo-French treaty made three years before, now blabbed about it to various members of the cabinet. The Earl of Shaftesbury was so shocked he began to ponder how England might be ruled by anyone except a member of the House of Stuart. By late 1673, with no support at home, it was clear to Charles that he had to terminate the war. Parliament forced Charles to make peace in a humiliating climbdown. The King's secret foreign policy was in tatters; so too was his relationship with London's financial powerhouse. When the peace treaty was signed there was public jubilation in London.

It took time for the city's financiers to recover from the default of the Exchequer. When they did, men like Sir John Banks took to lending solely on commercial ventures rather than to the Crown. Charles had to look elsewhere for funding. By now he had promoted the immensely capable Thomas Osborne to the post of Lord Treasurer, a position to which the cold and calculating Osborne was well suited. He immediately set about modernising the nation's finances.

The man who had taken it upon himself to carry out one of the most urgent and difficult tasks facing the Crown – and therefore the City of London – was far from a copybook hero. Even Osborne's friends found his character unappealing. John Evelyn, who had known him since they were young men travelling on the continent, described him as haughty. Osborne was criticised for being personally grasping, an attribute born of his lack of inherited money allied to the huge expenditure entailed in clawing his way to the top. On his way up the political ladder he ran up a debt of £10,000 and faced bankruptcy. He was seen as insincere and cunning, leading to Lord Shaftesbury's waspish remark that he had the qualities of a courtier.

Shaftesbury was correct. When introduced to the court by his friend and neighbour George Villiers, 2nd Duke of Buckingham, Osborne had taken to court life with relish, seeing London's political milieu as his gateway to power. Buckingham had wasted no time in showing Osborne the backbiting ways of politics. Together they had attacked Lord Clarendon and helped hasten his downfall following the disastrous second war with the Dutch.

Osborne's greatest strength was that he perceived his own future as connected to his ability to solve problems for the state. Largely thanks to Buckingham, he was appointed joint Treasurer to the Navy. His ambitions did not end there. He saw clearly that several national issues needed to be addressed: costs cut, the war ended, military pay redirected to settle debts, farming of customs reorganised so that more revenue would actually reach the Exchequer. Charles was lucky to have him. Osborne's efficiency earned him not only his appointment as Lord Treasurer but his elevation to the peerage, as Earl of Danby.

Osborne had an unlikely ally in his radical views, particularly regarding how to balance the national books. Slingsby Bethel was a disgruntled Commonwealth man grown wealthy as a merchant in Hamburg. As a sideline, having retired to London, Bethel wrote pamphlets on the country's ills as he saw them. His was the voice of London dissenters, longing to be recognised and given equal status. Bethel saw clearly that London's power lay in overseas trade, which he argued was impeded by a trade war with the Dutch. Bethel believed in free trade, a notion, at least in theory, supported by the Dutch themselves.

In *The Principal Interest of England Stated*, Bethel set out his blueprint for the ideal country. The King should be the champion of Protestantism, granting freedom to all dissenters so that they could use their natural propensity for hard work to enrich the nation, and should forge an alliance with the country's natural Protestant ally, Holland, supporting Protestantism against the ambitions of Louis XIV. Taxes should be kept low to encourage growth in trade. Finally, banks should be set up and the power of monopolies limited. Taking more than a few leaves out of the book according to the Dutch, Bethel's plan was in most ways admirable.[8]

Charles listened to many of Danby's proposals without acting. While Danby saw France as the enemy, Charles was all for negotiating more money from his secret benefactor, Louis.

Fortunately, thanks to Danby's modernisation of the Exchequer, tax revenue did improve – aided, paradoxically, by Charles's secret money from France. Danby knew about the secret deal and disapproved in principle, but understood it was necessary all the same. He negotiated a new agreement with the bankers ruined in the Great Stop.

War continued between the Dutch and the French, dragging on into the following decade. Following various internal intrigues, the Dutch leader de Witt was assassinated and Prince William of Orange came to power. He consolidated his position by marrying Mary, the Duke of York's daughter – a liaison proposed by Lord Danby and supported by Charles. Charles could not have realised that he had set in train the events that would ultimately lead to the overthrow of the House of Stuart, for even at this time, William had an eye on the English throne.

But it was the Duke's marriage to a Catholic princess that caused consternation in London, adding fire to the smouldering tensions between the city and its king. While York's children from his first marriage were both brought up as Protestant, it was taken as read that any progeny from the second would be Catholic, thereby making any male child a Catholic heir to the throne, providing Charles continued to be without legitimate offspring.* Shaftesbury revived a suggestion made by the Duke of Buckingham in the 1660s that Charles should divorce Catherine and marry an English Protestant, so ensuring a Protestant succession. Charles once more turned it down. The political mood in London was now more unstable than it had been since 1660.

---

* James's first wife, Anne Hyde, had died in 1671.

CHAPTER 21
THE MOOD OF THE CITY

As the 1670s wore on, a deteriorating public mood in London made the future of St Paul's Cathedral a matter of great public significance. Anti-Catholic and anti-French sentiment was running high, reflecting badly on the King and his new French Catholic mistress, as well as on the Duke of York, with his new Italian wife. The Anglican hierarchy was keen that any design for restoring St Paul's or building a new cathedral should be a visual affirmation of Protestantism. After the years of shilly-shallying, in 1673 Christopher Wren was appointed to design and build a completely new cathedral.

This vital commission was to run in parallel with all his other duties for rebuilding London. Wren's ideas of Protestantism were more aligned to those of the high Anglicanism of his father than to the traditions espoused by plain architecture and a preacher's pulpit at the end of the nave. Wren was the choice of a king rather than of a Protestant Reformation.

Below the hill where the old church had stood, London was well on the road to being rebuilt, thanks to the work of Wren,

Hooke and other surveyors and architects, with fine stone and brick houses lining thoroughfares that conformed to the new regulation widths. A new sewerage system was being installed. But everyone was kept guessing about the cathedral. What would Wren's design be like? In 1674, Wren invited the dean and chapter to the Convocation House where he and an assistant had been working for months. Wren unveiled a huge model built out of oak, limewood and plaster. It was on a scale of 1:25, and became known simply as the Great Model.

Its large scale enabled the church worthies to enter it and walk through it, as Wren intended, so gaining an idea of the interior space he planned to create. The model was intended to inform and reassure. It did the first only too well, the latter not at all. The problem was the design – that of a classical European Renaissance church with a vast dome in place of a spire; in other words, a Roman Catholic church, not an Anglican church at all. In the current mood nothing but a traditional, Gothic Anglican building would do. Wren started again. It was now seven years since the destruction of the old cathedral.

This time Wren produced a design that sought to marry the Gothic with the classical. Out of the middle of the dome grew an enormous spire. It was a hideous compromise. The clerics loved it: it was, they agreed, more in line with English church tradition. The King also accepted to it and gave it his warrant. This design became known as the Warrant Design. Wren promptly hid it away. He had no intention of building it.

Wren had permission from the King to make what detailed changes he saw fit. He promptly ditched the spire. Reverting to his favoured baroque design, he proceeded in secrecy, consulting no one, his church going up behind a wall of tarpaulins. The church he was building was strongly reminiscent of St Peter's in Rome – hardly the look of a Protestant church. Wren had not visited Rome, but in Paris he had admired the similar, though smaller, Church of the Val-de-Grace. To pay for the new cathedral, coal tax was increased. Hence the Protestant people of London would pay for their own, quite Catholic, cathedral.

While Wren proceeded, cautiously allowing no one but his workmen to see his drawings, a play was produced that came to epitomise the Restoration era. *Marriage à la Mode* by John Dryden opened at the King's House in the autumn of 1673 and took London by storm. The double plot, based on lost identities and star-crossed lovers, was a recognisable update on Jacobean themes. Dryden had borrowed much of it from John Fletcher, who had collaborated with William Shakespeare and succeeded him as house dramatist for the original King's Company around 1613.

Marriage à la Mode examined the state of seventeenth-century marriage and sexual attraction. Among families of wealth or position, sons and daughters habitually had to marry those they did not love in a sorry cycle that continued through generations. This was in contrast to the practice among the working population, where marriage for love was usual rather than an exception. Dryden humorously dealt with the heartache and cynicism of dynastic couplings. The well-to-do audience would have recognised it all too well, as enforcers, victims or both. The King, with his own unhappy marriage, was no exception.

Unlike the slow progress at St Paul's, the rebuilding of the city went on at a remarkable pace. By the mid-1670s, 8000 plots had been redeveloped. The problem was that 3500 of these new houses, put up by speculative builders, stood empty.

Some people were not keen on moving back into the old, walled city. The planners may have been at pains to develop a more fire-resistant fabric but at first the people preferred to make their homes elsewhere. Their choice was to go to the fast-expanding suburbs around the old city. For those who could afford it, the new West End, between the old city and Westminster, was the fashionable place to be. However, because of its attraction for those moving from elsewhere, the old city gradually filled up. Energetic young people arrived to fill the empty homes.

Outside the walls, speculators bought land and built on it at an enormous rate. So great was the speculative boom that Charles tried to rein it in by decree. This had little effect: there was just too much money to be made. Favoured developers could do what they wanted. George Downing, with his government position, was able to develop the street that was to bear his name – Downing Street. Aristocrats owning land between Whitehall and the old city either developed new streets themselves or sold the land to speculators like Nicolas Barbon, a physician trained at Leiden and Utrecht, who turned to speculative building.* Barbon became the greatest housebuilder of his time, often running roughshod over regulations in his race to develop much of the land between the city and Westminster. His housing schemes filled in much of the land north of the Strand and in present-day Bloomsbury.

As well as being a developer, Barbon was, like Sir William Petty, a proto-economist. One of his books espoused the value of housebuilding to the economy of a city:

---

* Barbon's full and correct name was Nicholas If-Jesus-Christ-Had-Not-Died-For-Thee-Thou-Hadst-Been-Damned Barbone, his name awarded by his father Praise-God Barebone, an influential Puritan during the Cromwellian era.

> Houses in the middle of a Town are of more value than those at the out ends; and when a Town happens to be increased by addition of New Buildings to the end of a Town, the old Houses which were then at the end, become nearer to the middle of the Town, and so increase in value.
>
> Houses are of more value in *Cheapside*, and *Cornhill*, than they are in *Shoreditch*, *White-Chappel*, *Old-Street*, or any of the Out-parts; and the Rents in some of these Out-parts have been within this few years considerably advanced by the addition of New Buildings that are beyond them. As for instance, the Rents of the Houses in *Bishopsgate-Street*, the *Minories*, &c. are raised from fifteen or sixteen pounds *Per Annum*, to be now worth thirty, which was by the increase of Buildings in *Spittle-Fields*, *Shadwells* and *Ratcliff-Highway*. And at the other end of the Town those Houses in the *Strand* and *Charing-Cross* are worth now fifty and threescore pounds *Per Annum*, which within this thirty years were not Lett for above twenty pounds *Per Annum*, which is by the great addition of Buildings since made in St. *James's*, *Leicester-Fields*, and other adjoyning parts.[1]

While building boomed from the old city to Whitehall, in Westminster political intrigue burgeoned. At the new parliamentary session that began on 7 January 1674, Shaftesbury warned that there were 16,000 Catholics in London ready to mount a rebellion. He asked Charles to order all Catholics to be banned from the city. Feelings ran high, with various anti-Papist and anti-York measures proposed and debated. When it looked as if the political opposition were about to attack the King himself, Charles prorogued Parliament.*

---

* It would not sit again until April 1675.

On 18 April, during Easter week, John Graunt, the haberdasher who had tried to produce a method to forecast plague epidemics and so protect his fellow Londoners, died of jaundice at home in Bolt Court, off Fleet Street, destitute and facing charges of recusancy. Following the success of his epidemiological works, and his elevation to the Royal Society, Graunt had quit his successful business as a haberdasher and taken employment with one of the companies supplying water to London, and later as a collector of hearth taxes. He had converted to Catholicism, but because of the Test Act he had lost his employment and his income.

Graunt's fall from grace was a salutary tale of how a person without social position was unable to kick against London's prevailing ethos and hope to thrive. His conversion to Catholicism meant that Graunt could no longer legally hold a government job, and he had no patronage or leverage to protect him. His wealthy friend Sir William Petty did nothing – whether because help was refused or because he did not offer is unknown. Graunt climbed a considerable way, but ultimately social order was restored at his expense.

His funeral took place at St Dunstan-in-the-West in the Strand, a hundred yards from his home. John Aubrey, who attended, described his funeral: 'His death is lamented by all good men that had the happinesse to knowe him; and a great number of ingeniose persons attended him to his grave. Among others, with teares, was that ingeniose great *virtuoso*, Sir William Petty, his old and intimate acquaintance.' Graunt, who wished to prevent the needless deaths of his fellow Londoners, had failed to prevent his own life descending to a miserable end.

By the autumn of 1674 there was some cause for celebration in London. A new mayor was installed – none other than the goldsmith and banker Sir Robert Viner, whose close friendship with the King and Lord Danby, alongside his role as a pre-eminent fixer between City and Crown, had helped to keep him financially afloat despite his huge losses in the Great Stop. Like each new mayor, Viner processed like a prince through the city, carried in a decorated coach under triumphal arches. As a sign of their friendship, the King attended his inaugural banquet. The new mayor was regaled in poetry celebrating the city's rebirth:

> Our ruines did shew, five or six years ago,
> Like an object of wo to all eyes that came nigh to us:
> Yet now 'tis as gay as a garden in May;
> Guildhall and th'Exchange are in Statu quo prius.[2]

It was said that when Charles tried to slip away, Viner, very drunk, followed him to his coach and broke with etiquette by laying a hand on the King's shoulder while entreating him to stay. Charles was reported to have quoted a line from a popular song – 'A man in his cups is as rich as a king', before agreeing to return to the feast.

There was less celebration on 29 September 1674, which came and went without much remark – this was the date stipulated in the 1670 Rebuilding Act by which time all temporary shelters for those made homeless in the Great Fire were supposed to have been pulled down. They were not; even though most private houses had been rebuilt, not all Londoners had been able to pay to have new homes erected.

On 2 February 1675 a frail 29-year-old man with a Derbyshire accent came to live in the city. He had an unusual address: the Tower of London. John Flamsteed was the son of comfortably off middle-class parents, Mary and William Flamsteed of Denby. The family carried on a business in nearby Derby, malting barley.* At the age of sixteen, John left school with the expectation he would go to Jesus College, Cambridge, to which he had been recommended by his school's headmaster. But John was sickly – from what is unknown – and stayed at home, helping in the business. He learned mathematics from his father and developed a keen interest in astronomy. His early accomplishments brought him to the attention of Sir Jonas Moore, the vastly rich Surveyor-General to the Ordinance and a mathematician of quality with an equally strong interest in astronomy. It was thanks to Sir Jonas that young Flamsteed was given digs at the Tower.

Sir Jonas, who was of Lancastrian farming stock, seems to have seen Flamsteed as another promising young man from the north, and decided to offer him some help in life. Sir Jonas had a plan to establish an observatory at Chelsea College, in which he was trying to interest the Royal Society. At the same time, under the patronage of the Duke of York, a committee was being set up to examine the possibilities for determining longitude via proposals put up by a French astronomer. Sir Jonas seized the moment to introduce Flamsteed, now his protégé, to the King. The young astronomer was quickly appointed assistant to the committee. The French ideas on longitude were rejected, but the committee recommended the establishment of an observatory.

Events now proceeded with extraordinary speed for Flamsteed. On 4 March, four weeks after his arrival in London, he was appointed the King's Astronomical Observator on £100 a year. Few outside the rarefied circle of the country's

* The process by which cereal grains are treated to change their starch into sugar, to be used in brewing or distilling.

top astronomers and mathematicians, a circle including Isaac Newton, Sir Christopher Wren and Sir William Petty among others, could have cared much about who was awarded the new position. For those in the know, Flamsteed seemed a good choice; he had developed knowledge of mathematics and astronomy at an early age, and had a determined, even stubborn character, together with a dogged, meticulous approach to work.

Work in building an observatory was almost as swift as John Flamsteed's elevation. The guiding purpose of the observatory was to increase the knowledge of the stars, so aiding navigation – critical to the country's growing maritime trade. The site, chosen by Christopher Wren, was not at Chelsea but on the hill behind Inigo Jones's Queen's House, on the site of Henry VIII's old palace at Greenwich. Working together once more, Wren and Robert Hooke designed the building, an octagonal tower-like structure of red brick dressed with stone. Using old foundations and recycled material from the palace, it was built in haste without a proper budget. Sir Jonas Moore paid for the astronomical equipment out of his own pocket. The Ordinance Office was responsible for the building works and thanks to Sir Jonas's interest in and patronage of Flamsteed, construction went on at a tremendous pace.

Upstream, on Ludgate Hill, it was a different picture. Despite a foundation stone ceremony, held on 21 June, there was little progress. Among those in attendance at the ceremony were Wren, his friend the Dean, and a small group of key personnel including the masons who would oversee the construction of the fabric of the cathedral. Master mason Thomas Strong laid the foundation stone, watched by his brother Edward and fellow master masons Joshua Marshall and Edward Pierce.

Strong came from a well-established Oxfordshire family of quarry owners.[3] He and Wren had first worked together a few years before on Oxford University's Sheldonian Theatre, and the relationship would last the rest of their lives: Following Thomas's death, it was his brother Edward who would finish St Paul's dome. The Strong quarry had possibly provided the limestone used by Inigo Jones for the lower storey of the Banqueting House at Whitehall; meanwhile stone from the quarry of the Marshall family went into the town hall in Abingdon. Both types of stone were particularly tough and weather-resistant while being sufficiently pliable to be carved.

Edward Pierce also hailed from an Oxfordshire quarrying family. He was a carver, an artist in both stone and wood. Each of these men had a team of masons working to them. Taken together with the teams of carpenters and others, the workforce ran into hundreds.

Now these highly skilled Oxfordshire men collected in London, brought by the vision of Wren and the needs of the city, to undertake the greatest commission of their lives. Unusually, a second foundation stone was laid. The honour went to master carpenter John Langland. The fact that neither stone was laid by Wren indicated something of his character. He was known to all as brilliant but self-effacing. Not only that, he had a reputation for having an affinity with those below him in social standing. These men, the master masons and carpenters, though educated in their trades at a high degree, generally, like Wren himself, had no private income to rely on. They all worked or they went without. Though his father had risen to be Dean of Windsor Castle – even then his tenure was interrupted by the Civil War – Wren's upbringing was that of a country rector's son. He appreciated the value of others no matter what their social status. Like his fellow former student at Westminster School, Robert Hooke, he depended on others for his advancement and station in life.[4]

At this auspicious moment, on the verge of the greatest work of his life, Wren stepped back to let others have their moment in history. With the self-belief of the visionary, he knew that if his radical plan for a new type of church building were to succeed, others would have to stay the course with him. This solemn but simple ceremony would have caused satisfaction among the little gathering. As events turned out, it marked an occasion full of promise and little else. Work would be stalled for some time to come.

The delays in building were twofold: the supply of money and of stone. The new coal tax to pay for the rebuilding was far from sufficient. The tax on sea-coal arriving at London docks from Newcastle was levied at fourpence halfpenny a cauldron (the equivalent of fifty-two and a half hundredweight, or 5880 lb). This brought in roughly £5000 per annum; far from enough. There was also the issue of how to carry thousands of tons of stone to the site. The stonemasons' quarries could not supply the enormous quantities of material required, nor could such vast amounts of stone be economically transported from Oxfordshire by road.

Hence, for the interior of the church, Wren chose a medley of stone, some of it from the Strong family quarries at Burford and Taynton, the rest from Devon and as far as Caen in France. This meant that some could be brought by sea. For the exterior, Portland stone was to be used. Wren specified this fine-grained stone for its durability and light, almost off-white, hue. He wanted his cathedral to glow in the sunlight above the city. There was another consideration: the Portland quarries were on the coast.

Portland in Dorset had once been a thriving and efficient centre for the quarrying, finishing and transportation of stone. The civil wars had put paid to that. Its quay, kept in excellent condition when Inigo Jones had been the King's surveyor, was now run down. The cranes were rusted and its roads rutted and in places washed away. Wren put forward proposals for restoration and re-energising the industry. The commissioners for rebuilding St Paul's agreed and appointed the experienced London stone merchant Thomas Knight as their agent in Portland.[5] So, while Londoners saw little or no evidence of a new cathedral rising, work was under way in Portland, rebuilding a dockyard and levelling roads from the quarry face to the water's edge.

Wren had other headaches. Once the massive task of clearing and levelling the site on Ludgate Hill was complete, it was discovered that the London clay was so unstable that foundations had to be dug much deeper than previously thought. Wren should have remembered the nave's leaning walls. Teams of navvies ended up digging down twenty feet before the masons could start putting in the stonework.

Bogged down with a multiplicity of troubles at the site on Ludgate Hill, Wren could take pleasure in how quickly the structure he and Hooke had designed was progressing on Greenwich Hill. Once the observatory was completed, Flamsteed proved to be a dedicated worker, meticulous to a fault.* While he established himself in the intellectual life of London, a debate on the application of astronomy was opening up inside the Royal Society. Mariners needed to do more than get a fix on the stars if they were to know their position. They needed to know their longitude. This necessitated a reliable watch that could record with a high level of accuracy the hours and minutes a ship sailed east or west. A row brewed inside the

---

* Flamsteed would go on to map the position of 2935 stars. Alas, he was so meticulous that he kept his findings under lock and key for years, allowing no one to see them, worried that he had failed properly to check over his computations. Finally, in a fit of frustration, his friend Edmund Halley stole the star charts and, together with Isaac Newton, published them without Flamsteed's permission.

society between rival factions. More was at stake than the glory of being first to develop a longitude watch; whoever gained a patent could become rich.

Among those competing were the society's secretary, Henry Oldenburg, and his rival, curator of experiments Robert Hooke. Hooke accused Oldenburg of double-dealing by revealing his work on the watch escapement to others without his permission. However, the King agreed to allow Hooke to demonstrate his watch to him. It looked as if Hooke's future was assured. The King tried out Hooke's watch and told him it kept the time well. Unfortunately, while Hooke's theory was correct, contemporary technology was insufficiently advanced to make his watch as accurate and reliable as required.*

It was a blow for Hooke, who had laboured all his life on many projects only to find he was constantly sidelined by events or thwarted by rivals. Just a year before the watch debacle he had clashed with Newton over the nature of light. Hooke conceived light as being composed of waves, while Newton thought it consisted of particles; today we know they were both partially right. Yet it was Newton's *Optics* that received all the attention and is still remembered today. Few remember that it was Hooke who first said that light travels in waves, or that Newton initially disagreed with him.

Ever since first crossing swords with Hooke, Newton had preferred to keep away from London. On 9 December, however, he made one of his rare visits to the city. Despite their bristly relationship, Newton was to present to the Royal Society a long paper on optics in which he speculated on the nature of light and how different colours were formed:

---

* It would be a hundred years before John Harrison demonstrated a watch that could keep time with sufficient precision to help mariners find their longitude.

> the agitated parts of bodies, according to their several sizes, figure, and motions, do excite vibrations in the æther of various depths or bignesses, which being promiscuously propagated through that medium to our eyes, effect in us a sensation of light of a white colour; but, if by any means those of unequal bignesses be separated from one another, the largest beget a sensation of a red colour; the least, or shortest, of a deep violet; and the intermediate ones, of intermediate colours.[6]

In his society diary, Hooke dryly noted only that 'Newton spoke on optics'.[7]

One day in 1675 – the exact date is unknown – the daughter of one of the most powerful men in the kingdom took a coach to Covent Garden to have her portrait painted by one of the most fashionable artists of the day. What was unusual was that the artist was a woman, Mary Beale. The sitter was the daughter of John Maitland, 1st Duke of Lauderdale, friend of Charles II, member of the government, Lord Commissioner of the Admiralty, Secretary of State for Scotland and President of the Privy Council of Scotland, which he ruled as his own private fiefdom.

The sitter, Lady Frances Hay, had married John Hay, the eldest son of the 1st Marquess of Tweeddale, at Highgate, near London, in 1666, the same year that John was elected a Fellow of the Royal Society. The future looked bright for the young couple but quickly turned sour when Lauderdale took against his new son-in-law, and the couple were forced to live on the continent for many years. In 1675, however, Lady Frances, already into her forties, came to London to have her likeness recorded.

There were notably few professional women painters at the

time, the pursuit usually being considered an amateur calling for ladies. One of the few exceptions before Mary Beale was Joan Carlyle (1606–79). The most famous of women painters active in England during the seventeenth century had been Artemisia Gentileschi (1593–1656), who worked with her father Orazio in the court of Charles I for a few years from 1638. Artemisia, who like her father was influenced by Caravaggio, was one of the most talented Italian painters of her period.

Mary Beale was born in 1633 to John and Dorothy Cradock in Suffolk. John was a country parson and an amateur artist who taught his daughter to paint; she went on to take lessons from Peter Lely and developed a style based on his. To a great extent, her studio flourished thanks to her work being similar to that of her mentor, and their stars to some degree shone and fell together. The Beale family lived and had studios at Covent Garden and then Fleet Street, while Mary's husband Charles acted as her business manager.* From the copious notes he left of his business transactions we know that in her best years Mary made around £200 a year, sufficient to keep herself, her husband and two sons in comfort if not luxury. She charged £5 for a head-and-shoulders portrait and £10 for a full-length study. For comparison, Samuel Pepys paid £17 to have his portrait painted by John Hayls.

Among Mary Beale's sitters were George Savile, 1st Marquess of Halifax, the proponent of the Test Act who became a favourite of Charles II, John Wilkins, Warden of Wadham College, Oxford, and the chief motivator behind

---

* Ellen Clayton in *English Women Artists* states that Charles Beale mixed pigments for the Board of Green Cloth. As the board was an administrative body, this is perhaps unlikely. The board gained its name from the baize cloth that covered the table around which it met. Charles's colour-mixing perhaps took place elsewhere.

the formation of the Royal Society, the physician Thomas Sydenham, and several notable clergy, including Gilbert Burnet, Bishop of Salisbury. She painted various society beauties, including the marvellously named Lady Style and Jane, Lady Leigh, whose portrait by Beale as a shepherdess might have passed as being by Lely if the brushwork were only finer. She also painted a portrait of Charles II, though this seems to be a copy of a painting by Lely.[8]

The portrait Beale painted of Frances Hay reveals her as a classically handsome woman rather than an aristocratic beauty, with a mass of black curls, a direct gaze and a straight nose set above a full mouth.[9] She looks as if she would not be a pushover in a debate. In several self-portraits, Beale displayed no tendency towards self-flattery. One such work is notable, showing Beale sitting in classical dress with her right hand resting on a canvas bearing two portrait sketches in oils of her sons. Beside her hangs her palette, scrubbed clean like a well-used domestic chopping board, ready for the next commission. Beale, the artist, wanted people to know that while she might be the proud mother of two children she kept a well-run studio.[10]

For a lesson on the comparatively poor state of British art at this time, it is instructive to compare Beale's self-portrait with Artemisia Gentileschi's *Self-Portrait as the Allegory of Painting*.[11] The two women had biographical details in common: both were taught by their fathers and both followed the style of established and successful artists. But the similarity ends there. While Artemisia's portrait is explosive, Mary's is banal. The cultural isolation of England that had begun in the reign of Henry VIII, coupled with a fashion during the Stuart and Cromwellian eras for portraiture above all else, conspired to stifle English artistic innovation. One cannot, for instance, imagine an English painter of the mid-seventeenth century having the inspiration to paint a portrait of a fellow artist in the form of a drawing consisting only of the image of a hand holding a brush, yet that is exactly what the French artist Pierre Dumonstier did when he visited Artemisia in Rome in 1625.[12]

Although a brief flowering of native baroque artists during the reign of Charles I, and into the Commonwealth, produced painters of the calibre of William Dobson and Samuel Cooper (who continued to work into the reign of Charles II), England had at this time little significant home-grown artistic momentum.* Perhaps another reason was that, from the Elizabethan age onwards, drawing and painting had been seen as largely amateur pursuits for men and women of the higher social classes, to be learnt as part of a rounded Renaissance education. The amateur's output could be highly prized; Charles II owned a cabinet containing paintings by, among others, Elizabeth Pepys and Susanna Evelyn. Even Nicolas Hilliard, a professionally trained goldsmith and limner who was painter to Elizabeth I, thought only 'gentlemen' should engage in painting.[13]

In the same year that Frances Hay went to Covent Garden to have her portrait painted, two of the most remarkable figures in London surreptitiously quit the city. The Frenchmen des Groseilliers and Radisson quietly left the city to which they had given so much, made for Dover and sailed for France. They had been beguiled by secret French promises of wealth if they abandoned the Hudson's Bay Company they had helped found, and once more used their expertise in the service of their homeland. Behind them, the two explorers left a profound legacy. Their

---

* Art that was intrinsically English both in form and content really only came about with the career of William Hogarth, beginning in 1721 with his engraving satirising the South Sea Bubble investment fiasco.

work on behalf of the British had been crucial in the company's early success, helping to lay the groundwork for British control over all of Canada more than a century later.

In France, the friends' hopes were dashed. They found they had little status and were refused the official positions they expected. Des Groseilliers, now in his mid-fifties, sailed across the Atlantic once more to recommence the arduous life of a peripatetic fur trader. Not long after, he was followed by Radisson, the latter once more in the employ of the Hudson's Bay Company, which by now mistrusted him too much to allow him to work at its London HQ, and insisted he return to Canada.

In the autumn of 1675, an anonymous pamphlet appeared in London, priced one shilling, and entitled *A Letter from a Person of Quality to his Friend in the Country*. Gaining instant notoriety, its price shot up to twenty shillings. Its author was said to be Lord Shaftesbury, now out of government, though John Locke may have written part of it. The pamphlet accused Lord Danby of plotting to install the monarchy with absolute and arbitrary power under divine right, without any say from Parliament. The rights of the political classes were therefore under attack, with the freedoms granted under Magna Carta under threat from a king who would reign without any countervailing force, such as the House of Lords, to restrict his will.

Another pamphlet that appeared around the same time, entitled *Two Seasonable Discourses Concerning the Present Parliament*, put forward the advantages for the King of holding regular parliaments. These would vote him more money, support the Church, grant dissenters freedom of conscience and permit freedoms to Catholics providing they continued to be banned from public office and bearing arms. Again, Shaftesbury was seen as the hand behind the polemic. Charles began to consider curtailing not only Parliament, but some of his former minister's personal rights. And so London, rife with rumour, stumbled uncertainly towards Christmas.

CHAPTER 22

COFFEE WARS AT HOME, REAL WARS IN THE COLONIES

On 30 December 1675, Robert Hooke left his lodgings in Gresham College and walked south down Bishopsgate towards the Royal Exchange to have a coffee and engage in the day's gossip. It was a mild day for December and the storms that had plagued the capital earlier in the month had cleared away. At the Exchange, Hooke turned right into Cornhill and then left at the church of St Michael. Going down the alleyway beside the church, Hooke made his way past scaffolding, stones and other paraphernalia of the masons and carpenters rebuilding what remained of the medieval church all but destroyed in the Great Fire.

Behind the church Hooke found his destination, Garraway's Coffee House. It was a journey of at most four hundred yards and one he took almost every day, knowing that at his journey's end he would find strong coffee, the company of people he knew, and interesting conversation. On this particular winter's day he found his fellow coffee aficionados in a state of shock, staring with disbelief at an item in that day's official government newspaper, the *London Gazette*.*

The cause of the consternation was a prominently displayed royal proclamation. The headline was set in that peculiar mix of upper and lower case used by printers of the time when at a loss how else to grab attention. With this item they need not have worried:

By the King.
A PROCLAMATION
FOR THE
Suppression of Coffee-Houses.
CHARLES R.

The proclamation ordered all coffee houses throughout the entire country to close by 10 January, in eleven days' time. Coffee houses, the proclamation stated, and the 'idle and disaffected' people who frequented them, had produced 'very evil and dangerous effects'. Magistrates across the realm were to recall all licences for the sale or retailing of coffee, chocolate, sherbet or tea on pain of a fine of £5 a month. Persistent offenders would face much more serious sanctions.

To be lumped in with the 'idle and disaffected' cannot have caused much delight for the highly industrious and monarchist Hooke and his fellow virtuosi, let alone the men of business who used coffee houses as offices. The assorted readers in Garraway's and hundreds of other coffee houses across London, as well as

* The *London Gazette* can claim to be Britain's oldest continuously published newspaper, having been established in 1665 when the royal court was at Oxford during the plague.

in many more all over Britain, read that these simple establishments 'fomented diverse false, malicious and scandalous reports to the defamation of His Majesties government'.

Charles was not the first Stuart king to try his hand at prohibition. His grandfather, James I, had issued a strongly worded jeremiad against tobacco in 1604, calling it a 'pernicious' and foul-smelling weed. But the immediate cause of his abrupt order was, of course, the appearance of the pamphlets written by Shaftesbury, Locke and their opposition allies, all avidly read and discussed.

London's coffee houses sold not only coffee but also the other beverages that were about to be banned, backed up by copious supplies of sweet tobacco from the farms in Virginia, with newspapers and pamphlets to read. Occasionally they served alcohol. On long, communal tables designed for conviviality lay cups, spoons, plates and smoking supplies such as clay pipes, jostling for space along with copies of the *London Gazette*, the latest unlicensed newssheets and broadsides, scandal-mongering pamphlets, satirical poems and political and social diatribes of every variety.

From the government's point of view, coffee houses were politically suspect, allowing their clientele to read a great amount of illegal material. The many scurrilous political satires appeared despite the efforts of the official censor, Roger L'Estrange. Had they been inspected, many houses would have fallen foul of the laws that forbade the publication of treasonable writings. The heterodox and liberal atmosphere of the coffee houses was seen as a breeding ground for political debate and dissent – and some were exactly that. The houses had become successful in their secondary role of providing meeting places for those who viewed either the King or his government with ill favour.

For such minds, there were the twin problems of the

King's attitude to Parliament, which bore strong similarities to that of his unfortunate father, and the question of the succession within a royal family that many saw as being composed mainly of Catholics, including the King's heir, his brother, and his many bastard children – not to speak of the Queen and the main royal concubine, Louise, Duchess of Portsmouth. Customers of the more politically minded coffee houses had had much to chew over since the Test Act had caught in its web the Duke of York himself. If the coffee-house malcontents had known about the secret treaty with France, there might have been real reason for insurrection to brew in the jangling minds of the coffee addicts. As it was, fear of popery combined with the pungent smell of black coffee and tobacco smoke to make for a heady mix increasingly viewed with alarm in Whitehall. To the devotees of the black bean the proclamation was as great a shock to the system as the strongest slug of Turkish coffee.

The coffee house fad had burst upon London twenty years before thanks to the travels of merchants, adventurers, diplomats and others in Asia and the Levant. The coffee trade was controlled by the Ottoman Empire, and exports to the West mainly originated through ports in Yemen. By the early seventeenth century, coffee drinking had become fashionable in the houses of members of elite circles. The first coffee house in England probably opened in Oxford in 1650, run by a Lebanese proprietor. In 1652, a coffee house opened in London; its proprietor had come to England with Daniel Edwards, a merchant who for many years had lived in Smyrna, trading with the Turks of Anatolia, and employing Pasqua Rosee, possibly born in Sicily of ethnic Greek stock, as some form of middleman or translator. Upon Edwards's return to London, Rosee came too. At his home near the church of St Stephen Walbrook, in the heart of the old city, Edwards treated his guests to Rosee's coffee. Word of Rosee's brew spread and Edwards selflessly supported Rosee's venture in going out on his own and opening a commercial coffee house, albeit a mere shed in the churchyard of St Michael's Cornhill, near where Hooke's favourite coffee house, Garraway's, later stood. The business flourished and the coffee fad took off. Soon a second coffee house opened, the Rainbow in Fleet Street, run by a former barber named Farr.

As coffee houses proliferated, the government set out to regulate them. In London, the Middlesex magistrates granted licences, initially to raise revenue for the Exchequer. To gain a licence a proprietor had to prove he had paid duty on the goods he sold. Later, once coffee houses took on differing characters, some becoming known for the dissenting political views of those who frequented them, the government came to see the licensing laws as a potential tool for political control.

There are many testaments to how vile this early coffee tasted. Yet it caught on. One clue to its popularity is contained in a poem lambasting the evils of alcohol – 'foggy ale' and the 'sweet poison of the treacherous grape' – and proclaiming coffee as heaven sent:

> Coffee arrives, that grave and wholesome Liquor
> That heals the stomach, makes the genius quicker
> Relieves the memory, revives the sad
> And cheers the Spirits, without making mad.[1]

To the puritanical or improving mind, coffee was God's antidote to alcohol, providing a convivial drink without intoxication. Not everyone was so enamoured of the dark brew. Early in the century, the treasurer of the Virginia Company, George Sandys, a vocal advocate of slave labour, reported from his travels to

Egypt and Constantinople that the Turks drank coffee 'blacke as soote and tasting not much unlike it'.[2] Despite such reservations, the coffee house arrived in London at exactly the right time. The population was eager for news, for new thinking, for debate. The city, though old, had a young population, keen for knowledge and ideas. If one wished to know what was happening, the place to go became the nearest coffee house. For the price of a cup, anyone, no matter what his social status, was welcome to join in the conversation. This was the era of the ascent of polite society – an ideal to be cherished if not often attained. Fuelled by caffeine, debate was lively. The rule that conversation should be respectful and civilised was not always adhered to, though argument resolved by fisticuffs was supposedly the preserve of the tavern.

Each coffee house drew its particular clientele. Those around the Royal Exchange attracted merchants and traders, those in the vicinity of Whitehall Palace were forums for political debate, those in the region of the Strand and Fleet Street were the haunt of journalists, while playwrights and members of the Royal Society picked and chose between them.

Coffee houses soon made their appearance in the printed media. Satires were written, as were plays. A play published in the 1660s and entitled *Knavery in All Trades, or, The Coffee House* has been attributed to the dramatist John Tatham, though it is so thinly written this seems unlikely. Pepys went to see it and pronounced it the 'most ridiculous, insipid play' he had ever seen. According to the play's printed title page, it was performed at Christmas by apprentices; in other words, by amateurs. Much of the play's action takes place in and around a coffee house and concerns the doubtful morality and honesty of most of the characters. It gives a disparaging verdict on the qualities of coffee: ''tis most pernicious to the brain, it fires the pericranium, disorders al the faculties, presents ideas most delusive,' opines one character, who amusingly goes on to claim that 'Brutus ... drank heartily of it when designed the death of Royal Cesar'[3] – a comment eerily presaging the fears of the royal court a decade after the play's appearance.

A further attack on the coffee house came with the publication of the anonymously written *Women's Petition Against Coffee*. The writer of this amusing and bawdy pastiche had undoubtedly sat through many a half-witted discussion in a coffee house. The petition was addressed to 'the Right Honorable the Keepers of the Liberty of Venus' on behalf of the women of Britain – 'Several Thousands of Buxome Good-Women, Languishing in Extremity of Want' because their husbands could no longer make love to them due to the disabling effects of coffee. The loss of sexual vigour was caused by nothing less than

> the Excessive use of that Newfangled, Abominable, Heathenish Liquor called COFFEE, which Riffling Nature of her Choicest *Treasures*, and *Drying* up the *Radical Moisture*, has so *Eunucht* our Husbands, and Cripple our more kind *Gallants*, that they are become as *Impotent* as Age, and as unfruitful as those *Desarts* whence that unhappy *Berry* is said to be brought.[4]

Impotence was not the petitioners' only complaint. Men stoked up on coffee could out-talk women: 'by frequenting these *Stygian Tap-houses*' they soon learned 'to exceed us in *Talkativeness*', holding wild discussions on major issues such as 'what colour the Red Sea is of; whether the Great Turk be a Lutheran or a Calvinist; who *Cain's* Father in Law was, *&c.*' Not only was the conversation tedious, but rather than replacing the taverns, the coffee houses actually 'pimped' for them:

> For when people have swill'd themselves with a morning draught of more Ale than a Brewer's horse can carry, hither they come for a pennyworth of Settle-brain, where they are sure to meet enow lazy pragmatical Companions, that resort here to prattle of News, that they neither understand, nor are concerned in; and after an hours impertinent Chat, begin to consider a Bottle of Claret would do excellent well before Dinner; whereupon to the Bush they all march together, till every one of them is as Drunk as a Drum, and then back again to the Coffee-house to drink themselves suber; where three or four dishes a piece, and smoaking, makes their throats as *dry* as Mount Aetna enflam'd with Brimflame; for that they must away to the next *Red Lattice* to quenc them with a dozen or two of Ale, which at last growing nauseous, one of them begins to extol the blood of the Grape, what rare Langoon, and Racy Canary may be had at the *Miter*: Saist thou so? cries another, *Let's then go and replenish there, with our Earthen Vessels*: So once more they troop to the Sack-shop till they are drunker than before; and then by a retrograde motion, stagger back to *Soberize* themselves with *Coffee*: thus like *Tennis Balls* between two Rackets, the *Fopps our Husbands* are *bandied* to and fro all day between the *Coffee-house* and *Tavern*, whilst we poor souls sit *mopeing* all alone till *Twelve* at night, and when at last they come to bed finoakt like a *Westphalia Hogs-head* we have no more comfort of them, than from a *shotten Herring* or a dried *Bulrush* . . .

The petition ended by asking for coffee to be banned for anyone under the age of sixty. Good old-fashioned ales should be provided in its place.

It is generally thought that coffee houses were exclusively male preserves, except for the maids or waitresses, the landlady, if there was one, and maybe a whore or two in the upstairs rooms. Such a picture is not entirely correct. Although the clientele was predominantly male, both Robert Boyle and Samuel Pepys tell us of women frequenting coffee houses; the latter describes going in a coach with his wife Elizabeth and her lady's companion Deborah Willet to a coffee house in Covent Garden on a Monday morning at ten o'clock. If Elizabeth and her maid could go, so could other women. So was the author of the pamphlet actually a woman? If so, Aphra Behn comes to mind as the most likely candidate.

The writer, though, was undoubtedly someone who preferred the company of an alehouse, making it more probable that the writer was male. Judging by the high quality of the writing, he or she was probably a poet or playwright, certainly one well used to writing sustained comedy. If the author were a man, the likely aspirant – or aspirants – for the honour must be looked for among the members of the 'Merry Gang', the professional wits who, like George Etherege or William Wycherley, could readily produce a humorous piece of writing. One thing we know for sure is that whoever the authors were, in person they were likely to enhance the conversation of any coffee house they entered.

The petition must have had some success, for it was followed up by a counter-blast, *The Men's Answer to the Women's petition Against Coffee*. Between them, these squibs undoubtedly caused considerable hilarity in coffee houses, taverns and anywhere else that the more lubricious members of society met. When the King's petition appeared the following year there was little mirth. The ban was put in place in January 1676, but before the languishing piles of imported coffee beans could rot, it was repealed. The power of commerce was greater than that of the Crown. There were hundreds of coffee houses in the city, providing the setting for all manner of business. Books were sold, auctions of goods held, shares in joint stock companies offered to the adventurous. Merchants had commercial interests not only in the importation of the small black beans but often in the coffee houses themselves. The fact was that the coffee trade had become important. It was closely allied to the major cash businesses of sugar and tobacco, both fed by widespread addiction to sweet coffee with an accompanying pipe to smoke, and both dependent upon the London-based slave trade. The coffee house had become such a part of the commercial fabric of London that a king could not will it away.

As the battle raged over the future of London's coffee houses, a much greater conflict was being fought out far away. Both battles were over personal rights – what today would be called civil rights. In America, animosity between English colonists and the native peoples had been increasing for some time. The colonists were greedy for land and did not consider it imperative to keep to agreements they made with the local inhabitants. For decades, London had allowed English colonies along the eastern seaboard of America to grow without control from home. Many of the earliest Puritan settlers had emigrated in order to set up colonies independent from the stifling religious orthodoxies they found at home. To a great extent they had succeeded in evading direct control from London. As long as the colonies paid their trading taxes and sent their cash crops home to England, they were kept on a very loose rein.

One of the problems with this arrangement in New England was that when it came to relations between the settlers and the Wampanoag people of Massachusetts, agreements were broken and land grabbed in an ad hoc manner. The indigenous population was in sharp decline, driven by imported

European illnesses and internal immigration to escape the invaders. It is estimated that by the 1670s there were 35,000 English settlers in New England and only 15,000 indigenous people.

In 1675, disagreements came to a head. The Wampanoag leader Metacom was suspicious of English ambitions. He foresaw that ultimately the English would take over everything and destroy his people. He set about putting together a coalition of tribes to resist the settlers.

In the resulting conflict – which would become known as King Philip's War* – Metacom's united tribes attacked more than half of the English settlements in New England. Out of a total of ninety settlements, fifty-two were either destroyed or partially burned down. The war spread from Massachusetts into other parts of New England and carried on through the winter. London sent reinforcements of 1000 extra troops, and in the spring of 1676 the English launched an offensive. Metacom was forced to retreat to Mount Hope, a small hill in Rhode Island. The English captured his wife and nine-year-old son and sold them into slavery in the West Indies. In August, Metacom's stronghold was overrun and he was shot dead. His head was put on a spike in Plymouth.

By the end of the war, 5000 indigenous people and 2500 English were dead. The native American population of New England never recovered. The war convinced Charles and his government that the colonies should be brought under stricter control. New governors were appointed with powers to ride roughshod over the wishes of local assemblies. Despite the introduction of more centralised control, under Charles's rule

* Metacom also had an English name, Philip, given to him by his father as a token of friendship between the Wampanoag and the settlers.

the colonies were not run as a pure exercise in imperial expansion but as economic units within the increasingly important transatlantic trade that fed London's economy.[5]

London's colonial problems were not confined to New England. Rebellions had broken out elsewhere. In 1675, slave uprisings were put down in Jamaica, leading to a declaration of martial law imposed by extra troops sent by London. In Barbados too a rebellion was brutally suppressed, with fifty-two Africans beheaded, burned alive or tortured to death by other gruesome methods. Among the island's large population of Irish indentured servants, disturbances took place on such a regular basis that the Irish workforce was phased out and replaced by one that was entirely African.

In the first English colony of Virginia, another threat arose to the colonial enterprise. An uprising that became known as Bacon's Rebellion almost led to the colony breaking completely free of London rule. For some time, there had been unrest among African slaves and indentured European servants, the latter for the most part slaves in all but name. Since the end of the British civil wars, Virginia had been a dumping ground for Irish rebels and English undesirables. Criminals rounded up across England were shipped to the colony. After the Restoration, former Cromwellian soldiers were transported along with the increasing numbers of London criminals, known as 'Newgaters'. Some of these former Roundheads led a series of small-scale insurrections.[6]

At the heart of the discontent in Virginia were the issues of land and taxes. Indentured servants, who had worked their passage to the new world, discovered upon gaining their freedom that their promised parcel of land rarely materialised. For the poor, taxation was harsh, based on a poll tax, which meant that the richest landowner paid the same as the poorest former indentured servant. On top of this, relations with the indigenous people were never good.

When a minor theft from a farm escalated into widespread butchery by both Europeans and the indigenous people, a hot-headed aristocratic planter called Nathaniel Bacon, who was descended from Elizabeth I's chancellor Francis Bacon, advocated an all-out war intended to exterminate the native peoples. The colony's governor, Sir William Berkeley – a cultivated man, a favourite of Charles II and an able and effective governor who experimented with new crops to improve the colony's economy – put forward a more reasonable approach. Matters came to a head during 1676, when elections to the ruling House of Burgesses turned into a mass rebellion of mostly freed indentured servants, led by Bacon. The appeal of the rebellion was based on Bacon's recognition of the abuse of the underclasses by the colonialist grandees; his intention was not only to take on the warring tribes and wipe them out, but to create a form of 'levelling', in what seems to have been a late flowering of the experimental and revolutionary political movements of the 1640s and '50s. When Bacon offered to free every slave and servant who rallied to his cause, hundreds of Africans and Europeans fled their plantations to answer his call. Bacon now had an army. They took the capital Jamestown and burned it to the ground.

Governor Berkeley sent word to London requesting reinforcements. Before the extra troops could arrive, however, Bacon died and his rebellion petered out. Hundreds of rebels were persuaded to surrender by false promises of pardons. Berkeley showed no mercy, hanging dozens. The King was not pleased with his old friend, saying, 'The old fool has taken more lives in his naked country than I have taken for my father's murder.'[7] When the thousand English troops ordered by London finally arrived in Virginia, they had nothing to do. Sir William was replaced and retired to his London mansion, where he died the following year.

With another attempted uprising having to be put down in Maryland, the colonial governors were under orders from London to find a solution to the growing unrest, which was again a result of inequality and suppressed expectations among poorer settlers.[8] In response, the governors played the race card. They passed laws depriving Africans and Native Americans of rights, downgrading their status relative to that of European servants. Freed Africans lost their right to own property and vote in elections, even the right to a family life. Enslaved Africans lost their right to freedom – even if their owners wished to free them.[9] Within a few years, Africans were to be enslaved in perpetuity, a status inherited by their sons and daughters.

Against the tumultuous background of the uprisings across the western colonies, the slave trade was expanding at a tremendous rate. In the five years before Bacon's Rebellion, London slavers shipped over 9000 men, women and children out of Africa; in the five years after it, 26,881 Africans were enslaved, a threefold increase. But although the uprisings threatened to destabilise the economic benefits accruing from the slave trade, London was slow to react. Partly this was because the colonies were designed to be self-regulating, but it was also because Charles's government had suffered considerable blows to its sense of security.

CHAPTER 23

CITY LIFE

With so much turmoil in the realm of foreign affairs during the mid-1670s, it would be easy to discount the wide variety of events simultaneously taking place in London. The shock of the war and disorder in the colonies had hardly died away before a very public attack was made on one of London's new institutions – the Royal Society.

The experimentalists were well used to criticism by now and must have considered themselves able to stand up to all types of sturdy argument, but the new assault was unexpected and difficult to counter. To their great surprise, the Royal Society's virtuosi found themselves lampooned on the stage. The play was Thomas Shadwell's *The Virtuoso*, performed by the Duke's Company at its sumptuous Dorset Gardens Theatre.

Shadwell came from an old family of minor gentry in Norfolk. He studied at Cambridge, left without gaining a degree and went to London to train as a lawyer, taking lodgings at the Inner Temple in 1658. His very first play, put on by the Duke's Company in 1668, when Shadwell was twenty-eight, dared to lampoon not just one fellow playwright but three, one of them being the pre-eminent John Dryden himself. In *The Sullen Lover* (the title role of which was played by the author's wife Anne), Shadwell mocked the kind of heroic tragedy written both by Dryden and Dryden's brother-in-law, Sir Robert Howard. Word quickly spread among the theatre-going public that Sir Robert was portrayed as Sir Positive At-All, an insufferably self-important know-all. Sir Robert's brother Edward, also a playwright and poet, was lampooned, it was said, as Poet Ninny. The play was a huge hit, with the Duke of York and a great number of London's society turning out to enjoy the fun. Its notoriety allowed it to run for twelve nights, making it a smash hit for the time.

Although not a man of money, Shadwell's wit and social prowess allowed him entrance to the company of well-bred and well-heeled Wits – the group including Charles Sedley, George Etherege, the Earl of Rochester, Charles Sackville, later Earl of Dorset, and the Duke of Buckingham – who dictated the prevalent London society taste for style over substance, and for wit over benevolence. Among this set, those who wished could write for the stage without having to write for money. Shadwell, like Dryden, was a professional writer, and so while others had the luxury of favouring witty conversation over the written word, Shadwell had no alternative but to survive by polishing his wit upon the page.

The plot of *The Virtuoso* centred on a character named Sir Nicholas Gimcrack, a rich virtuoso who carried out many oddball experiments, including giving a man a blood transfusion from a sheep, bottling air from different locations around the country to store in his cellar like wine and studying a frog to see how a man might swim on dry land. A particularly absurd moment saw Sir Nicholas read a bible by the light of a leg of pork in order to demonstrate phosphorescence. The play seemed to be perfectly in tune with the King's amused view – as reported by Samuel Pepys – of some of the experiments carried out by the Royal Society.

Many of Sir Nicholas's freakish experiments had actually been performed. One of the most notorious was the transfusion of animal blood into a human. On 23 November 1667, a Dr King (possibly the physician who would later be present in Whitehall Palace when Charles II was taken fatally ill) had transfused a small quantity of sheep's blood into a mentally challenged workman named Arthur Coga. Miraculously, Coga survived to receive twenty shillings for his pains. When asked why he thought sheep's blood was chosen for the experiment, he replied that it was symbolic, Christ being the Lamb of God.

There was much speculation over precisely who was the target of the play's satire – the Royal Society as a whole, the gentlemen amateurs, or the entire project of experimentalism?[1] It seems fair to say that while it was not an attack on the society per se, it was aimed at some of its activities. As Shadwell would have understood all too well, however, for any satire to work it must have a flesh-and-blood target, someone for the audience to hold in its collective mind's eye while it enjoyed the fun on stage. Indisputably, that person was Robert Hooke. No member of the Royal Society exemplified the ideal renaissance man better than he.

The Virtuoso of the play, Sir Nicholas Gimcrack, spends a great deal of his time viewing his menagerie of worms and insects through his microscope. When not so engaged, he views the geography of the moon through a telescope. The parallels with *Micrographia* are impossible to ignore. The possibility of human flight, suggested by no less a virtuoso than Robert Boyle, is used to great comic effect. It is unknown if Boyle went to see the play, but Hooke did, and he found the attack particularly hurtful. In his diary, he exclaimed, 'Damned Dogs!'

Hooke had by now many enemies, real and imagined. He found consolation in his unorthodox private life. He never married but had sex with a succession of maids. He shared his quarters with two relatives: young Tom Giles, the son of a cousin, and his niece Grace, to whom he became increasingly attached. When Hooke began keeping a private diary in 1672, Grace was already living with him. She was a vivacious young girl known for her good looks. Hooke doted on the girl, recording in his diary the necklaces and other items he bought for her.

On Friday 26 May 1676, a fire started among the ramshackle streets of Southwark, across the river from the walled city. Hooke took Grace to witness the flames of a second Great Fire. The pair watched from the top of the 200ft high Doric column he and his friend Wren had designed as a monument to the Great Fire, which was nearing completion. According to a contemporary account, the Southwark fire destroyed at least 500 houses, the meal market, several notable inns and 'the prison of the counter', a small gaol or compter dating from medieval times, used chiefly for the incarceration of debtors and religious dissidents.[2] Later estimates put the destruction at between 600 and 900 houses. Although this was very much smaller than the number lost in the Great Fire of 1666, it was still destruction on a very large scale.

As Grace grew up, Hooke's feelings towards her changed. On 4 June 1676, the couple had sexual intercourse for the first time. Hooke was a few weeks from his forty-first birthday. They continued to have intercourse until Hooke, perhaps in a fit of guilt, decided he should send her back to her family on the Isle of Wight. However, the separation did not take place; Grace continued as her uncle's lover, while becoming more attractive to other men. Hooke's diary records his anguish over these episodes when Grace took other lovers, though she continued to be attached to Hooke until his death.

Hooke's unorthodox private life may illustrate his lack of confidence. He was unable, or reluctant, to strike up relationships with women of his own social standing, preferring housemaids and his own much younger and less sophisticated niece. Perhaps he was all too aware of his own physical imperfections. Even his closest friend John Aubrey described his physical appearance as 'somewhat twisted'. A further blow to his esteem came when Isaac Newton, making one of his rare visits to London, remarked to him, 'If I have seen further it is because I stand on the shoulders of giants', doubtless ensuring that Hooke was under no illusions about his own position.

As if to remind people of his brilliance, Hooke chose 1676 to publish the solution to his anagram *ceiiinosssttuv*, which had gone unsolved since he first published it in 1660. He revealed the solution to be *ut tensio, sic vis* – as the tension, so the force. The phrase referred to Hooke's discovery of the relationship of force to the extension or retraction of springs. Hooke's Law, as it came to be known, stated that the force necessary to extend or depress a spring was directly proportional to the distance of extension or depression, expressed as $F = -kx$, where F is the force, x is the displacement of the spring and k is specific to the spring. Thus, for example, if a 50 gm weight stretched a spring by 2 cm, 100 gm would displace it by 4 cm.[3] The law, used widely today in science and engineering – in seismology, acoustics and molecular mechanics – would take its place in the history of technology as the basic principle behind devices such as the spring scale, the nanometer, or pressure gauge, and the mechanical clock.

The year 1676 saw success for Hooke in another area: architecture. On 29 August, the King went to Moorfields, where nine years before he had visited the homeless after the Great Fire. Now he came to view a new hospital for the insane, known as Bedlam or, more correctly, as Bethlehem Hospital. The old Bedlam, situated in the walled city near Bishopsgate, had burned down in the fire. Hooke's new hospital outside the city walls was a large, handsome classical building of forty-nine bays, built in a hurry in little more than a year.* When the King came to visit, Hooke realised that he had forgotten to give orders to carry out Wren's recommendation to widen the central path through Moorfields to the building, which would have allowed the King and his entourage to approach his building in style.[4] Somehow, for Hooke even his successes tended to be marred by some disagreeable incident or other.

At the Navy Office, Samuel Pepys wrestled with the inadequacies he felt the Dutch wars had highlighted in the Royal Navy. The problems, he thought, fell into three categories: the recruitment and training of officers, the provision of sufficient new ships, and the provisioning and maintenance of the fleet. In the mid- to late 1670s Pepys set out to remedy these problems. The Test Act, which had compelled James to resign as Lord High Admiral of the Navy, had the collateral effect of enhancing Pepys's career. With the Duke retired, the King put in place an Admiralty Commission to oversee control of the navy. Pepys was made its secretary, giving him enormous power. The navy was the single greatest enterprise in the kingdom, its monumental size and structure taking up the endeavours of tens of thousands, employed either directly or indirectly. It was not only the largest organised entity in England, it was

* The speed of building seems to have had unforeseen consequences. In 1800 the hospital was judged unsafe and a new one ordered to be built in Southwark.

the most important. Without the navy, mercantile capitalism could not operate and London would be unable to compete in international markets.

This was the body that Pepys set out to reorganise. In 1676 he instigated examinations for lieutenants, so moving command onto a professional basis and away from the old system of patronage and promotion through experience alone. The deficiencies of the navy's all-important victualling service had also long been of special interest to Pepys. The entire organisation of the navy was already under increasingly critical review, from the design of ships to the methods of supplying them; Sir William Petty had written on the subject some years before, for it was of great interest within the Royal Society, of which Pepys was a Fellow, as well as to the sailing-mad King.[5] Now, together with his recently appointed Surveyor for the Navy, Sir John Tippetts, formerly head of the naval dockyard at Portsmouth, Pepys put together an ambitious plan to build thirty identical frigates. It was the most sustained building programme the navy had ever known. Pepys used his considerable skills of persuasion to gain the agreement of the House of Commons to the necessary expenditure of £20,000 per ship, £600,000 in total.

One of Sir John Tippetts' protégés, a carpenter named William Keltridge, produced a manuscript containing measurements and detailed plans for the various types of ships required by the navy. This was followed by work by the skilled Hampshire shipwright Edmund Dummer, who had been appointed by Pepys as Controller of the Victualling Accounts as part of his programme of reorganisation and improved efficiency. Under Tippetts' guidance, Dummer drew up ideal plans of ships' hulls, based on vessels they surveyed at Harwich. From this, he produced a book of sectional drawings through the hulls of various ships, showing how the ideal sweep of their lines changed along the length of the vessel. In a letter to Pepys, Dummer expressed his dissatisfaction with the long-established practice of ship design being 'delivered man to man' rather than by 'maxims deduced from reason and experiments'.[6]

Dummer, Tippetts and Pepys had lofty ideas about how the new scientific approach might benefit the navy. But they were perhaps too ambitious for their time. What were required were more down-to-earth plans provided by men like Keltridge, on the basis of which ships might easily be built. The man chosen to oversee the construction of the new ships, however, was not Keltridge but the skilled ship designer and builder Sir Anthony Deane, the head of the naval shipyard at Woolwich. Known for building fast ships that handled well, Deane had come to Pepys's notice when he was still a young man at Harwich shipyard. At Pepys's encouragement he had written what has been described as the 'clearest account before the eighteenth century of how a ship's hull was constructed'.[7] According to Pepys, one of Deane's ships, the seventy-gun *Resolution*, launched in 1667, was 'the best ship by report in all the world'.[8]

Deane's reputation for constructing successful ships was enhanced by his gift of the gab and Pepys's patronage.[9] He was therefore the first choice when it came to shipbuilding in bulk. Pepys appointed him head of the important shipyard at Portsmouth, which had the capacity to construct large numbers of big ships. Building a large number of identical ships required great organisational ability and knowledge of naval architecture; it would however have the benefit of shared designs for masts, spars, etc., and the same advantages when it came to spare parts. What Pepys was proposing was nothing less than the creation of a centralised planning apparatus controlling a standardised fleet, run by uniformly trained men given the means to run successful campaigns at sea. His vision would pay off handsomely in the next century when Britain would become the premier world sea power.

There were further developments in the world of theatre as Thomas Killigrew's tenuous hold on the reins of the King's Men finally slipped from his grasp. The man who tugged them away from him was his son William, convinced he could make a better job of running the company than his father.

Having made Killigrew's and Davenant's original warrants hereditary, Charles could hardly interfere in a family spat over money. Unlike his former sparring partner Davenant, Killigrew was not steeped in the workings of the theatre. He saw it as one of a number of irons in the fire, all designed to make money, but none of which seemed to amount to much. He spent much of his time at court as the King's unofficial jester, although in between jokes he was always asking for favours, few of which amounted to anything much; the King preferred to keep him around rather than economically afloat.

It cannot have helped Killigrew's humour that in the same year, the Duke's players performed not only Shadwell's hit *The Virtuoso*, but the finest comedy of the age, *The Man of Mode, or, Sir Fopling Flutter*, by George Etherege, staring Thomas Betterton. The play remains the best example of a comedy of manners. Its convoluted plot revolves around a group of stylish characters trying to disentangle themselves from the wrong sexual partners – a situation caused largely by their being too clever for their own good – and all the while trying hard to retain their fashionable froideur. Within two years Killigrew would be dead at the age of sixty-six, having outlived Davenant by ten years.

*

In the world of music a teenage prodigy named Henry Purcell began to make a reputation in London. Purcell was born in St Anne's Lane, off Old Pye Street, in 1658 or 1659, two hundred yards from Westminster Abbey, where his father, Henry senior, a gentleman chorister at the Chapel Royal, had sung at Charles I's coronation. The younger Henry's fluent musicianship enabled him to display his genius early. At the age of twelve, while himself a scholar and chorister at the Chapel Royal, he wrote a choral piece for the King. He went on to be appointed organist at Westminster Abbey, and two years later was given a similar post at the Chapel Royal. As well as writing when required various sacred pieces and odes to the royal family, Purcell wrote a great deal of both religious and secular music.

Purcell's precocious skill at composition was soon noted in the theatrical world. In the cut-throat business of London's playhouses, customers had come to expect novelty. The playhouses' impresarios had to pander to a demand they themselves had created, coming up with new stage effects and songs on a regular basis, transforming plays old and new by the introduction of dances and songs. In this frenetic whirl, Purcell found himself much in demand. At the age of eighteen, he was asked to write music for two plays by the prolific Thomas Shadwell. These were the racy comedies of manners, *Epsom Wells* and *The Libertine.* He also wrote the music for plays by Dryden and Aphra Behn. The following year, he wrote the music for another of Shadwell's plays, an adaptation of Shakespeare's *Timon of Athens.* In these so-called dramatic operas, the lead actors recited their lines while musicians and singers filled out the dialogue with songs and musical interludes. The form was much admired at the time, largely thanks to William Davenant's shameless iconoclastic dicing and slicing of plays, no matter how good the original.

Despite his work for the commercial theatre, Purcell still found time to create operatic pieces including *Dido and Aeneas*, which with no spoken parts was the first true English opera. His masterpieces were to include a glorious *Te Deum* and *Jubilate*; an opera, *King Arthur*, with words by Dryden; and music for *The Fairy Queen*, an adaptation of *A Midsummer Night's Dream* written by Davenant, and Dryden's adaptation of *The Tempest*.

While young Henry Purcell was making his mark, the veteran poet Andrew Marvell became embroiled in a banking scandal. Two of Marvell's relatives, the merchants Robert Thompson and Edward Nelthorpe, headed a banking partnership taking in deposits from a large number of merchants and wealthy individuals. Thompson and Nelthorpe claimed they 'owned parts of East India shipping' (i.e. the East India Company) and that this was one of several 'advantageous and profitable trades' in which they invested. In other words, they speculated with their clients' money. They invested in silk, wine, lead mining in Wales, Russian trade and Irish linen, omitting 'nothing within the compass of our ingenuity'. When some of these speculative trades failed, word got out and there was a run on the bank. Unable to pay its depositors, soon it was adrift by £175,000.

Thompson and Nelthorpe had evolved their business into a new type of concern. Known as banker-scriveners, they took money in and issued paper (an IOU) for it, promising a return of around 4 to 6 per cent, while investing the deposits in other ventures. This new business arose because goldsmith-bankers could not keep pace with the need for investment in London's growing economy. With the population expanding, and likewise the various trades with the new colonies in America, Bermuda, Jamaica and Barbados, along with the existing trade from the Baltic and the Mediterranean and the growing trade with India and the East, there was too little silver or coinage to deal with demand. The scriveners took up the shortfall with paper pledges.

The combination of economic growth and the inflation due to the rapid influx of New World gold into European economies reinforced the need for a stable, centralised source of affordable credit. Unfortunately, there existed no such thing. All banking was run via goldsmiths, money scriveners, country banks and merchant bankers. Since goldsmiths already had stout vaults in which to store their gold, entrepreneurs entrusted their gold to them for safekeeping. It was not long before the goldsmith-scriveners realised that as well as investing the deposited money they could lend it out to others for a fee. This was the invention of modern British banking.*

Goldsmith-bankers carried out numerous types of banking transactions. They distributed to their clients notes or bills, which in turn went into circulation, being used in buying and selling bullion and in international currency dealings. These operations were theoretically self-limiting, restricted by the amount of gold on hand to lend against. While it is true that many goldsmiths practised a version of what is called fractional reserve banking, and typically put more notes into circulation than they could actually redeem, there was also a limit to creditors' faith in notes that were backed by an amount of gold that might not actually balance the paper. Having become in this way the equivalent of modern bankers, turning themselves into an investment vehicle using other people's money, that was the predicament in which Thompson and Nelthorpe found themselves.

Andrew Marvell rented a house in St Giles-in-the-Fields

---

* These receipts or notes from the goldsmith-bankers, often taking the form of a letter, are some of the earliest surviving cheques in England.

where Thompson and Nelthorpe could hide away from their creditors. The bankers published a pamphlet telling their creditors to be patient – the company was doing only what other banks were doing. They explained it was unfair of their creditors not to settle for the six shillings and eightpence in the pound they were offering. Had not another company recently settled for only eighteen pence in the pound? As with the Great Stop, the Thompson–Nelthorpe affair demonstrated that a bank was not always a secure place for one's money. The banking row would not be resolved until well into the next century.

Marvell meanwhile continued to take an active interest in politics, particularly in the question of the royal succession and the King's increasing wariness of Parliament.

Wary of mounting antagonism, Charles now ordered Shaftesbury – his one-time chancellor and now leader of the opposition – out of London. It had been noted in government circles that Shaftesbury continued to foment anti-government moves, entertaining various opposition figures at his home, the ancient and rackety Exeter House on the Strand. At first, Shaftesbury refused to go, because Secretary of State Joseph Williamson had not signed the King's order. Eventually he left for the country, but after a little time returned to London, setting up at Thanet House in Aldersgate Street. He and his allies distributed a pamphlet questioning the power of the monarchy, suggesting that Parliament could 'limit, restrain and govern the descent and Inheritance of the Crown itself'.[10] Because of his manoeuvres, Shaftesbury was put in the Tower, along with several other opposition figures, including Charles's one-time friend the Duke of Buckingham.*

---

* Buckingham and the others were released shortly after their incarceration; Shaftesbury was imprisoned until early 1678.

In the meantime, Marvell brought out a pamphlet on the threat of popery and Stuart-style arbitrary government.[11] Like Shaftesbury's broadside, Marvell's pamphlet railed against the prorogation of Parliament from November 1675 to July 1677; but it went further, suggesting some knowledge or suspicion of the secret deal Charles had done with Louis XIV.

Feelings were running high in the city and the Tory camp had to reply. In the event it was the censor, Roger L'Estrange, who responded, with a pamphlet titled 'An account of the Growth of Knavery'.[12] Soon, though, the war of words would turn to something more concrete, as London was shaken by rumours of a plot to murder the King.

CHAPTER 24

THE CITY CONVULSED

Charles first heard of a plot to kill him in the summer of 1678 as he went for his daily walk in St James's Park. Christopher Kirkby, an experimenter who had assisted the King at his alchemical laboratory, came up to the famously approachable monarch and warned him that Catholics were plotting to assassinate him.

By nature, Charles did not allow such tales to alarm him. Previous plots had dissolved into the air. But Kirkby insisted this one should be taken seriously. He said he could produce someone who had personal knowledge of the plot. Charles agreed Kirkby could bring what evidence he had to the Palace, and strolled on towards the park.

When Kirkby arrived for the arranged meeting at Whitehall Palace he brought with him an elderly clergyman called Israel Tonge, who fostered an obsessional belief that Jesuits were plotting against Protestant England. He told Charles that the Jesuits were plotting to kill him and the Duke of Ormond and cause rebellion in England, Ireland, Scotland and Wales. With the help of the French, they would place James on the throne or give it to the Duke of Monmouth.

Charles listened impassively. When Tonge produced a document he said would reveal all, Charles asked his servant William Chiffinch to arrange for the Earl of Danby, the first minister, to investigate. Charles appears to have thought that the matter would end there.

Kirkby and Tonge knew one another because they had once lodged in the same house in Vauxhall, where Kirkby had boasted of his access to the King. This engaged Tonge's attention, for he was already involved in fomenting one of the oddest conspiracies in British history. Some years before, he had come into contact with a failed clergyman named Titus Oates with whom he shared a hatred and fear of Catholicism.

Oates had recently returned to England from living abroad. He was a con artist; the one constant in his life was the wheedling of money by deception. Unfortunately for him, his skills at dissembling were usually undermined by his foul-mouthed conversation and disreputable habits. Even his father, a radical cleric, disliked him. Despite this, a career in the Church seemed a natural choice. Being by all accounts lazy and dim, Oates failed to gain a BA from Cambridge, then lied about his degree in order to be ordained in the Church of England. He was sacked from his parish for incompetence and homosexuality, before conning his way into several jobs, all of which ended in scandal. With his options running out, Oates managed to find employment as a Protestant curate in the household of the Duke of Norfolk, a leading Catholic. In 1677, at the age of twenty-eight, he converted to Roman Catholicism.

Seeking to turn his spiritual awakening to earthly advantage, Oates persuaded the Society of Jesus to enrol him in two Jesuit schools abroad, both of which later ejected him.[1] By 1678 Oates was in dire poverty. He discovered a lifeline in Tonge, the obsessive vicar who was now printing regular exhortations against the Catholic menace. Acting as a man who had seen at first hand the Jesuits' plots against England, Oates persuaded the gullible Tonge of his wish to reveal all. Tonge encouraged Oates to write down his experiences and his knowledge of the Jesuit plots.

To what extent Tonge was complicit in fabricating the evidence rather than being merely a gullible stooge is unknown, though he was at first the main engine of the enterprise.[2] According to Roger L'Estrange, the official censor turned satirist, 'the original design was to remove the Queen and to destroy the Duke of York'.[3] Oates's motives remain a matter for conjecture, as he maintained to the end that his invented evidence of a plot was true.

Egged on by Tonge, Oates wrote forty-three papers on Popish plots. There had, he claimed, already been many attempts upon the life of the King; one had been foiled only because the weapons used by the assassins failed to fire their silver bullets. The first minister, Danby, thought it best to treat the claims with respect. After reading the papers provided by Tonge, Danby realised that neither the ageing cleric nor the eccentric chemist Kirkby alone could have compiled the evidence of multiple plots and schemes. Tonge reluctantly arranged for Titus Oates to come briefly out of the shadows to swear the truth of his evidence before a magistrate, Sir Edmund Berry Godfrey.

Among the most sensational of Oates's claims was that the Duchess of York's former secretary, Edward Coleman, was a conspirator. In this Oates scored an unwitting bull's-eye. Coleman had converted to Catholicism in the early 1660s and was said to have played a part in the conversion of the Duke of York. As a secretary for the Duchess of York, he had carried out a private mission to forge links with, and raise money via, Catholic priests close to the crowns of France and Spain. What better name for Oates to pick as a member of his fictitious plot? Coleman had been in private contact with Catholic priests who had the ear of Louis XIV, as well as that of the simple-minded Charles II of Spain. Two years before, the Earl of Danby and the Bishop of London had learned of Coleman's activities and removed him from his post in the Duchess's household.

Two weeks after Godfrey witnessed Oates's deposition, he vanished. His body was found five days later, 17 October, on Primrose Hill, with his own sword driven through it. Examination showed that Godfrey had been dead when impaled; the cause of death had been strangulation. The murder was the event Oates and Tonge required for their plot to be taken seriously. Suddenly it was the talk of London.

A few days after Godfrey's death, and thanks to the Duke of York urging his brother to take matters seriously, Tonge and Oates were called before the Privy Council to be interrogated. Charles attended and personally quizzed Oates on his evidence, discovering many inconsistencies. Oates stuck to his story, which by now he had embellished with more details. The entire inglorious confection was composed of names and events squirrelled away by Oates during his time with the Jesuits, and now to be spewed forth with the addition of a huge plot to overthrow Protestant England and Scotland. His list of plotters numbered more than five hundred Jesuits and many Catholic nobles and their associates.

Charles ordered Oates to be arrested as a false witness; he thought Oates and Tonge had invented the entire conspiracy as 'some artifice, and did not believe one word of the plot'.[4] Unfortunately, he was almost alone in seeing through the conspirators' fictions. Parliament ordered that Oates be freed and provided all assistance in tracking down the plotters. He was given an income of £1200 a year and an apartment inside Whitehall Palace. Charles must have been intensely irritated.

Talk in the salons, political clubs and coffee houses was dominated by speculation about James. How would the Papists be contained if he succeeded his brother? Should he be allowed to succeed? If not, who might replace him? Lack of money forced Charles to reconvene the Parliament he had prorogued eighteen months earlier in irritation at its attempts to bring in ever-tighter controls on religious observation. In his formal speech from the throne, he revealed the Popish Plot, calling it 'a design against my person by the Jesuits'. The news was delivered almost as a throwaway line, Charles saying only that it involved 'foreigners contriving to introduce popery amongst us'.

Charles, as we have seen, disbelieved in the plot, and was far from keen to have it investigated by Parliament. If members of the Commons started probing they might stumble upon 'many things that were yet to be concealed'.[5] Charles's prime concern was keeping a lid on the secret payments from Louis of France. Danby had been instructed to bypass Parliament and leave the allegations of conspiracy for the judges to pursue. Always a hardliner on Catholic issues, and the most devious of men, he disobeyed his master, making details of the allegations available to the Commons. The King, though furious with Danby, had no option but to go along with him and announce the plot.

The effect was immediate. In the words of the politician Sir John Reresby, the country 'took fire'. In his memoirs, Reresby recalled, 'It is not possible to describe the ferment which the artifices of some and the real fear and belief of others concerning his plot put the two Houses of Parliament and the greatest part of the nation in.' Over the coming weeks even the most level-headed were persuaded that the King was in imminent danger from Papist assassins and the very future of

Protestantism was in the balance. In London, Catholics went in fear of violence from mobs that toured the streets chanting anti-Catholic slogans.

The furore developed into a threat to the throne itself, with the Earl of Shaftesbury playing a major part. Probably the ablest politician of the reign, Shaftesbury had helped restore Charles to the throne but had become increasingly alienated from the King because of his absolutism. Shaftesbury was the dominant figure among the loose grouping of constitutional monarchists, Presbyterians and radicals who would come to be known as the Whigs. Few historians think he ever believed in Oates's plot, but he found it a useful weapon. He orchestrated an anti-Catholic campaign that had the crown wobbling on Charles's head.

Shaftesbury showed his hand a week after Charles's speech. In the Commons, the Earl's ally Lord Russell tabled an address calling for the removal of the Duke of York 'from His Majesty's presence'. In the following days a similar address demanded the banishment from Whitehall of the Queen and all her retinue. Then came a bill to ban Catholics from sitting in either house. The Lords voted by the narrowest of margins to exempt York.

It was a limited reprieve in a darkening situation. Orders went out to arrest priests and Jesuits. Catholics were barred from the court, the army, and then from London. Search parties were sent to arrest those who had failed to leave the city. London's prison population soared. The round-up netted some 2000, held in Newgate, the Fleet, the Marshalsea and other gaols. The anti-Catholic purge put the position of the King's chief mistress Louise de Kérouaille and even of the Queen herself under question, if not actual threat.

In the midst of the turmoil, London's greatest annual spectacle – the Lord Mayor's Day – took place. Everyone turned out to watch the procession as the new mayor, Sir George Edwards, a grocer, made his way to Westminster to pledge his allegiance to the Crown. As usual, the procession included representatives of all strata of London life, ranging from pensioners and apprentices all the way up to aldermen and sheriffs. It was a chance for London to express civic pride and enjoy itself. Each year a series of elaborate pageants, chiefly written by Thomas Jordan and designed to illustrate a specific theme, was laid on at points along the route. In 1678 the theme was overseas trade and the East India Company. The choice was made by the sponsoring guild, which changed year by year. This year it was the grocers, whose overriding interest was in foreign trade. Billowing scenes of exotic Asian plenty erupted across the old city, with pasteboard elephants (the symbol of the EIC) carrying luscious baskets of vegetable and mineral riches. Indian youths, imported to add verisimilitude to these visions of excess and wealth, held bowls overflowing with spices. From beneath the visual bombast, actors dressed for the part read long panegyrics on the wonders and virtues of London.

In Jordan's verse, the message was clear: no one should mess with London and its ancient rights, for the city was where the wealth of the nation lay. A subsidiary message was no less important: this was a Protestant city, engaging in Protestant trade and holding allegiance to a Protestant Crown.

By the spring of 1679, London was still in the throes of anti-Catholic sentiment and rumours of plots and counter-plots. The atmosphere remained virulent. In April anti-Catholic venom swerved towards Samuel Pepys and his close associates. Pepys was correctly seen as the Duke of York's man. Even with the Duke removed from his position as admiral, Pepys still suffered from rumours that made him suspect of recusancy. Of course, although Pepys had long been close to the Duke he was not a Catholic. Despite this, he and the shipbuilder Sir Anthony Deane were suspected of espionage. Charged with leaking secret documents to the French, on 22 May they were sent to the Tower.

Pepys's powerful Whig enemies wished to depose anyone with connections to the Duke, while suspicion fell on Deane because of his association with the King himself. On Charles's orders four years before, Deane had gone to France to design and build two sporting yachts for Louis XIV. This was enough to place him under suspicion. The prosecution had great difficulty constructing a case against either man and on 9 July Pepys and Deane were released on bail, although it would take until June the following year for the charges to be dropped.

During the height of the crisis, in 1679, Charles was taken seriously ill and took some months to recover. The nature of the illness is not understood, but it may possibly have been heart trouble brought on by good living or the stress of dealing with a major national emergency.* In September, Charles banished the Duke of Monmouth to the continent, in order to prevent his continuing role as a rallying point for Whig dissent; his supporters included those who saw him as an alternative Protestant heir to the throne. By November he was back – without permission. Crowds turned out in London and elsewhere to greet him.

The Popish Plot mania was to last three years. At the height of his fame Oates was hailed by many as the saviour of the kingdom, a notion he held on to until the end of his days. He adored his fame and made much of his sudden elevation from poverty to well-fed celebrity:

---

* He was to fall ill again the following May. These bouts may have been the first manifestations of a stroke, from which Charles would die in 1685.

> I had my guard of Beefeaters to protect me from being insulted or assassinated, my ten pounds a week duly paid without deductions, Venison Pasties and Westphalian Hams flew to my table without sending for, I was as much stared at, at the Amsterdam Coffee House and at Dick's as a Foreign Ambassador, when he makes his entry through Fleet Street.[6]

The plot hatched by the gullible Tonge and the exploitative Oates ultimately led to the execution of fifteen innocent men, among them the hapless Edward Coleman. Shortly after the murder of Sir Edmund Godfrey, one of the Queen's servants had been arrested on suspicion of his murder, taking the plot right to Catherine herself. The accused servant, Miles Prance, himself a Catholic, was tortured in Newgate, admitted his guilt and named three others. He then recanted his confession and veered between admissions and denials of guilt until on his evidence the three luckless individuals he had named were executed.

The flames fanned by the plot reached their zenith in the summer of 1679 with a series of trials and executions. The trials caused a sensation in London, which by now was stoked up into a fervour of anti-Catholicism. All those found guilty declared their innocence. Charles himself believed them to be so, though it was politically expedient for him to let all fifteen go to their deaths.

Amidst the crisis, it was believed by some that the Duke of York, sent by the King into exile in Brussels, was plotting a coup. The Duke of Monmouth, who had been sent to Scotland to crush a Covenanter uprising, was asked to return to London.* He did so, in late November 1680, to great jubilation on the

* The Covenanters were a Scottish Presbyterian movement named after the biblical covenant between God and the Israelites.

streets of the city. With the King refusing to call a Parliament to discuss the deteriorating situation, a huge petition was organised in London. Some 20,000, including Shaftesbury, signed it. The King's response was to announce he would call another Parliament, saying he would listen to reasonable proposals to deal with people's concerns, barring any discussion of the royal line of descent. In other words, he would listen but not act.

Finally, a backlash began against Oates and the Popish Plot. A turning point was reached when Oates accused the Queen's physician, Sir George Wakeman, of plotting to poison the King with the assistance of the Duke of York. When this clearly ridiculous charge went to court, Wakeman was acquitted. Although his trial helped turn opinion against Oates, the hunt for plotters went on. The final victim of Oates's fabrications was the blameless Catholic Archbishop of Armagh, Oliver Plunkett, hanged in July 1681 for complicity in the plot. With this final travesty, the country had had enough of Popish plots. Oates was told to leave Whitehall Palace. In response, he made accusations against the King and the Duke of York. They were accusations too far. Oates was accused of sedition and taken to the Tower.

As the grotesque nonsense of the Popish Plot played out, the interlinked and more important political struggle over the royal succession continued to pose danger to the House of Stuart. Many feared the country might stumble into a new civil war.

The Popish Plot, and the ensuing exclusion crisis, during which concerted efforts were made to have the Duke of York prohibited from succession to the throne, caused political turmoil throughout London. Public figures found themselves forced to make open declarations of support for one side or the other, for or against the royal family, especially the Duke. John Dryden declared himself for the King against the emerging Whigs, who were primarily opposed to the Duke of York because of his Catholicism. Whipped up by the King's enemies, crowds paraded through the capital in November, carrying effigies of the Pope to be burned. Similar demonstrations would be repeated each November during the rest of Charles's reign.

The King was widely criticised in Whig circles for his 'effeminacy', a seriously derogatory charge in the seventeenth century, meaning a lack of both 'masculine' leadership and sexual potency. Proof was offered in the fact that the Queen had failed to provide an heir and that he preferred pawing – in Evelyn's telling phrase, 'toying' – his mistresses rather than having sex.[7] Even though the slurs on the king's sexuality were obviously without foundation – he had many illegitimate children – they had a political point: that he was effeminate or ineffectual in dealing with the perceived threat of French Catholicism that was spreading into the land.[8]

Towards the end of 1679 a vicious anonymous satire appeared, attacking the King, his French Catholic mistress Louise, Duchess of Portsmouth, the King's on-off favourite the Earl of Rochester and others. Rumours began to circulate that the author was John Dryden, despite the fact he was poet laureate. On the night of 18 December, as Dryden made his way home from Will's Coffee House to Gerrard Street in Soho, he was attacked by a gang of thugs armed with cudgels. The assailants staged their ambush in a dark alleyway beside the Lamb and Flag pub in Rose Street, Covent Garden. It was rumoured they had been hired by Rochester, whose friendship with the poet had turned to loathing following a literary spat. Other rumours put the blame on the Duke of Monmouth, or on the Duchess of Portsmouth, anxious to defend herself from public defamation.

A reward was offered for information as to the identity of the attackers. They were never identified. In fact, the true author of the satire was not Dryden, but John Sheffield, the Earl of Mulgrave. The agent behind the misdirected attack on Dryden was indeed his former friend Rochester, who wrote a form of confession, saying he would leave 'the repartee to black Will with a cudgel'.[9] By the distorted code of the day, it was thought quite honourable to hire a gang to attack someone from whom one had received some slight or insult. Despite the severity of the assault, Dryden recovered.

In reaction to those promoting various Exclusion Bills, designed to deny James the throne, a posthumous book was published in 1680 setting out the arguments for monarchy and the divine right of kings. This was Sir Robert Filmer's *Patriarcha*, written almost fifty years before, during the period when Charles I ruled without calling a Parliament.[10] According to Filmer, the correct form of government was based on the model of a family ruled by its father. *Patriarcha* was the subject of much debate, particularly as it came at a time when the House of Stuart was under assault from former members of the government, senior political opposition figures, and an increasingly vocal and restive London population.

Soon afterwards John Locke began writing *Two Treatises of Government*, in which he argued against the view that civil society was best controlled by divinely ordained paternalism, asserting that the only legitimate form of government was by consent. Locke's work was in part an answer to Filmer and partly a reaction to the exclusion crisis. The political heat around the crisis was intensifying, fuelled by Locke's patron, Lord Shaftesbury and allies including Lord Russell. In the political upheavals following various attempts to have James removed from the royal line of inheritance, London was further wracked with rumours of plots and counter-plots.

It was certainly true that new groups of conspirators had arisen from an unexpected quarter. Far from being in the old Cromwellian mould, they were aristocrats. This was not so strange as it might first appear, for the attack was not on the Crown itself but on the possibility of a Catholic succeeding to the English throne. The aim was to reform the monarchy rather than to destroy it; as Shaftesbury put it, they didn't want democracy. In 1680 an Exclusion Bill passed the Commons but was defeated in the Lords. The Commons was prepared to consider an alternative, whereby the powers of a Catholic monarch would be limited. Charles refused to consider it. By this time, the London mobs were parading effigies of the Duke of York through the streets.

With so much at stake, it is hardly surprising that the government stepped in to censor the theatre. During the period of the exclusion crisis many plays, both old and new, were banned. Several of Shakespeare's history plays dealing with his recurring themes of power and monarchy fell foul of the ban. Plays by Shadwell, a Whig, were banned, as were works by Dryden, a Tory.[11]

The problem was not so much the criticism of monarchy but the fear of incitement of the rabble.[12] Quite how a theatre frequented by the well-to-do was likely to pander to the rabble was hard to explain. Dryden was so incensed by his work being caught up in the government's paranoia that he wrote a public broadside against its actions – a bold action for the poet laureate. Dryden had another reason to feel aggrieved; he had recently written perhaps his greatest work, the political poem *Absalom and Achitophel*, in which he defended Charles II despite his philandering and castigated his enemies, including the Whig leader Lord Shaftesbury, for not sticking by the monarchy.[13]

*

In the winter of 1680, in the midst of the political turmoil, two comets appeared. Comets were seen as a portent of some great or dreadful event. The appearance of two comets, as had also occurred fifteen years before, was surely an omen of an event of cataclysmic importance. The sighting caused consternation in London. The people remembered the comets that had appeared in 1664 and 1665, and which had subsequently been said to have foretold the plague and fire. Pamphlets appeared, filled with foreboding about the new celestial appearances. One of these, entitled 'An Alarm to Europe by a late prodigious Comet', claimed to offer a 'predictive discourse' on some of the comet's 'sad effects' on England, Scotland, Ireland, France, Spain, Holland, Germany, Italy 'and many other places'.[14] It was one of many attempts to cash in on the natural phenomena of the times. Astrology was still of great interest to many, especially physicians, so the notion of portents was not in any way unusual. The Astronomer Royal, John Flamsteed, had an abiding interest in the subject, though he tended to keep it under his hat, in much the same way that Isaac Newton never wrote a letter to the Royal Society about his life-long interest in alchemy.[15]

While some pondered the astrological significance of the phenomenon, it rekindled the interest of Newton in astronomy. Moreover, it was the comet, rather than the fabled falling apple, that would initiate his work on gravity. At Greenwich, Flamsteed proposed that the comets, seen in November and December, were not two but one body moving towards the sun, then going behind it and finally moving away from it. At first Newton disagreed with Flamsteed, but later he realised the Astronomer Royal was correct. Much to Flamsteed's annoyance, his friend and one-time assistant Edmund Halley allowed Newton access to measurements and data compiled by Flamsteed. As a result, Newton was able to theorise that like planets, comets went around the sun in elliptical orbits. It was this work that formed the basis of *Principia Mathematica.*

Astonishingly, none of the astrologers making use of the appearance of the comet were able to foretell what was about to happen. In answer to the turmoil of the exclusion crisis, and following repeated prorogations of Parliament, the King decided in the spring of 1681 to inaugurate absolute rule. The promised Parliament met on 21 March, not in its ancient berth in the old Palace of Westminster but in Oxford, a venue chosen by the King as a site well removed from London, where hordes hostile to the Duke of York had staged demonstrations through the winter. The Parliament barely met until the House of Commons brought in another Exclusion Bill, whereupon Charles promptly dissolved it. It had sat for one week. The signal was clear that Charles no longer wished to be pulled this way and that by those who despised his brother or his brother's religion, or who mistrusted the King's own political or religious inclinations.

In future Charles would rule if not as an absolute king, like his cousin Louis XIV in France, then at least without calling Parliament. The promises made in the Declaration of Breda were forgotten. Within the space of three years, 1679–81, three Parliaments had been elected, all of which had taken issue with the King over the question of the succession. From now on, Charles would rule without calling another Parliament. As for Shaftesbury, Charles had tried to neutralise the Whig leader by bringing him into the government and making him President of the Privy Council on the enormous sum of £4000 a year – a patent bribe. Now he sacked him, along with several other government officers who had dared to voice criticism of the King's policies at home and abroad.

In March Charles had made a new secret deal with Louis

XIV. It allowed him to dissolve Parliament for good. In return for the sum of £4 million, payable over four years, Charles once again promised support for France's expansionist policies. As England already had a treaty with Spain, this led to confusion in foreign policy. When Louis threatened the Spanish Netherlands and Spanish-controlled Luxembourg, Spain asked Charles for help under the terms of the treaty. Charles procrastinated until Louis took Luxembourg and the Spanish Netherlands. It became clear to the political opposition in London that Charles had made some sort of new deal with Louis. Further political tension in the capital ensued.

The King's finances, though, were now much improved. Together with reforms in tax collection put in place by Sir George Downing and the Earl of Danby, the stream of money from customs and excise duty greatly increased. But the nagging questions about the King's religion, his closeness to France and the future of the throne continued to be the talk of London's coffee houses and political salons.

The theatres were far from silent about the political situation. Charles was now interfering directly with aspects of London's government, influencing the appointment of magistrates and officers of the trained bands. Plays were written from both the Tory and Whig perspectives. In *The Duke of Guise*, Dryden commented severely on Monmouth's aspirations to succeed his father and chastised the Whigs for their support for the Duke:

> Do what in coffee houses you began;
> Pull down the Master, and set up the Man.[16]

A more strident tone was adopted by Thomas D'Urfey in *The Royalist*, equating Whigs with the republicans who had escaped execution at the start of Charles's reign. They should, he declared, be hanged 'That have deserved it twenty years ago'.[17]

In *The Lancashire Witches*, Thomas Shadwell took the Whig side, dedicating the published edition of the play to Shaftesbury. But it was John Crown, who wrote both pro-Tory and pro-Whig plays, thereby bending with the wind to maintain a living, who best summed up the sorry state of London's political and public life when he admonished his upper-class audience at the Duke's Theatre:

> 'Tis pleasant, Sirs, to see you fight and brawl
> About religion, but have none at all.[18]

CHAPTER 25

THE FALL OF MADAM CRESWELL AND THE MIGRATION OF CRIMINALS

As London's population, from the lowest to the highest, continued to quarrel over the Popish Plot, one of the city's most colourful characters was forced into retirement. In 1681, London's foremost brothel-keeper, Elizabeth Creswell, was sent to gaol for 'thirty years of bawdry'. Creswell ran a string of brothels across the city, catering to all price ranges and tastes. Her best establishments, it was claimed, were frequented by the King himself, though there is no evidence for this. They were certainly frequented by London rakes, some of whom may well have been members of Charles's court. Creswell was the foremost of a large number of Londoners who made their living one way or another from sex. Thanks to her establishments, the city's pox doctors had a steady trade, while the city's many sweating houses always had customers hoping to sweat the pox from their pockmarked bodies.

Little or nothing is known about Elizabeth Creswell's background. She was said to have been born into a middle-class family in Kent, though there is no proof of that. What is certain is that she thrived in London by being good at business. She never married and took to prostitution in order to support herself. By the 1650s she was running a brothel in Bartholomew Close, a few hundred yards north of St Paul's Cathedral. She was diligent at scouring the countryside for new girls to bring into the city and for attracting well-bred women who had fallen on hard times. By keeping up her product range, and being adept at advertising her services, she ensured a loyal client list. She lived in style and was much represented in satires, plays and broadsides. Occasionally her brothels were attacked – most violently during the Easter apprentice riots of 1668 – but in general her businesses were protected thanks to her well-connected clientele.

Madam Creswell was a target for those who supported the Duke of York during the exclusion crisis. Possessing a strongly Protestant perspective on the monarchy, she publicly and financially supported the Whig point of view. For her time, Creswell was unusual – she was a woman who became financially independent through her own endeavours, albeit from running a string of brothels, and publicly took part in the most important political debate of her time. Her choice of profession seems to have been purely pragmatic; as Aphra Behn also discovered, there were few employment options open to women capable of doing better than selling victuals or gloves and ribbons from a basket in the street.

With sexual licence went sexually transmitted diseases. Remedies were many and varied, ranging from purging to herbal remedies and, in extreme cases, the use of toxic substances including mercury. In seventeenth-century London, sexually transmitted diseases were rife and were looked upon as a natural hazard of love. All sections of society were at risk, from the lowest labourer to London's social elite. In some ways, the latter had more to fear, having both the leisure to indulge in promiscuous behaviour that increased the chances of catching an infection and the money to pay for the most dangerous remedies.

The most feared scourge of the sexually active was syphilis, known as the pox and sometimes as 'the French disease' – so-called because of the belief it had come from France, even though it may originally have reached Europe from North America or Africa, or simply have been around since the dawn of mankind. Physicians usually referred to it as *lues* (after the neo-Latin for plague) *venerea*. It spread rapidly through Europe in the sixteenth century and by the middle of the seventeenth had reached epidemic proportions in London. The pox was so ubiquitous that it was frequently referred to in private correspondence and public newssheets, as well as in plays, ballads and satires. 'A pox on you!' was a common insult.

Treatment was difficult and haphazard.* Under the current state of medical knowledge, there was no proper understanding of the underlying nature of the disease or its causes. A further complication was that gonorrhoea and syphilis were sometimes mistaken for one another, for in their initial stages they could present similar symptoms. Despite these drawbacks, some treatments appeared to work. Around London, sweating houses – sweating tubs, as they were known – were common, where those afflicted with the pox could be subjected to extreme heat and hope to sweat their way to a cure. The irony

---

* The cause of syphilis would not be known until 1905, when the disease was shown to be caused by the bacterium *Treponema pallidum*.

is that the ailment itself could also cause sweating. A cure there would seem to be, but of a kind, for the initial signs of syphilis tend to disappear in anything from ten to forty days, while the disease lurks on inside waiting to wreak terrible harm in later years.

Fortunately for Charles, when he and Louise contracted syphilis, they had the best doctors available to treat them. One of the personal physicians to the King was Richard Wiseman, an experienced and thoughtful man who wrote a handbook for doctors.[1] Dedicated to Charles, it was the distillation of a lifetime's work, primarily as a former ship's doctor, dealing with all the marvellous and shocking assaults inflicted on humanity at large. There were eight treatises, each one on a particular ailment. The first four were concerned with naturally occurring conditions such as tumours, ulcers, haemorrhoids and The King's Evil, or scrofula (the King's miraculous power to cure the last of these was carefully acknowledged). In the second group the experience of an old ship's doctor shone out from the subject headings: wounds caused by knives or swords, gunshot wounds, fractures, and venereal disease.

Wiseman described *lues venerea* as a

> venomous contagious disease gotten either immediately or mediately from an impure coition . . . I say immediately or mediately, because it is very manifest that not only the persons so copulating are infected but also the children derived from such parents, and nurses that suckle such children, and any other child that sucks upon those nurses; and so forwards.

He was talking here about both gonorrhoea and syphilis, for he, like others of the time, thought of the former as an initial manifestation of the latter. So what was there to do?

> Now the known remedies, all or some of which we use in this cure, are Bleeding, Purging, Vomiting, Salivating, Sweating, Cordials and Opiates; to which we may add Dietetical directions, especially Alternative Drinks, and Topics.
>
> Concerning Phlebotomy, tho' it do not cure the Disease, yet in the very beginning of it we usually let blood, to calm the fermenting Humours, and dispose them for evacuation, and prescribe a Clyster before or after.

Purging was carried out by administering potions made up of posset or whey, mixed with senna, rhubarb, sarsaparilla, cremor tartari, manna, tamarind, etc.

It was not only sweating houses that mimicked the effect of the disease itself; sweating was also the result of that other common treatment for those who could afford it, mercury. Mercury was administered by absorption topically through the skin, from mercury-filled compresses, or by taking mercury pills. The latter was far and away the most harmful. Mercury poisoning at first caused salivation, followed by worsening symptoms including inflammation of the mouth, mouth ulcers, rotten teeth, bad breath, inflammation of the intestines, increased heart rate, kidney failure and finally death.

> In the case of pain we add a grain or more of laudanum. Mercury thus mixt with purgatives it is from which we must expect our main success. For though the other may purge strongly, they of themselves have not virtue to check the malignity of even the lesser species of this disease.
>
> This I the rather add, because of the wickedness of many Pretenders, who will in this Cure declaim against the use of mercury, in which if they speak honestly, and follow their

Judgements (and do not give it at the same time when they speak against it, as many do) they will prolong their cure to no purpose, and meet with disgrace at last; it being very sure, that no species of it will be cured without it.

I have myself made, and seen endeavoured by some worthy late practitioners in our Faculties without Mercury, but by omitting of it, our Cures were rendered tedious and unsuccessful, the Ulcer the while spreading and breaking out fresh in some parts while we were endeavouring to Cure them in others, the Disease becoming more fierce in some of them whilst their bodies were purged with Caharticks without mercury.

The methods of salivating are divers, but all by mercury ... When we design Salivation by Mercurius Dulcis, we give it from 20 to 25 grains and sometime to thirty, either in a spoonful of white bread and milk ... or in some such like cordial ...

Mercury amalgamated with gold doth vomit and raise Salivation ...

The humours being evacuated by salivation and purging, Sweating will be necessary ...

Mercury is used both externally and internally.

Condoms were not yet widely available – they would become so in the 1700s, made from oiled silk, or the innards of various animals, including fish bladders. The rudimentary condoms that did exist were perfunctory and for use not to protect from the pox but to prevent pregnancy.

Madam Creswell's luck ran out not because of the pox but the magistrates. Perhaps the public mood changed and her influential clients were no longer able to protect her, or her enemies in the Tory faction brought influence to bear on the authorities.

Either way, she was charged and found guilty of earning a living by vice. She was imprisoned in the Bridewell prison, situated between Fleet Street and the Thames, beside the River Fleet, and rebuilt after the Great Fire on its original site as a large, grey, stone institution arranged around two courtyards.

Within two years of her incarceration, Creswell found herself unwittingly providing the *nom de plume* for the anonymous writer of a new work entitled *The Whore's Rhetorick*, a salacious tale masquerading as an instruction manual for a prostitute.[2] In this work, Madam Creswell instructed the daughter of a ruined Royalist family how to live by her sexual wiles, a theme exploited in similar works, most notably in *The English Rogue*.

Madam Creswell died in prison, possibly of tuberculosis. The probably apocryphal story was told that she made provision for her funeral in advance, paying a preacher a handsome fee to speak at her funeral but say nothing of her profession. Come the funeral, the preacher supposedly said of the deceased, 'She was born well, she lived well, and she died well; for she was born with the name of Creswell, lived at Clerkenwell and died in Bridewell.'[3]

The writer of *The Whore's Rhetorick* was not in fact anonymous, nor was the work entirely new. Its original author was Ferrante Pallavicino and it had been published in Italian forty years before. Now it was translated and amended for an English readership.[4] Erotic literature was widely available in Restoration London, which had alongside its famous, racy theatre a much racier underground literary world where anonymous works circulated to a well-heeled and leisured class. Demand was sufficiently brisk to support a market for imported material in foreign languages. On 8 February 1668, Samuel Pepys bought an example from his habitual bookseller John Martin at the Sign of the Bell in St Paul's churchyard. *L'Ecole des Filles*, by

Michel Millot and Jean l'Ange, had been published in France in 1655. The following day, Pepys described going to his room and reading it: 'A lewd book but what do me no harm to read for information's sake,' he recorded. Realising he was not being truthful to his secret diary, Pepys added, 'But it did hazer my prick para stand all the while and una vez to discharger.' In plain words, he masturbated. After he finished, he burned the book, 'that it might not be among my books to my shame'.[5] Though image mattered to Pepys, he was unable to control posterity as well as he hoped, for his encoded diaries, with their difficult shorthand and deliberate mix of foreign and slang words for salacious passages, were ultimately cracked.

L'Ecole and *The Whore's Rhetorick* were early examples of a genre known as whore's dialogues, erotic books written in the form of cod lessons for the education of innocent young women, often with tongue-in-cheek instructions on how to avoid the pitfalls of debauchery. They were very popular during the Restoration era. In the same year *The Whore's Rhetorick* appeared, another first-person narrative, *The London Jilt*, was published; it purported to be by a well-born young woman whose parents had fallen on hard times and left her to make her own way by prostitution.[6] Here a familiar strain appeared: the foreword written by a person (male) purporting to be the editor of the memoir, and to have only the best interests of everyone, men and women, at heart. Of the Jilt, the author says: 'She is set here before thee as a beacon to warn thee of the Shoals and Quick-sands, on which thou wilt of necessity Shipwrack thy all, if thou blindly and wilfully continuest and perseverest in steering that course of Female Debauchery, which will inevitably prove at length thy utter Destruction.'

What follows is not, as suggested by the foreword, a warning of the perils of debauchery, but a hypocritical about-turn by the author to produce a first-person narrative whose object is to titillate the reader with stories of the harlot's busy schedule and the rightness of her calling. The eponymous Jilt goes so far as to warn against marrying a virgin: 'for two persons that are Novices and unexperienced in Copulation, the children they get are commonly Fools, which is a thing People ought to be more careful of than any other.'[7]

The London Jilt became the second best seller of the age, beaten only by *The English Rogue.* The narrator Cornelia tells us that after her father was ruined by trickery she and her mother were forced into prostitution. What follows is both a history of Cornelia's sexual encounters and an account of her need to make a living in a world that gives her few options. Whereas Aphra Behn was able to turn to writing to stay afloat, the fictional Cornelia's talents lie in a different direction and she is forced to make use of what she has to offer. The Jilt therefore gives us a picture of what life could be like for women in London in the situation those such as Cornelia and her mother found themselves. Their circumstances were, one feels, no different from those experienced by Elizabeth Creswell, or by Nell Gwyn's mother when she found herself without a husband and with two daughters to feed. In Mrs Gwyn's case, one of them at least – Rose – became a common prostitute, while the other – Nell – became a courtesan, a prostitute in silk. From these examples we can see that the events narrated by the fictional Cornelia reflected real life for many women in Restoration London.

Despite censorship, anonymous works of erotica and soft pornography thrived, indicating that an official softly-softly approach existed regarding such material. It has been argued that the public espousal of sexual themes was a propaganda weapon used by Tory apologists against Puritanism.[8] It is little wonder that modern feminist writers have paid considerable attention to what has for long been a forgotten work.

The London Jilt was not the kind of book the average bookseller would have stocked. Anyone wanting a copy had to go to a bookseller where they were already known, or directly to the publisher. To obtain a copy, a customer in the know would have turned south off Fleet Street, past the newly built Bell Tavern – the only pub designed by Christopher Wren – and down Bride Lane, towards Wren's more notable St Bride's Church, an ancient place of worship going back thousands of years to pre-Christian times, and now rebuilt in classical style.* Past the church, next door to the Bear Tavern, could be found the shop of Henry Rhodes, an established publisher of pornography and erotica.

As *The London Jilt* was published by a firm specialising in such matter, one is led to conjecture that the anonymous author was someone already successful in the new genre of fictional memoir. The finger has been pointed in the direction of both Richard Head and his publisher Francis Kirkman.[9] *Jilt* was a success among the middle and upper classes of England, as well as across the Atlantic among the God-fearing Puritans of New England.

It was no accident that a plethora of anonymous books on similar themes appeared around this time. The Licensing of the Press Act 1662 had expired in 1679 and had not been renewed. The first Licensing Act, passed in 1637, had set up an official censor, made it illegal to publish any book without official permission, restricted publishing to London, Cambridge and Oxford, and placed strict rules on journalism. This meant that

---

* Though rebuilt in a breathtaking four years, 1671–5, St Bride's did not receive its unique 'tiered wedding cake' spire until 1701 as funds were yet to be raised.

for some time the only official publication in London was the government's own *Gazette*. For many years the censor had been Roger L'Estrange, a virulent anti-Parliamentarian and staunch royalist, who saw his role as being to dampen criticism of the Crown and support the monarchy at all costs. Even L'Estrange was unable to keep down the anonymous peddlers of salacious literature. They flourished, like so much else, in London's underworld market. These anonymous books did not gain the fame of later works whose authors were proclaimed on the title page, but they did establish the market for them, setting the tone and providing the form and often the content. When the Licensing Acts lapsed, a small but active underground publishing trade was able to rise to the surface and flourish.

Without these mid-century anonymous writers, later works such as Daniel Defoe's *Moll Flanders* could not have been written. Defoe's 'sempiternal bawd' Moll, telling us her story in a first-person narrative, was a true successor to those characters in the pages of *The English Rogue* and *The London Jilt*. Such anonymous novels were as important in the social mix of London as the theatre. Because of the necessity for their authors to hide their identities, these books have not stayed the test of time as well as certain plays of equally questionable merit or taste. In their way, though, they told the same kind of tale that was popular on the stage. Like the playwrights, they took their cue from Jacobeans John Fletcher and Ben Jonson, giving us stories of silly men gulled by clever women, and roguish men getting one over on the gullible.

The trade in sexual exotica in London illustrated more than merely an appetite among the moneyed classes for vicarious thrills – they illustrated a healthy publishing and bookselling trade in the capital. By historical accident the printing trade had grown up around Fleet Street, one of Caxton's apprentices having set up shop in the area in the fifteenth century. To keep up with changing tastes, booksellers became publishers, and publishers became writers. By the 1660s London had a thriving publishing trade along Fleet Street itself and in the alleys and streets running off it. Plays sold well, as did satire and poetry. The trashy new novels that satisfied the desires of city men found their upmarket mirror in poetical works, which could sell equally well. Much of the popular work was misogynistic, reaching its zenith (or nadir, if one prefers) with Robert Gould's long ode, *Love given O'er, or a Satyr against the Pride, Lust and Inconstancy Etc of Woman*. Its title spoke for its content and attitude, and it quickly sold out its numerous printings. The printing presses of Fleet Street were seldom fed with the ink of human kindness.

Apart from Madam Creswell, another famous bawd and brothel-keeper with notable social connections also died in prison. Damaris Page was born around 1610 and in 1658 she married a James Dry in Bermondsey. Little else is known about her early life except that she was charged with bigamy, having supposedly already married in 1640, but was acquitted.[10] We know that Page made considerable money from her brothels, becoming a property owner and developing housing in The Highway, a Roman road running from Tower Hill eastwards through Shadwell and Wapping to Limehouse. The area was predominantly populated by sailors and their families, along with others connected with London's seafaring business. Page's brothels, such as the Three Tuns, near the walls of the Tower in Stepney, were regularly frequented by sailors.

At a Trinity House dinner, Admiral Sir Edward Spragge once let it be known that as long as Mrs Page lived 'he was sure he would not lack men'. From what Sir Edward let slip, it would appear that Page provided a press-gang service, whereby merchant seamen would be plied with drink and forcibly signed up to the navy. This interchange at a dinner between powerful men provides a window into the seedy world of London's docklands where the needs of the navy coalesced with the services of the city's brothel madams. According to Pepys, John Evelyn, ever the moralist, suffered great 'affliction' on hearing what the admiral had to say.[11]

Page was something more than an infamous brothel-keeper: she became the embodiment of a new public theatre of sexuality given expression in newssheets and printed satires, as well as on the stage. In 1668 she became embroiled in a scandal created by satirists attacking the Countess of Castlemaine. A satire called 'The Poor-Whores Petition' was supposedly written by Damaris Page and Mother Creswell; Page's brothel, like Creswell's, had been set upon in the apprentice riots of Easter week. These disturbances were a traditional outlet for the frustration of apprentices, who were not allowed to marry and had not the money, if they so wished, to become clients of brothels. That year the disturbances had been particularly violent, stoked by political unrest over a perception in the city that the Crown was not delivering on promised reforms enabling greater freedom for nonconformist sects. The satire was addressed to the Countess Castlemaine and was wildly funny.

The petition, claiming to be from the 'Undone Company of Poor Distressed Whores, Bawds, Pimps and Panders', addressed itself to 'The most splendid, illustrious, serene and eminent Lady of Pleasure, The Countess of Castlemaine'. The petitioners claimed that through the actions of 'rude and ill-bred boys' they had lost the practice of their 'venerial pleasures – A trade in which your Ladyship hath great Experience'. The petitioners pleaded for speedy relief from the rioters 'that a stop may be put unto them before they come to your honour's palace, and bring contempt upon your worshipping of Venus, the great Goddess whom we all adore'. It went on to make a sideswipe at Barbara's Catholicism, winding up by promising that in return for her help to the 'inferior whores' they would promote Barbara's 'honour, safety and interest'.

Of the many satires published during the seventeenth century (or at least those that have survived), the 'Poor-Whores Petition' was among the finest. Perhaps its only comic equal was that other great mock petition, 'The Women's Petition Against Coffee'. The 'Poor-Whores Petition' chose as its basis an event of genuine and disquieting unrest, during which violence had to be faced down by troops called out by the government. The undercurrent of unhappiness with Stuart rule was not directly alluded to; the petition went instead for the King's disliked mistress, who in turn stood for the London mob's hatred of Catholicism. Homing in on Castlemaine in such a wicked and subversive manner, the petition pretended to be on her side while giving her, the monarchy and Catholicism in general a good kicking.

While Londoners of all creeds were generally God-fearing and went to church on a Sunday, Creswell and Page represented an amoral undercurrent in the city, created out of need more than desire. Without a trade it was easy to starve in London. People born without money had to do what they could to make a living. For the masses, survival beyond early childhood was something of a miracle, and even then the battle was only just beginning. Most of London's inhabitants lived a life in which they constantly both feared and hoped for what tomorrow might bring. A set of mid-seventeenth-century cards depicting London street sellers and their cries, once owned by Samuel Pepys, illustrates the lives of some of these Londoners: women dressed in long skirts of rough material carrying their goods – fish, oysters, buttons, puddings – as often as not in baskets on their heads, and men selling toasting forks, second-hand boots, firewood, meat or music played on a fiddle. This was the London of those who slept in overcrowded houses and spent much of their lives on the street.

It was also the London of thievery, violence, burglary, murder and more. Extortion rackets and kidnappings were common. Former soldiers down on their luck were for hire for any sort of criminal exploit. Many of those in London's gaols were not criminals, merely debtors. While the Tower of London accommodated those accused of treason and wayward aristocrats who had fallen foul of the King, debtors were put in the Bridewell, Ludgate prison or one of the lesser gaols south of the river.

The line between success and failure, between freedom and debtor's prison, was a fine one, easily crossed. The distinguished physician and chronicler of the plague, Nathaniel Hodges, ended his life in prison, despite the medical establishment recognising the value of his work during the plague. The Royal College of Physicians invited him to give the annual Harveian Oration, a lecture founded by William Harvey, the discoverer of the circulation of blood. Harvey had stipulated that the lecture should be given to extol the virtues of the college and to exhort its members to improve medicine through experimentation. During the plague Hodges had done just that, putting old remedies to the test. Yet, soon after his recognition, came his fall. His medical practice failed and he ran into debt from which he never recovered. Hodges died in a cell in Ludgate prison in 1688 and was given a funeral service in his parish church, St Stephen's Walbrook. The church, seriously damaged in the Great Fire, had been remodelled by Wren, who gave it an enormous dome based on that of St Paul's, almost straddling the width of the building. This innovative church was a fitting venue for a eulogy for a man who strove at great personal risk to revolutionise medical practice.

A major element of London's criminal class was made up of religious dissenters. Thanks to various Acts, those who did not conform to the rites of the Church of England were gradually criminalised during the reign of Charles II, with stricter and stricter sanctions against them. It must be emphasised that these laws were enacted because of the views of Parliament and the Anglican bishops. Charles himself was well known to have broad-minded views on religion, having been defeated by Parliament in several attempts to liberalise the law. By the middle years of his reign, hundreds of Quakers in London were either in gaol or in hiding, or had taken themselves off to the colonies in America. Even there, these criminalised people could not always find peace, for the early Puritan settlers of Massachusetts (those who called themselves Pilgrims) were quite hostile to their fellow nonconformists.

On 4 March 1681, Charles gave the astonishing gift of 45,000 acres to a Quaker and former convict, making him the largest non-royal landowner in the Western world. The land was in America and the recipient was William Penn the Younger. Given the untold numbers of men who had to trim, change their political spots, twist and turn one way or the other to thrive or merely survive in the whirlpool of seventeenth-century England, the case of Penn is singular and peculiar.

From an early age Penn was interested in nonconformist religious ideas, finally settling on the ideology of the Quakers, whose belief in the spiritual equality of all, high or low, man or woman, did not sit well with the institution of monarchy. Yet Penn was a friend and confidant of the Duke of York, the heir to the throne. It has been speculated that what drew the two men together was their unity in difference.[12] Both belonged to groups that suffered under the Test Act: the Duke, forced as a Catholic to resign as Lord High Admiral of the Navy; Penn, the Quaker, unable to swear any form of oath and so also barred from official office.

Penn was imprisoned in Newgate and the Tower for his heretical beliefs, which held that no man was beneath the King; the Duke saw rioters in the streets of London call for his Catholic head. Apart from their personal beliefs, both men had strong experiential reasons for exposing religious intolerance.

William Penn was a Londoner, born in 1644 in the family home on Tower Hill, in the shadow of the fortress and prison he would grow to know well in later years. His mother was Margaret Jasper, the daughter of a wealthy Rotterdam merchant, and his father Admiral Sir William Penn, himself a prime example of one who could turn in the wind to stay at the top. During the Civil War Sir William had been a naval commander for the Parliamentary forces. When it became clear that the King was returning from exile, he made sure he was on the *Royal Charles* when it sailed to bring Charles home. He then fought with valour under the command of the Duke of York during the Second Anglo-Dutch War. By all accounts he was a clever and courageous officer but a devious and untrustworthy colleague.[13] His later neighbour and fellow employee of the Navy Office, Samuel Pepys, had a low opinion of him as a man but was taken by his intelligence.[14]

Under Charles II, Sir William was appointed a Commissioner of the Navy. He hoped his son would use his undoubted intelligence and charm to forge a career under the patronage of the royal family, as he had himself. Young William had different ideas.

Beginning at Oxford University, William developed an interest in nonconformist religion that would ultimately lead to him being asked to leave. His father became so annoyed by the young man's beliefs that he threw him out of the family home, lashing him with a cane. After a time, William and his father were reconciled; it also appears that he and the university reached an understanding, only for young Penn to be sent down again later. The cause of the trouble was that William had fallen under the radical religious and political spell of the Quaker leader George Fox. The Quakers believed no one was above God, not even a king; therefore they did not support the monarchy. They also refused to swear oaths, making life difficult in a country ruled by those determined that its servants should swear oaths of allegiance and demonstrate their religious orthodoxy via the sacraments of the Anglican Church. The Quakers believed no person should act as an intermediary between another person and God. This led to the idea of the inner light, or the revelation of God within the individual.

Penn campaigned for religious rights for minorities, writing pamphlets that resulted in his spending time in the Tower. Along with other sects, Quakers were seen as heretics, and under the increasing intolerance of those who strayed from Anglican orthodoxy, membership of the sect was punishable by deportation. Penn was undeterred and developed a heterodox group of friends, including the republican theorist Algernon Sidney, later campaigning for him in two parliamentary elections.

In 1670, Sir William suffered a fatal illness and, knowing he was dying, appealed to the King and the Duke of York to protect his son. In view of Sir William's service to the Crown, they agreed to do so.

Throughout the kingdom, persecution of Quakers intensified. Many now saw the only way forward to be emigration to

America. Even there, all would not necessarily go well for them. Puritan settlements in New England were often as wary of Quakers as were Anglicans and the courts at home. Penn, who had inherited a large fortune from his father, joined with a group of prominent Quakers to purchase the colony of West Jersey. Despite his many transgressions in the eyes of the monarchy, by 1681 he gained such prominence that Charles II granted him ownership of a substantial tract of land, partially in settlement of a debt owed to Penn's father, put at the sum of £16,000, but also to provide a safety valve against religious intolerance at home. By helping Penn promote the notion of religious freedom in the New World, Charles was potentially freeing himself from one of the country's many perplexing religious problems. Penn's idea was to found a colony of Quakers, free of monarchy, able to exercise their beliefs and to establish a religious Garden of Eden. The first 150 to travel to the new colony were, like Penn himself, Londoners, Quakers from the north of the city who keenly felt the oppression of the Anglican Church.

The grant of a large tract of colonial land to one individual was not in itself unusual. By becoming proprietor of Pennsylvania (newly named after his father), Penn was in a line of colonial proprietors, taking charge of land on behalf of the King, who remained the ultimate owner. Previously established proprietary colonies included Maryland and Newfoundland. Colonies could be run in other ways, too. Virginia and Massachusetts had been established by joint stock companies. If other means failed, a new area of settlement could be set up directly as a royal colony, run by a governor on behalf of the King.* Penn's warrant allowed him

* Such a system existed widely well into the twentieth century, most notably with India run by a viceroy. Today, the Queen nominally owns territories including the British Virgin Islands, run on her behalf by governors, with locally elected representatives.

almost complete control over his new territory as a 'seigniniorie': 'To Have, hold and possesse and enjoy the said tract of Land, Countrey, Isles, Inletts and the other premises, unto the said William Penn, his heires and assignes, to the only proper use and behoofe of the said William Penn, his heirs and assignes forever.'

In return, Penn was to pay the King and his heirs 'two Beaver Skins to bee delivered att our said Castle of Windsor, on the first day of January, in every yeare'. On a more practical note, Penn was to give the king 'the fifth parte of all Gold and silver Oare, which shall from time to time happen to bee found within the Limitts aforesaid'. Sadly for all concerned there was precious little precious metal to be found.

More practical were the rules governing the right to trade to and from the new colony, 'Provided alwayes, that they pay such customes and imposicions, subsidies and duties for the same to us, our heires and successors, as the rest of our subjects of our kingdome of England, for the time being shall be bound to pay, and doe observe the acts of Navigation and other lawes in that behalfe made.'[15]

Quakers in the new lands were split on many issues, including the ownership of slaves. Penn was in favour of slavery and had slaves of his own, though he did say that they should be well treated and should be freed upon his death. Thus the distasteful labours of the London slave trade fed a free workforce for egalitarian Pennsylvania.

Some of the slaves who came to Pennsylvania were landed by Boston merchants who skirted the embargo on all slave trading except via ships of the Royal African Company. The Bostonians evaded contact with the English traders off West Africa by sailing all the way to Madagascar to buy their slaves. Other Pennsylvania slaves were bought from neighbouring American colonies or from Barbados and Jamaica.

Notwithstanding the new colony's at best ambivalent position on slavery, Penn endowed Pennsylvania with radical ideas on government that would help form the basis for the American Constitution and of modern democracies in general. It was an unexpected outcome for a colony founded by individuals branded criminals and heretics at home. Even more unexpected was the fact that they were aided and abetted by a king.

CHAPTER 26

THE CITY COWED, THE CITY TRIUMPHANT

The propaganda battle fought out on the London stage gradually became of less consequence. Not that the political situation had improved – far from it. But the power of the theatre, if it had existed at all, was now on the wane.

Audiences were not increasing but declining. The unrest that had begun with the Popish Plot continued to be felt. Rather than put their fears aside for an hour or two in the theatre, the people of London chose to shun the pleasures of the stage. Since the death of Sir William Davenant in 1668, the quality of theatrical offerings had been patchy, with great plays and productions followed by the drab and makeweight. Though highs and lows were only to be expected in the theatre, quality had in recent years deteriorated greatly. To maintain a steady flow of new and familiar productions, interposing new plays with boiled-up versions of Shakespeare and Fletcher and offering endlessly thrilling *coups de théatre*, was a task that only those with the finest management skills and theatrical nous could handle. To keep up the momentum in just two theatres was too much to ask.

With the slump in attendance figures, in 1682, the King's Company, its management always rather ramshackle, collapsed completely. The Duke's Company, though better run under the management of Thomas Betterton, was also in financial difficulties.

The two companies amalgamated under the direction of the Duke's Company management, with Betterton the guiding light. The new United Company made Wren's Theatre Royal its headquarters. The Duke's Company theatre at Dorset Square had always suffered from poor acoustics and the opportunity was taken to abandon it. The United Company had a monopoly on London theatre. Despite Betterton's guidance, standards slipped further, fewer new plays were commissioned and a downward spiral began. Over a previous four-year period, sixty-eight new plays had been staged in London, the equivalent of twenty-seven a year. In the first four years of the United Company only nineteen new productions were put on, barely five a year. Actors' conditions and pay suffered. The trouble was that Betterton did not have absolute control, and constant squabbling rendered clear financial and artistic objectives impossible. In truth, the United Company was far from united.

As the theatre writhed within its self-made existential crisis, real life-or-death intrigue was taking shape in political circles. Among the nascent Whig alliances, extreme constitutional measures, not dissimilar to those that had led up to the deposition of Charles I, were being contemplated. In the salons of grand houses in Westminster and the home counties, plots to oust the government were considered, shelved, or discovered.

Senior figures including Lord Shaftesbury pondered ways to overthrow Charles II and the House of Stuart for ever, and to install the type of representative government envisaged by John Locke. In 1682 Shaftesbury became embroiled in discussions for a plan to depose the King and put his eldest illegitimate son, the Duke of Monmouth, on the throne.

In London, feeling still ran high on both sides of the exclusion debate. The annual 5 November bonfire night demonstrations were held on 6 November, the fifth being a Sunday. Almost as soon as bonfires were lit, Tory crowds appeared, chanting pro-York slogans, and began to put out fires tended by anti-Yorkists. Rioting ensued. The homes of well-known Tories were attacked; Roger L'Estrange's house was ransacked. The trained bands were called out but were unable to contain the crowds. Disturbances continued until the morning. Four days after the rioting, the government banned all fireworks and bonfires during public celebrations.

Charles had never forgotten the failure of the City to fund the second Anglo-Dutch War. He decided to clip the wings of the powerful Corporation, the City's governing body. The Corporation dated from Anglo-Saxon times and had evolved over the centuries. Unlike the City of London, which had a royal warrant dating from the time of William the Conqueror, no royal charter seemed to have been issued for its governing body: the Corporation just was – it had always been. Charles took advantage of this lack of a defining legal foundation by issuing a writ questioning the Corporation's powers. *Quo Warranto* ('By What Warrant?') directly attacked the Corporation's authority, taking away its ability to award franchises or licences to trade. This was a huge blow to the City, aimed at reinforcing the monarchy's power, prestige and coffers.

Thanks to a partisan ruling by the court of the King's Bench in 1683, Charles got his way.* By withdrawing the Corporation's power, he was able to enforce his rule more closely over the City, appointing a Tory mayor and sheriffs. With major figures in the political opposition crushed, he now operated a government that was openly one-sided, favouring the Cavalier or Tory elements over all others. To the dismay of most, he dissolved the commission that had controlled the navy and reinstated his brother, the Duke of York, as head of the navy, a position he had had to resign years before when his Catholicism had become an issue.

In the same year that Charles clipped the wings of the City of London, a plot against the Crown was uncovered that appeared to be the most dangerous yet. It was revealed shortly after Charles's return to London from Newmarket, where he went regularly for the racing. According to an informant, a plot had been hatched to assassinate the King and the Duke of York as they made their way back to the capital from Newmarket. The plan was to ambush the King and his entourage as they approached a narrow section of road at an old manor called Rye House near Hoddesdon in Hertfordshire.

The scale of the plot, and even whether or not it in fact existed, have been hotly debated. In any event, the attack never took place, but it was used as the pretext for removing many of Charles's most outspoken political enemies. It was the perfect moment for Charles to take the initiative and crush the Whig opposition. Those rounded up included members of the main parliamentary opposition, including Lord Russell, a virulent promoter of Exclusion Bills in the House of Commons. Once the round-up began, the Earl of Shaftesbury, also a promoter of

---

* Six years later, in 1689, following the Glorious Revolution, the order was rescinded, reinstating the Corporation.

bills to exclude York, was charged with treason, but was found not guilty by a sympathetic jury of Londoners.

Before he could be returned to the Tower and tried again before a less amenable jury, Shaftesbury fled abroad. His protégé John Locke, feeling his position was now untenable, also fled, taking with him his unfinished manuscript of *Two Treatises of Government*. Locke knew that if the government discovered a copy of his work, particularly the *Second Treatise*, in which he argued for democratically elected government in place of divinely appointed kings, he would be tried for treason.

On Thursday 12 July the trial of the accused conspirators began at the Old Bailey before Judge Jeffreys. The five accused of high treason were William, Lord Russell, John Rouse, Captain Thomas Wallcot, Captain William Blake and William Hone. The evidence against them was that 'the Lord Howard, Colonel Shepherd a Vintner in Cornhill, &c. who Deposed, that he had been at divers Consuls in order to raise Rebellion and Leavy War, and a General Rising throughout the Kingdom, and that a Declaration had been drawn to that purpose, and a Survey taken of the King's Guards at the Savoy and Muse, in order to Surprize them, &c.'[1]

The trial lasted three days. Except for William Blake, who was acquitted, the accused were found guilty and sentenced to execution. On 20 July they were hanged at Tyburn. Others were rounded up and imprisoned but not hanged. They included the Earl of Essex, who committed suicide after being imprisoned in the Tower. The Duke of Monmouth admitted his involvement in plotting against the King, then recanted and fled abroad. In all, twelve men were executed for their part in one plot or another against the King. The list included several aristocrats, including political theorist Algernon Sidney, who believed people had the right to choose the type of government they wanted. At his trial for treason, Sidney had the unique experience of hearing his own works – which, published posthumously, were to have a profound impact on the genesis of the American Constitution – read out in evidence against him.[2] The clampdown on conspirators, whether actually engaged in plots or not, put a temporary cap on schemes against the Crown.

The winter at the start of 1684 was one of the coldest on record. As usual during severe winters at that period, building work stopped on all major projects, including at St Paul's Cathedral. Temperatures stayed below freezing point for weeks on end. The low temperatures brought the danger that rain could enter the stonework already erected, freeze and crack the masonry. Sackcloth and straw were used to protect any vulnerable walls, but frost still caused some damage. The affected stones would be replaced in the spring.

The Thames froze over and a fair was held on the ice. The Frost Fair was one of a number held during the seventeenth century, beginning in the winter of 1608–9. During the severe frost of 1658–9, the fair had become so popular that there were said to be more people on the river than in the streets. During the winter of 1662–3 the sport of skating was introduced from Holland. The King watched skaters on the Thames but did not join in.

The ice fair held during the winter of 1683–4 was the greatest of all, with the Thames frozen over for two months. On Candlemas Day (2 February) 1684, a whole ox was roasted on the river near Whitehall Palace. The King and Queen went to see it and Charles was reported to have tried some. Londoners took to the ice in their thousands. John Evelyn was among them:

> Coaches plied from Westminster to the Temple and from several other stairs too and fro, as in the streets; sleds, sliding

> with skeetes [skates], a bull-baiting, horse and coach races, puppet plays and interludes, cooks, tipling and other lewd places, so that it seemed to be a bacchanalian triumph, or carnival on the water.[3]

Among the novelties, a printer named Croom sold, at sixpence each, souvenir cards on which would be printed the purchaser's name and the date, together with the information that the card was printed on the Thames. The King bought one. Croom was said to have made £5 a day, ten times a labourer's weekly wage.

The cold weather was a cause not only for merriment but of hardship, as Evelyn explained: 'The fowls, fish and birds, and all our exotic plants and greens universally perishing. Many parks of deer were destroyed, and all sorts of fuel so dear that there were great contributions to keep the poor alive.' Returning to his pet subject of London's dreadful air quality, he continued: 'London, by reason of the excessive coldness of the air hindering the ascent of the smoke, was so filled with the fuliginous steam of the sea coal . . . that one could hardly breathe.'[4]

As London stood still in the icy air, its population was acutely aware that the political world was in ferment. The old problems of the relationship between Church, Crown and Parliament still haunted the capital. As Charles II moved into late middle age, the city moved into its own mature phase. The scars of the fire had mainly healed. Charles's health deteriorated gradually while London grew in strength. London was now the pre-eminent city in Europe, if not the world, having outstripped Amsterdam and Paris in trade. Of course, France and Spain remained the leading continental powers. But London sat at the centre of an international trade encompassing the Far East, India, Africa, the West Indies and America. The increase in trade brought new hurdles to cross: finance was always in short supply, while the bullion market could not keep up with the needs of investment. But no nation could challenge England's power on the oceans, with the old enemy the Spanish no longer a serious sea power and the Dutch cowed despite previous English military disasters.

Since the Great Fire, architecture had flourished, as had the building of grand houses in the countryside around the city for merchants, bankers and the nobility. Thanks to Inigo Jones's lead, Thomas Webb's expertise and the genius of Christopher Wren and of his pupil Nicholas Hawksmoor, the architecture of London changed. In the new streets and buildings, classicism was the order of the day. Britain would never look the same again. From now on, when any stately home was to be built or remodelled, columns, pilasters and porticos were the thing. Finally, London itself had been redesigned to resemble other imperial European cities. The city's population had increased from 350,000 in 1660 to more than 500,000. This growing populace was accommodated in suburbs, the first dispersed urban developments of their kind in the world.

London's accelerated growth was of continuing interest to Sir William Petty. Petty took London to mean the entirety of the metropolis, including the old city within the walls, the liberties outside the walls, all of Westminster, the new developments Barbon was responsible for building between Westminster and the old city, Southwark and the suburbs that spread outwards into parts of Middlesex and Surrey. In all, Petty counted 84,000 houses. Taking an average residency rate of eight people per house, he reckoned that London's population by 1682 had grown to 672,000.

In *An Essay Concerning the Multiplication of Mankind*, Petty outlined how this figure had been arrived at using the same basic information employed by his friend Graunt – the parish bills of mortality – and estimating the difference between the number who were born each year and the number who died. Petty's figures relied on a series of assumptions that did not bear close scrutiny. If he was correct, then London had almost doubled in size since Graunt's estimation of 384,000 only twenty years before. His far from accurate basic figures and assumptions led him to calculate that the city would double in size every forty years. Fortunately, he was incorrect, for such a growth rate would have put a great burden upon skeletal public utilities such as water and sewerage.* However, Petty foresaw no difficulties with a large population; in fact, he considered size to be an advantage in several spheres of public and commercial life: 'As to the administration of justice. If in this great city shall dwell the owners of all the lands, and other valuable things in England; if within it shall be all the traders, and all the courts, offices, records, juries, and witnesses; then it follows that justice may be done with speed and ease.'[5]

Petty believed that taxes were necessary for the good governance of society and that rich and poor should shoulder their burden proportionately. A great city such as London was of greater benefit to the national wealth owing to the size and industry of its populace. This meant it could generate more taxes, which could be collected more economically thanks to the confined urban setting:

> As to the equality and easy levying of taxes. It is too certain that London hath at some time paid near half the excise of England, and that the people pay thrice as much for the hearths in London as those in the country, in proportion to the people of each, and that the charge of collecting these

* Although wrong, Petty was, in ways, ahead of his time. With better hygiene and health care, by the 1800s Britain's population almost doubled every fifty years.

> duties have been about a sixth part of the duty itself. Now in this great city the excise alone according to the present laws would not only be double to the whole kingdom, but also more equal. And the duty of hearths of the said city would exceed the present proceed of the whole kingdom.

Others saw it differently. For his part, William Penn envisaged a land of equality and opportunity for all, with each inhabitant playing his or her equal part in a Utopian dreamscape, while the property developer Nicholas Barbon saw the city as a repository for individual free enterprise.[6] Petty understood society differently from either – as an economic organism serving a central cause, the state itself. When it came to foreign trade he saw a tremendous advantage in having a large concentration of labour. 'Whether more would be gained by foreign commerce? The gain which England makes by lead, coals, the freight of shipping, &c., may be the same, for aught I see, in both cases. But the gain which is made by manufactures will be greater as the manufacture itself is greater and better.'

The reason for this was a profound insight on Petty's part that would be most significant when large-scale manufacturing became the norm. What he recognised was the benefit of the division of labour and economies of scale:

> For in so vast a city manufactures will beget one another, and each manufacture will be divided into as many parts as possible, whereby the work of each artisan will be simple and easy. As, for example, in the making of a watch, if one man shall make the wheels, another the spring, another shall engrave the dial-plate, and another shall make the cases, then the watch will be better and cheaper than if the whole work be put upon any one man.

Such economies of scale already operated. It was one of the reasons why the Dutch were able to build ships more quickly than the English. In Dutch shipyards, a specialised workforce worked on specific parts of each ship only – the keel and main ribs of the hull, the planking and decking, the masts, general fitting out, and so on. This enabled ships to be built on a form of production line, whereas in England each ship was built individually with shipwrights doing many different jobs.

Petty himself had used the advantages brought by economies of scale to his work in Ireland as a surveyor for Cromwell. The task of surveying the entire island, noting the area and ownership of all arable land, was a massive one. Petty completed it in a very short time thanks to his employment of a workforce who needed very little skill, because each man was allotted a specific task which could be quickly taught and applied. Petty's methodology was among those used in surveying London for rebuilding after the Great Fire.

In almost all important fields outside politics and the theatre, London was thriving. Although monopolistic trade was increasingly seen more as a hindrance than a help, overseas trade was buoyant. Barbon made an interesting observation regarding political writers from Livy to Machiavelli: none of them had mentioned trade as being one of the key ingredients in the affairs of state. Trade, he observed, exercised 'great influence ... in the support and welfare of States and Kingdoms'.[7] According to Barbon's thesis, free trade was one method by which rulers could ensure the stability of the state.*

The sciences were forging a way out of blind superstition

* What seemed a solid proposition in the seventeenth century has proved to be less so in recent times.

and magic towards a world of reason and empirical observation. Belief in witchcraft and astrology were on the wane, battered by the new philosophy's rationalist demand for evidence. Medical science was making strides in exploring and understanding the body, and illness was seen less frequently as an opportunity to ply the patient with ineffectual or harmful potions. Tentative steps were even being made towards an understanding of the nature of the human mind.

In January 1684 the city played host to an historic scientific meeting when the three sparring partners Isaac Newton, Edmund Halley and Robert Hooke met at the Royal Society. By now they were uneasy in one another's company, but science had forced them together. They discussed the thorny problem of showing mathematically why planets did not move in circles around the sun, as Copernicus had said, but elliptically. Early in the seventeenth century, Johannes Kepler had come to the same conclusion but had been unable to produce a satisfactory proof. The laws pertaining to gravitation and the movement of planets had engaged the members of the Royal Society and their circle since the 1660s. Hooke now claimed he had reached a mathematical proof of planetary movement and of what became known as the inverse-square law governing gravitational attraction. Since Hooke produced no physical evidence of this work his claims were greeted with scepticism by Newton. Halley, a better mathematician than Hooke, had reached a partial derivation of the inverse-square law, but had failed to make a proof for its general application.

Newton was spurred by the conversation to go away and provide what the other two had failed to do. This was the impetus to complete work he had begun as early as 1665 and was to become his masterwork, *Philosophiae Naturalis Principia Mathematica*.

He became obsessed by it, for his personal appearance changed; he became scruffy, often neglected to eat, and between May 1684 and April 1686 ceased to make entries in his record books on his longstanding work in alchemy.

When Newton produced his proofs and prepared to publish the *Principia*, Hooke petulantly demanded recognition of his prior work in the field. The dispute between the two men has caused a great deal of argument and speculation over the years. Perhaps the best comment on the issue is that of the eighteenth-century French astronomer Alexis Clairaut, who acknowledged the work of both men but pointed out that Hooke's exaggerated claims served 'to show what a distance there is between a truth that is glimpsed and a truth that is demonstrated'.[8]

In the same year that Newton began sustained work on the *Principia*, a critical voice was raised against the great machine that was increasingly enriching London – the slave trade. Two pamphlets were published questioning the methods and legitimacy of slavery. Their writer and publisher was Thomas Tryon, a wealthy London merchant and self-made man. Born in Gloucestershire in such poor conditions that he worked as a child labourer in the wool spinning industry, Tryon was then employed as a shepherd. In his spare time he learned to read and write. Having mastered these basic skills he went to London and managed to find an apprenticeship to a hatter. His master converted him to the beliefs of the Anabaptist sect, but Tryon read the works of the German mystic Lutheran Jacob Boehme and became an independent thinker, combining Christian and eastern mystical texts into a personal religious theory.

Tryon then set out on an individual path to a spiritual and moral life. He became a fervent pamphleteer, espousing vegetarianism, kindness to animals and a questioning attitude to slavery. When Tryon had visited Barbados in the 1660s with the intention of setting up a hat business, what he saw repulsed him. He returned to London and set up home in the fashionable leafy village of Hackney. In 1684 he published two essays, 'The Negro's Complaint of their Hard Servitude and the Cruelties Practised Upon Them' and 'A Discourse in Way of Dialogue, between an Ethiopean or Negro Slave and a Christian, that was His Master in America'.[9]

Tryon did not go so far as to say all slavery should be banned. His argument was that the hardship inflicted on slaves was unchristian. Given the importance of the slave trade to London and the colonial economies, his broadsides had little or no impact. They were, however, a sign that it was not only Quakers who were wondering about the morality of what was being done in the name of progress and trade. About the same time several other pamphlets were published that argued about the issue of slavery. One powerful voice raised in support of anti-slavery measures was that of Josiah Child, the mercantile grandee who had made the East India Company virtually his private fiefdom.

From London, Child watched over every corner of the company's empire with a ferocious attention to detail. He kept an iron grip on the activities of the overseas agents. Long gone were the freewheeling days of William Langthorne and Sir Streynsham Master. The current agent in Madras, William Gifford, was completely under Child's thumb.

Under the EIC, Madras had expanded rapidly. By 1684 its population was around 300,000. In a city of such a size, control over slaving was bound to be difficult. While Langthorne had, it seems, privately encouraged slavery, Master had been tasked with curtailing it, though without success. On 10 July 1684, at the behest of Child, Gifford introduced a law backed by a new Court of Admiralty to try those suspected of slavery. This stricter regime was not to last – within a year, Madras was upgraded by the EIC to a so-called presidency, and its first president, the Boston-born merchant Elihu Yale, was a strong proponent of slaving.* He insisted that every ship bound for England should carry at least ten slaves.

Like most of his predecessors, Yale became wealthy through private trading, before he too was removed because of his corruption. Perhaps alluding to his corrupt private dealings and participation in the slave trade, his tombstone carries a poem containing the following lines:

> Much good, some ill he did; so hope all's even
> And that his soul thro' mercy's gone to heaven[10]

It would not be until 1693 that the first printed pamphlet would appear that explicitly argued against keeping slaves. It was published anonymously in New York and directed at the slave-owning Quaker society of Pennsylvania.[11] The monopoly enjoyed by the Royal African Company had always been unpopular in Bristol, from where most of the transatlantic trade was carried out. After prolonged lobbying, the city's merchants and ship owners had it lifted – even though, long before then, as we have seen, the monopoly was increasingly ignored. Though London would lose much of its slave trade as the century closed, its financial clout continued to grow along with the power and wealth of the East India Company, which ultimately grew to rule India.

*

---

* The famous American university was named after him.

While London thrived, the King did not. Old illnesses continued to afflict him. He may have had gout, he may have been feeling the symptoms of pulmonary disease, it may have been the syphilis he had contracted a decade before – any one of these diagnoses is possible. One thing is certain: Charles had tired of London. He had faced down Parliament, seen the Whigs destroyed as a force, reasserted his legitimacy and that of his heir, the Duke of York, and taken power from the City, withdrawing the Corporation's warrant and imposing his royal will on the appointment of all office bearers from the mayor to the aldermen. There had been plots on his life, at least one of which had involved his own eldest son, on whom he doted. Now – although these difficulties had been caused not by London but in many cases by the Crown's inability to rule in accordance with the will of the people – he felt he should move away from the scene of his troubles.

In AD 26 the Roman emperor Tiberius had moved from Rome to the island of Capri, tired of political wrangling and in fear of assassination. On Capri he built the fortified Villa Jovis, a pleasure palace Suetonius tells us was a scene of debauchery.[12] Now Charles planned to leave London and rule from Winchester, the ancient seat of the kings of Wessex. He commissioned Christopher Wren to build a great palace in the baroque style to rival Versailles, where he would rule a frenchified court, surrounded by his Catholic Queen, his French mistress and his Catholic brother, well away from the troublesome Protestants of the House of Commons and the City of London. The palace was to be sited on a hill beside the ancient castle, designed around a series of courtyards, with formal gardens descending to the River Itchen. Charles informed Wren that the building must be completed in great haste.

Wren was able to keep up with the building works at

Winchester as well as his other projects in London only thanks to a young clerk in his office named Nicholas Hawksmoor. Wren promoted Hawksmoor to deputy surveyor at Winchester, giving him responsibility to oversee the provision of finished drawings to be used by the builders. The new palace was being erected at a ferocious rate.

In the meantime, Charles was forced to continue to reside in the haphazard maze of Whitehall Palace, a place he had come to hate as much as London itself.

CHAPTER 27
DEATH AND LEGACY

On 6 February 1685, Charles Stuart, King of England, Scotland and Ireland, died at the age of fifty-four, not in his new palace at Winchester, but at his hated Whitehall. He had collapsed five days before, early in the morning of 1 February, after spending an evening in the company of his *maîtresse-en-titre*, the Duchess of Portsmouth, and two of his former lovers, Barbara, Countess Castlemaine, and Hortense Mancini. The soiree had been held in the Duchess's grand apartment in Whitehall Palace. Silver vases and urns graced inlaid French furniture, grand tapestries – a present from Louis XIV of France, presenting Arcadian dreamscapes in which sat French regal palaces – covered the walls. Those gathered in the grand room could have imagined they inhabited a glowing, golden world beside the River Seine rather than an ageing palace beside which the oily Thames washed London's sewage in and out with the tide. London's filthy streets and grimy intrigues seemed far away. According to those present, the King had never been in better spirits.

Over the days that followed, Charles floated in and out of

consciousness before abandoning the faith of his father and his people and accepting the last rites of the Roman Catholic Church. The cause of his death is unknown, though the symptoms indicate he suffered a series of strokes. His demise left an unresolved dilemma over the fate of the throne and the Church. There were no legitimate children to inherit, so the crown went to his openly Catholic brother James. Charles had resisted calls to divorce and remarry or to declare his Protestant first son, James, Duke of Monmouth, legitimate. One can only conjecture as to his desires for the realm, for he left no instructions. However, he refused the ministrations of an Anglican priest, opting instead for the last rites of the Catholic Church. Whether he wished the country to convert to the Catholic faith is open to debate, as is the question of how this was to be achieved under James in the face of fierce opposition.

As self-appointed master of the revels, Charles had presided over a profound change in behaviour among Londoners, albeit only for a few at first. During his reign, attitudes regarding sexual freedom and freedom of individual expression began to change. Between the intellectuals of London's literary and theatrical world and the new hedonists such as Rochester and Behn, the idea of the individual began to shine more brightly than that of society in general. From these small beginnings in the West End of London, life would never be the same again. A few years after Thomas Hobbes wrote that mankind must be protected from itself by tyranny, with all the crushing conformity that implied, the age of the individual was at hand. John Locke, with his more generous view of mankind, saw individuals as capable of engaging in collectively choosing their ruler or rulers.

Politically, Charles ruled at the tipping point between two worlds. Culturally and religiously he was a liberal, while politically he was an authoritarian. Several London residents wrote profoundly important works thanks to the political and social schisms that developed during his rule. John Milton, a native Londoner resident in the city almost all his life, produced *Paradise Lost*, one of the finest laments for lost freedom ever written, as a direct result of Charles coming to the throne. Though it never mentions the King by name, *Paradise Lost* was the greatest correction or indictment of his reign. Milton saw Charles, and all members of the House of Stuart, as a danger to society.

Another London resident, John Dryden, wrote the satirical poem *Absalom and Achitophel* in praise of Charles as a king and as a man. These works by Milton and Dryden may be taken as the opposite poles of Londoners' feelings about their ruler.

Charles had begun his era with a series of actions that boded well for London and Londoners. He proclaimed religious tolerance, meaning that Presbyterians and nonconformists, of whom there were many, would be able to worship as they wished. In fact, the introduction of the revised Anglican Book of Common Prayer, which was out of Charles's hands, drove a wedge between many Anglican sects, and introduced a schism which continues to this day. However, Charles failed to control the series of Acts of Parliament excluding those who did not participate in the Anglican Eucharist from holding public office. This had a major effect on the make-up of many public bodies in London, throwing several Londoners out of office. The initially cordial relations between city and monarch gradually turned to enmity, fuelled by the question of the royal succession and the Popish Plot. Finally, Charles took an autocratic hold of London, dissolving its ancient Corporation and placing his own candidates in the offices of Lord Mayor and sheriffs. To some extent, Charles was as much a victim of circumstance as the city, though his wish to rule like a French king was a decisive factor in the breakdown of his relations with his capital.

In other areas, Charles's relations with London were more beneficial and fruitful. When a group of high-minded individuals came to him asking for his imprimatur for a Royal Society, he gladly gave it. Not only that, but Charles actively encouraged experimentation to produce navigational aids, including the elusive quest for a clock to fix longitude at sea. He also had an observatory built on land he donated to encourage the mapping of the skies. Thanks to Charles II, zero degrees longitude is measured at Greenwich, forming the basis of mean solar time at noon (though Greenwich Mean Time has recently been superseded by Coordinated Universal Time). Though he was a keen advocate of the new empirical sciences, Charles's support for any cause rarely ran to financial backing – he was a spendthrift and never had sufficient funds to support his family, never mind any institutions. There was also the fact that Parliament underestimated the funds necessary to fund the monarchy.

One enterprise where Charles did provide finance was the Company of Royal Adventurers Trading into Africa, later renamed the Royal African Company. The King, his brother James and their cousin Rupert were key instigators of this joint stock company, set up for the purpose of sending traders to West Africa and returning first with gold and then with slaves. The importance of Charles and his family in making London the pre-eminent slaving city in northern Europe cannot be overestimated. During Charles's reign, the royal family and many of the most important figures in the City benefited hugely from the wealth brought into London by the slave trade. In the final five years of Charles's life, the numbers of slaves conveyed by London-based ships out of Africa rose to 37,854, double that in the previous period. If we estimate that each slaving ship carried on average a little fewer than 200 slaves, we can work out that almost every week a ship left London for the doleful triangular voyage to Africa, across the Atlantic and home again.

Paradoxically, Charles's support for such ventures also held them back. By his insistence on granting royal warrants to monopolistic companies, Charles prevented other enterprising merchants from joining in the trade. It was only with the lifting of these monopolies on the accession of William III that the slave trade grew to the enormous levels that enriched investors and practitioners throughout Britain, providing the engine for the ascendancy of the British Empire.

On a less contentious note, Charles enriched London in other ways. By restoring its theatre he brought fun and entertainment back to those who could afford it. In turn, the theatre became a mirror for his licentious and amoral court, with the characters of the Restoration fop or wit becoming English archetypes. By licensing women to appear on the public stage, Charles brought to the stage both sexuality and new possibilities of portraying human emotion. By giving theatre warrant holders free rein, he enabled the London stage to catch up with continental production practices and perhaps surpass them. For those who could not afford to attend the theatre, the reintroduction of public celebrations brought gaiety back to London: May Day celebrations, fairs, Lord Mayor's Day, Christmas celebrations and the rest all contributed to restoring sparkle to Londoners' often difficult, unhealthy and short lives.

Charles's role in promoting new architecture deserves a special mention. Without a king who, like his father before him, appreciated the attractions of neoclassicism, London might have looked very different today. Charles left a string of unfinished royal buildings behind him, but in a stroke of inspired patronage, he promoted the work of the young Christopher Wren, directing him away from other possible careers towards architecture. For the shape and look of much of London today, we must thank Charles and Wren, along with Wren's friend and collaborator Robert Hooke and a handful of other architects and planners.

In a time of patronage, Charles could be as astute or as blind as the next man. Of several key areas where he chose wisely, his support of Samuel Pepys's reorganisation of the Royal Navy must stand as his most important legacy for the future of Britain. Thanks to London's greatest diarist, the navy was restructured into an efficient, properly trained fighting organisation. Thanks to Charles's backing, the structure was put in place of the force that went on to overcome Napoleon's navy. Britain thereby became master of the seas, greatly boosting London, the country's great trading hub and, until the industrial revolution, the engine of the nation's wealth and turmoil. Modern Britain was created in London.

Given an impossible hand, Charles occasionally played it well, but as he became more embattled he reverted to autocratic ways that did him little favour. Throughout it all, London, the financial, economic and political heart of the nation, survived fire and plague to become the largest city in Europe. Restoration London provided the building blocks for modern life. By setting the scene for so much of modern political, sexual, scientific and economic thought and freedoms, making ready for the Age of Enlightenment, Charles II's London, it could be argued, has made us all.

EPILOGUE

So what of the characters who made London great during Charles's reign? How did they fare after his death and what legacy did they, their works and ideas leave?

Christopher Wren lived to the age of ninety-one, more than long enough to see his great cathedral finished in 1710. His joyous baroque style would not thrive, losing out to a more restrained, perhaps more English, love of Palladianism, which went on to become the style of Empire. Nevertheless, Wren was one of the first in the modern age to see architecture as the means to represent national character. For Wren, architecture was not simply style, it was the embodiment of an ideal of the nation at its best.

Wren epitomised a new age in architecture. The design of buildings, once the task of the artisanal architect/mason, became that of the educated gentleman. The major transitional figures in the process were Inigo Jones, who brought neoclassicism to England, and Wren himself, who made architecture into poetry, though towards the end of his life Wren regretted expending his talents on architecture, saying he wished he been a physician.[1]

In medieval times, English architecture had been

predominantly under the control of the Church. As a result of the religious and political upheavals of the seventeenth century, old beliefs came under question. In the face of a less certain faith, classicism seemed to lead the way back to some form of verity, to ancient roots of civic and spiritual knowledge that could be tapped to restore a sense of balance. With this realisation, the educated classes took over architectural practice from the master builders, so that architecture became one of the attributes an educated man might have at his disposal. The new breed of architect did not necessarily have to earn a living from it (though Wren did), but needed to demonstrate an understanding of its form and rules. This change led to the rise of practitioners like James Gibbs, the Earl of Burlington and John Vanbrugh. The face of England, and of Britain, would be changed for ever.

Thanks to Wren, Hawksmoor and those they enthused, new ideas in architecture bloomed in London. Classicism ensured that the architect's patron was seen as a person not only of substance but also of taste. The building of a new Palladian house could transform any country landowner or city merchant from rustic gent or city slicker into the epitome of enlightened and cutting-edge culture. Thus was born the rash of neoclassicism across the nation that culminated in the Barratt home in Dulwich, south London, bought by Margaret and Denis Thatcher – a red-brick suburban villa with an ersatz classical porch stuck on the front. How Inigo Jones, the boy from Smithfield, would have wept.

The London street changed utterly during the time of Charles II. Before the Great Fire, a typical London streetscape consisted of rows of medieval houses of different heights, each with its own patterns of wooden beams interposed with variously shaped areas of plaster. After the fire, the typical new street was a vista of conformity, with rows of identical terraced houses, each one the same width – usually fifteen feet – and of identical detailing and height. This uniformity was partly due to the Rebuilding Act of 1667 and to the massive programme of reconstruction carried out by the developer Nicholas Barbon to the west of the old city. The need to rehouse the displaced, together with the need to house a growing population, led to the development of the eighteenth- and nineteenth-century streets we know today. The Georgian and Victorian townscape had arrived.

To his great credit, Charles commissioned religious music from the precociously talented Henry Purcell. Perhaps fittingly, Purcell's groundbreaking works came not from commissions for sacred music but from the profane world of Greek myth. *Dido and Aeneas*, written around 1680, but not performed until 1688 or 1689 – and then only at a girls' boarding school in Chelsea – was the first English opera to feature continuous music. Until then, and despite Sir William Davenant's best efforts, all English opera had consisted of spoken dialogue interspersed with lyrics set to music. *Dido* was an opera as we would understand the term today and is still much performed. It is no exaggeration to say it is one of the glories of English music.

Following Charles's death, Purcell wrote music for the coronation of James II. He continued to write prolifically, including music for the funeral of Queen Mary II – some of which, with verses by Dryden, was played at Purcell's own funeral. Purcell was the first undoubted genius of British musical life. His music has stimulated, or been adapted by, composers including Michael Nyman and Benjamin Britten. It has been used for over a hundred film soundtracks and has inspired The Who, the Pet Shop Boys and Sting. This last should not surprise us too much, for Purcell was the quintessence of the baroque, the spiritual core of modern popular music's exuberant appeal, with its soaring chords, synthesisers, string sections, sampling and fast-cut video.

Purcell died in his thirties, at the height of his powers, and was buried in Westminster Abbey. By the time of his death, possibly of tuberculosis, he had changed the course of music. His resting place is dominated by the organ loft, where he spent so much of his professional life.

In the sphere of literature, John Dryden went on to publish his momentous translation of Virgil in 1697, a great public achievement for which he was paid £1400. Dryden's translations made many Latin classics accessible to the average reader for the first time. And where would today's rap or hip-hop artist be if Dryden had not made the heroic couplet (rhyming pairs of lines in iambic pentameter) the standard form in English poetry?

Without Dryden's lead, we would have no plays by his greatest disciple, William Congreve, one of the first writers able to retire early on the proceeds of his work. Congreve had arrived in London determined to make his mark. He soon found his way to Will's Coffee House in Covent Garden, where Dryden held court, and became a devotee. With London's theatrical revival failing badly, it was 25-year-old Congreve who came to the rescue. The situation facing London's premier playhouse, the United Company, had become so precarious that the company tore itself apart, with the more talented actors anxious to break away to breathe life into the city's theatrical heart while it still had a beat. Thomas Betterton, Mrs Barry and others set up their own company. They opened with Congreve's *Love for Love*, which was a smash hit. Congreve wrote his play in the high style of the sexual comedies of manners he learned from

Dryden. It was the last great hurrah for bawdy comedy dressed up in fine Restoration clothes.

Congreve had a knack of coining the phrase that lingered. In *Love for Love*, it was the line that described a daily staple of tabloid journalism, taken from the line 'O fie, miss, you must not kiss and tell.' His later play, *The Mourning Bride*, provided misanthropists everywhere with 'hell has no fury like a woman scorned'. And what would romantics everywhere do without 'music has charms to soothe the savage breast'?

Congreve was a Whig, a member of the Kit-Kat Club, a political and literary fraternity, and mixed in high society. He supposedly fathered a child by Henrietta Godolphin, the daughter of John Churchill, 1st Duke of Marlborough, and gave up the theatre to live on his royalties. He took up politics with minor success. All his writing for the theatre was done in a five-year period from 1695 to 1700. After that, tastes changed, but today Congreve seems to epitomise the high style of comedy that we have come to associate with the sexualised court life under Charles II.

To many, the style of theatre that evolved during Charles's reign was merely an abasement of the finer qualities of the Elizabethan and Jacobean theatre. Whatever one's taste, there is little doubt that Carolinian theatre lacked either the depth or poetry of the earlier theatre. And by 1698, time was being called on what some saw as the amoral excesses of the Restoration stage. The most powerful blast against the style of Dryden, Wycherley, Vanbrugh, Congreve and the rest came from a renegade Anglican cleric named Jeremy Collier. Unlike previous panegyrics lambasting those opposed to the writer's point of view, Collier went to great pains in giving examples drawn from the works in question. The main thrust of his argument was that in Restoration comedies the morally reprehensible were not punished for their licentious acts. Nor did he mince his words: 'Being convinced,' he wrote, 'that nothing has gone farther in Debauching the Age than the Stage Poets, and Play-House, I thought I could not employ my time better than in writing against them.'[2] There followed 280 pages of argument. Women were, said Collier, treated roughly on the stage, blasphemy went unpunished, and there was a lack of modesty and a general tone of profanity. Warming to his theme, Collier chastised the playwrights for cherishing passion and rewarding vice. Comedy, as known in the ancient world, he reminded his targets, was no laughing matter; the writer who 'minds nothing but the matter of *laughing*, is himself ridiculous'. He ended by saying that playwrights had 'the most need of repentance of all men living'.

John Vanbrugh laughed off Collier's attack. Dryden, who had survived Rochester's goons, had little to fear from a renegade cleric's words.* But Congreve took the criticism badly. Collier's condemnation may have contributed to his decision to give up writing for the theatre, although it undoubtedly concerned Congreve and his contemporaries that public taste was turning away from the brittle, knowing Restoration wit towards a gentler commentary upon the passing scene. Charles himself would have smiled at Collier's tirade – after all, he had once answered Bishop Burnet's chiding by saying that God would not punish a man for having fun.

Newton's *Philosophiae Naturalis Principia Mathematica* (usually referred to simply as the *Principia*) was published in 1687, a distillation of work begun some years before. One of the most

---

* Collier, though ordained, refused to recognise William and Mary and so was unlicensed by the Anglican Church.

important works in the history of science, the *Principia* set out Newton's laws of gravitation and of motion, establishing the ground for the modern discipline of mechanics. In 1696 Newton left Cambridge and moved to London as Warden of the Royal Mint. In 1703 he became president of the Royal Society. Two years later, he was knighted by Queen Anne. Newton's international prestige helped to rekindle interest in the society, which became a focus for the enhanced experimental abilities of researchers in the eighteenth century.

A row over Robert Hooke's claims to earlier authorship of some of the ideas in the *Principia* was never resolved. But if one man represented the Royal Society in its early aims and aspirations it was Hooke. Many superlatives have been used to praise him, including the assertion that he was England's Leonardo. After Hooke's death in 1703, Newton gained his revenge over his old sparring partner; it was said he destroyed the only known portrait of Hooke.* In 1712, he further displayed his ruthlessness when he and Edmund Halley pilfered more work from their supposed friend John Flamsteed and published a pirated edition of his sky atlas. Flamsteed had only himself to blame, for upon his appointment he had been tasked with producing star charts useful in navigation and had then procrastinated for years, delivering nothing of practical value. Halley and Newton both produced the goods, as it were, and thereby justified their greed for Flamsteed's figures.

London had another important advantage in the world of science: the German émigré Heinrich 'Henry' Oldenburg. It was largely thanks to Oldenburg that so many works, scientific,

---

* His image seemed lost to us until 2005 when Professor Liza Jardine published her biography of Hooke, reproducing what she claimed was a portrait long subject to misattribution. However, Andreas Pechtl and William Jensen have since separately argued the portrait is in a fact that of the Flemish chemist J.-P. van Helmont.

political and philosophical, were printed in English – one of the greatest innovations of the age in Europe. It is not known if he encouraged Robert Hooke to write his *Micrographia* in English, though he may well have done. Only a few decades before, all similar works had been published in Latin, the common language of Western learning. During the reign of Charles II, English became the chief language of international intellectual activity. This was the result of the deliberate policies of a few men. First, Oldenburg published his scientific newsletter in English and then funded what became the *Transactions of the Royal Society*, still published today in English. Second, a small group within the Royal Society, with John Wilkins at the centre, sought to find a form of language precise enough to express the technological exactitudes of the new mechanical science.[3] After a few efforts, these attempts were discarded. Having more elasticity than Latin (which proved to be quite unsuited to scientific debate) and being found amenable to development in order to meet new challenges of expression, English became the default scientific tongue.

With so many new observations being made, it is unsurprising that substantial numbers of words were coined, or first appeared in print, at this period. Although William Shakespeare holds the record for the highest number of newly coined English words (or at least for their first appearance in print), at 1582, John Evelyn coined no fewer than 491 new words, Robert Boyle 360, the botanist John Ray 342 and Hooke 68.[4] The mercurial adaptability and the reactive fluidity of the English language helped to push science forward almost as much as the Baconian revelation of reductive investigation itself.

During the reign of Charles II the Royal Society's importance first grew and then gradually decreased. After an initial flurry of excitement, the society to some extent lost its way, with many of its founders losing interest, failing to pay their subs, or simply not having experimental aptitude. There were too many dilettantes and gentlemen and not enough men like Hooke with the ability and inclination to engage fully in experimental work.

One of the contemporary criticisms made of the early mechanical experiments was that they seldom if ever had any practical value. A substantial proportion of the suggested experiments that Hooke was expected almost single-handed to set up were ludicrous, unnecessary or so ambitious as to be well nigh impossible. On one occasion he was asked to 'develop an engine to kill whales'[5]. The idea of Hooke, a creature of the city, bent over a prototype harpoon gun at the prow of a ship lashed by wind and waves in whale-rich waters off the Azores is hard to resist.

Despite many drawbacks, some very significant advances of great practical use were made. Among the most important were Isaac Newton's work on motion, gravity and light, Hooke's law of springs, his universal joint, the anchor escapement* and the balance spring watch, developed independently by both Hooke and Dutch scientist Christiaan Huygens. The other work to have immense significance, carried out by a variety of people, was on steam. Robert Boyle employed the French experimenter Denis Papin, who built on Boyle's and Hooke's vacuum pump to develop what he called his steam digester, in which the pressure of steam could be regulated. Experimental work on steam would reach fruition within a few years of Charles's death. In 1698 Thomas Savary patented the first steam engine. Hooke lived on to correspond with Thomas Newcomen, who built the first steam-powered water pump, of huge importance to

---

* Credited by some to Hooke and by others to clockmaker William Clement. Hooke seems to have been the earlier.

the development of the deep mine coal industry, which in turn powered the industrial revolution.

In 1689, with the absolutist Stuart brothers no longer in charge and the constitutionalist William on the throne, John Locke was able to publish *Two Treatises of Government*, refuting the promotion of absolutism and monarchy put forward by Robert Filmer in his influential *Patriarcha* of 1680. Locke laid out the natural rights of man to 'life, health, liberty or possessions'. These ideas were to be discussed by Samuel Adams and Thomas Jefferson and would resurface in the American Declaration of Independence as 'life, liberty and the pursuit of happiness'.

A few months later, Locke published his hugely influential *An Essay Concerning Human Understanding*, giving birth to the empiricist school of philosophy. The idea for the work had germinated during a meeting between Locke and Thomas Sydenham in Lord Shaftesbury's house in 1671, shortly after Locke arrived in London. It was of immense importance for Enlightenment philosophers such as Berkeley, Hume, Kant and Rousseau.

London in the age of Charles II also gave us statistics. Despite its baleful reputation, the development of statistical analysis was of first-rank importance. Thanks to the pioneering work of John Graunt and William Petty, a new science developed that would allow other great changes to take place. Without a way of measuring social and physical events accurately and then holding them up to analysis, various occupations are impossible. Statistical analysis proved to be the key to running an economy, to keeping tabs on expenditure and estimating income via taxes. It was also the key to scientific work requiring careful comparison between groups of results, or packets of information. Along similar lines, huge advances were also made in surveying, which would have great utility in the redevelopment of London after the fire, and in the future layout of new towns and cities. Without accurate measurement, the perfect Vitruvian city could not be built.

When Charles took ill and died at the beginning of 1685, he left the country in an uncertain state, but London itself was secure. Although its ancient freedoms and privileges had been taken away by the Crown's tightening hold, such a state of affairs would not last long. The calamity of the Great Fire had been overcome by the vitality of the city's people, making way for the future Georgian metropolis that epitomised the British Empire in its pomp. New ideas on trade, taxation and revenue were realised during Charles's reign, leading London to become the dominant trading city of its time. To this day, the City of London has remained a centre of trade rather than of industrial finance. In this rather odd way, the City stood outside and slightly apart from the industrial revolution. In Restoration London the system of using debt to finance trade grew radically, allowing London to expand its overseas trade at a rapid rate. State debt became commonplace – something that today causes palpitations among British politicians. The idea of starting up a national bank was edging closer. Despite the misgivings on all sides, the year before Charles's death a bill to form such a bank went before the Ways and Means Committee of the House of Commons. It was passed by twelve votes, and there the matter rested. It was never put before the House. Of course, debate did not stop there, but it would be another ten years before a national bank came into existence.*

By 1685, other important institutions and policies were already in place that would help London and Britain become the

* For a short description of how this came about, see Appendix V.

pre-eminent international capitalist force. It had been a slow process, but mercantile capitalism finally reached its apogee in London during the mid-1600s. International capitalism had grown from the novel supply of New World gold and silver bullion in the preceding century, with the tiny Italian city state of Genoa becoming the first state to use bullion in order to develop its mercantile activities.[6] The baton of supremacy passed from the Genoese to the Dutch and thence to the East India Company. During the reign of Charles II, and under the guidance of Samuel Pepys, from the third Anglo-Dutch War onwards, the development of a large, well-armed navy ensured England's dominance of international trade.[7]

During Charles's reign, England's role in the transatlantic slave trade also increased massively. The first decade of the Royal African Company's existence saw the country's share in the trade rise from one-third to three-quarters.[8] Once the African Company's monopoly was broken by Parliament after the accession of William III, the number of slave voyages increased massively.[9] In the period 1685–9, the number of exported slaves rose to 90,000.[10] Even then, demand was so great that it became obvious London's monopoly on slaving was holding the slave labour industry back. But it took until 1720 for Bristol to approach the capital in numbers of slaves embarked in Africa, before going on to eclipse it in the 1730s when over a five-year period Bristol traders shipped 106,532 slaves against London's 64,905. By the 1750s, Liverpool had outgrown both London and Bristol, shipping 129,984 Africans in the decade.[11] In fifty years, from its inception in 1672 until the 1720s, the Royal African Company shipped more African slaves than any other organisation in the dreadful history of the transatlantic slave trade.

The sea route that launched London into a dominant position

in world trade and finance was not the transatlantic run, but the route east from London to Bombay. When the Portuguese gave Bombay as part of Queen Catherine's dowry it was a little trading post on the western seaboard of India. Over time, the East India Company used this foothold to expand its trading in India and beyond. Within ten years the population of Bombay had increased from 10,000 to 60,000, and it continued to expand thereafter.* The EIC, like the Royal African Company, was given the right by royal warrant to engage in war and take foreign land by force. By the end of the seventeenth century, the company was so powerful that it was able to undertake military action against individual Indian rulers over trade agreements. This set the scene for the EIC to become a supra-national power with its own army and the ability to fight wars and eventually establish its rule over much of India. By this means Britain would go on to build up surplus capital and increase its domestic production. Out of this emerged the industrial revolution and the British Empire. Thanks to the instruments largely created or developed in London during Charles's reign, Britain would become the world's most important capitalist power until overtaken by the United States in the nineteenth century.

Today, it is possible to have an experience close to that of the intellectually curious seventeenth-century Londoner. To do so one has to begin with a tube ride to Chancery Lane. On emerging onto High Holborn the journey back in time begins. On the south side of High Holborn stands Staple Inn, one of the few remaining examples of Tudor architecture in London. Thanks to its location outside the area destroyed by fire, Staple

---

* By the time of India's independence from British rule in 1947, Bombay – now Mumbai – had a population of 2.3 million.

Inn stands as a fine evocation of what London looked like before the conflagration.

From here it is a short walk east along High Holborn to Barnard's Inn, an eighteenth-century office block for lawyers. Turning down an alleyway towards the back of the building, one comes to a half-timbered fifteenth-century hall. This is Gresham's Hall, today home of the eponymous college, which long ago moved from its original site in Bishopsgate. The college still holds weekly free lectures as it did in the days of Wren, Hooke, Petty and the rest. If one doesn't wish to make the journey, however, one can watch the lectures on the internet. Joseph Glanvill's imagining of 'magnetic waves that permeate the ether' comes instantly to mind. How the original members of the Royal Society would have loved that.

Among Robert Boyle's papers is a handwritten 'wish list' of twenty-four advances he would have liked to see come to pass. Among them was 'the prolongation of life'– thanks to improved hygiene, diet and modern medicine, life has indeed been prolonged. He wished for 'the recovery of youth, or at least some of the marks of it, as new teeth, new hair coloured as in youth', a wish fulfilled thanks to dental implants, hair colouring and follicle implanting. There is also the wish for 'the cure of diseases at a distance or at least by transplantation', which has come about in part in the form of organ transplants. Boyle wished for 'potent drugs to alter or exalt imagination ... appease pain, procure innocent sleep, harmless dreams, etc', all come to pass thanks to pharmaceutical advances.[12]

Despite such intellectual fireworks, to sum up the inquiring mind of mid- to late seventeenth-century London, it is to Robert Hooke we must turn, in particular to his engraving of the humble leaf, taken from *Micrographia*. This one image may stand for all the extraordinary events and discoveries in

London during the rumbustious and turbulent reign of Charles II. Having observed the structure of a piece of cork, Hooke then turned his attention to a leaf and noticed the same arrangement on a much smaller scale. The leaf was made up of repeated, tiny interlinked structures. He called these structures 'cells', from the Latin *cella*, meaning a small room. It would take until 1847 for cell theory to develop, but Hooke had helped to create the pathway for cell biology. He and other seventeenth-century investigators had, with their microscopes, set the ball rolling towards the double helix of DNA – what we now call 'the building blocks of life'.

APPENDIX I: THOMAS MUN, ENGLAND'S TREASURE

Thomas Mun's instructions to his son John on how to be a good merchant, written in 1628, published as *England's Treasure*, in 1664:

> My Son, In a former Discourse I have endeavoured after my manner briefly to teach thee two things: The first is Piety, how to fear God aright, according to his Works and Word: The second is Policy, how to love and serve thy Country, by instructing thee in the duties and proceedings of sundry Vocations, which either order, or else act the affairs of the Common-wealth; In which as some things doe especially lend to Preserve, and others are more apt to Enlarge the same: So am I now to speak of Money, which doth indifferently [unconsciously] serve to both those happy ends. Wherein I will observe this order, First, to show the general means whereby a Kingdome may be enriched; and then to proceed to those particular courses by which Princes are accustomed to be supplyed with Treasure. But first of all I will say something of the Merchant, because he must be a Principal Agent in this great business.

The Qualities which are required in a perfect Merchant of Forraign Trade.

The love and service of our Country consisteth not so much in the knowledge of those duties which are to be performed by others, as in the skilful practice of that which is done our selves; and therefore (my Son) it is now fit that I say something of the Merchant, which I hope in due time shall be thy Vocation: Yet herein are my thoughts free from all Ambition, although I rank thee in a place of so high esteem; for the Merchant is worthily called The Stewart of the Kingdoms Stock, by way of Commerce with other Nations; a work of no less Reputation than Trust, which ought to be performed with great skill and conscience, that so the private gain may ever accompany the publique good. And because the nobleness of this profession may the better stir up thy desires and endeavours to obtain those abilities which may effect it worthily, I will briefly set down the excellent qualities which are required in a perfect Merchant.

1. He ought to be a good Penman, a good Arithmetician, and a good Accountant, by that noble order of Debtor and Creditor, which is used only amongst Merchants; also to be expert in the order and form of Charter-parties, Bills of Lading, Invoices, Contracts, Bills of Exchange, and policies of Insurance.
2. He ought to know the Measures, Weights, and Monies of all foreign Countries, especially where we have Trade, & the Monies not only by their several denominations, but also by their intrinsic values in weight & fineness, compared with the Standard of this Kingdome, without which he cannot well direct his affairs.

3. He ought to know the Customs, Tolls, Taxes, Impositions, Conducts and other charges upon all matters of Merchandise exported or imported to and from the said Foreign Countries.
4. He ought to know in what several commodities each Country abounds, and what be the wares which they want [lack], and how and from whence they are furnished with the same.
5. He ought to understand, and to be a diligent observer of the rates of Exchanges by Bills, from one State to another, whereby he may the better direct his affairs, and remit over and receive home his Monies to the most advantage possible.
6. He ought to know what goods are prohibited to be exported or imported in the said foreign Countries, lest otherwise he should incur great danger and loss in the ordering of his affairs.
7. He ought to know upon what rates and conditions to freight his Ships, and ensure his adventures from one Countrey to another, and to be well acquainted with the laws, orders and customs of the Insurance office both here and beyond the Seas, in the many accidents which may happen upon the damage or loss of Ships or goods, or both these.
8. He ought to have knowledge in the goodness and in the prices of all the several materials which are required for the building and repairing of Ships, and the diverse workmanships of the same, as also for the Masts, Tackling, Cordage, Ordnance, Victuals, Munition and Provisions of many kinds; together with the ordinary wages of Commanders, Officers and Mariners, all which concern the Merchant as he is an Owner of Ships.

9. He ought (by the diverse occasions which happen sometime in the buying and selling of one commodity and sometimes in another) to have indifferent if not perfect knowledge in all manner of Merchandise or wares, which is to be as it were a man of all occupations and trades.
10. He ought by his voyaging on the Seas to become skilful in the Art of Navigation.
11. He ought as he is a Traveler, and sometimes abiding in foreign Countreys to attain to the speaking of diverse Languages, and to be a diligent observer of the ordinary Revenues and expences of foreign Princes, together with their strength both by Sea and Land, their laws, customes, policies, manners, religions, arts, and the like; to be able to give account thereof in all occasions for the good of his Countrey.
12. Lastly, although there be no necessity that such a Merchant should be a great Scholar; yet is it (at least) required, that in his youth he learn the Latin tongue, which will the better enable him in all the rest of his endeavours.

APPENDIX II: THE NAVIGATION ACT 1660

Here is the first clause of the Navigation Act of 1660, setting out its wide-ranging and restrictive powers (for the complete Act see 'An Act for the Encourageing and increasing of Shipping and Navigation', in *Statutes of the Realm*, vol. 5, 1628–80, ed. John Raithby, 1819):

No Goods shall be imported to or exported from Asia, Africa, or America, but in English Ships, and Master and Three-fourths of Mariners English.; Penalty.; Admirals, &c. empowered to seize and bring in as Prize all Ships offending.; Proceedings in case of Condemnation.

FOR the increase of Shiping and incouragement of the Navigation of this Nation, wherin under the good providence and protection of God the Wealth Safety and Strength of this Kingdome is soe much concerned Bee it Enacted by the Kings most Excellent Majesty and by the Lords and Co[m] mons in this present Parliament, assembled and the Authoritie therof That from and after the First day of December One thousand six hundred and sixty and from thence forward noe Goods or Commodities whatsoever shall be Imported into or

Exported out of any Lands Islelands Plantations or Territories to his Majesty belonging or in his possession or which may hereafter belong unto or be in the possession of His Majesty His Heires and Successors in Asia Africa or America in any other Ship or Ships Vessell or Vessells whatsoever but in such Ships or Vessells as doe truely and without fraude belong onely to the people of England or Ireland Dominion of Wales or Towne of Berwicke upon Tweede, or are of the built of, and belonging to any of the said Lands Islands Plantations or Territories as the Proprietors and right Owners therof and wherof the Master and three fourthes of the Marriners at least are English under the penalty of the Forfeiture and Losse of all the Goods and Commoditves which shall be Imported into, or Exported out of, any the aforesaid places in any other Ship or Vessell, as alsoe of the Ship or Vessell with all its Guns Furniture Tackle Ammunition and Apparell, one third part thereof to his Majesty his Heires and Successors, one third part to the Governour of such Land Plantation Island or Territory where such default shall be commited in case the said Ship or Goods be there seised, or otherwise that third part alsoe to his Majesty his Heires and Successors, and the other third part to him or them who shall Seize Informe or sue for the same in any Court of Record by Bill Information Plaint or other Action wherin noe Essoigne Protection or Wager of Law shall be allowed, And all Admiralls and other Commanders at Sea of any the Ships of War or other Ship haveing Co[m]mission from His Majesty or from his Heires or Successors are hereby authorized and strictly required to seize and bring in as prize all such Ships or Vessells as shall have offended contrary hereunto and deliver them to the Court of Admiralty there to be proceeded against and in case of condemnation one moyety of such Forfeitures shall be to the use of such Admiralls or Commanders and their Companies to be divided and proportioned amongst them according to the Rules and Orders of the Sea in [cases] of Ships taken prize, and the other moyety to the use of his Majesty his Heires and Successors.

APPENDIX III: ROBERT BOYLE'S DESIDERATA

A list of twenty-four developments Boyle wished to see in the future.

The Prolongation of Life.
The Recovery of Youth, or at least some of the Marks of it, as new Teeth, new Hair colour'd as in youth.
The Art of Flying.
The Art of Continuing long under water, and exercising functions freely there.
The Cure of Wounds at a Distance.
The Cure of Diseases at a distance or at least by Transplantation.
The Attaining Gigantick Dimensions.
The Emulating of Fish without Engines by Custome and Education only.
The Acceleration of the Production of things out of Seed.
The Transmutation of Metalls.
The makeing of Glass Malleable.
The Transmutation of Species in Mineralls, Animals, and Vegetables.

The Liquid Alkaest and Other dissolving Menstruums.
The making of Parabolicall and Hyperbolicall Glasses.
The making Armor light and extremely hard.
The practicable and certain way of finding Longitudes.
The use of Pendulums at Sea and in Journeys, and the Application of it to watches.
Potent Druggs to alter or Exalt Imagination, Waking, Memory, and other functions, and appease pain, procure innocent sleep, harmless dreams, etc.
A Ship to saile with All Winds, and A Ship not to be Sunk.
Freedom from Necessity of much Sleeping exemplify'd by the Operations of Tea and what happens in Mad-Men.
Pleasing Dreams and physicall Exercises exemplify'd by the Egyptian Electuary and by the Fungus mentioned by the French Author.
Great Strength and Agility of Body exemplify'd by that of Frantick Epileptick and Hystericall persons.
A perpetuall Light.
Varnishes perfumable by Rubbing.

APPENDIX IV: BRIEF OBSERVATIONS CONCERNING TRADE AND INTEREST OF MONEY, BY JOSIAH CHILD, 1668

The prodigious increase of the Netherlanders in their domestick and forreign Trade, Riches, and multitude of Shipping, is the envy of the present, and may be the wonder of all future Generations: And yet the means whereby they have thus advanced themselves, are sufficiently obvious, and in a great measure imitable by most other Nations, but more easily by us of this Kingdom of England, which I shall endeavour to demonstrate in the following discourse.

Some of the said means by which they have advanced their Trade, and thereby improved their Estates, are these following:

First, They have in their greatest Councils of State and War, trading Merchants that have lived abroad in most parts of the World; who have not onely the Theoretical Knowledge, but the Practical Experience of Trade, by whom Laws and Orders are contrived, and Peaces with forreign Princes projected, to the great advantage of their Trade.

Secondly, Their Law of Gavel-kind, whereby all their Children possess an equal share of their Fathers Estates after their decease, and so are not left to wrastle with the world in their youth, with inconsiderable assistance of fortune, as most of our youngest Sons of Gentlemen in England are, who are bound Apprentices to Merchants.

Thirdly, Their exact making of all their Native Commodities, and packing of their Herrings, Codfish, and all other Commodities, which they send abroad in great quantities; the consequence whereof is, That the repute of their said Commodities abroad continues always good, and the Buyers will accept of them by the marks, without opening; whereas the Fish which our English make in Newfound-Land and New-England, and Herrings at Yarmouth, often prove false and deceitfully made, and our Pilchards from the West Country false packed; seldom containing the quantity for which the Hogsheads are marked in which they are packed.

And in England the attempts which our fore-fathers made for Regulating of Manufactures, when left to the Execution of some particular person, in a short time resolved but into a Tax upon the Commodity, without respect to the goodness thereof; as most notoriously appears in the business of the AULNAGE, which doubtless our Predecessors intended for a scrutiny in o the goodness of the Commodity; and to that purpose a Seal was invented, as a signal that the Commodity was made according to the Statutes, which Seals it is said, may now be bought by Thousands, and put upon what the Buyers please.

Fourthly, Their giving great incouragement and immunities to the Inventors of New Manufactures, and the Discoverers of any New Mysteries in Trade, and to those that shall bring the Commodities of other Nations first in use and practise amongst them; for which the Author never goes without his due Reward allowed him at the Publique Charge.

Fifthly, Their contriving and building of great Ships to sail with small charge, not above one third of what we are at, for Ships of the same Burthen in England; and compelling their said Ships (being of small force) to sail always in Fleets, to which in all times of danger they allow Convoy.

Sixthly, Their parsimonious and thrifty Living, which is so extraordinary, that a Merchant of one hundred thousand pound estate with them, will scarce spend so much per annum, as one of fifteen hundred pounds Estate in London.

Seventhly, The education of their Children, as well Daughters as Sons; all which, be they of never so great quality or estate, they always take care to bring up to write perfect good hands, and to have the full knowledge and use of Arithmetick and Merchants Accompts; the well understanding and practice whereof, doth strangely infuse into most that are the owners of that quality, of either Sex, not onely an ability for Commerce of all kinds, but a strong aptitude, love, and delight in it; and in regard the women are as knowing therein as the men, it doth incourage their Husbands to hold on in their Trades to their dying days, knowing the capacity of their Wives to get in their Estates, and carry on their Trades after their Deaths: Whereas if a Merchant in England arrive at any considerable Estate, he commonly withdraws his Estate from Trade, before he comes near the confines of old Age, reckoning that if God should call him out of the World, while the maine of his Estate is engaged abroad in Trade; he must lose one third of it, through the unexperience and unaptness of his Wife to such Affairs, and so it usually falls out.

Besides, It hath been observed in the nature of Arithmetick, that like other parts of the Mathematicks, it doth not onely improve the Rational Faculties, but inclines those that are expert in it to thriftiness and good Husbandry, and prevents both Husbands and Wives in some measure from running out of their Estates, when they have it always ready in their Heads what their expences do amount to, and how soon by that course their ruine must overtake them.

Eighthly, The loweness of their Customs, and the heighth of their Excise, which is certainly the most equal and indifferent Tax in the World, and least prejudicial to any People, as might be made to appear, were it the subject of this discourse.

Ninethly, The careful providing for, and employment of their Poor; which is easie to demonstrate can never be done in England comparatively to what it is with them, while it's left to the care of every Parish to look after their own onely.

Tenthly, Their use of BANKS, which are of so immence advantage to them, that some not without good grounds have estimated the profit of them to the Publick to amount to at least one million of pounds sterling per annum.

Eleventhly, Their Toleration of different Opinions in matters of Religion: by reason whereof many industrious People of other Countreys, that dissent from the Established Government of their own Churches, resort to them with their Families and Estates, and after a few years cohabitation with them, become of the same Common interest.

Twelfthly, Their Law-Merchant, By which all Controversies between Merchants and Tradesmen are decided in three or four days time, and that not at the fortieth part (I might say in many cases not the hundredth part) of the charge they are with us.

Thirteenthly, The Law that is in use among them for transference of Bills for Debts from one man to another: This is of extra-ordinary advantage to them in their Commerce; by means whereof, they can turn their Stocks twice or thrice in Trade, for once that we can in England; for that having sold our Foreign Goods here, we cannot buy again to advantage, till we are possest of our Money; which it may be we shall be six, nine, or twelve Months in recovering: And if what we sell be considerable, it is a good man's work all the Year to be following Vintners, and Shopkeepers for Money. Whereas, were the Law for Transferring Bills in practise with us, we could presently after sale of our Goods, dispose of our Bills; and close up our accounts. To do which, the advantage, ease, and accommodations it would be to Trade, is so great, that none but Merchants that have lived where that custom is in use, can value to its due proportion.

Fourteenthly, Their keeping up PUBLICK REGISTERS of all Lands and Houses, Sould or Mortgaged, whereby many chargable law Suits are prevented, and the securities of Lands and Houses rendred indeed, such as we commonly call them, REAL SECURITIES.

Lastly, the lowness of Interest of Money with them, which in peaceable times, exceeds not three per cent Per annum; and is now during this War with England, not above four per cent at most.

APPENDIX V: NOTES ON THE FORMATION OF THE BANK OF ENGLAND

Throughout the seventeenth century London looked to Amsterdam for inspiration on how to manage its financial affairs. One of the benefits of a national bank was seen to be, from the Dutch model, that interest rates could be kept low. When the Bank of Amsterdam was founded in 1609 the English saw this as a way forward, but were unable to find a means of setting up their own version until after the iron hand of the Stuarts was released from the economic levers. Ironically, the very thing that London's merchants most envied about the Dutch would only be made possible when a Dutchman became king. The Bank of England was formed in 1694, six years after William arrived with his army.

There had been many schemes for a national bank throughout the century. John Banks's remark to Samuel Pepys that the Exchequer was too far from the Exchange was an aside to a debate that seldom went away. In 1658, Samuel Lambe, a London merchant, wrote a detailed design for a national bank and sent it to the House of Commons for consideration by the Grand Committee for Trade, setting out 'Proposals for managing England's economic and trade conditions'.[1] Lambe could not have chosen a worse moment. The country was in turmoil and his idea was forgotten about.

In another irony, one of the reasons for a bank not being formed was that the House of Commons – whose members one would have thought of as natural allies of London's merchant classes – did not want the King to use the bank as a means of raising money and bypassing Parliament. There was the added concern that a bank could be taken over entirely by the King, taking away any financial leverage Parliament might have had. The lessons of the Great Stop were never far away. A move to form a National Bank of Credit in 1683 came to nothing for much the same reason that previous efforts foundered: fears of the King making the bank his own and sidelining Parliament. Not everyone in the City of London was keen on the establishment of a national bank. The goldsmiths were set against it, fearing – rightly – that it could end their near-monopoly on loans. Even if it did not do so, it would undoubtedly have a severe effect on the high rates of interest they could charge.

If any one person can be said to have founded the Bank of England, it was a Scot, William Patterson.* Patterson made his money in London, trading with the slave colonies in the West Indies. Like many merchants trading overseas, Patterson was acutely aware for years that the banking system needed reform and enlargement to take account of expansion both in trade and in government. In 1691 he proposed 'to form a company to lend a million pounds to the Government at six percent [plus £5000 "management fee"] with the right of note issue'.[2] The following

---

* Interestingly, it was an Englishman who in 1695 created the Bank of Scotland. This was John Holland, a merchant born in London in 1658. His father, a ship's captain, was a friend of Samuel Pepys.

year his proposal was turned down by the parliamentary committee set up with the express purpose of pondering how to raise money to pay for the war with France. The reason, to quote Halley Goodman, a historian of the Bank of England, was a residual fear that permeated both sides in Parliament:

> The primary political groups which were in opposition were the Jacobite supporters of the deposed King James and the landowning Tories. Both groups feared that the government would be strengthened and their own influence diminished by the establishment of a national bank. The Catholic Jacobites thought that the creation of the bank would weaken France's monarchy. The Tories, in turn, thought that the bank 'would lead straight to socialism' or a commonwealth. The Tories also opposed the Bank because it would strengthen King William III's power by making it easier for him to obtain money; this would make it less likely for the House of Stuart to be restored.[3]

Patterson made another proposal – this time to lend the government £2 million. This also foundered. A year later, in 1693, the Commissioner to the Treasury, Lord Montagu, stepped in, suggesting Patterson try yet again. Patterson, having been bitten by political opponents twice before, took the precaution of writing a pamphlet setting out the benefits of a national bank. Despite the usual criticisms (plus a new one that the bank might allow William III to become an absolutist king like his Stuart predecessors), on 25 April 1694 Patterson's plan was included in the Tunnage Act (also known as the Bank of England Act) and was passed by both Houses of Parliament. The act was a compendium of measures, both to raise duties and to raise money by other means, as outlined in its odd opening description:

> An Act for granting to their Majesties several Rates and Duties upon Tunnage of Ships and Vessels, and upon Beer, Ale, and other Liquors, for securing certain Recompences and Advantages in the said Act mentioned, to such Persons as shall voluntarily advance the Sum of Fifteen hundred thousand Pounds towards carrying on the War against France.

In the event, the act allowed a national bank – the Bank of England – to be set up as a corporation. The sum of £1.2 million was loaned to the government, allowing William III to continue his war with France, which had begun in 1690 and continued to 1697. In fact the bank was privately run, its only client being the government. Thus the longstanding and curious relationship between governments and bankers, in which they are inexorably intertwined, was established. The bank remained in private hands until it was nationalised in 1946.

Given the current state of banking practice, with banks routinely lending many times their capital, it is interesting to note that under the rules by which the Bank of England was set up, initially its borrowing and lending could not be greater than its capital.

NOTES

1 A City of Expectation

1 John Aubrey, *Brief Lives*, 1715.
2 Anthony Munday, *Mayoral Pagent Book*, quoted in Christine Stevenson, *The City and the King*, 2013.
3 A.E. Wrigley and R.S. Schofield, *The Population History of England, 1541–1871: A Reconstruction*, 1989.
4 Fernand Braudel, *The Perspective of the World*, 1985.
5 John Stowe, A *Survey of the Cities of London and Westminster*, 1720.
6 John Milton, *The Readie and Easie Way to Establish a Free Commonwealth*, 1660.
7 Ibid.
8 John Downes, *Roscius Anglicanus*, 1708.

2 The King Comes In

1 Declaration of Breda, 1660, http://www.constitution.org/eng/conpur105.htm
2 *Middlesex County Records*, vol. 3, 1625–1667.
3 Edward Hyde, 1st Earl of Clarendon, *History of the Rebellion*, 1702–4.
4 Samuel Pepys, *Diary*.
5 Charles II, *Letters*, ed. Arthur Bryant, 1968.
6 Thomas Macaulay, *The History of England*, 1848.
7 Hyde, *History of the Rebellion*.
8 John Evelyn, *Diary*, vol. 1, 1901, http://www.gutenberg.org/

files/41218/41218-h/41218-h.htm#tn_png_296a

9 Hyde, *History of the Rebellion.*

10 Lucy Hutchinson, *Memoirs of the Life of Colonel Hutchinson*, 1806.

3 Theatrum Redux!

1 Aubrey, *Brief Lives.*

2 Ibid.

3 William Davenant, *Madagascar with other Poems*, 1638.

4 A. Nethercot, *Sir William Davenant*, 1938.

5 Leslie Hotson, *The Commonwealth and Restoration Stage*, 1928.

6 *Mercurius Fumigosus*, 12–19 September 1665.

7 Hotson, *The Commonwealth and Restoration Stage.*

8 Alison Latham, ed., *Oxford Companion to Music*, 2002.

9 Evelyn, *Diary.*

10 Don Jordan and Michael Walsh, *The King's Revenge*, 2012.

11 Gilbert Burnet, *A History of My Own Time*, 1715.

12 Proceedings of the Old Bailey, http://www.oldbaileyonline.org

13 *The Speeches and Prayers of the Regicides*, Thomason Tracts, BL, 1660.

14 Evelyn, *Diary.*

15 Hyde, *History of the Rebellion.*

4 Something for Everyone?

1 Pepys, *Diary.*

2 Aristotle, *Politics*, Book I.

3 Quoted in Benjamin A. Rifkin, *Human Anatomy, Five Centuries of Art and Science*, 2005.

4 Giraldus Cambrensis, *Topographia Hibernica*, 1187.

5 PRO SP 29/5 74.

6 Ibid.

7 PRO SP 29/5 74.1.

8 John Bold, *John Webb, Architectural Theory and Practice in the Seventeenth Century*, 1989.

9 Sir William Sanderson, *Compleat History of the Life and Raigne of King Charles*, 1658.

10 Margaret D. Whinney, 'John Webb's Drawings for Whitehall Palace', *Proceedings of the Walpole Society*, vol. 31, 1942–3, 1946.

11 Aubrey, *Brief Lives.*
12 Anthony Wood, *Anthenae Oxonienses,* 1813.
13 PRO SP 29/5 74.
14 Lisa Jardine, *On a Grander Scale: The Outstanding Life of Christopher Wren*, 2002.
15 W.H. Kelliher, *DNB.*
16 BL Add. MS27962, 17 January 1661.
17 Hotson, *The Commonwealth and Restoration Stage.*
18 Christopher Wren, *Parentalia*, 1750.

5 Rivals

1 Geoffrey Smith, 'Long, Dangerous and Expensive Journeys: the Grooms of the Bedchamber at Charles II's Court in Exile', *Early Modern Literary Studies* 15, 2007; BL, Copy of a Letter Written by Mr Thomas Killigrew, Manuscript 27402, fos. 69r–71v.
2 Venetian State Papers.
3 CSP Dom, 1660–1.
4 G.E. Bentley, *The Jacobean and Caroline Stage*, 1941; 1968.
5 Downes, *Roscius Anglicanus.*
6 Edward A. Langhans, 'The Theatres', in *The London Theatre World 1600–1800*, ed. Hume, 1980.
7 PRO; Admiralty Papers of the Navy Board.
8 George Frederick Zook, *The Company of Royal Adventurers*, 1919.
9 Pepys, *Diary.*
10 Richard Ligon, A *True and Exact history of the Island of Barbadoes*, 1657.
11 Trans-Atlantic Slave Trade Database, Emory University, www.slavevoyages.org
12 Ibid.

6 The Crowning of a King

1 Peter Earle, *The Making of the English Middle Class*, 1989.
2 Raphaelle Schwartzberg, *Becoming a Goldsmith in the Seventeenth Century*, LSE Working Papers 141/10, Department of Economic History, LSE 2010.
3 Richard Grassby, *The Business Community of Seventeenth Century England*, 1995.

4 John Evelyn, *Fumifugium*, 1661.
5 Mark Jenner, *The Politics of London Air: John Evelyn's Fumifugium and the Restoration*, 2013.
6 Evelyn, *Fumifugium*.
7 Stowe, *Survey of the Cities of London and Westminster.*
8 Ibid.
9 Anon., *In Praise of the choice company of philosophers and witts who meete on Wednesdays weekely at Gresham College*, Ashmolean MSS, reprinted in *Notes and Records of the Royal Society of London*, vol. 5, 1948, attrib. William Godolphin.
10 David Scott, *Leviathan: The Rise of Britain as a World Power*, 2013.
11 John Ogilby, *The relation of his Majestie's entertainment passing through the city of London*, 1662.

7 'Too Great an Honour for a Trifle'

1 John Wallis, *Account of Some Passages of his Life*, 1700.
2 John Evelyn, letters on 3 and 29 September 1659, in *Diary*.
3 J.A. Bennett, *The Mathematical Science of Christopher Wren*, 1982.
4 Ibid.
5 Jardine, *On a Grander Scale*.
6 Ibid.
7 Ibid.
8 Francis Bacon, *New Atlantis*, 1627.
9 Robert Hooke, *Folio*, MSS Royal Society, www.livesandletters.ac.uk/cell/Hooke/Hooke.html
10 Robert Boyle, *Collected Works*, 1772.
11 Henry Power, *Experimental Philosophy*, 1663.
12 Robert Boyle, *New Experiments Physico-Mechanicall, touching the Spring of the Air, and its effects, made in the most part using a New Pneumatical Engine*, 1660.
13 Anon., *In Praise of the Choyce Company of Philosophers and Witts*.
14 Hooke, *Folio*.
15 House of Lords Journal, 5 September 1660.

8 Foreign Adventures

1 Pepys, *Diary*.
2 Figures extrapolated from The Trans-Atlantic Slave Trade Database.

3 CSP Dom, quoted in Liza Picard, *Restoration London*, 1997.
4 Pierre Mignard, *Louise de Kérouaille, Duchess of Portsmouth*, National Portrait Gallery, London, NPG497.
5 *Mercurius Publicus*, 30 May 1662.
6 Charter of Carolina, 1663, http://avalon.law.yale.edu/17th_century/nc01.asp
7 Wren Society Papers, Oxford, vol. 13, 1924–43.

9 Trade Wars

1 Figures extracted from the Trans-Atlantic Slave Trade Database.
2 http://higherpraise.com/outlines/text_misc_cs/article4056.html
3 Trans-Atlantic Slave Trade Database.
4 William Davenant, *Macbeth*, 1674; Christopher Spencer, ed., *Five Restoration Adaptations of Shakespeare*, 1965.
5 Thomas Mun, *England's Treasure by Foreign Trade*, written 1628, pub. 1664.
6 Edward Misselden, *Free Trade, or The Meanes to Make Trade Flourish*, 1622.
7 Thomas Mun, *A Discourse of Trade from England Unto the East-Indies*, 1621.
8 Mun, *England's Treasure.*
9 Evelyn, *Diary.*
10 G.F. Steckley, ed., *The Letters of John Paige, London Merchant, 1648–58*, London Record Society 21, 1984.
11 *An Act for Increase of Shipping, and Encouragement of the Navigation of this Kingdom*, October 1651.
12 *An Act for Confirming an Act Entituled an Act for Encouraging and Increasing of Shipping and Navigation*, etc., 1661.
13 Burnet, *A History of My Own Time.*
14 Calendar of Manuscripts of Marquis of Bath, HMSO 1980, https://archive.org/stream/calendarofmanusc05bath/calendarofmanusc05bath_djvu.txt

10 A New World of Science

1 J.G. Marcus, *A Naval History of England*, vol. 1, 1961.
2 Evelyn, *Fumifugium.*
3 Robert Hooke, *Micrographia*, 1665, BL C.175.e.8.

4 Ibid.
5 Joseph Glanvill, *Plus Ultra*, 1668.
6 Francis Bacon, *Instauratio Magna*, The Oxford Francis Bacon, 2000.
7 *Philosophical Transactions of the Royal Society*, vol. 1, 1665.
8 Ibid.

11 The Year of the Flea

1 Jardine, *On a Grander Scale*.
2 National Archives, *Rules and Orders to be observed by all justices of the Peace, Mayors, Bayliffs and other Officers for the Prevention of the Spreading of the Infection of the Plague*, SP29/155 f102, 1666.
3 Daniel Defoe, *A Journal of the Plague Year*, 1722.
4 Ibid.
5 John Graunt, *London's Dreadful Visitation*, 1665.
6 Nathaniel Hodges, *Loimologia*, 1720.
7 Ibid.
8 Hugh G. Dick, *Students of Physic and Astrology*, quoted in Michael MacDonald, 'The Career of Astrological Medicine in England', in Ole Peter Grell and Andrew Cunningham, eds, *Religio Medici*, 1996.
9 Peter Levens, *The Pathway to Health*, 1587–1664.
10 Grell and Cunningham, eds, *Religio Medici*.
11 Mark Jenner, 'Quackery and Enthusiasm', in Grell and Cunningham, eds, *Religio Medici*.
12 Thomas Gale, quoted in Jenner, 'Quackery and Enthusiasm', in Grell and Cunningham, eds, *Religio Medici*.
13 Thomas Sydenham, *Observationes Medicae circa Morborum acutorum historiam et curationem*, 1676.
14 Nicholas Culpeper, *Herbal*, 1649.
15 Evelyn, *Diary*.
16 Ibid.
17 Hodges, *Loimologia*.
18 Evelyn, *Diary*.
19 Ibid.
20 Pepys, *Diary*.
21 Hodges, *Loimologia*.
22 Numbers 11.33; Jeremiah 21.6.
23 Defoe, *A Journal of the Plague Year*.
24 Ibid.

25 Quoted in Hans Fantel, *William Penn: Apostle of Dissent*, 1974.
26 Ian Mortimer, *Dying and the Doctors*, 2009.
27 Bart K. Holland, 'Treatments for Bubonic Plague, Reports from seventeenth century British epidemics', *Journal of the Royal Society of Medicine*, vol. 93, June 2000.

12 Pestilence, War and Fire

1 John Evelyn, letter to Wren, Wren Society Papers, Vol. 13.
2 Wren, *Parentalia.*
3 Wren Society Papers, Vol 13.
4 Ibid.
5 Sir John Banks to Pepys, *Diary.*
6 National Archives, E179 database; Hearth Tax Online, hearthtax.org.uk
7 Pepys, *Diary.*
8 *London Gazette*, 2 September 1666.
9 Ibid., 10 September 1666.
10 Leo Hollis, *The Phoenix*, 2008.

13 The Aftermath

1 Venetian State Papers.
2 Trans-Atlantic Slave Trade Database.
3 John Dryden, *Annus Mirabilis*, 1667.
4 Jardine, *On a Grander Scale.*
5 Evelyn, *Diary.*
6 Quoted in David Hughson, *London, An Accurate History and Description of the British Metropolis*, 1805.
7 Ibid.
8 Proceedings of the Royal Society.
9 Robert Hooke, *Diaries*, ed. Richard Nichols, 1994.
10 Emma Wilkins, 'Margaret Cavendish and the Royal Society', *Notes and Records of the Royal Society*, May 2014.
11 Robert Boyle, *A Free Enquiry into the Vulgarly Received Notion of Nature*, 1686.
12 Margaret Cavendish, *Observations upon Experimental Philosophy*, 1666.
13 John Locke, *Anatomie*, written with Thomas Sydenham, 1668, quoted in Wilkins, 'Margaret Cavendish and the Royal Society'.

14 Pepys, *Diary.*
15 Margaret Cavendish, *The Description of a New World, called the Blazing World*, 1666.
16 Hooke, *Folio.*
17 Joseph Glanvill, written 13 October 1667, published in *Letters and Poems in Praise of the Incomparable Princess, Margaret, Duchess of Newcastle*, 1676.
18 Thomas Hobbes, *Considerations upon the Reputation . . .*, 1680.
19 Joseph Glanvill, *Sadducismus Triumphatus*, 1681.
20 Hollis, *The Phoenix.*

14 A Star is Born

1 John Dryden, *Works*, ed. Sir Walter Scott, 1808.
2 Charles Beauclerk, *Nell Gwyn.*
3 Ibid.
4 Katherine Eisaman Maus, 'Playhouse Flesh and Blood', *English Literary History*, vol. 46, no. 4, 1979.
5 *Covent Garden Drollery*, 1672, text read by Mrs Reeves.
6 Pepys, *Diary*, 22 August 1667.
7 Geoffrey Smith, in *Thomas Killigrew and the Seventeenth Century English Stage*, ed. Philip Major, 2013.
8 John Dryden, *Secret Love, or The Maiden Queen*, 1669.
9 John Spurr, *England in the 1670s: This Masquerading Urge*, 2000.
10 Burnet, *A History of My Own Time.*

15 The Threat from Abroad

1 Stowe, *A Survey of the Cities of London and Westminster.*
2 Pepys, *Diary.*
3 C.D. Chandaman, *The English Public Revenue, 1660–1688*, 1975.
4 See Jenny Uglow, *A Gambling Man, Charles II and the Restoration*, 2010.
5 Andrew Marvell, *Last Instructions to a Painter*, 1667.
6 Ibid.
7 Ibid.
8 Brian Lavery, *Empire of the Seas*, 2009.
9 See Ronald Hutton, *Charles the Second*, 1989.

10 Burnet, *A History of My Own Time*.
11 J. Douglas Cranfield, *Heroes and States*, 1999.

16 New Territories

1 Peter (Pierre) Esprit Radisson, *Voyages of, Being an account of his travels and experiences among the North American Indians, from 1652 to 1684*, 1885.
2 Richard Hakluyt, *The Principal Navigations, Voyages, Traffiques and Discoveries of the English Nation*, ed. E. Goldsmid, 1884–1890.
3 Robert Filmer, *Observations Upon the Original of Government*, 1652; *Patriarcha*, 1680.
4 John Locke, *Two Treatises on Government*, pub. anonymously 1689.
5 Ibid.
6 Quoted in Alfred O'Rahilly, 'Aquinas versus Marx, Part I', *Studies*, vol. 31, no. 124, 1942.
7 William Petty, *Treatise on Taxes*, 1662.
8 William Petty, *Economic Writings*, reprint 1963.
9 John Evelyn, *Tyrannus, or The Mode*, 1661.
10 Josiah Child, *Brief Observations Concerning Trade and Interest of Money*, 1668.

17 Law and Order

1 Don Jordan and Michael Walsh, *White Cargo*, 2007.
2 Ibid.
3 Abbot Emerson Smith, *Colonists in Bondage: White Servitude and Convict Labor in America, 1607–1776*, 1947.
4 BL, Miscellaneous Sheets 74/515 L2.
5 Ned Ward, *A Trip to Jamaica*, 1698.
6 Jordan and Walsh, *White Cargo*.
7 Ibid.
8 Pepys, *Diary*.
9 John Dryden, *Upon the Three Dukes Killing a Beadle*.
10 CSP Dom., April 1671.
11 *Survey of London*, vol. 36, 1970: http://www.british-history.ac.uk/survey-london/vol36/pp185-192#fnn7
12 Pepys, *Diary*.
13 William Winstanley, *Lives of the Most Famous English Poets*, 1687.

14 Daniel Defoe, *The Fortunes and Misfortunes of the Famous Moll Flanders*, 1722.
15 Richard Head, *The English Rogue Described in the Life of Meriton Latroon; a Witty Extravagant; Comprehending the Most Eminent Cheats of Both Sexes*, 1661; 1672.
16 Richard Head (attrib.), *The French Rogue*, 1672.
17 John Graunt, *Natural and Political Observations Made upon the Bills of Mortality*, 1662.
18 Old Bailey records: http://www.oldbaileyonline.org/browse.jsp?id=t16740429-5&div=t16740429-5#highlight

18 A Spy in the Family, the Court and the Theatre

1 Don Jordan and Michael Walsh, *The King's Bed*, 2015.
2 Mary Ann O'Donnell, *The Cambridge Companion to Aphra Behn*, 2004.
3 Ibid.
4 CSP Dom, vol. CLXXII, 1666.
5 Aphra Behn, *Works*, ed. Montague Summers, 1915.
6 Ibid.
7 Ibid.
8 Colley Cibber, *An Apology for the Life of*, 1740.
9 Ibid.
10 Evelyn, *Diary*.
11 Pepys, *Diary*.
12 Robert Gould, *Love Given Over, or a Satyr against the Pride, Lust and Inconstancy, Etc, of Woman*, 1683.
13 Evelyn, *Diary*.
14 Montague Summers, *The History of Witchcraft*, 1926.

19 Trading in People and Money

1 Beckles Willson, *The Great Company*, vol. 1, 1900.
2 Scott, *Leviathan*.
3 G.E. Aylmer, 'Sir Martin Noell', *DNB*, 2004.
4 Ligon, *A True and Exact History of the Island of Barbadoes*.
5 Pepys, *Diary*, various entries.
6 Jordan and Walsh, *The King's Bed*.
7 National Archives: British History Online –

http://www.british-history.ac.uk/no-series/london-aldermen/hen3-1912/pp168-195

8 Pepys, *Diary.*
9 Halley Goodman, 'The Formation of the Bank of England', *Penn History Review*, vol. 17, 2009.
10 Pepys, *Diary*
11 David Cuthbert Coleman, *Sir John Banks, Baronet and Businessman*, 1963.

20 War and Enterprise

1 East India Company Court Minutes, 11 September 1672.
2 John Fryer, *A New Account of East India and Persia*, 1698.
3 Ibid.
4 Thomas Seccombe, *DNB*, 2004.
5 Abraham Eraly, *The Mughal World: Life in India's last Golden Age*, 2007.
6 Makrand Mehta, *Indian Merchants and Entrepreneurs in Historical Perspective*, 1991.
7 Ibid.
8 Slingsby Bethel, *The Principal Interest of England Stated*, 1671.

21 The Mood of the City

1 Nicholas Barbon, *Apology for the Builder*, 1685.
2 Thomas Jordan, *The Goldsmiths Jubilee, or, Londons Triumphs . . . performed October* 29, 1674.
3 Janet Jarvis, *Christopher Wren's Cotswold Masons*, 1980.
4 Jardine, *On a Grander Scale*, 2002; Kerry Downes, *The Architecture of Wren*, 1988.
5 Harold F. Hutchinson, *Sir Christopher Wren*, 1976.
6 Isaac Newton, *Hypothesis explaining the properties of light*, in Thomas Birch, *The History of the Royal Society*, 1757.
7 Hooke, *Diaries.*
8 Mary Beale, *Portrait of Charles II*, Inverness Art Gallery.
9 Mary Beale, *Portrait of Frances Hay, Marchioness of Tweeddale*, Moyse's Hall Museum, Bury St Edmunds.
10 Mary Beale, *Self-Portrait*, c. 1665, National Portrait Gallery, NPG1687.

11 Artemisia Gentileschi, *Self-Portrait as the Allegory of Painting*, Royal Collection, Hampton Court Palace: https://www.royalcollection.org.uk/collection/405551/self-portrait-as-the-allegory-of-painting-la-pittura
12 Pierre Dumonstier II, *Right Hand of Artemisia Gentileschi*, British Museum, Drawing Collection, Nn,7.51.3.
13 Kim Sloan, in *The History of British Art 1600–1870*, ed. David Bindman, 2009

22 Coffee Wars at Home, Real Wars in the Colonies

1 Anon, quoted in Wolfgang Schivelbusch, *Tastes of Paradise*, 1992.
2 Sir George Sandys, Robert Hooper ed., *The Poetical Works of Sir George Sandys*, ed. Robert Hooper, 1872.
3 John Tatham, attrib., *Knavery in All Trades, or, The Coffee-House*, 1664.
4 Anon., The Women's Petition Against Coffee, 1674.
5 David Scott, *Leviathan, The Rise of Britain as a World Power*, 2013.
6 Robert Beverley, *The History and Present State of Virginia*, 1947.
7 Quoted in Charles A. Goodrich, *A History of the United States of America*, 1825.
8 Jordan and Walsh, *White Cargo*, 2007.
9 Ibid.

23 City Life

1 See Albert Borgman, *Thomas Shadwell, His Life and Comedies*, 1928; Thomas Mayo, *Epicurus in England*, 1934; Joseph Glide, 'Shadwell and the Royal Society', *Studies in English Literature 1500–1800*, vol., no. 3, 1970; Marjorie Hope Nicolson and David Stuart Rhodes, eds, *The Virtuoso by Thomas Shadwell*, 1976; 1992, and others.
2 Anon., *A True Narrative of the Great and Terrible Fire in Southwark on Fryday, 26th May, 1676*, 1676.
3 For this illustration and its development, see www.4physics.com/phy_demo/HookesLaw/HookesLawLab.html
4 Hooke, *Diaries*.
5 William Petty, *Treatise on Naval Philosophy*, Royal Society, Classified Papers, vol. 20, March 1685.
6 Celina Fox, 'The Ingenious Mr Dummer', *British Library Journal*, 2007.

7 Brian Lavery, 'Charles Anthony Deane', *Oxford Dictionary of National Biography*, 2004.
8 Pepys, *Diary*.
9 Brian Lavery, *Empire of the Seas*, 2010.
10 Anthony Ashley Cooper et al., *Some Considerations on the Question . . .*, 1676.
11 Andrew Marvell, *An Account of the Growth of Popery and Arbitrary Government in England*, 1677.
12 Roger L'Estrange, *The Parallel, or an Account of the Growth of Knavery, under the Pretext of Arbitary Government and Popery. With some Observations on a Pamphlet (of A Marvell) entitled An Account of the Growth of Popery, etc.*, 1678.

24 The City Convulsed

1 Roger L'Estrange, *Titus Oates, his Case, Character, Person and Plot*, 1685.
2 Roger L'Estrange, *History of the Times*, 1687.
3 L'Estrange, *Titus Oates*.
4 Sir John Reresby, *Memoirs*, 1734; 1821.
5 *Grey's Debates*, 21 October 1678.
6 Titus Oates, A *sermon preached at an Anabaptist meeting in Wapping on Sunday the 9th of February by the Rev T.O.*, 1699.
7 Thomas Povey to Samuel Pepys, quoted in Pepys, *Diary*.
8 Susan J. Owen, *Restoration Theatre and Crisis*, 1996.
9 John Wilmot, 2nd Earl of Rochester, *Letters*, 1981.
10 Filmer, *Patriarcha*.
11 Owen, *Restoration Theatre and Crisis*.
12 John Dryden, *The Vindication*, 1679.
13 John Dryden, *Absalom and Achitophel*, 1681.
14 John Hall, *An Alarm to Europe*, 1681.
15 Lesley Murdin, *Under Newton's Shadow*, 1985
16 John Dryden, prologue to *The Duke of Guise*, 1682.
17 Thomas D'Urfey, prologue to *The Royalist*, 1682.
18 John Crown, *The Misery of Civil War*, 1680.

25 The Fall of Madam Creswell and the Migration of Criminals

1 Richard Wiseman, *Eight Chirurgical Treatises*, 1776.
2 Anon., *The Whore's Rhetorick*, 1683.

3 J. Granger, *A Biographical History of England*, 1775.
4 Ferrante Pallavicino, *La Rhetorica delle Puttane*, 1642.
5 Pepys, *Diary*.
6 Anon., *The London Jilt, or The Politick Whore*, 1683, ed. Charles H. Hinnant.
7 Anon., *The London Jilt*.
8 Melissa M. Mowry, *The Bawdy Politic in Stuart England, 1660–1714*, 2004.
9 Roger Thompson, 'The London Jilt', *Harvard Literary Bulletin* 23, 1975.
10 Faramerz Dabhoiwala, 'Damaris Page', *DNB*, 2004.
11 Samuel Pepys, *Pepys's Navy White Book and Brooke House Papers*, 2004., ed. R Latham, 1995.
12 Vincent Buranelli, 'William Penn and James II', *Proceedings of the American Philosophical Society*, vol. 104, no. 1, 1960.
13 David Hannay, *Empire of the Seas*, 1911.
14 Pepys, *Diary*.
15 Pennsylvania State Archives, www.phmc.state.pa.us

26 The City Cowed, the City Triumphant

1 Proceedings of the Old Bailey, http://www.oldbaileyonline.org/browse.jsp?id=t16830712-3&div=t16830712-3#highlight
2 Algernon Sidney, *Discourses Concerning Government*, 1698.
3 Evelyn, *Diary*.
4 Ibid.
5 William Petty, *Essays on Mankind and Political Arithmatic*, ed. Henry Morley, 2014.
6 Nicholas Barbon, *A Discourse of Trade*, 1690.
7 Ibid.
8 Alexis Clairaut, translated in W.W. Rouse Ball, *An Essay on Newton's Principia*, 1893.
9 Thomas Tryon, *Friendly Advice to the Gentlemen-Planters of the East and West Indies*, parts 2 and 3, 1684.
10 Benjamin Trumbull, *A Complete History of Connecticut, Civil and Ecclesiastical*, 1818.
11 Anon., *An exhortation and caution to Friends concerning buying or keeping of Negroes*, 1693.
12 Suetonius, *De Vita Caesarum*.

Epilogue

1 Christopher Wren, *Parentalia*, 1750.
2 Jeremy Collier, *A Short View of the Immorality and Profaneness of the English Stage*, ed. Yuji Kaneko, 1996, first published 1698.
3 John Wilkins, *Essay Towards a Real Character, and Philosophical Language*, 1668.
4 For a list of new words see the website Robert Hooke's London: http://hookeslondon.com/2014/03/29/hooke-and-english/#more-185
5 Hooke, *Diaries*.
6 Joseph A. Schumpeter, *Capitalism, Socialism and Democracy*, 2008.
7 Giovanni Arrighi, *The Long Twentieth Century: Money, Power and the Origins of Our Times*, 2010.
8 William Pettigrew, *Freedom's Debt, The Royal African Company and the Politics of the Atlantic Slave Trade, 1672–1752*, 2013.
9 Ibid.
10 Figures extrapolated from the Trans-Atlantic Slave Trade Database.
11 Ibid.
12 Boyle, *Collected Works*. For a photograph of the handwritten list, go to the Royal Society's online Boyle papers: http://blogs.royalsociety.org/history-of-science/2010/08/27/robert-boyle-list/.

Appendix V

1 Samuel Lambe, *The humble representation of Samuel Lambe of London, merchant*, 1659.
2 Quoted in Halley Goodman, 'The Formation of the Bank of England', *Penn History Review*, vol. 17, 2009.
3 Ibid.

BIBLIOGRAPHY

An Act for Confirming an Act Entituled an Act for Encouraging and Increasing of Shipping and Navigation, etc., 1661

An Act for Increase of Shipping, and Encouragement of the Navigation of this Kingdom, October 1651

Anon., *An Exhortation and Caution to Friends Concerning Buying or Keeping of Negroes*, 1693

Anon., *A True Narrative of the Great and Terrible Fire in Southwark on Fryday, 26th May*, 1676

Anon., *Character and Qualifications of an Honest, Loyal Merchant*, 1686

Anon., *The Life of Titus Oates*, 1685

Anon., *The London Jilt, or The Politick Whore*, 1683, ed. Charles H. Hinnant, 2007

Anon., *The Whore's Rhetorick*, 1683

Anon., *The Women's Petition Against Coffee*, 1674

Aristotle, *Politics*, Book I

Arrighi, Giovanni, *The Long Twentieth Century: Money, Power and the Origins of Our Times*, 2010

Ashley Cooper, Anthony, et al., *Some Considerations upon the Question, Whether the Parliament is Dissolved, by its Prorogation for 15 Months?*, 1676

Aubrey, John, *Brief Lives*, 1715, ed. Andrew Clark, 1898
Aylmer, G.E., *The Struggle for the Constitution 1603–89*, 1963
Bacon, Francis, *New Atlantis*, 1627
—— *Instauratio Magna*, The Oxford Francis Bacon, 2000
Ball, W.W. Rouse, *An Essay on Newton's Principia*, 1893
Barbon, Nicholas, *Apology for the Builder*, 1685
—— *A Discourse of Trade*, 1690
Beauclerk, Charles, *Nell Gwyn*, 2005
Beer, G.L., *The Origins of the British Colonial System*, 1908
Behn, Aphra, *Works*, ed. Montague Summers, 1915
Bennett, J. A, *The Mathematical Science of Christopher Wren*, 1982
Bentley, G.E., *The Jacobean and Caroline Stage*, 1941; 1968
Bethel, Slingsby, *The Principal Interest of England Stated*, 1671
Beverley, Robert, *The History and Present State of Virginia*, 1947
Bold, John, *John Webb, Architectural Theory and Practice in the Seventeenth Century*, 1989
Borgman, Albert, *Thomas Shadwell, His Life and Comedies*, 1928
Boulton, Jeremy, 'Wage Labour in Seventeenth Century London', *The Economic History Review*, New Series, vol. 49 no. 2, May 1996
—— *Neighbourhood and Society: A London Suburb in the 17th Century*, 2005
Boyle, Robert, *New Experiments Physico-Mechanicall, Touching the Spring of the Air, and its Effects, Made in the Most Part Using a New Pneumatical Engine*, 1660
—— *A Free Enquiry into the Vulgarly Received Notion of Nature*, 1686
—— *Collected Works*, 1772
—— photograph of the handwritten list of hoped-for

inventions: www.bbk.ac.uk/boyle/boyle_papers_index.htm
Braudel, Fernand, *The Perspective of the World*, 1985
Bucholz, Robert, and Ward, Joseph, *London: A Social and Cultural History* 1550–1750, 2012
Buranelli, Vincent, 'William Penn and James II', *Proceedings of the American Philosophical Society*, vol. 104 no. 1, 1960
Burnet, Gilbert, *A History of My Own Time*, 1674–85, 1617
Calendar of Manuscripts of Marquis of Bath, HMSO 1980, https://archive.org/stream/calendarofmanusc05bath/calendarofmanusc05bath_djvu.txt
Cambrensis, Giraldus, *Topographia Hibernica*, 1187, PRO SP 29/5 74
Cary, John, *An Essay on the State of England in Relation to its Trade*, 1695
Cavendish, Margaret, *Observations upon Experimental Philosophy*, 1666
—— *The Description of a New World, called the Blazing World*, 1666
Chandaman, C.D., *The English Public Revenue, 1660–1688*, 1975
Charles II, *Letters*, ed. Arthur Bryant, 1968
Charter of Carolina, 1663
Child, Josiah, *Brief Observations Concerning Trade and Interest of Money*, 1668
—— *A New Discourse on Trade*, 1692
Cibber, Colley, *An Apology for the Life of*, 1740
Coleman, David Cuthbert, *Sir John Banks, Baronet and Businessman*, 1963
Collier, Jeremy, ed. Yuji Kaneko, *A Short View of the Immorality and Profaneness of the English Stage*, 1996, first published 1600

Cranfield, J. Douglas, *Heroes and States*, 1999
Crouch, John, *Mercurius Fumigosus*, 12–19 September 1665
Crown, John, *The Misery of Civil War*, 1680
Culpeper, Nicholas, *Herbal*, 1649
Davenant, William, *Madagascar with Other Poems*, 1638
—— *Macbeth*, 1674
—— *Five Restoration Adaptations of Shakespeare*, ed. Christopher Spencer, 1965
Davies, J.D., *Pepys's Navy: Ships, Men and Warfare*, 2008
Davies, Kenneth Gordon, *The Royal African Company*, 1957
Davis, Ralph, *The Rise of the English Shipping Industry in the Seventeenth and Eighteenth Centuries*, 1962
Declaration of Breda, 1660, http://www.constitution.org/eng/conpur105.htm
Defoe, Daniel, *A Journal of the Plague Year*, 1722
—— *The Fortunes and Misfortunes of the Famous Moll Flanders*, 1722
Dick, Hugh G., 'Students of Physic and Astrology', *Journal of the History of Medicine*, vol. 1 no. 3, 1946
Dowdell, E.G., *A Hundred Years of Quarter Sessions*, 1932
Downes, John, *Roscius Anglicanus*, 1708
Downes, Kerry, *The Architecture of Wren*, 1988
Dryden, John, *Annus Mirabilis*, 1667
—— *Secret Love, or The Maiden Queen*, 1669
—— Prologue and Epilogue to *Marriage a-la-Mode*, pub. in *Covent Garden Drollery*, 1672
—— *The Vindication*, 1679
—— *Absalom and Achitophel*, 1681
—— Prologue to *The Duke of Guise*, 1682
—— *The Works of John Dryden*, ed. Walter Scott, 18 vols, 1808
D'Urfey, Thomas, prologue to *The Royalist*, 1682
Earle, Peter, *The Making of the English Middle Class*, 1989

—— *A City Full of People: Men and Women of London 1650–1750*, 1994
East India Company Court Minutes, 1672
Eraly, Abraham, *The Mughal World: Life in India's last Golden Age*, 2007
Evelyn, John, *Fumifugium*, 1661
—— *Tyrannus, or The Mode*, 1661
—— *Sylva, or a Discourse of Forest Trees*, 1662
—— *Diary*, ed. Bray, 1901
Fantel, Hans, *William Penn: Apostle of Dissent*, 1974
Filmer, Robert, *Observations Upon the Original of Government*, 1652
—— *Patriarcha*, 1680
Fox, Celina, 'The Ingenious Mr Dummer', *British Library Journal*, 2007, Article 10
French, Roger, and Wear, Andrew, *The Medical Revolution of the Seventeenth Century*, 2008
Fryer, John, *A New Account of East India and Persia*, 1698
Garfield, John, *The Wandering Whore*, in five parts, 1660–1664
Glanvill, Joseph, *Plus Ultra*, 1668
—— *Letters and Poems in Praise of the Incomparable Princess, Margaret, Duchess of Newcastle*, 1676
—— *Sadducismus Triumphatus*, 1681
Glide, Joseph, 'Shadwell and the Royal Society', *Studies in English Literature 1500–1800*, vol. 10, no. 3, 1970
Godolphin, William, attributed, *In Praise of the Choice Company of Philosophers and Witts Who Meete on Wednesdays Weekely at Gresham College*, Ashmolean MSS, reprinted in *Notes and Records of the Royal Society of London*, vol. 5, 1948
Goodman, Halley, 'The Formation of the Bank of England', *Penn History Review*, vol. 17, 2009

Goodrich, Charles A., A *History of the United States of America*, 1825

Gould, Robert, *Love Given Over, or a Satyr against the Pride, Lust and Inconstancy, Etc, of Woman*, 1683

Granger, J., A *Biographical History of England*, 1775

Grassby, Richard, *The Business Community of Seventeenth Century England*, 1995

Graunt, John, *Natural and Political Observations made upon the Bills of Mortality*, 1662 etc.

—— *London's Dreadful Visitation*, 1665

Grell, Ole Peter, and Cunningham, Andrew, eds, *Religio Medici*, 1996

Grey's Debates, 21 October 1678

Hakluyt, Richard, *The Principal Navigations, Voyages, Traffiques and Discoveries of the English Nation*, ed. E. Goldsmid, 1884–1890

Hall, John, *An Alarm to Europe*, 1681

Halsbury's Statutes of England and Wales, 3rd edn, 1985

Hannay, David, A *Short History of the Royal Navy*, 2 vols., 1898, 1911

—— *Empire of the Seas*, 1911

Harper, L.A., *The English Navigation Laws*, 1939

Harris, Tim, *London Crowds in the Reign of Charles II*, 1987

Hatcher, John, *The History of the British Coal Industry*, 1993

Head, Richard, and Kirkman, Francis, *The English Rogue Described in the Life of Meriton Latroon; a Witty Extravagant; Comprehending the Most Eminent Cheats of Both Sexes*, 1661 (1672)

Head, Richard (attrib.), *The French Rogue*, 1672

Hearth Tax Online, hearthtax.org.uk

Hobbes, Thomas, *Leviathan*, 1651

—— *Considerations Upon the Reputation, Loyalty, Manners, & Religion of Thomas Hobbes of Malmsbury*, 1680

Hodges, Nathaniel, *Loimologia*, 1720

Holland, Bart K., 'Treatments for Bubonic Plague, Reports from seventeenth century British epidemics', *Journal of the Royal Society of Medicine*, vol. 93, June 2000

Hollis, Leo, *The Phoenix*, 2008

Hooke, Robert, *Folio*, MSS Royal Society: www.livesandletters.ac.uk/cell/Hooke/Hooke.html

—— *Micrographia*, 1665, BL C.175.e.8

—— *Diaries*, ed. Richard Nichols, 1994

Hooper, Robert, ed., *The Poetical Works of Sir George Sandys*, 1872

Hotson, Leslie, *The Commonwealth and Restoration Stage*, 1928

Howe, Elizabeth, *The First English Actresses*, 1992

Howell, James, *Londonopolis*, 1657

Hubbard, Eleanor, *City Women: Money, Sex and the Social Order in Early Modern London*, 2012

Hughson, David, *London, An Accurate History and Description of the British Metropolis*, 1805

Hunter, L., and Hutton, S, *Sisters of the Royal Society*, 1997

Hutchinson, Harold F., *Sir Christopher Wren*, 1976

Hutchinson, Lucy, *Memoirs of the Life of Colonel Hutchinson*, 1806

Hutton, Ronald, *The Restoration*, 1985

—— *Charles the Second*, 1989

Hyde, Edward, 1st Earl of Clarendon, *History of the Rebellion*, 1702–4

Inwood, Stephen, *The Man Who Knew Too Much: The Inventive Life of Robert Hooke*, 2003

Jardine, Lisa, *On a Grander Scale: The Outstanding Life of Sir Christopher Wren*, 2002

—— *The Curious Life of Robert Hooke*, 2003

Jarvis, Janet, *Christopher Wren's Cotswold Masons*, 1980
Jenner, Mark, 'Quackery and Enthusiasm' in Grell and Cunningham, eds, *Religio Medici*, 1996
—— *The Politics of London Air: John Evelyn's Fumifugium and the Restoration*, 2013
Jordan, Don, and Walsh, Michael, *White Cargo*, 2007
—— *The King's Revenge*, 2012
—— *The King's Bed*, 2015
Jordan, Thomas, *The Goldsmiths Jubilee, or, Londons Triumphs . . . performed October* 29, 1674
Lambe, Samuel, *The humble representation of Samuel Lambe of London, merchant*, 1659
Langhans, Edward A., 'The Theatres', in *The London Theatre World 1600–1800*, ed. Hume, 1980
Lavery, Brian, *The Arming and Fitting of English Ships of War 1600–1815*, 1987
—— *Empire of the Seas*, 2010
L'Estrange, Roger, *The Parallel, or an Account of the Growth of Knavery, under the Pretext of Arbitrary Government and Popery. With some Observations on a Pamphlet (of A Marvell) entitled An Account of the Growth of Popery, etc.*, 1678
—— *Titus Oates, his Case, Person, Character and Plot*, 1685
—— *History of the Times*, 1687
Levens, Peter, *The Pathway to Health*, 1587, etc., to 1664
Ligon, Richard, A *True and Exact history of the Island of Barbadoes*, 1657
Lillywhite, Bryant, *London Coffee Houses*, 1963
Locke, John, *Anatomie*, written with Thomas Sydenham, 1668
—— *Two Treatises on Government*, 1689
MacDonald, Michael, 'The Career of Astrological Medicine in England', in Grell and Cunningham, eds, *Religio Medici*, 1996

Marcus, J.G., A *Naval History of England*, vol. 1, 1961

Marvell, Andrew, *Last Instructions to a Painter*, 1667

—— *An Account of the Growth of Popery and Arbitrary Government in England*, 1677

Masson, D., *The Life of John Milton*, 7 vols, 1859–94

Maus, Katherine Eisaman, 'Playhouse Flesh and Blood', *English Literary History*, vol. 46 no. 4, 1979

Mayo, Thomas, *Epicurus in England*, 1934

Mehta, Makrand, *Indian Merchants and Entrepreneurs in Historical Perspective*, 1991

Mercurius Publicus, published and written by Henry Muddiman, 1659–1662

Middlesex County Records, 1625–1667, 1638–1751

Milton, John, *The Readie and Easie Way to Establish a Free Commonwealth*, 1660

—— *Paradise Lost*, 1667 etc.

Milton, Philip, 'John Locke and the Rye House Plot', *The Historical Journal*, vol. 43 no. 3, 2000

Misselden, Edward, *Free Trade, or The Meanes to Make Trade Flourish*, 1622

Miyoshi, R., 'Recent Studies on Sir William Davenant', *Restoration and Eighteenth Century Theatre Research*, vol. 28 no. 1, 2013

Mortimer, Ian, *Dying and the Doctors*, 2009

Mowry, Melissa M., *The Bawdy Politic in Stuart England, 1660–1714*, 2004

Munday, Anthony, *Anthony Munday's Mayoral Pagent Book*, 1605

Mun, Thomas, A *Discourse of Trade from England Unto the East-Indies*, 1621

—— *England's Treasure by Foreign Trade*, written 1628, pub. 1664

Murdin, Lesley, *Under Newton's Shadow*, 1985
Nethercot, A., *Sir William Davenant*, 1938
Newton, Isaac, *Hypothesis explaining the properties of light*, in Thomas Birch, *The History of the Royal Society*, 1757
Oates, Titus, *A sermon preached at an Anabaptist meeting in Wapping on Sunday the 9th of February by the Rev T.O.*, 1699
O'Donnell, Mary Ann, *The Cambridge Companion to Aphra Behn*, 2004
Ogilby, John, *The relation of his Majestie's entertainment passing through the city of London*, 1662
Old Bailey records: http://www.oldbaileyonline.org
O'Rahilly, Alfred, 'Aquinas versus Marx, Part I', *Studies*, vol. 31, no. 124, 1942
Owen, Susan J., *Restoration Theatre and Crisis*, 1996
Oxford Dictionary of National Biography, 2005
Pallavicino, Ferrante, *La Rhetorica delle Puttane*, 1642
Pepys, Samuel, *Diary*, ed. Robert Latham and William Matthews, 1970–83
—— *Samuel Pepys's Navy White Book and Brooke House Papers*, ed. Robert Latham, 1995
Pennsylvania State Archives, www.phmc.state.pa.us
Pettigrew, William, *Freedom's Debt, The Royal African Company and the Politics of the Atlantic Slave Trade, 1672–1752*, 2013
Petty, William, *Treatise on Taxes*, 1662
—— *Treatise on Naval Philosophy*, Royal Society, Classified Papers, vol. 20, March 1685
—— *The Economic Writings of Sir William Petty*, reprint of his collected works, 1963
—— *Essays on Mankind and Political Arithmatic*, ed. Henry Morley, 2014

Philosophical Transactions of the Royal Society, vol. 1, 1665
Picard, Lisa, *Restoration London*, 1997
Porter, Roy, *London: A Social History*, 1994
Power, Henry, *Experimental Philosophy*, 1663
Proceedings of the Old Bailey, www.oldbaileyonline.org
Radisson, Peter (Pierre) Esprit, *Voyages of, Being an account of his travels and experiences among the North American Indians, from 1652 to 1684*, 1885
Records of the Navy Board and the Board of Admiralty, PRO ADM 106
Reresby, Sir John, *Memoirs*, 1734, 1821, etc.
Rifkin, Benjamin A., *Human Anatomy, Five Centuries of Art and Science*, 2005
Rodger, N.A.M., *The Wooden World*, 1998
Rules and Orders to be observed by all justices of the Peace, Mayors, Bayliffs and other Officers for the Prevention of the Spreading of the Infection of the Plague, PRO SP29/155 f102, 1666
Sanderson, Sir William, *Compleat History of the Life and Raigne of King Charles*, 1658
Schivelbusch, Wolfgang, *Tastes of Paradise*, 1992
Schumpeter, Joseph A., *Capitalism, Socialism and Democracy*, 2008
Schwartzberg, Rafaelle, *Becoming a Goldsmith in the Seventeenth Century*, LSE Working Papers, 141/10, Department of Economic History, LSE, 2010
Scott, David, *Leviathan, The Rise of Britain as a World Power*, 2013
Shadwell, Thomas, *The Virtuoso*, ed. Marjorie Hope Nicolson and David Stuart Rhodes, 1992
Shoemaker, R., *Prosecution and Punishment: Petty Crime and the Law in London and Rural Middlesex 1660–1725*,

Cambridge Studies in Early Modern British History, 2008
Sidney, Algernon, *Discourses Concerning Government*, 1698
Sloan, Kim, in *The History of British Art 1600–1870*, ed. David Bindman, 2009
Smith, Abbot Emerson, *Colonists in Bondage: White Servitude and Convict Labor in America, 1607–1776*, 1947
Smith, Geoffrey, *Long, Dangerous and Expensive Journeys: the Grooms of the Bedchamber at Charles II's Court in Exile, Early Modern Literary Studies*, Issue 15, 2007; British Library, Copy of a Letter Written by Mr Thomas Killigrew, Manuscript 27402, ff. 69r-71v
—— in *Thomas Killigrew and the Seventeenth Century English Stage*, ed. Philip Major, 2013
Speeches and Prayers of the Regicides, Thomason Tracts, BL, 1660
Spence, Craig, *London in the 1690s: A Social Atlas*, 2000
Sprat, Thomas, *The History of the Royal Society of London*, 1667
Spurr, John, *England in the 1670s: This Masquerading Urge*, 2000
Steckley, G.F., ed., *The Letters of John Paige, London Merchant*, 1648–58, London Record Society 21, 1984
Stevenson, Christine, *The City and the King*, 2013
Stone, Laurence, *Family, Sex and Marriage in England 1500–1800*, 1977
Stowe, John, *A Survey of the Cities of London and Westminster*, 1633, 1720
Suetonius, *De Vita Caesarum*
Summers, Montague, *The History of Witchcraft*, 1926
Sydenham, Thomas, *Observationes Medicae circa Morborum acutorum historiam et curationem*, 1676

Syfret, R.H., 'The Origins of the Royal Society, January 1696/7', *Notes and Records of the Royal Society*, vol. 5 no. 2, April 1948

Tatham, John, attrib., *Knavery in All Trades, or, The Coffee-House*, 1664

Thomas, Keith, *Religion and the Decline of Magic*, 1971

—— *The Ends of Life: Roads to Fulfilment in Early Modern England*, 2009

Thompson, Roger, 'The London Jilt', *Harvard Literary Bulletin* 23, 1975

Trans-Atlantic Slave Voyages, Emory University, slavevoyages.org

Trumbull, Benjamin, A *Complete History of Connecticut, Civil and Ecclesiastical*, 1818

Tryon, Thomas, *Friendly Advice to the Gentlemen-Planters of the East and West Indies*, parts 2 and 3, 1684

Tumbleson, R.D., 'The Triumph of London, Lord Mayor's Day Pageants and the Rise of the City', in *The Witness of Times*, ed. Keller and Schiffhorst, 1993

Uglow, Jenny, A *Gambling Man, Charles II and the Restoration*, 2010

Venetian State Papers: CSP Dom, 1660–1

Wallis, John, *Account of Some Passages of his Life*, 1700

—— Letter to Dr Thomas Smith, in *Transcripts of Writings of Dr John Wallis (1616–1703), Mathematician*, c. 1830

Ward, Joseph, *Metropolitan Communities: Trade Guilds, Identity and Change in Early Modern London*, 1997

Ward, Ned, A *Trip to Jamaica*, 1698

Whinney, Margaret D., 'John Webb's Drawings for Whitehall Palace', *Proceedings of the Walpole Society*, vol. 31, 1942–1943, 1946

Wilkins, Emma, 'Margaret Cavendish and the Royal Society', *Notes and Records of the Royal Society*, May 2014

Wilkins, John, *Essay Towards a Real Character, and Philosophical Language*, 1668

Willson, Beckles, *The Great Company*, Vol. 1, 1900

Wilmot, John, 2nd Earl of Rochester, *Letters*, 1981

Winstanley, William, *Lives of the Most Famous English Poets*, 1687

Wiseman, Richard, *Eight Chirurgical Treatises*, 1776

Wood, Anthony, *Athenae Oxonienses*, 1813

Wren, Christopher, *Parentalia*, 1750

Wren Society Papers, Oxford, 1924–43

Wrigley, A.E., and Schofield, R.S., *The Population History of England, 1541–1871: A Reconstruction*, 1989

Zahedieh, Nuala, *Making Mercantilism Work*, Transactions of the Royal Society, 6th series, vol. 9, 1999

Zook, George Frederick, *The Company of Royal Adventurers*, 1919

ACKNOWLEDGEMENTS

It is a wonderful gift to be allowed to write about people, to say what one thinks of them – the good, the bad, the great, the misguided and the entertaining. This task is made not easier but less hazardous when those under scrutiny are dead, as with the *dramatis personae* of this book. But this section is the place to write about the living – about those without whom this book would not have been born.

The gift of being asked to write this book was bestowed by Tim Whiting, my publisher at Little, Brown. For this, and for his unflappable support and faith, much gratitude. My thanks are due to all at Little, Brown who have helped to see this book through to completion. Commissioning Editor Claudia Connal's kindness and support was always unwavering. When she left for new challenges elsewhere, Dominic Wakeford picked up the project at a late stage. In view of this, his clarity of direction was all the more remarkable. Dom's wise counsel ensured a rough first draft moved through to a final manuscript. Thanks also go to Senior Project Editor Nithya Rae, whose clear-headedness has been a blessing, especially as she also had to take on the project at a late point when her stalwart predecessor Iain Hunt left for new pastures. I must also thank the meticulous Steve Gove for his copyediting; Picture Research Manager Linda Silverman who, as always, provided marvellous pictures; and Bekki Guyatt, who designed the arresting cover. And I must thank Ted Vallance, Professor of Early Modern British Political Culture at Roehampton University, for his penetrating comments on the manuscript and for helping to steer me away from some seventeenth-century political quicksand I might otherwise have headed into.

Finally, I must say a few words about my friend and long-standing collaborator, Michael Walsh. Shortly after this book was commissioned, Mike had to bow out of what was set to be yet another enjoyable partnership when he was hit by a chronic illness. This was to have been our fifth book together. We first met more than thirty years ago when working on ITV's investigative current affairs series *World in Action*. After we separately left the series, we continued to make television programmes together. From writing documentary scripts it was a natural, if daunting, progression to writing books. With his encyclopaedic knowledge of English history and a nose for a good story, Mike was always a pleasure to work with. While writing *The King's City* I missed what for many years had been our regular editorial meetings in the 'office' – in reality, a pub halfway between our homes in West London. Sadly, Mike died just a few weeks after this book was first published in the UK in July 2017. With great determination and physical effort he had attended the launch party; his presence there gave me, and many others who knew him, immense pleasure. I still go to the 'office' and when I do I make sure I raise a pint to his memory.

INDEX